A GENERAL VIEW OF
EUROPEAN LEGAL HISTORY

AND OTHER PAPERS

Munroe Smith

A GENERAL VIEW OF EUROPEAN LEGAL HISTORY

AND OTHER PAPERS

BY

MUNROE SMITH

AMS PRESS, INC.
NEW YORK
1967

For his editorial work on this volume I wish
to thank my husband's colleague and friend

HESSEL E. YNTEMA

GERTRUDE H. MUNROE SMITH

NEW YORK
October, 1927

FOREWORD

By FRANK J. GOODNOW, LL.D.,

President of The Johns Hopkins University

MY acquaintance with Munroe Smith began in 1882 when as a student in the Law School and the newly established School of Political Science at Columbia, I heard his lectures on Roman Law. Later on, in 1883, I was appointed lecturer on Administrative Law in the new School of Political Science and from that time on until 1913 was thrown into almost daily contact with him. The members of the faculty of the School were all comparatively, some very, young men. We all were enthusiastic in our endeavors to make the new experiment a success, and to no one more than Munroe Smith belongs the credit for the reputation and influence which subsequently attached to the School.

One of the ventures which we entered upon was the Political Science Quarterly. This journal was started in 1886. It was agreed by all of us that Munroe Smith was the man who should become Managing Editor. And no happier choice could possibly have been made. The accurate scholarship and finish of literary expression which characterized even his college years had become emphasized as he had grown older. Indeed his desire that everything that was published in the Quarterly should be both correct and properly expressed was so great that he gave of his time without stint to attain the only result with which he would be satisfied. Yet withal he was so tactful and kindly in his criticism that anyone who had the benefit of his suggestions could not help feeling that a favor had been conferred upon him, and was far from having any of that resentment which so commonly attaches to criticism. I was one of those who frequently had the benefit of his suggestions. I owe him a debt which I never repaid, and as I look back on our life together at Columbia I can never recall an instance when I felt anything but gratitude to him although in not a few cases his criticism was anything but superficial.

Munroe Smith's intellectual attitude was not exclusively critical. He was himself a productive and accurate scholar. But the years which he devoted to the editorship of the Political Science Quarterly — years of tireless and conscientious work which came at a time when his productive capacity was at its greatest — seriously handicapped him in his productive work.

Munroe Smith wrote a number of books, principal among which were " Bismarck and German Unity," " Out of Their Own Mouths," and " Militarism and Statecraft." He studied in Germany just after the Franco Prussian War when Bismarck's figure towered over all Europe. No wonder that such a character made a deep impression upon the young American student. He read almost everything that was written about Bismarck. It is not surprising that his contribution to an understanding of Bismarck's life and work became almost a classic in its field. The " Militarism and Statecraft " was in large measure the attempt to show how Bismarck would have acted in the 1914 crisis. The conclusion reached is aptly set forth in the title.

But Munroe Smith's main contributions to the studies which he loved are to be found in the articles which he wrote. Many of them are devoted to comparatively small portions of a large subject. His knowledge was encyclopedic, but he had no ambitions to thresh old straw. Indeed his methods of work were inconsistent with the production of *magna opera*, certainly in the sense of size. His desire for absolute accuracy made it impossible for him to place great reliance on the conclusions of others. His insistence on perfection made it necessary for him to go over and over again what he had written in the hope of improving what he had done. I remember he told me once that every time he sat down to write a little critical devil perched upon his shoulder and kept insisting upon changes. Another time he said that he thought no one could attain perfection in prose unless he also wrote verse, that the habit developed in writing verse of searching for the right word was invaluable when the writing of prose began. Munroe Smith did himself write verse although little of his verse has been published.

In closing this very inadequate sketch of Munroe Smith I can not refrain from saying how much his death affected me. Thirty or more years of intimate companionship, the love of a student for a teacher to whom a great debt has remained unpaid, the admiration of a colleague for work which is now finished all make it a privilege as well as a duty to record in this poor way my impressions of his life and his work, as well as my affection for a man of remarkable sincerity, of unusual kindliness, and of great ability. He has gone, it is true, but the work which he did will go on. He not merely contributed to the advancement of his chosen subject. He played as well an important part in the reorganization of higher education in the United States which began fifty years ago.

TABLE OF CONTENTS

A GENERAL VIEW OF
EUROPEAN LEGAL HISTORY

AND OTHER PAPERS

By

MUNROE SMITH, J.U.D., LL.D., J.D.

LATE BRYCE PROFESSOR OF EUROPEAN LEGAL HISTORY
COLUMBIA UNIVERSITY

I

A GENERAL VIEW OF EUROPEAN LEGAL HISTORY [1]

IN my study of European legal history I have been increasingly impressed by the fact that in the central and western countries of continental Europe, which today form independent statês, each with its own separate body of laws, the development of private or civil law during the past fourteen centuries has been essentially similar. The whole movement has been European. And yet no writer has attempted to deal with it from this point of view. There are numerous histories of Italian law, of French law, of Spanish law and of German law. There are also histories of the legal development of many of the smaller European countries. But there exists no general history of European law.

It is, of course, recognized that in each of these countries there were important bodies of law that were common to all: the feudal law, the canon law and the law merchant. It is also recognized that until very recent times none of these countries had anything approaching common and uniform private law. Controversies not governed by either feudal or ecclesiastical or commercial law were determined primarily, even in modern times, by local or provincial custom; and in none of these countries, except perhaps in those of German speech, were these customs sufficiently similar to be called national. Even in German-speaking countries there were marked differences between the customs of the northern and those of the southern territories. All the local and provincial customs of western and central Europe were blends, in varying proportions, of Roman, Teutonic and

[1] Reprinted from *Actorum Academiae Universalis Jurisprudentiae Comparativae*, vol. i. (*Mémoires de L'Académie Internationale de Droit Comparé*. Tome i.) Berolini, apud Herman Sack; Londini, apud Sweet & Maxwell; Parisiis, apud Marcel Rivière. 1927.

specifically mediæval elements, and in each instance the proportion was determined far more largely by the racial composition and economic development of each local group than by its position in the political màp of Europe.

In the later middle ages the Roman law, as set forth in the law books of Justinian, was accepted in most parts of central and western Europe as subsidiary law, to be applied in all cases in which neither feudal nor ecclesiastical nor commercial law was applicable, and in which neither local nor provincial custom furnished any rule on which a decision could be based. Through this reception of the ancient Roman law, modern Europe obtained a fourth body of continental law — a subsidiary body of rules and principles which filled all the chinks and crevices in the private law.

Until the nineteenth century, accordingly, the ordinary life and social relations of all the peoples of western and central Europe were governed in part by local and provincial laws, in part by European laws. Not until the nineteenth century was there in any of the great modern states of central and western Europe any such thing as national civil law. The modern national states of the Continent first obtained such law by codification, and national codification was itself a European movement.

A history of European law, written from a European rather than from the modern national point of view, would begin by indicating the conditions existing in Europe in the early centuries of the Christian era. Europe, so far as it was then civilized, formed part of the Roman Empire. This empire, which included all the chief commercial peoples of the ancient world, except the Chinese, and all the important industrial areas of western civilization, formed one vast economic domain of substantially free trade. Roman rule had established on land and on sea a hitherto unknown peace and legal security. The military roads of the empire were also highways of commerce, such as have not since existed in the East and only in the nineteenth century again in the

West. In this empire the commerce of the world attained a development that was not again equalled until the nineteenth century.

This world empire was governed by a uniform world law. In the extension of Roman rule over the Mediterranean basin — a movement which began in the third century B.C. — the Romans did not impose upon the conquered provinces their own civil law. For their provincial subjects they gradually developed, partly in provincial courts, but particularly in the court of the foreign prætor at Rome, a different body of rules, substantially uniform as regarded movable property and obligations. These rules were based on very ancient commercial customs, possibly carried from Babylon through Phenicia to the Mediterranean, in any case long recognized in Mediterranean trade. To this customary law, which the Romans appropriately called *jus gentium,* their legal genius gave more precise formulation and more systematic presentation. This law was so superior to their own civil law for commercial purposes that it was applied in controversies between Roman citizens and Rome's provincial subjects; and it was so much more equitable and progressive that before the close of the republican period it was accepted almost in its entirety for the determination of controversies between Roman citizens themselves. For these their older civil law was not indeed abolished, but it was overridden by the reformatory activity of the city prætor. Thenceforth the relation of the Roman civil law and the newer prætorian law was singularly like that which was established centuries later between common law and equity in England. In both instances the new law was official law, *jus honorarium,* based on governmental authority; and in both instances it was created by the development of new remedies. The substantive rules of English equity appeared in the decisions of the chancellors; those of the Roman prætorian law in the instructions given to the judices in the prætorian formulas. In its form the edict was legislative; but the significance of the prætorian promises of actions and exceptions was revealed only in the formulas, to which the edict was but an index; and since the wording of the formulas and their interpretation were always subject to modification as new cases suggested new points of view, the Roman prætorian law, like English equity, was in reality what the English call case law, and a French writer has described as " cette législation occulte qui s'appelle la jurisprudence."

When Caracalla conferred Roman citizenship upon all the free inhabitants of the Roman world, what was left of the old Roman civil law was indeed extended over the entire empire, but in this now uniform world law the *jus gentium* remained the dominant element. In the earlier imperial period, particularly in the second and third centuries, this world law was further developed by the decisions of an imperial supreme court, the auditory of the prætorian prefect, and was brought to a degree of refinement which has again been reached only in the most modern legal systems. In the Pandects of Justinian we have a digest of the decisions of this great central court, drawn almost entirely from the writings of imperial judges.

The decline of the Roman Empire in the fourth and fifth centuries was but a part of a wider movement, a decline of the entire ancient civilization. There was in these centuries a marked economic retrogression, of which the causes are still a matter of dispute. What we call the fall of the West Roman Empire was brought about by the irruption of northern barbarians, mainly of Teutonic stock. At the close of the fourth century and the beginning of the fifth, whole tribes of Germans had been permitted to settle within the borders of the empire on their agreement to defend these borders against the other Germans behind them; and before the year 476, when a leader of German mercenaries dethroned the West Roman emperor, German kings were already in possession of many of the West Roman provinces.

Into this mass of victorious barbarism some elements of Mediterranean civilization had previously been filtering; first through Greek and Roman traders, later through Christian missionaries. Many of the German tribes, notably the Burgundians, the Vandals, the Goths and the Langobards, had accepted Christianity before they swept across the Danube or the Rhine. The German invaders were familiar also with the Roman military and civil organization and administration. In the later imperial period, the German element in the Roman armies and in the imperial bodyguard itself had steadily increased, and service in this guard led not infrequently to the highest offices in the empire.

Given these earlier relations, it is not surprising that the Germans who overran Italy and the western provinces had no notion that they had destroyed the Roman Empire. They regarded it as still existing. The Vandal, Gothic and Burgundian kings who established their authority in the Danubian provinces, in Italy, in southern Gaul, in Spain and in Africa, regarded themselves as governors of imperial provinces and described their armies as imperial armies. They sought formal recognition of their authority from the emperor at Rome, so long as there was still such an emperor. Later, in several instances, they sought it from the emperor at Constantinople.

Unlike the heathen invaders of Britain, or the heathen Franks in their first occupation of northern Gaul, these Christian conquerors did not seize all the land held in private ownership. They followed, in most instances, the Roman military practice and quartered themselves, or rather thirded themselves, on the provincial proprietors. This system of settlement, which scattered the Germans through the Roman civilian population, helps to explain the fairly rapid acceptance by the German conquerors of the vulgar Latin speech and the gradual amalgamation which has produced the modern Italian, French and Spanish nations. Amalgamation was blocked at the outset by religious differences. The Vandals, the Goths, the Burgundians and the Langobards had been converted by missionaries who held Arian tenets, and they came into an empire in which Arianism had become a heresy. Sooner or later, however, all these Germans accepted the Nicene creed; the Franks, like the Saxons in England, passed directly from heathenism to orthodox Christianity; and the religious bar to intermarriage disappeared.

The German conquerors, however, did not subject themselves to the rules of the Roman law. According to their theory, the law governing each person was that of his tribe, and this law each tribesman carried with him everywhere. From this point of view it logically followed that the provincials, who were regarded as members of one great Roman tribe, were entitled to live by their own Roman law. Illogically, but quite intelligibly, it was also held that in controversies between Germans and Romans German tribal law should prevail.

The German tribal laws had however been modified, even before their invasion of Roman territory, by trade relations with the Mediterranean world. In the earliest written German laws fines and compositions were no longer measured in cattle but in Roman coin. And with their acceptance of Christianity the Germans accepted, in theory at least, the Christian view of marriage. The German nobles, indeed, who in the time of Tacitus " had many wives on account of their nobility," long remained imperfectly monogamous, notably in mediæval Spain; but here as elsewhere the " wife of benediction " had a status superior to that of other wives. The church was able to secure also the recognition of testaments. On the other hand, the Roman law, by which the provincials were in theory living, was gradually modified in some important respects by their acceptance of Teutonic customs. This was largely due to further economic retrogression and a general reversion to simpler social conditions. To such conditions Teutonic tribal customs, because they were more primitive, were in some respects better adapted than were the refined and progressive Roman rules. For example, the independent property rights of married women, recognized in Rome before the close of the republican period, soon fell into abeyance. In the later customs and laws of mediæval Europe, even in Latin countries, the control of the wife's property was usually in the hands of the husband. In theory, marriage established a "community" of goods, a sort of partnership, but the wife was a silent partner. The so-called Roman law, by which the provincials lived, was "broken," like their Latin speech.

The period from the fifth to the ninth century may be described as a period of interpenetration and reciprocal modification of Roman and German legal institutions. During these centuries the smaller German kingdoms were replaced by broader unions. The earliest of these, the Ostrogothic kingdom, extended for a time from the Danubian provinces to southeastern Gaul and included a great part of Italy. In this kingdom the continued existence of the Roman Empire was strongly emphasized. King Theodoric insisted that he and the emperor at Constantinople were joint rulers of a single empire, *unum corpus*. He even asked the East Roman emperor to confirm some of his appointments. Early in the sixth century he issued a brief code of laws, in order, as he stated, that barbarians and Romans alike might know what rules they were to observe. This kingdom, however, was soon overthrown by the armies of Justinian, and its legislation exercised no appreciable influence upon the later development of Italian law. Nor did the temporary re-union of Italy with the East Roman Empire in the sixth century exercise any abiding influence. Before the close of the century northern Italy fell under the rule of new invaders, the Langobards. In the development of the Langobard law, which at first was almost purely Teutonic, we find an increasing infiltration of Roman rules, particularly after the Langobards abandoned the Arian heresy. Their laws remained in force when their kingdom was conquered by Charlemagne, and Lombard law in its further development constituted an important element in Italian law.

The Visigothic kingdom in southwestern Europe was established earlier and lasted much longer than that of the

Ostrogoths. Visigothic kings obtained control of southern Gaul and of the greater part of Spain early in the fifth century; and after their expulsion from Gaul by the Franks they reigned in Spain until the beginning of the eighth century, when nearly all Spain was conquered by the Moors.

In this, as in the other German kingdoms established on Roman soil, the Goths at first lived by Gothic law and the provincials by Roman law. In both fields there was important legislation. For the use of his Roman subjects King Alaric II promulgated in the year 506 a handbook of Roman law, made by a committee of provincial Roman lawyers and accepted by an assembly of bishops and other provincial notables in Gascony. This Roman law of the Visigoths or, as it is more commonly called, this Breviary of Alaric, was largely used in Gaul and in the German portions of the Frank Empire, whenever Roman law was invoked as personal law. Until the twelfth century it was indeed almost the only source from which Roman law was drawn in western Europe, except by ecclesiastical writers.

Written statement of Visigothic law began earlier, in the latter part of the fifth century. It is believed that a palimpsest, now in the Paris National Library, gives a portion of this ancient Gothic code in its original form. If so, this is the oldest existing bit of written German law, antedating the famous Salic law.

The development of Visigothic legislation went on without interruption until Spain was overrun by the Moors. In the middle of the seventh century, however, an important change took place: the Roman laws were put out of force and the Visigothic laws were imposed on all the inhabitants of the kingdom. But the Visigothic code was already largely Romanized. After the acceptance of orthodox Christianity by the Visigothic kings, all revisions of this code were evidently made by ecclesiastics. It is attested that they were approved by the Visigothic Council, in which the prelates largely outnumbered the barons. In the end, at the beginning of the eighth century, the Visigothic code had become distinctly ecclesiastical in form, and on the whole more Roman than Gothic in substance.

Here we have the first attempt to fuse Roman law, civil and ecclesiastical, and German law in a single code. It is doubtful, however, to what extent the rules laid down in this code actually governed the life of the people. The Visigothic kingdom was frequently torn by civil discord and was at times in a state of anarchy. After the Moorish conquest we find, in the little Christian kingdoms that survived in northern Spain, institutions and rules characteristically Teutonic and unrecognized in the Visigothic code. Because of this prompt reversion of the Spanish people to more primitive customs and rules, it seems probable that this great code, in many respects singularly progressive, was never fully enforced, and that its rules represented rather the aspiration of churchmen to put their moral ideals on the statute book than a serious effort to enforce them — a tendency that is not confined to ecclesiastics and seems in some cases to inspire modern legislation.

The latest of these empires, that of the Franks, was by far the most important. At the close of the eighth century it included all those parts of continental Europe which were Christian and which recognized the spiritual supremacy of the bishop of Rome. To all contemporaries it must have seemed a thoroughly appropriate recognition of this fact that, on Christmas Day, 800, Charlemagne, king of the Franks and Langobards, received from the bishop of Rome the Roman imperial crown. The imperial tradition was still a living force. It had indeed gained new strength through the development of the idea that all Christian peoples ought to form a single great commonwealth.

Over against this reëstablished West Roman Empire stood only one other important political organization, the East Roman or Byzantine Empire. Between these two empires ran lines not only of political separation but also of official language. More important than these was a third line of cleavage, that of religious antagonism. The division of the

Christian world into two great churches, the Roman Catholic and the Greek Orthodox, had profound and enduring results. The eastern Slavs were converted to Christianity by Greek missionaries, and the Mediterranean civilization, which came to central and western Europe from Rome, came to them from Constantinople. Thenceforth the development of eastern and southeastern Europe, not in religion only but also in politics and in law, proceeded on separate lines.

In the Frank Empire the tribal notion of law prevailed as fully as in the earlier German kingdoms. In this empire, however, no superiority was attributed to Frank law over any other German tribal law, nor was any German tribal law permitted to override the Roman law. As often as legal transactions took place or legal relations were to be established between persons living by different laws, it was recognized as necessary either to observe the forms required by each law or to determine which should be chosen. In legal controversies between persons living by different laws, it was necessary to decide which of the two laws should govern the forms of pleading and the decision of each disputed point. Before the dissolution of the Frank Empire a considerable body of rules had been established governing these conflicts of law, and that great body of modern law which we call international private law may rightly be said to have its earliest roots in the laws of the Frank Empire.

In this empire we find also the beginnings of a general or common law of the realm, overriding all the tribal laws and Roman law. No such codification as that which Spanish churchmen had elaborated was attempted; but cases could be drawn by royal writ, and were drawn with increasing frequency, from the local courts to the king's court, and in this court neither Frank law nor any other tribal law nor Roman law governed the decisions. Each case was to be decided *secundum aequitatem*. In the reign of Charlemagne the activity of this central court was supplemented by a division of the realm into judicial districts, into each of which two itinerant justices were sent each year to ride circuit and to hold courts. Here was already the judicial machinery which was set up in England three centuries later by Henry II and by which the English common law was gradually built up. In the Frank Empire there were also the beginnings of general legislation by royal ordinances. At the close of the Frank period the more important ordinances were submitted for approval to the magnates of the realm, secular and spiritual, convoked in annual assembly. In the Frank Empire, however, these judicial and legislative organs were developing law for a far wider area than England, for the greater part of central and western Europe. If this empire had held together and if its law-making organs had remained active, the greater part of Europe would to-day be governed, as England has long been governed, by uniform law.

After the dissolution of the Frank Empire Europe fell into political chaos. Authority was so divided and subdivided that, even in those countries in which royal authority was first gradually consolidated, no efficient organs for the development of common law could be established. The kings had too little power to draw appeals to their courts. The assemblies of magnates, secular and spiritual, gradually enlarged by the admission of representatives from the cities, were chiefly solicitous to preserve and increase their rights and immunities, and were therefore little interested in general legislation.

The progressive legislation of the Frank Empire, except where its provisions had been introduced into the various tribal laws and were thus in some measure preserved as local usages, lapsed into desuetude. Europe was governed primarily by customary laws. These gradually ceased to be personal and became local. The individual was subjected primarily, if he were serf or tenant, to the custom of the manor; if he were a freeman, to the custom or law of the county or city.

Across this maze of customs there stretched, in the tenth and following centuries, two European bodies of law: the feudal law and the ecclesiastical law. Both systems had older roots. The economic basis of feudalism was serfdom, the tillage of the soil by men bound to the soil. In the conquered Roman provinces the Germans found almost all the agricultural land in the ownership either of the emperor, of municipalities, of ecclesiastical foundations or of secular magnates (*potentes*), and most of these estates were tilled by serfs. In the German portions of the Frank Empire there was from the outset a similar class, described as " half free," but as a rule the land was tilled in small parcels by freeholders. Before the end of the Frank period, however, great landed estates had developed here also, and the great majority of the German freeholders had been forced into the position of lessees or of serfs. At the same time, both in the Latin and German territories of the empire, slaves to whom definite holdings had been assigned for tillage (*servi inquilini*) were gradually rising to the higher status of serfs.

In the Roman Empire many of the great estates enjoyed what was already termed immunity, and in the Frank Empire a similar immunity was extended to the great estates, ecclesiastic and secular, in the German territories. In both empires, immunity meant only what we should today describe as limited powers of local government. In no case were the lords of these estates immune against the central authority. In the political disintegration of Europe which followed the fall of the Frank Empire, every lord of a manor became substantially the sole ruler of his domain. His independence was limited indeed by his duties to his overlord, but the overlord had no authority over his vassal's underlings.

Of the higher feudal tenures, the earliest to develop was tenure by knight service. This first took definite form in the Frank Empire. In the time of Charles Martel, when the Moors swept from Spain into Gaul, it was found necessary to meet the Moorish light cavalry, against which the German infantry was of little value, by the development of a superior heavy cavalry. Armored knights were already to be found in the retinues of the king and of the magnates, but far greater numbers were needed. The problem of their equipment and maintenance was solved by a sweeping confiscation of church lands, justified by the peril of Christendom. These lands the Frank rulers distributed in large tracts among their most trusted followers, who redistributed them among their followers on the condition of knight service. The whole process resembled the award of a public-service contract to a few responsible contractors and the sub-letting of the work to subcontractors. In this process we have, perhaps, the origin of the chain of intermediate tenures between the king of each country and the holders of knight fees. And in the principle that a subcontractor is directly responsible only to the person with whom he has contracted we have perhaps the origin of the rule of continental feudalism that " the man's man is not the lord's man " — a rule which produced that disintegration of political authority which followed the break-up of the Frank Empire and which reduced direct royal power to a shadow.

Once definitely established in the military organization of Europe, the principle of tenure by service was gradually extended into other fields. In the Frank Empire dukes, margraves and counts were in theory, and in practice also through the reign of Charlemagne, royal officers holding their position at the king's pleasure. Under the later and weaker Frank rulers, as previously in the Visigothic kingdom, these offices came to be held for life; and after the disruption of the Frank Empire all these offices, and also the great court offices, were regarded as heritable fiefs, and the royal lands which had been held as the appanage of such offices, their yield amounting to salary, were treated as land held on the tenure of political service. Land held by ecclesiastical dignitaries or foundations, in so far as it was not burdened with the duty of military service, was similarly regarded as held on the tenure of religious and charitable services — in the Norman-English phrase, tenure of frankalmoign.

The feudal law thus became the public law of mediæval Europe. It became also the private law of Europe as regarded land tenures. Nearly all the land in the open country was held on some feudal tenure, and the towns also had their feudal lords. There were, however, extensive territories in which the land was never feudalized. In Scandinavia feudalism gained little or no foothold. The same was true of the forest cantons of Switzerland. These territories may be said to have had no middle age; they passed almost directly from primitive Teutonic to modern conditions. And in other parts of Europe — for example, in Westphalia and in the Basque provinces of Spain — we find throughout the middle ages a free peasantry with fairly substantial holdings. In the towns, as these grew in population and in wealth and fought or bought themselves free from their feudal lords, municipal courts of final jurisdiction were established and feudal tenures disappeared.

For the development of the feudal system by legislation there existed, after the dissolution of the Frank Empire and during the following four centuries, no organs of wider authority than the diets or estates of the Holy Roman Empire and of the western kingdoms, and the activity of these bodies was confined to the field of public law. For the development of the feudal law by judicial interpretation, authority was even more widely dispersed. The imperial and royal courts had original jurisdiction only over the immediate feudatories of the crown. From the courts of these and of the lower mesne lords, and from the manorial courts, there was, as a rule, no appeal to any higher tribunal. In spite of these conditions, which favored an unlimited diversity of judgments, the feudal law remained essentially European. The substantial uniformity of its rules resulted primarily from the fact that the social and economic bases on which they rested were everywhere similar. Variations and changes were European rather than local. Throughout Europe, for example, the serfs on ecclesiastical domains enjoyed a status superior to that imposed on the serfs of nobles and knights.

In Spain and in France, as in England, the serfs on royal domains had an even better position. Economic changes, operating throughout central and western Europe, everywhere produced similar results. When the supply of agricultural labor was lessened by the movement of population to the towns, the position of the serfs was bettered. When this movement slackened, there was a corresponding deterioration of the servile status. As regarded the higher feudal tenures, also, the development of the law was European rather than national. Everywhere lay fiefs became heritable; almost everywhere female succession was permitted in default of male heirs; and, with few exceptions, the exclusive right of the first-born disappeared, fiefs becoming divisible. Uniformity of law was largely promoted by imitation, and particularly by the recognition accorded in this, as in other branches of mediæval law, to the written word. Certain early compilations, notably the Lombard *Libri Feudorum*, obtained general recognition as authoritative statements of feudal law.

To comprehend the great influence exercised in the middle ages by the Christian church, we must remember that on the church rested in the main the task of perpetuating the ancient Mediterranean civilization and adapting it to mediæval conditions. Not only were the mediæval rulers dependent upon the clergy, as the only educated class, for the efficient conduct of their civil administration, but many of the social duties which are today discharged by the state, notably education and poor relief, were necessarily discharged by the church, because the mediæval state attempted little more than the defence of its frontiers and the maintenance of internal peace. We must also remember that the Teutons, although their personal morality, like that of many other barbarians, was in some respects superior to the morality of civilized society, had little notion of social morals. To train them in social morality was perhaps the chief task of the mediæval church; and for the successful performance of this task the machinery employed by the church — peri-

odical confession, penance, exclusion from the sacraments
·and excommunication — was assuredly efficient and possibly indispensable.

In the strictly legal field we should note that throughout
the later middle ages the church exercised a practically exclusive jurisdiction over its clergy.   Clerks charged with
crime were amenable solely to ecclesiastical jurisdiction, and
even civil suits against them were commonly brought in the
ecclesiastical courts.   Over the laity also the Christian
church exercised a very wide jurisdiction, extending over
many matters which the Roman law regarded, and modern
law again regards, as falling within the exclusive jurisdiction of the secular courts.

The roots of ecclesiastical jurisdiction are to be found in
the Roman Empire.   The church had, of course, disciplinary
jurisdiction over its clergy and, as it developed a hierarchic
organization, this jurisdiction became increasingly effective.
In the later Christian period, when a clergyman was charged
with crime, the church was usually granted a stay of proceedings in the secular court until the ecclesiastical court
had investigated the matter.   If this court found the clergyman guilty it unfrocked him.   He then appeared in the secular court as a layman, and the scandalous spectacle of a
clergyman in the dock was avoided.   Acquittal by the ecclesiastical court, however, was no bar to the course of secular justice.

In the Frank Empire, after protracted controversy, the
church succeeded in withdrawing its clergy from the
jurisdiction of the ordinary criminal courts.   If the accused person was found innocent, no further proceedings
could be taken against him.   If, however, he was found
guilty, he was delivered to the secular power for punishment.

Of greater importance was the jurisdiction of the ecclesiastical courts over the Christian laity.   This also had
its roots in the Roman Empire, partly in the disinclination
of the early Christians to submit their controversies to the

heathen courts, but chiefly in the wide jurisdiction assumed by the church over the sins of its members. In the Roman Empire, even after Christianity became the state religion, this jurisdiction was extra-legal. The sanctions by which the church enforced its moral code were moral, not legal. The penalty of excommunication was indeed extraordinarily severe; it amounted to ostracism and assumed increasingly the features of a boycott. It had, however, no direct effect upon the legal status of the excommunicated person.

In the Teutonic kingdoms, however, at least when these kingdoms became not only Christian but orthodox, legal force was attached to excommunication. It became a European rule that an excommunicate who failed to make his peace with the church within a year and a day was *ipso jure* outlawed. Given this secular sanction, it is hard to see why the so-called Penitentials, in which sins and the appropriate penalty for each sin were elaborately catalogued, were not law books in the strictest sense of the word.

In these kingdoms, however, and even in the Frank Empire, the church courts claimed no exclusive jurisdiction in matters satisfactorily regulated by the secular law. As long as the rules on which the church insisted were embodied in the tribal laws or in supplementary legislation, the church was content to leave their application to the secular courts. It could always fall back, if necessary, on the concurrent jurisdiction which it exercised over sins.

In all these kingdoms, and particularly in the Frank Empire, the relation between church and state, in spite of occasional conflicts, was that of coöperation rather than of rivalry. Under Charlemagne this coöperation reached its highest development. After his death, however, the attitude of the church began to change. It became increasingly evident that the unity of the empire could not be maintained, and it was felt that the position of the church must be strengthened. Without an emperor to protect it, it would need greater independence. We find accordingly, in the ecclesiastical utterances of the middle decades of the ninth century, an increasing exaltation of spiritual over secular authority and an increasing demand for the independence of the church and for its more efficient organization under the central authority of the pope.

An important part of this movement for the greater independence of the church was the demand for an exclusive jurisdiction of the ecclesiastical courts in many matters of importance, particularly in matrimonial cases. This it obtained, and it gained at the same time an increasing jurisdiction, concurrent with that of the secular courts, both in criminal and in civil cases.

For the development of the ecclesiastical or canon law the church had adequate central organs. Legislative power was exercised by its councils and an extensive ordinance power was vested in the pope. From the ordinary ecclesiastical court, that of the bishop, appeals ran to Rome; and the pope, as universal ordinary, had an unlimited original jurisdiction. The judicial authority vested in the bishops and the pope was not, as a rule, directly exercised. The church developed a body of trained ecclesiastical lawyers, an ecclesiastical bar; and from this bar judges were drawn. The judicial authority of the bishop was usually delegated to a *subrogatus* of adequate legal training, and that of the pope was exercised by a bench of learned judges. It was chiefly through decisions rendered by the central court at Rome that the canon law was elaborated and refined. It was largely because of its superior judicial organization and the more refined and progressive character of its law that the church was able to secure so broad a field of jurisdiction as it held throughout Christendom during the later middle ages. Within the field recognized as ecclesiastical, the judgments of the church courts received secular recognition and support.

Ecclesiastical procedure was based on that of the late Roman Empire. In criminal cases it was inquisitorial in the technical sense, in that the court had not to wait for formal accusation by any complainant, but might take jurisdiction on information or on common report. In both criminal and civil cases procedure was inquisitorial in the popular sense of the word, in that the ecclesiastical judge sought to discover the facts by direct examination of the parties and of the witnesses. This is, of course, necessary in all cases where a judge has to render decision on the facts.

As compared with procedure in the local secular courts of the middle ages, ecclesiastical procedure was rational and progressive. It was, however, cumbrous and slow, because testimony was largely taken in the form of depositions — a practice which made cross-questioning of witnesses impossible except by taking further depositions — and because, for the purpose of eventual appeal, all testimony, pleadings and judgments had to be put into written form.

Gratian's famous digest of the statutory and case law of the church, made about 1140, was so thorough and so exact that in practice it was accepted as authoritative. Later compilations, made under papal authority, were simply supplements to Gratian's digest, and consisted even more largely of case law. In 1582 there was published, under the authority of Gregory XIII, a revised official edition of Gratian's digest and of the supplementary collections. This constituted, until our own day, the *Corpus Juris Canonici*.

When it was issued, the pope's writs were no longer running throughout Europe; but in most Protestant countries Protestant ecclesiastical courts long continued to exercise much of the jurisdiction previously held by the courts of Catholic Christendom. In these Protestant church courts the older canon law was applied, except where variant rules had been introduced after the Reformation.

Of later development, but of no less importance, was a third body of European law, the law merchant. In inland towns it was developed at periodical markets or fairs, such as that held in our own day (at least until the recent world war) at Novgorod in Russia — fairs to which merchants came from great distances. In seaports visited by trading vessels the law merchant was in continouus development. At the fairs and in the seaport towns mixed courts were commonly instituted, in which foreign and local merchants sat together and found judgments. In these courts the commercial customs of different regions met and waged a peaceful contest for mastery, in which the better custom tended to prevail.

It was especially in the courts of the seaport cities that common commercial law was developed, and it was in the courts of the Italian cities that a common maritime law was first established. From Italy this law spread to Spain and France and, following the lines of sea trade, to the Netherlands, to Germany, to England and to Scandinavia. From the seaports rules which were applicable to trade in general struck inland, following the routes of land trade. Both by sea and by land still other commercial customs spread through Europe; and just as the maritime law of Pisa served as a model for that of Barcelona, that of Barcelona for that of Oléron, that of Oléron for that of Wisby and that of Wisby for that of Bristol, so the custom of Lombard bankers spread throughout Europe and created a uniform law governing drafts and bills of exchange.

That Italy exercised a preponderant influence in the development of the law merchant was apparently due to the fact that Italian cities first contested the supremacy of Constantinople in the oriental trade and first revived Mediterranean trade on a large scale; but it was due also to the fact that the Italian cities were not making wholly new law. These cities were in close touch with the East, where the Mediterranean custom of merchants, as embodied in the Roman *jus gentium*, had never lost its authority. Building on such foundations the Italian cities constructed better law than was being made in Spain, in France or in Germany.

It is commonly said that the law merchant of the middle ages was simply mercantile custom. But here, as in all cases in which custom is said to have made law, we notice that the only customs that were binding were those which were recognized and enforced by courts. What enabled the merchants to transform their custom so largely into law was the fact that they had their own courts.

Certain compilations of maritime law obtained general recognition throughout Europe. The *Consulate of the Sea,* which appeared at Barcelona in the thirteenth century, the *Charte d'Oléron* and the *Waterrecht* of Wisby formed a continuous chain of maritime law, extending from the eastern Mediterranean to the Straits of Gibraltar and along the coasts of the Atlantic to the North and Baltic seas.

In England these three great bodies of European law, the feudal law, the canon law and the law merchant, enjoyed the same authority as on the Continent. William the Conqueror brought to England the Frank feudal law in the fuller development which it had attained in the tenth and eleventh centuries. He and his successors, however, took good care that the disintegrating tendencies of continental feudalism, which had made the dukes of Normandy so largely independent of the French crown, should not be developed in England. The continental doctrine that the man's man was not the lord's man obtained no recognition. The direct authority of the king over all the inhabitants of England was asserted from the outset, and on the whole effectively maintained.   When Henry II established a centralized judicial organization, his courts at once took jurisdiction of feudal cases, and under his successors the lower feudal courts, except those of the manor, were soon deprived of all real authority. The fact that one of the first fields in which a common law of England was effectively developed was that of feudal law had the result that the English law of real property today retains more traces of the feudal system than the law of any continental European state.

Of the law merchant the king's courts assumed no general control until the Tudor period. Until that period commercial cases were decided, as on the Continent, in independent commercial courts. When commercial cases were drawn into the royal courts the law merchant, except in admiralty cases, ceased to be a separate body of law. It became, especially through the decisions of Lord Mansfield, an integral part of the English common law. As earlier in Rome, the general law was itself so far commercialized as to meet all the needs of trade.

Ecclesiastical law was administered in special ecclesiastical courts until the nineteenth century, and, as on the Continent, the general canon law of Europe, as it existed before the Protestant Reformation, furnished the starting point for all further developments. The theory that before the time of Henry VIII England was governed by a special " king's canon law " is, as Maitland has demonstrated, a legal fiction.

The fact that the ecclesiastical law and the law merchant were not originally English but European law, and the resultant fact that a special training was desirable for their interpretation and application, led to the development of a special bar for ecclesiastical and admiralty cases. The members of this bar had their offices, not in the Inns of Court, but in Doctors' Commons. And today the special character of these European elements in the English law is emphasized in the existence of a special judicial division of Probate, Divorce and Admiralty. In the United States admiralty jurisdiction is exercised exclusively by the federal courts; and in many of our states we still have special courts of first instance dealing with fragments of the ecclesiastical law; courts variously described as surrogates' or orphans' or probate courts.

The great difference between English legal development and that of continental Europe is to be found in the fact that in England the royal courts instituted by Henry II speedily created a common custom of the realm, while on the Continent there was, at the time, no similar development. On the Continent, all cases that were neither feudal nor ecclesiastical nor commercial were decided, until a much later period, by local courts of the popular type, from whose decisions there was commonly no appeal. When the royal or princely authority became sufficiently consolidated to establish local courts composed of learned judges, and to draw appeals to central courts of the same character, local and provincial customs were too firmly established to be ignored in judicial decisions, and all that the new appellate courts could accomplish was to develop subsidiary law. In the application of the customary law, the mediæval rule that local law took precedence over provincial law, and provincial law over general territorial law, was almost universally observed until the nineteenth century, except where the general rule was established by legislation. General legislation, however, whether proceeding from diets or estates of the mediæval type or from the expanded ordinance power of autocratic rulers, dealt almost exclusively with matters of governmental organization and administration, including judicial procedure, and with criminal law. Until the period of national codification, there was little legislation in the field of private or civil law.

Throughout central and western Europe there was, in the eleventh and following centuries, urgent need of new and more refined law. The revival of commerce was but one phase of a wider movement, a general economic advance. There was a simultaneous industrial development. Land ceased to be the chief form of wealth; personal property grew in variety and in importance. These profound and sweeping changes required new law. In England the new law that was needed was provided to some extent by acts of Parliament; to a greater extent by the further development of the common law; but chiefly by the rapid development of equity. On the Continent the new law required could not be created by legislation, because there were here no efficient organs of general legislation. It could not be developed in the feudal or in the ecclesiastical courts, because the cases in which new law was most needed were not within their competence. The feudal courts had but slight and incidental jurisdiction over personalty. The ecclesiastical courts had such jurisdiction only in the administration of testaments, in the distribution of the goods of intestates and in matrimonial cases. Over contracts the feudal courts had no jurisdiction, nor had the church courts such jurisdiction, except in cases of vows, oaths and pledges of faith, and in cases of usury, which meant the taking of any interest on loans of money. In these matters the doctrines of the church were not an aid but an obstacle to economic and legal progress. Nor could even the commercial courts develop all the new law that was needed, because they had no jurisdiction except over strictly commercial controversies. The only courts that were in theory competent were the popular courts. These, however, were not so organized as to be able to adapt their ancient customs to the needs of a changing social order. In the open country these courts were composed of the resident land-holders: nobles and knights and, in some districts, free peasants. The city courts were composed, in most cases, of officials whose duties were primarily administrative.

From the point of view of comparative jurisprudence the composition of these local courts was abnormal. In the normal development of law decisions are either rendered by experts or virtually controlled in questions of law by expert opinion. In the very earliest stages of legal development the interpretation of custom and its application in controverted cases is usually controlled by priests. In early law, as in religion, priests are the custodians of tradition, and its authoritative interpretation rests in their hands. At a later period secular experts emerge by a sort of natural selection. In the later centuries of the Roman Republic the rulings of the unlearned magistrates and the decisions of the *judices* were virtually determined by the expert opinions of unofficial jurisconsults. In the early German tribal courts judgments were always formulated by a few " wise men " or " law speakers." In the final stages of legal development, judgments are rendered by official experts, that is, by

learned judges. In continental Europe, however, until near
the close of the middle ages, judgments were rendered in the
popular courts by judges destitute of any legal training, except what they might acquire in trying and deciding controversies.

Abnormal again, and a fatal impediment to the development by judicial decisions of the new law that was needed,
was the general lack of higher courts of appellate jurisdiction.
Courts of justice are legal laboratories. Their decisions are
social experiments. The rule laid down, especially in a case
involving a novel question, is a tentative rule. If it does not
work well, it is subject to modification in later and similar
cases. In courts of justice, as in other laboratories, conclusions of value are reached only gradually by repeated experiments, and their value is in proportion to the number
and variety of the experiments. In a purely local court no
such number nor any such variety of cases is presented for
consideration and judgment as in a court to which cases
are brought from a wider area. In imperial Rome cases
came to the supreme imperial court from the whole area of
western civilization. In England cases came to the royal
courts of Westminster from an entire kingdom. Later, appeals ran to the Privy Council from all parts of the British
Empire.

In the self-governing cities of the Continent, indeed,
greater progress was made than in the rural districts in the
task of adapting the local laws to the new social and economic conditions. City judges were in most cases better
qualified for their duties than were the rural judges. Attainment of official position in a self-governing community
implies a higher degree of ability than the inherited possession of land. In the cities, moreover, notably in the city
republics of Italy, there was earlier and more frequent legislation in the field of private law than elsewhere on the Continent. In some cases there was apparently, as in many
countries today, too much legislation. Dante's complaint
that his fellow citizens changed their laws as often as the

fashion of their dress might well be echoed by a modern satirist. Despite such aberrations, European city laws were clearly more progressive, and have exercised a greater influence upon modern European civil law, than any other contemporaneous local or territorial laws. At the best, however, in spite of the extent to which the laws of the older and more important cities were imitated or borrowed in their entirety by other cities, the city laws were provincial, not European, nor even national. There was need at the time not only of progressive law but also, and even more, of general law; and the development of variant city laws represented a new element of diversity and of resultant inconvenience — an inconvenience that was intensified by the simultaneous increase of inter-regional relations and of individual changes of domicile. Conflicts of law were so frequent as to give a marked stimulus to this branch of legal literature.

The reception of the law books of Justinian as subsidiary law for nearly all western and central Europe — an event which gave to Europe a fourth great body of continental law — is to be explained, first, by the general need for new and more refined law, and second, by the non-existence of law-making or law-finding organs that could supply the new general law that was needed. From this point of view we are able to understand why the Roman law was not received or not completely received in certain parts of Europe. It was not received where it was not needed. It was accordingly not received in countries where economic conditions were still so simple that the old laws and customs were still satisfactory. Therefore it was not received in Scandinavia, for instance, nor in the old forest cantons of Switzerland. In other countries where new law was needed the Roman law was not received, or at least not fully received, because in these countries adequate law-making or law-finding authorities were already in existence or in process of development. In England, for example, and in the Spanish kingdoms of Aragon and of Castile, the law books of

Justinian were not received, or not directly and fully received, because in these countries there were adequate legislative organs and royal courts of appeal. In northern France, where royal authority was consolidated earlier than in southern France, royal courts of appeal were established at the critical period when Roman law was sweeping over Europe, just in time to make it unnecessary to receive Roman law in its entirety. In most parts of the Continent, however, new law was needed and there were no legislative or judicial organs that could supply it. Accordingly, the law books of Justinian were fully received, not only in territories where the local customs were largely Roman and where the people believed that they were living by Roman law, as was generally the case in central and southern Italy and in southern France; they were received also in northern Italy, where Lombard law prevailed, and in Germany and in the Netherlands, where the local customs were even more distinctly Teutonic.

In the popular courts so refined a law as the Roman could not well be applied until there were learned advocates to state and explain its rules, nor even then could it be satisfactorily applied by unlearned judges. If Roman law were to be used in the civil courts, these courts must have, what only the church courts had so far possessed, a legally trained bar from which learned judges could be drawn. This need was first met in Lombardy, where law schools were developed in the eleventh century, and in the twelfth century it was more fully met in other parts of Italy, notably at Bologna. Here provision was made for the detailed study of the law books of Justinian, and this study attracted such masses of students that it seems to us today as if the supply of Roman civil lawyers must have greatly exceeded any conceivable demand for their services. To Bologna and to other Italian universities came law students by the thousands. They came not only from Italy and the French *pays de droit écrit*, but also from Germany and the Netherlands, where the Roman law was not yet received, and from other countries where it was not destined to be received. Some of these students were or intended to become clergymen, and were studying the Roman civil law in order to prepare themselves more fully to practice in the ecclesiastical courts; but many, apparently the majority, were laymen who did not intend to become priests. Why then were so many laymen studying a law which they could hardly expect to use in the secular courts of their own countries?

Of those who were consciously fitting themselves for a definite career, some indeed intended to teach Roman law in their native countries, but a far greater number were probably preparing themselves for governmental service. For several centuries the emperors, kings and princes of Europe had been forced to depend for expert administrative service upon the clergy, as the only educated class. After the dissolution of the Frank Empire, frequent and increasingly acute conflicts had arisen between the rulers of Europe and the ecclesiastical authorities. In these conflicts the secular rulers could not but doubt whether their ecclesiastical chancellors and ministers gave them whole-hearted support. The intensive study of the Roman civil law produced a new learned class, and emperors, kings and princes were prompt to draw into their service men of this class on whose undivided allegiance they could confidentially rely. That seems to be the chief reason why students came in such numbers from all parts of western and central Europe to study Roman civil law in Italy. Today we should call them students of political science. If they failed to secure positions in the central or local administration of any kingdom or principality, they might at least anticipate employment in some city.

For the complete reception and practical application of the Roman civil law, it was obviously necessary that the local courts of the older popular type should be replaced by courts of learned judges and that from each local court appeal should run to some higher court of the same character. In the self-governing cities the substitution of learned judges for the unlearned municipal magistrates could be, and was for the most part, effected by the cities themselves; but elsewhere courts of the new type could be established only by royal or princely authority, and only by such authority could higher courts be established to which appeals should run from the city courts as well as from the courts of the open country. What legal historians call the development of the learned judiciary was, from the political point of view, the replacement of the popular courts by official courts. This change was made possible by the growing power of the kings and princes. At the outset it seems to have encountered little opposition. In many cases the change met a popular demand. The inability of the unlearned judges to adapt the archaic customs of the popular courts to new conditions brought these courts into discredit; and in many instances complaints of denial of justice and prayers for relief, addressed directly to the territorial rulers, gave support, if not the first impulse, to the development of the new courts.

The reception of the Roman law was facilitated by the persistence of the Roman imperial tradition, which found expression in the theory of " continuous empire." In the sense in which the theory was most widely accepted, continuous empire meant that all existing political authority was somehow derived from the old Roman empire. The roots of this theory have already been indicated. It gained a new basis when the Frank kings became Roman emperors, and it was further strengthened when the title of Roman emperor was connected with the German crown. The Hohenstaufen emperors in their conflicts with the papacy cited Roman law texts against papal decretals. In 1165 Frederic II declared that he followed in the footsteps of his predecessors, the sacred emperors, especially Constantine, Valentinian and Justinian, and that he revered their sacred laws as divine oracles.

These were something more than claims advanced by the emperors; the theory of continuous empire was accepted even by ecclesiastical writers. An Italian canonist, Huguccio, wrote about the year 1200:

The Roman law binds the Romans and all who are subject to the Roman emperor. What of the French and English and other ultra-montanes? Are these bound by Roman law and held to live by it? I answer, certainly; for these either are subject or ought to be subject to the Roman emperor; for in the Christian world there is but one emperor, although in the different provinces there are different kings under him.

This extension of the theory was of course rejected by the kings of England, of France and of Spain, but it seems to have been regarded as a menace to their independence that could not safely be ignored. It is recorded that on one occasion, when a German king who was also Roman emperor paid a visit to England, he was not permitted to land until he had disclaimed political authority in that island. Assertion of independence is also to be found in the fact that the kings of England and of Spain were not infrequently described as emperors. In these precautions and protests we have no rejection of the theory that all European authority was derived from the Roman Empire. What was asserted was that imperial authority had been so divided that the Roman emperor of the German nation was not the superior of the western kings.

If all mediæval kings and independent princes were successors of the Roman emperors, it logically resulted, as Huguccio declared, that the laws established by their predecessors must everywhere be applicable. We find, in fact, that as early as the tenth century jurists of Barcelona were describing the special law of their province as municipal law and the Roman law as common law. Accordingly it appears that not only in the territories of the Holy Roman Empire but also in other parts of the Continent, the theory of continuous empire was of some value in facilitating the reception of the Roman law. It has always been found desirable to discover a legal basis for revolutions.

In many parts of Europe, in which the law books of Justinian were not received as having direct legal authority,

the Roman law was either received in its entirety, although
in a different form, or partially received through the acceptance of many of its principles and rules. In Castile, for example, the Roman law was virtually received by the enactment in the fourteenth century of the "Law of the Seven
Parts." In Aragon the Roman law was not received, either
directly or indirectly, as general subsidiary law; but, as in
other parts of Europe, gaps in the law were filled by what
is today called a "particular" reception of special Roman
rules. Such a particular reception took place in northern
France, where, as a French jurist neatly said, Roman law
was received *non ratione imperii sed imperio rationis*. In
England, the process of partial reception of Roman rules
had been under way in the common law courts almost from
the time of Henry II. In the development of a common
custom of the realm the English royal judges frequently
filled gaps in the law by adopting Roman rules, usually without acknowledgment of their source. In the court of equity
even more Roman law was introduced. In the ecclesiastical
courts the basis on which the so-called "private" canon law
was developed was, as elsewhere throughout Christendom,
the Roman civil law; and with the law merchant not a little
Roman law came into England, as was fully recognized by
Lord Mansfield. To an even greater extent such a particular reception of Roman law took place in Scotland before
the union of this kingdom with England.

Throughout Europe, even in such countries as the Scandi-
navian kingdoms and the forest cantons of Switzerland,
where Roman law was not received in the middle ages because economic conditions did not require new law, there
was, earlier or later, what legal historians call a "scientific"
reception of the Roman law. From the thirteenth century
on, statements of local and provincial customs were increasingly presented in an arrangement, and frequently in a terminology, borrowed from the Roman law. In England itself the first systematic statement of the law in the great work
of Bracton was based, both in arrangement of topics and in

the statement of general principles, on a famous and widely circulated Italian handbook of Roman civil law, the *Summa* of Azo. It is for this reason that in those parts of the Continent in which the law books of Justinian were never received, and even in England at the present time, the study of Roman law is regarded as a valuable and even necessary part of legal education.

In this chapter of European legal history we have a remarkable fulfillment of an ancient prophecy. Early in the fifth century, when German conquerors had swept through the Roman Empire from the Danubian provinces to Spain, the Gallo-Roman statesman and poet, Claudius Rutilius, exhorted Rome to look forward to the future triumph and perpetual influence of her laws.

> *Porrige victuras Romana in saecula leges*
> *Solaque fatales non vereare colus.*

For the interpretation of this fourth great body of European law and for its adaptation to mediæval and modern conditions there was no central European court, such as existed in Rome for the interpretation and development of the Roman canon law. But in this case, as in the case of feudal law and in that of commercial law, a substantial unity of interpretation was obtained by imitation. The interpretation worked out in the Italian universities from 1100 to 1250, digested and made readily available in the so-called " gloss " of Accursius, was accepted throughout Europe as authoritative; and throughout the middle ages and even in more modern times, writers and judges in all parts of the Continent were familiar with and frequently cited the writings of jurists and the decisions of judges in European countries other than their own. We have today an exact parallel in the interpretation and development of English common law and equity, in that decisions rendered in England and in the self-governing commonwealths of the British Empire are frequently cited in American courts, and American decisions in England and in all parts of the British Empire that are governed by English law.

The complete or partial reception of the Roman law in the later middle ages not only met immediate and pressing needs, but was also, on the whole, of permanent advantage. It had, however, for a time at least, some serious disadvantages. In some matters the law of the ancient Mediterranean world was not so well adapted to mediæval conditions as were the local customs. In theory it was everywhere recognized that the Roman law had only subsidiary force, that local custom was to govern every decision if any local rule could be discovered which fitted the case. The learned judges, however, trained in the Roman law and its fervent admirers, regarded variant local usages with disfavor. Legal writers described these usages as barbarous, asinine, established by men devoid of reason. In the new learned courts it became the established rule and practice that a plaintiff need not invoke local usage if he could base his claim on Roman law. If he could do this, it was for his adversary to plead a contrary local rule. In all cases where a local rule or usage was invoked, the learned courts required proof of its existence and its general recognition. When the local rule was unwritten, it was not easy to satisfy the learned judges that it was generally recognized and should be applied. The result was that in some matters an established local usage which was well suited to existing conditions was overridden by Roman law. This naturally aroused resentment, especially in German-speaking countries; and with the completed reception of the Roman law there arose a wide-spread reaction against "the foreign laws."

The hostility to the foreign laws had, however, other grounds. In the popular courts, in which the judges, as a current phrase ran, decided each case according to established custom and their five sound senses, a litigant had little need of counsel. He might indeed find it advisable to employ an expert pleader who was familiar with the es-

tablished forms of complaint and of answer, but such assistance was not expensive. With the establishment of learned
courts, applying a highly refined law, written in a language
intelligible only to the learned class, the aid of learned counsel became indispensable, and the fees of such counsel were
found burdensome. A German saying ran: " ' Now we have
got them ' said the lawyer to his client, but he meant his
client's dollars."

There were frequent complaints also of delay in the administration of justice. This was largely due to the introduction of appeals; but the evil was aggravated by the system of procedure, which was based on that developed in the
ecclesiastical courts. In these, as has been already noted,
procedure was cumbrous and slow. Men accustomed to the
cheaper administration of justice in the popular courts
found this delay of justice the more exasperating because
it meant still larger fees to counsel. For these grievances
the foreign laws were primarily held responsible, but to a
large extent responsibility for all the inconveniences which
followed the acceptance and attended the administration
of the foreign laws was imputed to the learned lawyers themselves. This, of course, was unjust; but throughout the
course of legal history we find similar criticisms and protests when a stage of social and economic development is
reached in which law necessarily ceases to be simple because life itself has become complicated. I know of but
one historical period in which no popular criticism appears
to have been directed against the legal profession, namely
the Roman republican period, and in that period the jurists
gave advice gratuitously.

A Castilian poem of the fifteenth century complains:

At the king's court there are more than sixty judges, audi-
tors and notaries, sitting in imperial state and drawing endless pay, besides a hundred and ninety doctors; and in forty
years they have not finished a single case. When a case
comes to argument the digest is cited, as are also the writings
of Guittoncino, Bartolus, Baldus, Juan Andrés and Enrique;

and when the case has been thoroughly argued, the advocates discover a point of error and begin all over again. In the land of the Moors one alcalde deals with civil and criminal cases, and one long day is enough to render equal-handed justice in any case. There there are no Clementinae or other decretals, no Azo or Rodbertus, but common sense and the good doctrine that shows all men how they are to live together.

In Germany more formal protests began to appear at the close of the fifteenth century. In 1497 the Bavarian knighthood complained: " Many things are done in contravention of established usage, whence arise deceptions, errors and confusion; for these professors of the law do not know our customs, nor if they knew them would they be willing to make any concession to them." In 1514 the duke of Württemburg was requested by the Estates to appoint as judges in his court " honest and sensible men from the nobility and the cities and such as are not doctors, that verdicts may be rendered in accord with established usage and that his Highness's poor subjects may not be unsettled and confounded." Many similar complaints might be cited. In the demands advanced in the German peasant insurrection of 1525 we read: " No doctors of laws, be they clerks or laymen, shall be suffered in any court, in any trial, or in any princely or other council; for the law is harder for them to unlock than for the layman, nor are they able to find the key until both the parties are impoverished and ruined." It is then suggested that these doctors " be employed to read and to preach the Holy Gospels instead of ruining folk by their delays and evasions." And at the close of the eighteenth century one of the reasons given for the projected preparation of an Austrian code was " to protect oppressed innocence against the ordinary arts of the advocates."

The rule established in the learned courts, that local customs must be proved, and the difficulty of proving unwritten customs gave a marked stimulus to the presentation of local and provincial laws in written form. Such compilations had been made in earlier times, but the thirteenth century produced a far greater number. This and the five following centuries may be described as the period of particularistic codification. Many of the earlier compilations were treatises, not codes, and were the work of private writers. Of these law books the most famous were Eike von Repkow's "Mirror of the Saxons" and Beaumanoir's "Custom of Beauvoisis." Such private compilations were gradually replaced by official statements. In France, for example, all the local and provincial customs were ultimately put into written form by royal commissioners. In some territories, notably in the separate Spanish kingdoms, in the Norman kingdom of Sicily and in some of the larger German territories, codes were enacted which covered an area far wider than that of a French province. It should be noted, however, that these codes, like the provincial codes of France, had as a rule only subsidiary force. It should be noted also that wherever the Roman law had been completely received, it retained ultimate subsidiary authority. The Prussian code of 1794 represented the first serious attempt, since the Visigothic code, to establish for an entire kingdom rules overriding variant local and provincial customs, and to deprive the Roman law of subsidiary authority. This code, of course, was not a national code, since the kingdom of Prussia was then, at least in theory, and afterward became in fact, a part of a wider national organization.

National civil law, as distinguished on the one hand from European law and on the other from local and provincial law, was first established in the nineteenth century, and first of all in France. The demand for a French civil code was widely voiced, at the beginning of the revolution of 1789, in the complaints and demands sent from all parts of the kingdom to the Estates General. These complaints were largely directed against the existence of different laws for different classes. Very general, however, was the complaint against the diversity of local laws and customs, which made Frenchmen living in different villages legally strangers each to the other. These protests were accordingly directed in part against the application in France of European laws, particularly feudal law and ecclesiastical law, and partly against the diversity of local customs. Against the law merchant there was no protest. This indeed had been put into the form of a French code in the reign of Louis XIV.

Revolutionary legislation abolished feudalism, clerical privileges and ecclesiastical jurisdiction. In 1804 the Code Napoleon abolished all the various provincial and local customs, deprived the Roman law of its authority, and thus established uniform national civil law.

In all the principal countries of Europe legal conditions were much the same as in pre-revolutionary France. From the point of view of legal uniformity they were no better in Spain, where each of the old kingdoms retained its ancient laws and customs. In Italy and in Germany, when these countries obtained national organization, there was a similar diversity of laws. In each there were different codes, some of them modern, and in Germany there was an extraordinary variety of ancient local customs. In each of the great national states of modern Europe, except in Spain, uniform civil law has been established by the enactment of civil codes. In Spain the attachment of Aragon and of some of the smaller provinces to their ancient separate law was so strong that in these provinces subsidiary force only was given to the civil code adopted in 1889. The example of the larger states of the Continent has been followed by the smaller. The movement has been European.

Most of these modern European codes exhibit a strong family resemblance. This is largely the result of imitation. The Italian civil code is based on that of France, and the Spanish civil code on those of France and of Italy. Nearly all the codes of the smaller European states are based on the French model. The one great national code which is not based on the Code Napoleon is the German civil code. This has had a marked influence upon the Swiss federal code. At present there are but two groups of European civil codes,

the Latin and the German-Swiss; and in comparing the codes
of these two groups we find a substantial accord which far
outweighs their material and formal differences. All the
European codes belong to what is aptly termed the modern
Roman law group.

In the preceding review of European legal history, stress
has been laid on the supra-national character and essential
unity of the whole movement, because, in the writer's opinion, this unity is obscured by the presentation of the movement in separate national histories. The chief phases of the
European movement are indeed fully described in the vast
body of literature dealing with the history of feudal, of
ecclesiastical and of commercial law, with the continuous
influence of Roman law through the earlier middle ages,
and with the reception of the law books of Justinian as subsidiary European law; but the separate treatment of each
of these great movements does not create the same impression that would be produced by a general history of European law. In the national legal histories the influence of
each of these great bodies of European law is of course
recognized; but the fact that each has its special literature,
in which its European character is emphasized, almost inevitably leads the national historian to dwell chiefly upon
the degree of influence which each has exercised upon the
legal development of his own country, and to insist rather
upon minor variations than upon fundamental similarities
in his own as compared with other countries. The national
point of view leads him also to devote to the local and provincial customs of his own country a degree of attention
that is out of proportion to their intrinsic importance and to
the degree of influence they have exercised in shaping the
existing civil law.[2]

[2] In the " Continental Legal History " series, published under the auspices of the Association of American Law Schools, the first volume attempts
to give a " General Survey " of continental legal history. The other volumes
are translations of standard works on the legal history of the more important
continental states, and on the special topics of commercial law, criminal law

The writers of these national histories are of course familiar with the special histories of each of the great bodies of European law, but the great majority of their readers are not. For admission to the bar, candidates are usually examined on mediæval and modern legal history only as this is presented in the legal histories of their respective countries. In the existing state of European legal historiography this is all that can reasonably be required. The result is to create, even in the legal profession, a false impression concerning the extent to which the existing law of each continental country is the product of that country's special history, and therefore an expression of its national life and character.

Efforts to attain a greater international harmony of legal rules, to create anything approaching world law, are impeded far less by national interests than by national sentiment. Not only in commercial law, in the narrower sense of the term, but also in many fields of general civil law, notably in the law of personal property and of contractual and quasi-contractual obligations, countries that have reached a similar stage of economic development have little or no interest in the maintenance of variant rules. In these fields, different rules are historical accidents rather than the expression of national characteristics. National sentiment, however, regards national law as an essential element of the national life, second in importance only to a common language. Where a national law is the product of a historical development reaching back, as in the case of the English common law, through many centuries, instinctive reluctance to abandon settled rules for the sake of attaining world law is intelligible. The attachment of even a province to its peculiar law, when this law has deep roots in the past, is

---

and judicial procedure, these topics being treated from the continental point of view. In the absence of any general history of continental law, the residuary " General Survey " is compiled from the nationalistic literature; and the failure of this volume to give a clear view of the essential unity and continental character of the whole movement strikingly illustrates the inadequacy, for any such purpose, of the material to be found in the legal histories of the several European States.

equally intelligible, and we have seen that the devotion of Aragon and other Spanish provinces to their ancient *fueros* was strong enough to prevent the establishment of common national law in Spain.　In the other continental states, even in Switzerland, where attachment to cantonal law delayed for decades the enactment of a federal civil code, provincial sentiment has been unable to prevent the establishment of common national law.　National sentiment, however, will prove a more serious impediment to the attainment of greater unity of law in Europe; and this sentiment is strengthened by the belief, even though this belief be largely an illusion, that the different civil codes of the Continent have ancient roots in the special history of each country.　As Wordsworth puts it:

" Assent is power; belief the soul of fact."

II

THE DOMAIN OF POLITICAL SCIENCE [1]

THE term " political science " is greatly in need of definition. Technical terms should have a limited and exact meaning; but this particular term is used vaguely, not by the laity alone but by professed experts. These speak sometimes of a " political science," at other times of a plurality of " political sciences." Again, the sciences which are commonly described as " political " are often designated as " social "; and besides the various " social sciences " there appears to be a " social science."

A more exact use of these terms is certainly desirable. This, it seems to me, is more likely to be obtained by endeavoring to establish the respective domains of the sciences in question and their relation to each other, than by laying down dogmatic definitions, the practical value of which is often overrated. A neat definition is a very attractive thing. It seems to offer the conclusion of wisdom in portable form. It is, in fact, the condensed result of a great deal of hard thinking; but to understand it, to appreciate what it includes and what it excludes, the thoughts of the definer must be thought over again until the disciple has gained the same outlook over the subject as the master — and then he no longer needs the definition.

Social science, in the broadest sense, deals with all the relations of man in society; more precisely, with all the relations that result from man's social life. It may be questioned whether it is proper to speak of *a* social science. We certainly have no general social science in the sense in which we have particular social sciences. In politics, in economics,

[1] Reprinted from the Political Science Quarterly, vol. i, no. 1, March 1886, pp. 1–8. This leading article was published upon the establishment of the *Political Science Quarterly* by Professor Munroe Smith, who was then and for many years thereafter editor.

in law and in language, we are able to some extent to trace phenomena to their causes, to group facts under rules and rules under principles. But the laws which underlie man's social life as a whole have not been grasped and formulated. Social science or sociology, if we use the term, is therefore simply a convenient general expression for a plurality of social sciences. But social science is used in another and a narrower sense. The various social sciences do not cover the entire field of man's social life. There are portions of that field — *e.g.*, movement of population, vice and crime — which lie beyond the domain of the older and better-defined sciences; in which the preliminary work of exploration has only recently been undertaken; and in which little has been accomplished beyond the collection of data by statistical observations. For lack of a more definite term,[2] social science is used in a restrictive sense to describe these newly-entered domains of investigation.

Among the social sciences we find some which are designated as the political sciences. Political science signifies, literally, the science of the state. Taken in this sense, it includes the organization and functions of the state, and the relation of states one to another. But what are the political sciences? Are they subdivisions, or special branches of the science of the state? Economic science is obviously regarded as one of the political sciences, for the term " political economy " is used more often than " economics " and commonly in quite as broad a sense. But economic science does not occupy itself simply with the state. It is the science of wealth. It deals with the finances of the state, but it deals also with the accumulation, exchange and distribution of wealth by individuals. But the political sciences may perhaps be taken to be those which deal with the relations of man in the state, *i.e.*, with all the relations which *result* [3]

---

[2] For the science of population the Germans are beginning to use the word *Demologie*. This new science, strictly speaking, lies only in part within the circle of the social sciences; in part it reaches out into natural science, *i.e.*, biology.

[3] This limitation is obviously necessary. The mere fact that certain relations exist in the state does not make them political; otherwise, in the present stage of civilization, all social relations would be political. The question is: Do the relations exist *because of* men's living in and under the state?

from man's political life. But is economic science a purely
political science even in this sense? Do we not find, for example, private property and barter among people who, like
Homer's Cyclops, know no other social organization than
that of the family? If economics be a political science,
much more must law be so. Law, like economic science,
deals with many relations not resulting from man's political
life — *e.g.*, property and family relations — but its rules are
at least formulated by state organs, and enforced by governmental machinery. Nevertheless, law is not commonly
classified as one of the political sciences. It seems preferable, under these circumstances, to recognize but one political
science — the science of the state. The relations with which
this science deals may, of course, be subdivided and treated
separately. We may separate the relations of states one to
another — the international relations — from the national.
We may divide the national relations into questions of state
organization and state action. We may distinguish between
the various functions of the state. But there is no good reason for erecting these various groups of questions into distinct political sciences. The connection of each with all is
too intimate.

In endeavoring to distinguish political science from the so-
called political sciences, I have no thought of denying the
close connection which subsists between political science, as
here defined, and the sciences of economics and law. On the
contrary it is a chief object of this article to demonstrate the
inter-dependence of these sciences. In defining them we
emphasize the point of view rather than the field of view —
the side from which social relations are regarded rather than
the relations themselves. Thence arises an impression
that the domains of these sciences are more distinct than is
really the case.

> *Leicht bei einander wohnen die Gedanken,*
> *Doch hart im Raume stossen sich die Sachen.*

Each of the three sciences we are now considering holds a
large proportion of its territory in common with one or both

of the others. Law and politics have common ground in the organization and operation of government in the single state. Law and economics are both concerned with all commercial transactions. The theory of governmental administration is largely economic; and state-finance is a part of the administrative system of the state, is based on economic theory, and is regulated by law. The relative position of these sciences may be indicated by drawing three circles or ellipses, each of which intersects the other two, with a very considerable space occupied by all in common. Nor is the ground which these three sciences cover, proper to them only. All the social relations with which politics, law and economics have to do lie within the domain of ethics. Duty, loyalty, honesty, charity — these ideas are forces that underlie and support the state; that give to law its most effective sanction; that cross and modify the egoistic struggle for gain.

Politics, law and economics — political, legal and economic science — these two classes of terms have thus far been used indiscriminately. But it is obvious that the politician and the lawyer are not necessarily political or legal scientists, any more than a man who busies himself in devising new means of gaining wealth is an economist. Primarily, of course, the difference is in the aim. Science aims at the discovery of truth. But the methods must be such as are adapted to realize this aim. What then are the methods of the social sciences? All the various methods employed may be grouped under one term — *comparison.* The single fact means nothing to us; we accumulate facts that seem akin; we classify and reclassify them, discarding superficial and accidental similarities as we discover deeper substantial identities. We accumulate and compare facts from our own and from foreign countries; we accumulate facts from the immediate and more remote past, and compare them with each other and with present facts. Statistics, comparative legislation, history — these are means and modes of accumulating facts for comparison.

The ancillary relation which these studies bear to the social sciences is often lost from view. We speak of an historical science, of a science of comparative legislation, of statistical science — and thus apparently coördinate these studies with the social sciences of politics and economics, law and ethics. But they should not be so coördinated. History, for example, is not a social science in the same sense as economics, for it does not deal with a definite group of social relations. It is a mode of investigating all sorts of social relations. The same is true of statistics and comparative legislation.

I have not the slightest intention of denying the existence of a science of history, of statistics, or of comparative legislation. There are methods of accumulating and using facts (?) that are inaccurate and deceptive. The number of these methods is as unlimited as the ingenuity of ignorance. There are, on the other hand, methods of collecting, testing, sifting and using facts that give approximately accurate and trustworthy results. These are properly called scientific methods. They are limited in number; and the most important are those which we call the sciences of history, of statistics, and of comparative legislation. But the relation of these sciences to the social sciences is not coördinate, but auxiliary.

Of all these auxiliary sciences, the most important is history. All other methods of comparative study may be said to operate on a single plane — the plane of the present. History gives to the social sciences the third dimension, and thus indefinitely increases the range of comparison. But it does far more than this. To the application of the historic method we owe the discovery that social institutions persist and at the same time change from generation to generation and from century to century; that these changes, in the case of each single institution, are not fitful but steady, and are of such a nature that we involuntarily borrow words which describe the processes of organic life, and speak of their " growth " and " decay "; and when we take a further step, and compare the social institutions of the present time, in their totality, with those of earlier and still earlier periods until tradition vanishes in the " infinite azure of the past," we discover a constant tendency from the simple to the complex, a constantly increasing differentiation of form and specialization of function; so that we borrow another phrase from the science of biology, and speak of the " evolution " of states and law, of art and language. The sociologists have borrowed the word from the naturalists, but not the conception. Before the naturalists made the word technical, German philologists had demonstrated the evolution of language, and a German jurist had said: Law is not made, it grows; it is as much a part and a product of a nation's life as is its speech.[4]

We have already seen that the domains of politics, economics and law are largely coincident. From that coincidence alone would result a close interdependence. This interdependence is greatly increased by the use of the comparative and especially of the historical method. To use statistics safely, the sociologist must take into account the entire social condition of the state in which the statistics are gathered. Political or legal as well as economic differences may make the statistical reports of two states upon the same subject valueless for comparison. The intelligent use of foreign legislations by the jurist, the economist, or the student of politics, implies not only an acquaintance with the general principles and technical structure of foreign law, but also a knowledge of the political and economic conditions of the country in and for which each particular law was made. But it is in historical investigation that this interdependence of the social sciences becomes most sensible; and it is through historical investigation that we gain insight into the cause of this interdependence. It is rarely possible to stamp an historical fact as exclusively political, legal, or economic. The student will naturally approach it from one of these sides, and is in danger of failing to see the others; but a one-sided

[4] Savigny, *Beruf unserer Zeit* (1815).

view is never a true view. Take, for example, the agrarian bill of the younger Gracchus. To the economist, its principal interest lies in the attempt to break up the *latifundia,* the great cattle-ranches, and to reëstablish small agricultural holdings. To the lawyer, the chief points of interest are the tenure by which the *latifundia* were held, and the proposed inalienability of the new properties. To the student of politics, it is a phase in the struggle between the senatorial oligarchy of Rome and the democracy of the peninsula. But to view the fact truly, each of the three should be able to see it on all sides.

If we seek to trace through history the evolution of the state, we find each step in its development recorded in the evolution of law and explained to a great degree by economic changes. The transformation of the nomadic clan into the local community and of the tribe into the primitive state is accompanied and conditioned by the development of agriculture. The substitution of aristocracy for kingship in the ancient world, and the analogous development of feudalism in mediæval Europe, are results of the development of private property in land. The substitution of monarchy for aristocracy, and of democracy for monarchy — the cycle through which Aristotle already saw the little states of the ancient world moving — and the similar substitution, in modern Europe, of absolutism for feudalism and of democracy for absolutism — these further changes are necessitated by the development of commerce and the increasing weight of movable wealth.

If it is the evolution of law upon which our attention is primarily bent, we find that in primitive society rules which we should to-day call legal are inextricably blended with moral precepts and religious dogmas. Properly speaking, there is neither religion nor morals nor law in this stage of social development, for these distinctions are not yet drawn. The only sanction of these undifferentiated rules is religious fear and the moral sense of the community. But as the tribe becomes territorially fixed and the state takes form, the physical power of the state begins to be applied to compel obedience to a certain portion of these traditional rules, and law begins to separate itself from religion and ethics. As civilization becomes more complex, the state plays an increasingly important part, and the domain of law widens. But every step in its development, as in that of the state, is conditioned to a great extent by economic changes.

Finally, if we take economics as the immediate object of investigation, we find that the operation of the social forces with which this science primarily concerns itself is constantly modified by the development of ethics and law. In the struggle for existence into which men enter with unequal endowments, it is at first the physically weaker who goes under, and the physically stronger who survives; but the cruder forms of violence are gradually tabooed by ethics, and at last law interposes its imperative *vim fieri veto,* ends the reign of force, and makes the plane of struggle intellectual. Then cunning and fraud take the place of brute strength; but law meets fraud with equitable interposition, and develops a system of checks that grows more complex and refined as the increasing ingenuity of man develops subtler forms of iniquity.

It is a result of the entire preceding discussion that political, economic and legal science are so interdependent that the investigation of any one of the three implies the investigation of both of the others. Choose which you will, the others are necessary auxiliaries. But of the three, the science of the state is assuming more and more the dominant position. The principal legal question of the day, in our country, is: To what organ or organs of the state shall the development of law be entrusted — to the judicial *and* legislative, or to the legislative alone? This is the essence of the question of codification. Behind this is rising a second question, which Europe has met and answered and which we shall soon be called upon to answer: Shall the development of law be partly local and partly national, or national only? Both of these questions are political. Again, the burning economic questions of the day all turn on the advisability, the extent or the method of state interference: between landlord and tenant, in Great Britain; between capitalist and laborer, in Germany; between corporations and the public, in the United States.

The conception of the state as a mere protective association against external force and internal disorder is antiquated. The state is everywhere exercising other functions than the protection of person and property and the enforcement of contract. Whether the increasing importance of the state be deplored or applauded, the fact remains that it is rapidly becoming, if it is not already, the central agency of social evolution.

III

STATE STATUTE AND COMMON LAW [1]

CODIFICATION has been a subject of debate in this country for about half a century. There has been discussion enough one might naturally assume, if not to settle the question, at least to illuminate it upon all its sides and to furnish all the data for its settlement. Nevertheless, the most important side of the question has scarcely been examined. The attention of the debaters has been centred upon the direct results of codification — upon its immediate advantages or disadvantages. It may be shown, I think, that the direct results for good or for evil are much less considerable than the friends and opponents of the movement have maintained, and that the question of real moment is this: How will codification affect the development of our law in the future? development of the codifying state?

1. What will be the effect of codification upon the legal development of the codifiying state?

2. What will be the effect of the general adoption of state codes upon the general development of American law?

About the first of these questions there has been much debate, although the issue has not always been clearly formulated. The second question, so far as I know, has not even been put.

I

The law of the American colonies, like the rest of their civilization, was English; and the development of American law, however modified by new conditions and alien grafts, has been and is a growth from English roots. The English law which the colonists brought with them and by which they lived — avowedly, in most cases; actually, where they

[1] Reprinted from the *Political Science Quarterly*, vol. ii, no. 1, March, 1887, pp. 105–134; vol. iii, no. 1, March, 1888, pp. 134–164.

did not avow it — was case law, *i.e.*, judge-made law. It had
been developed by the courts. It could be changed by king
and people, acting together in Parliament, and such changes
were made from time to time; but they did not compare in
number or importance with the changes made by the courts.
Besides the law-interpreting power — which is always to a
greater or less extent a law-making power — vested in the
ordinary courts, the chancellor wielded the law-overriding
power of the crown, the old Germanic right of the king to
substitute equity for law; and every student of English legal
history knows to what an extent the latter power was exercised.

The United States emerged from the war of independence
with this body of English judge-made law as the basis of
their legal development. As means of legal development
they had all the English factors: the interpreting power of
the ordinary courts; the extraordinary powers of the courts
of equity; and statute, or act of legislature. They had also
the English theory of the relative power of these three law-
making organs, according to which equity overrides common
law, and statute supersedes both. In addition to these, they
devised a fourth form of law, dominating all the others. The
people themselves, in state and nation, created written constitutions. As constitution-making power, the people legis-
lates directly; and such legislation overrides, of course, all
ordinary statute.

In studying the development of our law during the past
century, we observe, in the first place, that the extraordinary
powers of equity have counted for relatively little. The creative movement of English equity had spent itself long before the separation of the colonies. It had left a tolerably
well-settled body of rules superimposed upon the common
law, and the courts of equity had come to limit themselves
to interpreting and applying these rules. In the United
States, the tendency has been to intrust the enforcement of
both bodies of law to one set of courts; and we have come
to use the phrase " common law " as including equity, *i.e.*, as

including all judge-made law. The word will be so used in the remainder of this paper.

All the other law-making factors have continued active and productive. The highest courts of the different states have continued to modify and develop the common law by decisions; the legislatures have issued annual or biennial volumes of session laws; and the people, from time to time, has revised and modified its state constitutions. But when we examine the legal development in our states more closely, we see a marked tendency of the superior law-making power to encroach upon and narrow the field of the inferior. Our state constitutions limit the power of the legislatures. Many of their provisions are restrictive in form, prohibiting the legislature from doing certain things; all are restrictive in fact, since the legislature must legislate in accordance with the constitution. And the constitution-making power has by no means confined itself to the domain of the organic public law; the provisions of the state constitutions, particularly in the newer states, touch every branch of the law, public and private, and their scope widens with each revision.[2] In like manner, we find the legislatures encroaching upon and narrowing the power of the courts; not expressly by restrictive statutes, but in fact. Whenever a legislature regulates by statute a matter previously governed by common law, it diminishes *pro tanto* the power of the judiciary. This is obviously true whether the statute change the rule of common law or not. As long as the rule rests upon decided cases, the judiciary can in fact change it by re-examination and re-interpretation of the cases in point. As soon as the rule becomes statutory, the court is restricted to the interpretation of the particular form of words which the legislature has seen fit to employ. The same limitation of the judicial power may sometimes be accomplished when a new statute is passed to meet an entirely new question, if the matter be one with which the courts might have dealt. The legislature, in such cases, seizes ground which the courts might have occu-

[2] Stimson, *American Statute Law*, preface.

pied. So whether it simply re-enacts or changes or adds to the common law, each legislative act invades and lessens the power of the courts. The moment any relation of our social life is regulated by statute, the development of the law governing that relation is substantially barred to the courts and must be obtained from the legislature.

From this point of view, " codification " of the law is simply an attempt to do all at once and once for all what appears to be going on gradually without codification. For codification, in so far as it is opposed and has become a subject of debate in the United States, does not mean the orderly arrangement of that portion of the law which is already statutory, — nobody objects to periodical revision of statutes, — but the transfer from the courts to the legislature of the future development of all our law; the elimination, as far as may be, of the judiciary as a factor in the making of our law.

This issue has seldom been squarely presented. American lawyers are not in the habit of arguing abstract questions, and the question of codification never becomes a burning one until the bar of a state is actually confronted with a draft code. Then the discussion necessarily turns, to a great extent, upon the merits or demerits of the particular code which is proposed for adoption.[3] Of course the general question is also discussed; but the real issue is commonly darkened by arguments, or assertions rather, of an extremely absurd kind. The opponents of codification have sinned in this respect almost as grossly as its friends.

The anti-codifiers have maintained again and again that it is " impossible " to reduce the common law to statutory form. If by that they merely mean to say that no human ingenuity can construct a series of statutes, or a code, which shall answer every possible legal question justly and *directly, i.e.,*

---

[3] This has notably been the case in New York. The so-called " Field code " is opposed on the ground that it is unscientific in structure and inaccurate as a presentation of existing law. It was vetoed on that ground by Governors Robinson and Cornell; and on that ground it was rejected by the legislature in 1885 and again in 1886.

by the simple application of one or more sections to the case in point, without resort to deduction or to inference from analogy, — if they merely mean to deny the possibility of codification in this sense, no sane person will dispute their position.   But no sane person at present proposes to make such a code.[4]   On the other hand, if they mean to say that the common law cannot be crystallized into forms of words and set forth in rules, the answer is, that this is not only possible, but is in fact precisely what the English and American courts have been doing ever since they began to decide cases.   No case was ever decided without affirming or modifying an old rule or setting up a new one.   If at the outset a rule is stated too broadly or too narrowly, if its first formulation is crude and unsatisfactory, it is narrowed or extended by subsequent decisions — in other words, it is amended — until it becomes satisfactory.   But at every stage of its development the common law is just as truly a body of positive rules as is any book of statutes.

[4] Bentham contemplated the establishment of such a code.   He did not think it could be perfected at first essay; but it might gradually be perfected, he thought, by a series of additions.   The courts were to have no power of filling open places; the code should be made complete by statutory amendment.   See his *General View of a Complete Code of Laws,* ch. 31 and 34; *Works,* Bowring's ed., vol. III, pp. 205, 206, 209, 210. — The idea was a common one in the eighteenth century.   " New law-books were demanded, which, by their completeness, were to give a mechanical certainty to the administration of justice.   The judge was to be relieved from the necessity of exercising his own judgment and restricted to the literal application " of the provisions of the code.   Savigny, *Beruf unserer Zeit,* 3te Aufl., S. 5. — The Prussian Landrecht of 1794 was meant to be a code of this sort.   The codifier attempted to forecast all possible questions.   " The consequence of this was the introduction of numerous casuistic passages, which were based on no general principles, and which, therefore, instead of making the law clear, gave the best possible basis for doubts."   Die neueren Privatrechts-Kodifikationen, S. 366, in Holtzendorff's *Encyklopädie der Rechtswissenschaft,* 4te Aufl., 1882.   The courts were not to decide doubtful points, but to ask for instructions from a legislative commission in Berlin.   The legislation thus obtained was to be added to the code.   One such supplement was issued, April 11, 1803; after this, the construction of the law was left to the courts.   *Ibid.,* S. 366–368. — The Prussian experiment has never been repeated.   The code Napoleon provides, in art. 4: " The judge who shall refuse to render decision under pretext of the silence, the ob-·scurity, or the insufficiency of the law, is to be prosecuted as guilty of denial of justice."   The penalty is fine and suspension (code pénal, art. 185). — None of the codes adopted or proposed for adoption in the United States have attempted to realize the Benthamite ideal.   Mr. David Dudley Field has expressly repudiated it.   See his article on codification in the *American Law Review,* vol. xx, no. 1, pp. 1, 2.

On the other hand, one of the favorite arguments of the codifiers is equally baseless. They assert that everybody " has a right to know the law " — which nobody disputes — and that codification will make the law intelligible to everybody — which is nonsense. For a codifier necessarily does one of two things. He either states the existing rules of law in the technical language in which they are already clothed, or he restates them in other words which are not technical, and which " everybody understands." In the first case it is obvious that the layman is little advantaged. It may be easier for him to find the rule, but it is no easier for him to understand it. In the second case, he appears to be better off — but is he? Every lawyer knows that the restatement of a legal rule in popular phraseology simply makes its application uncertain. He knows that the law is clothed in technical phraseology simply because it is necessary to have words of which the meaning is absolutely certain. He knows that the only difference between a technical phrase and a phrase of common speech is that the one has a definite sense and the other a variety of possible meanings. But it has always been singularly difficult to get this fact through the head of the average layman. Every doctor of theology or medicine, every scientific man, every artist, every tradesman and every mechanic uses in his own science or business technical terms which are unintelligible to the outsider. Even when the term is explained, it is quite likely that the outsider will not understand the explanation, because it involves the understanding of other things unknown to him, the knowledge of which is part of the science or craft in question. Now all these people use technical terms for the same reason that the lawyer uses them — because they need terms of definite meaning. This necessity, felt in the simplest trade, is greatest in the sciences. And yet all these people demand that the law, the oldest and perhaps the most complex of sciences, shall speak the language of the hearth and the street. It seems a waste of effort to combat such a demand, resting upon such a delusion. But if it be a waste of effort, it is not because the delusion is obvious, but because it is imperishable.

Not a few lawgivers have shared it, and have attempted to " popularize " the law. The result has always been the same. As soon as a set of new, vague, and " popular " terms is bundled into the written law, the courts proceed to give them, by construction, that definiteness of meaning which legal science requires — and which in fact the people themselves demand, for the people demand that law shall be certain. That is, a set of new technical terms is constructed.[5] In the meantime, not even the lawyer knows what the written law means; and the layman is worse off than before, because he thinks he knows what it means. He is not to blame; he has been told, by those who ought to know better, that the law can be made perfectly intelligible to him. He therefore attempts to act as his own lawyer — with the proverbial result. Of course he is made no wiser by the event. He simply abuses the " pettifogger " on the other side, who by captious construction has wrested the statute from its true meaning, and the judges who have decided inequitably on " technical " grounds. He will not recognize that the law is a science, and that a science cannot be mastered without study.

Much less can he be brought to understand that the law is simplified in proportion as it becomes more scientific, and that there is no other way given among men by which it can really be simplified. The relations of man to man in civilized society are not few or simple, but infinitely varied and complex; and if the legislator attempts to set up positive rules directly regulating every possible relation, there can be no limit to the number of the rules. Legal science analyzes and classifies these relations, and finds general rules to govern the relations which it has formed. The further this process is carried, the more simple the law becomes. The jurist who finds a rule burdened with a number of arbitrary exceptions

---

[5] So in California. See J. N. Pomeroy, *The Civil Code in California,* pp. 7, 17, 18 *et passim.*

and sets in its place a rule that includes the exceptions, or who brings a number of apparently isolated rules under a single principle of which they are henceforth corollaries, — he it is who simplifies the law. He does not make it any more intelligible to the layman, but he makes it easier for the advocate and the judge to master and apply it.

There is, then, nothing in the nature of the rules of common law which prevents their being enacted as statutes; and there is nothing in such enactment which makes the rules simpler or more intelligible. The only direct result which can be accomplished by codification is to make the rules more accessible. Upon this point the advocates of codification lay great stress. The common law, they say, is scattered through an immense number of cases. Reports of decisions have been accumulating for centuries and already fill thousands of volumes. It is in this chaos of cases that we must search for the rules of our law. The number of cases cited in briefs and decisions is appalling. Why should we not collect the rules of the law in a code?

The argument seems a strong one. The evils deplored are undeniable, particularly the multiplication of citations. But are these evils wholly due to the nature of case law? Would they be wholly removed by collecting the rules of the common law in a code? Is it true that the lawyer and the judge have to search through hundreds of cases to find the *rule* which they need, or do they search for guidance in the *application* of the rule to the concrete case before them? I do not believe there are two answers to these questions. Now if the multiplication of citations is due to the attempt to find guidance in the application of the rule, — to find, if possible, a case running " on all fours " with the case before the court, — what will it avail us that the rules themselves are in a code? They will still be interpreted and applied in the light of old and new cases, until our adherence to precedent becomes less slavish, and our lawyers acquire more of that independence in juristic thinking which characterizes the bench and the bar of France and Germany. Nothing but a complete reform in our legal science will give them that independence; a code will not do it.

It may be admitted, then, that codification will make the *rules* of the law somewhat more accessible; but the greatest difficulty, that of their *application*, is not lessened. This distinction is extremely important. It greatly lessens the force of another argument which constantly appears in the discussion of the code question, and upon which the friends of codification lay great stress. They say that the common law is not only inaccessible but uncertain; that it is not only difficult to find the law in the constantly increasing mass of cases, but that careful exploration discloses important contradictions and conflicts in the law. Here again it will be found, in almost every instance, that the conflict of authorities is in reference to the application of a rule which is itself undisputed. How will this evil be abated by putting these well-settled rules into a code? Where the conflict of authorities is serious, it doubtless indicates that there is something wrong about the rule — that it is ill formulated. What will it profit us, if that is the case, to have the ill formulated rule made statutory? We shall be worse off than before, by as much as it is harder to get an act of legislature than a decision of the highest court. —I exclude the hypothesis that the codifier is to find that happier formulation which the courts have been vainly striving to discover, because, in the first place, the advocates of codification themselves insist that a code shall simply enact the existing rules, not change them; and because, secondly, it is not to be assumed that we shall be able to get our codes made by men possessed of more than the average wisdom of the wise men of their own day.

That the uncertainty of the law lies almost entirely in the *application* of its rules is a truth that would soon come home to us if our law were wholly statutory. In the case law which has grown up about the codes of France and Germany, there are quite as serious contradictions and uncertainties as in the case law of any state in our Union. He

who would satisfy himself that this is true of French law
need not struggle through the voluminous *Jurisprudence
Générale* of Dalloz; any standard handbook of French civil
law will answer the purpose. In fact, we need not go so
far afield for our evidence. We have been living under a
constitutional code for a century. It was drafted by able
men, wise in statecraft and learned in the law. They sensibly used, as far as possible, words and phrases whose
meaning had been settled by centuries of constitutional
conflict and judicial interpretation. Has there been no uncertainty in the construction of our Federal constitution?
Is there no uncertainty to-day?

Unfortunately we have here again to deal with a delusion that seems indestructible. Neither reason nor experience seems to shake it. It is as old as the XII Tables and
as new as the proposed civil code of New York.

The points thus far made may be summarized as follows: Codification of the common law is perfectly feasible
if too much is not attempted. It is not possible to make a
code that will settle everything, that will wholly free the
courts from the duty and deprive them of the power of interpreting and applying the law; but it is quite practicable
to make a code that shall contain the positive rules which
now rest upon decisions. The immediate results of such
codification will not be very great. The law will be made
somewhat more accessible; but it will not be made any more
intelligible, nor much more certain; nor will the practice of
citing cases be abandoned. But the ultimate results may
be quite serious. As soon as the rules that now rest upon
decisions become statutory, they are withdrawn from the
control of the courts. The judges retain a certain power
of construction, but have no longer the power of change.
Judicial legislation comes to an end, and the development
of the law passes wholly into the hands of the legislatures.
Is this a thing to be desired? The question, as was said
at the outset, must be divided: (1) Is such a change in
the interest of the people primarily affected, the people

of the codifying state? (2) Will it be better for the whole people, the people of the United States, that the law now made by the judges be henceforth made by the legislatures of the different states?

Neither of these questions can be intelligently discussed until we know *what part* of the law the change will affect — what part of the law, if any, has generally escaped enactment and still rests upon cases. And the second question cannot be satisfactorily answered until we know how far the state legislatures are modifying and adding to the general or common law, and how far their innovations are producing divergences and conflicts of law. Until these preliminary questions of fact are answered, the discussion has no solid footing; it is in the air. But no one can answer these questions who has not made minute study and careful comparison of the statute law of all our states. It is fortunate for my present purpose that I have been able to obtain an answer which rests upon and derives authority from such a study of our state laws.

II [6]

In all our states, it appears, there has been or is now in progress a gradual invasion of common law by statute, and consequently a gradual transfer of the law-making power from the courts to the legislatures; but unless codification is attempted, this movement stops short of the goal toward which it is apparently tending. A considerable part of the common law is cast in statutory form, a considerable part of their law-making power is taken from the judges, — and then every one seems to be satisfied, and nothing more is done until the code question arises. Mr. Stimson tells us that in the older states the gradual encroachment of statute upon common law ceased half a century ago, and that it is only in the younger states that it is still going on. This fact is extremely interesting and suggestive. Codi-

---

[6] Part II of the article on State Statute and Common Law as originally published in *Political Science Quarterly*, vol. ii, pp. 115–118, was by Mr. Frederic J. Stimson and is not here reproduced.

fication is demanded because of general evils alleged to be inherent in the nature of case law and general advantages that are to flow from the reduction of the whole law to statute. It is a *doctrinaire* demand. Our ordinary statutes are not made for *doctrinaires*. They are made to redress concrete evils and to satisfy concrete wants. If now the legislatures of the older states, during the past fifty years, have found no concrete evils to remedy and no concrete wants that lack satisfaction in the body of the common law — what is the inference as to the existence of the alleged general evils?

But how are we to account for the fact of encroachment followed by the cessation of encroachment; that is, how are we to account for *both* phenomena?

Judicial legislation is often assailed upon the ground that it is " undemocratic." It is said to be contrary to the genius of popular government that judges should make the law. The law, it is argued, is meant to realize the interests of the people, and the people is the best judge of its own interests. The law should, therefore, be the expression of the popular will; and the more directly the people is represented in legislation, the more completely does its will find expression. Whether this reasoning is sound or not, it cannot be doubted that the great majority of the American people thinks it sound. We have here a leading article in the orthodox democratic faith, based upon a deep-rooted popular instinct. And we have here, I think, the explanation of several phenomena in our legal history. The desire of the people to realize its will as directly as possible, explains the unpopularity of an appointed judiciary holding office for life. Such judges are too little dependent upon the people; accordingly, the people makes the office elective and limits its tenure. Even then the longer term and the traditions of the judicial office make the judges far more independent than the representatives who are sent annually or biennially to the capital. It is accordingly quite in harmony with the democratic idea that the legislature should despoil

the judiciary of its law-making power. But there is still a
more direct method by which the popular will can find expression. As constitution-making power the sovereign people declares its desires directly. That it has only to say
yes or no to propositions framed by representatives or delegates does not seem to lessen the glad sense of power wielded
directly. It is, therefore, quite in harmony with the democratic idea that the constitution-making power is encroaching more and more upon the legislatures. A similar phenomenon is observable in Switzerland, where the *referendum,* or
direct appeal to popular vote, is constantly becoming more
frequent [7] — But if all this is true, if it is the democratic
instinct which causes all these changes, including the encroachment of the legislatures upon the powers of the judiciary, why is the movement not carried through to its legitimate conclusion? How shall we account for the fact that
in our oldest states the legislatures steadily widen the bounds
of their activity for half a century, and then for the next
fifty years leave the judiciary undisturbed within its narrowed domain? By what securer title do the courts retain
this remnant of their former power? How is their continued
and undisturbed exercise of the law-making power to be
reconciled with the imperious desire of democracy to formulate its policy either by elected representatives or by *plébi-
scite?*

Another ground upon which judicial legislation is often
assailed is its cumbrousness, slowness, and alleged general
ineffectiveness. These accusations all touch the method;
and it cannot be denied that the method invites criticism.
In view of the history of our common law, it is an exaggeration to pronounce the method ineffective; but it cannot
be denied that it is cumbrous and slow. Judicial legislation
is hampered by the fiction that the courts do not make law,
but only find it. Nobody really believes in the fiction, but
few judges have been bold enough to defy it openly. Ac-

---

[7] De Laveleye, The Recent Progress of Democracy in Switzerland,
The Nineteenth Century, August, 1885.

cordingly, when new law is needed, the courts are obliged to " find " it, and to find it in old cases. This can commonly be done by re-examination and re-interpretation, or, at the worst, by " distinction." By a combination of these means, it is even possible to abrogate an old rule and to set a new one in its place. When the old rule is sufficiently worm-holed with " distinctions," a very slight re-examination will reduce it to dust, and a re-interpretation of the " distinguish-ing " cases will produce the rule that is desired. But all this takes time; and the process, scarcely intelligible to the layman, arouses his discontent. If it were intelligible to him, its apparent absurdity might arouse other and stronger emotions. — Here again we have grounds that seem sufficient to explain the gradual transfer of legisla-tive power from the courts to the assemblies; but here again we are confronted with the question: Why does the movement stop uncompleted? Why is it arrested precisely during the half-century which has witnessed the greatest changes in our social and economic life? Are there por-tions of the law in which the slow and cautious legislation of the courts is preferable to the apparently more effective operation of the statute; and, in the gradual adjustment of boundaries between our law-making powers, have we unconsciously drawn a logically defensible line of demarca-tion?

I believe this to be the case. I think there is an inherent difference between the law of which the people and its representatives have assumed control, and the law which has been left in the hands of the courts. If this can be demonstrated, if we have reached an adjustment — or, to use Mr. Stimson's word, an equilibrium — which is capable of scientific interpretation, the fact is one of no little weight; for it shows that the adjustment is not accidental.

The division which has unconsciously been established, in the older states where no civil codes have been adopted, corresponds very closely to a distinction drawn by the Roman jurists. They clothed the distinction in words

which have come to-day to bear a different meaning, *viz.,*
public and *private* law. They defined public law as that
portion of the law " which looks to the common weal " ;
private law as that portion " which looks to the advantage
of individuals." [8] This distinction includes in the domain
of public law much that we call private law; it includes
all those rules governing relations between individuals, of
which the purpose is not, primarily, to guard the interests
of the persons directly affected, but the interests of the
public.[9] But in whatever words we clothe the distinction,
it is a real one. It is doubtless true, on the one hand, that
all rules of law are intended *ultimately* to subserve the interests and secure the welfare of individuals; if not of every
individual at least of the majority. It is equally true, on
the other hand, — and it is, in fact, but another form of
the same statement, — that all law is *ultimately* intended
to secure the welfare of the entire community; that it all
rests upon social interests. But the general social interest
is realized in part by imposing positive restrictions upon
the activity of the individual, — for example, by punishing him for his acts, — and in part by giving play to the
egoistic impulse and securing to the individual the fruits
of his activity. We therefore find that, in fact, a portion
of our law is *primarily* intended to realize the social interest
or " public policy," and that another portion is *primarily*
meant to secure the advantage of individuals.

If now we attempt to separate the different portions of
our law by the test above indicated, we shall doubtless agree
that political or constitutional law, criminal law and pro-

---

[8] *Digest,* 1, 1, 1, § 2.

[9] Hence the rule: " Public law is not set aside by pacts of individuals,"
which implies that private law may thus be set aside. *Digest,* 2, 14, 38; 50,
17, 45, § 1. *Cf.* 11, 7, 20, *pr.*; 26, 7, 5, § 7; 27, 8, 1, § 9; 35, 2, 15, § 1;
38, 1, 42. This rule would be unintelligible if their conception of private
law had been as broad as ours. The mediæval jurists had somewhat the same
distinction in mind when they divided law into *jus imperativum* and *jus dis-
positivum;* a distinction which modern jurists retain, and which the Germans
express in the terms *zwingendes* and *nachgiebiges Recht.* But the old Roman
distinction comes out most clearly, to-day, in the doctrine of the conflict of
laws, when we say that foreign law will not be applied in derogation of a *lex
fori* which rests upon " *public policy.*"

cedure, lie clearly on the one side of the dividing line, and a great part of our private law on the other. Civil procedure occupies an intermediate position; it is chiefly intended to realize and enforce the legalized interests or " rights " of individuals, but the organization of the courts and the rules of evidence and of appeal are mainly determined by the general or social interest. When we examine more closely the body of the private law, we shall at once recognize that the social interest is extremely direct and strong in the matters of marriage and divorce, and the property relations of husband and wife; in respect to the devolution of property by succession, especially *ab intestato;* and in respect to the whole law of immovable property. This leaves upon the other side of the line the law of torts,[10] and the law of personal property and of contract; and here it will hardly be questioned that the social interest is best realized by giving freest play to individual activity.

How has the law actually been divided between our three law-making factors? The political law stands in our constitutions; but not the political law only. There are numerous provisions in these instruments touching other parts of the law. All of these express the strongest and most direct public interests. That is the reason they are put into the constitutions: the public interest at stake is so strong and direct, that the people desire not merely to bind the courts, but also to tie the hands of the legislatures. The criminal law, Mr. Stimson tells us, has become mainly statutory. The legislatures have also made extensive inroads upon the law of the family, of inheritance, and of real property. Within these general divisions of the law, the careful reader of Mr. Stimson's statements will see that the legislatures have regularly possessed themselves of precisely those matters in which the social interest is greatest. The law of torts, of personal property, and of contract has

---

[10] The law of torts is closely akin to criminal law as regards the matters with which it deals; but it is separated from criminal law by the precise distinction now in question — the distinction of the private or individual from the public or social point of view.

been comparatively little touched by statute. This domain is therefore left to the courts.[11] The constitutional provisions which touch upon the law of contracts are general in their character, not regulative of detail. They are, in effect, negative provisions. They are intended to guarantee the freedom of the individual against encroachment. The legislatures are not to be permitted to interfere with the individual in this domain, because the public interest that might demand interference is deemed less weighty than the higher interest that demands freedom.

One of the questions raised in the preceding pages has already found its answer. The desire of the sovereign power in the state to realize its policy with greatest possible directness — a desire which has led the American people as constitution-making power to encroach upon the legislatures, and which has impelled the legislatures to invade and narrow the domain of judicial legislation — this desire has not resulted in the complete withdrawal of our private law from the control of the courts, because here the dominant interest is that of the individual, and the chief interest of society is to make sure that his activity shall have free play.[12]

---

[11] Mr. Stimson tells us that the law of notes, bills, and negotiable paper has been largely enacted; and that the law of interest and usury has been subject not merely to much enactment but to much change. There has also been much statutory innovation in the law of choses in action. In the last case (choses in action), the aim of the statutes has been not to restrict but to enlarge the domain of individual freedom, by creating new actions and by making actions assignable. In the law of interest and usury, the statutory restrictions have been dictated by a strong — although perhaps a mistaken — idea of public policy. The enactment of the law of notes, bills, *etc.*, rests, I think, upon a different ground, which will be explained later.

[12] The result of the foregoing discussion — *viz.*, that public law (in the Roman sense) must needs be developed by statute, while private law (again in the Roman sense) need not be so developed — was really reached inductively, in the way indicated in the preceding pages. Taking the data furnished by Mr. Stimson, I set myself to see whether any intelligible line of demarcation had been drawn, in our oldest states, between statute and common law. When I found such a line, it did not escape me that very much the same division had been established in the Roman empire between the imperial *leges* and the boay of case law, the *jus*, — a division not obliterated by Justinian, but preserved in the digest and codex. Nor did it escape me that Savigny, in his "Vocation of our Time," drew the same line between the field of statute law and that of jurisprudence. Savigny, indeed, employed a different nomenclature to describe these two portions of the law; calling that which expresses the social or public interest the

A second question remains to be answered; *viz.*, the question whether, in this domain of social life, the making of law by decisions offers any advantages over the making of law by statute. In this domain the social interest, as I have said, demands the freest possible play of individual activity; *i.e.*, the freest play compatible with equally free play for all others. There must be free play, but there must also be fair play. The problem is to determine what is and what is not fair play; *i.e.*, to establish the rules of the game. And the question now under consideration is: Shall these rules be made by the umpires, — the judges, — or by the legislatures?

At bottom, it is the sense of justice, *i.e.*, the ethical feeling, of the people and the time which really decides what is and what is not fair play. The rules, if they are rightly drawn, simply express this feeling. But to draw them rightly is not an easy matter. There are many relations of daily life in which every layman *feels* the principles of justice more accurately than the most skilful jurist can *express* them. In some cases the difficulty seems insurmountable, and the attempt is practically abandoned. Every legal system, for example, sets up rules which determine the consequences of fraud and negligence; but no court or lawgiver has ever succeeded in fixing a definite standard of honesty or due care. In a number of the most common and most important contractual relations, the Roman prætor simply directed the *judex*, or referee, to

---

" political element " of the law, and the other portion, for reasons which will presently be indicated, the "scientific element " ; but he had the same distinction in mind. I was not aware, however, until after the preceding pages had been written, that Mr. James C. Carter, of the New York bar, had not only insisted upon this distinction in our own law, but had employed the same terms, " public " and " private " law, to describe it. See his admirable essay, *The Proposed Codification of our Common Law,* New York, 1884. The substantial identity of his conclusions and mine has naturally strengthened my belief in the correctness of my induction. A distinction which has commended itself alike to Roman jurists of the third century and to German and American jurists of the nineteenth, is probably a valid one; and a distinction which has established itself, by a natural and unconscious adjustment, in both Roman and English law, — the only legal systems which have passed through a normal and complete evolution, — is surely a valuable one.

award what was due *ex fide bonâ, i.e.,* according to his sense
of fair play; and the most elaborate codes of modern
Europe have not gone much further.[13] The Roman standard of ordinary diligence was *diligentia boni patris familiæ,*
the carefulness of a substantial citizen; and the phrase has
come down *verbatim* into the code Napoleon.

In a second and the most numerous class of questions,
the difficulty is not insuperable; but the task is still far
from light. As I have already urged, the relations of social
and especially of commercial intercourse are endlessly
varied in their details, — it is the very freedom of motion
granted the individual in this domain that makes them so,
— and it is impossible to lay down rules that will directly
cover every special question. Only general rules can be
posited; and the formulation of such rules is eminently
the work of juristic science.[14] I have not now in mind the
science of the study and the lecture room. This kind of
science has done good work in discovering the general principles upon which the rules of positive law rest, in showing
their organic interdependence, and in throwing the whole
mass of rules into systematic form; but it is not this clois-
tered science that discovers and formulates the rules themselves. This is done by the science that is in constant contact with the daily life of the street and the market. It
would perhaps be more accurate to call this the *art* rather
than the science of law.[15] The masters of this art have always been, and always will be, the men who pass their lives
in applying the law, *i.e.,* the bench and the bar. It was
this class that worked out the rules of private law in Rome,
and it is this class that has made the English common law.
It is customary to emphasize a distinction of method in
the development of the two systems, to point out that in

[13] The proposed civil code of New York has not gone much further.
In section 987 an attempt is made, in sub-sections 1–4, to enumerate the
possible forms of fraud, but sub-section 5 confesses failure by adding:
"Any other act fitted to deceive." And section 989 declares: "Actual
fraud is always a question of fact."

[14] It is for this reason that Savigny called this portion of the law the
"scientific element."   [15] So Jhering, *Geist des römischen Rechts.*

Rome the jurists made the law by *opinions,* and in our system the judges make it by *decisions*; but it should be remembered that the opinions of the Roman jurists on points of law were in effect decisions. In both systems the law is made by the same class, the legal profession; and in both systems it is made in the same way, by the decision of concrete cases.

It is universally conceded that the Roman jurists were masters in the art we are considering, — the art of finding rules to govern the manifold transactions and relations of individuals, — and yet, as long as the Roman jurisprudence was at its best, the work was never completed. Like our own judges, the Roman jurists found it practically impossible to give their rules final form. New cases were constantly arising that brought out new sides of familiar relations, and necessitated the revision of the rules. The Roman jurists, like the English courts, never had anything but " working " rules, subject to continual modification.

The difficulty which they experienced and which we experience — the difficulty, or rather the impossibility, of giving final form to the rules of private law — does not lie wholly in the complexity of the relations of private life. It is largely due to the fact that these relations, like all things human, are in constant flux and change, and that the law must change with the relations it governs. Whether the law be statute or case law, it must incessantly be amended. If it be statutory, it can be amended only by *enactment;* if it be case law, it may be amended by *decision.* When a case arises which shows that an existing rule of common law was originally ill formulated, or has ceased to express the existing sense of justice, it is in the power of the courts to amend the rule. They can often do this by re-examining the old cases and showing that the spirit of previous decisions justifies the amendment; that their predecessors would have phrased the rule differently if they could have foreseen the concrete case now presented. If they cannot amend the law in this way, they can do it by " distinction."

But, say the advocates of statutory legislation, you are wronging the man who has acted in accordance with the rule laid down in the previous decisions. You are subjecting him to loss by retro-active legislation. The latter statement is perfectly true; the man *is* subjected to loss by retro-active legislation. But is he really wronged, and does he really deserve sympathy? In the case supposed, the court modifies the rule because the application of the old rule will work manifest injustice to the other party. Does not the man who invokes the old rule know this? Is he not trying to obtain an unjust advantage by means of the law? [16] Even if this be not the case, it may be a less evil occasionally to injure one man by retro-active legislation than to wrong a series of men by upholding an inequitable rule. If the former evil attaches itself to judicial legislation, the latter evil is inherent in statutory legislation. How long must an inequitable statute work injustice, and how many people must be injured by its operation, before the demand for change becomes strong enough to set the legislature in motion and secure the necessary amendment?

This, I think, is the chief advantage of judicial legislation, *viz.*, ease of amendment. Ease of amendment is desirable in a great part of the private law because constant amendment is necessary. Constant amendment is necessary, first, because of the difficulty of formulating satisfactory rules for the endlessly varied relations of our social life, and

---

[16] Every system of jurisprudence must see to it that no one is permitted to do fraud by means of the law — " *Ne cui dolus suus per occasionem juris civilis contra naturalem equitatem prosit.*" *Digest*, 44, 4, 1, § 1. This end is largely secured in our law by the " equitable powers " of the courts, as it was in Roman law by the similar powers of the prætor. But the power of our courts to amend the rules of ordinary common law works in the same direction. Mr. Carter puts the matter admirably: " The unwritten law, . . . in dealing with any novel conditions of fact which the variety of human affairs present, can address itself . . . to the simple office of applying the standard of justice to the particular case. *All men count and rely upon this.* They engage in their transactions without the aid of a professional expert, without knowing or caring to inquire what the rules of law may be, with no other guide than honest intention and ordinary prudence; but in the full confidence that the rules of law which govern their transactions, should they ever be challenged, would be the simple dictates of justice and common sense intelligently ascertained and applied." *The Proposed Codification of our Common Law*, p. 37.

secondly, because these relations are constantly changing. And it should be noted that when such a change occurs and a really new rule is required, the advantage of judicial (and, conversely, the disadvantage of statutory) legislation is greatly augmented. If it is hard to find the proper form for *any* rule of private law, it is especially hard to find it in the case of a *new* rule designed to meet novel conditions. A series of attempts will in any case be necessary before the desired result is obtained; before a rule is found broad enough to include all the cases that should be included, and narrow enough to exclude all those that should be excluded. If this series of experiments is judicial, the community will be forced to endure a period of legal uncertainty. If the experiments are statutory, the number of changes will not be less, the period of experiment will be much longer, and during this period the community will be subjected to a reign of positively inequitable law.

The advantage here ascribed to judicial legislation has always been recognized and emphasized by the opponents of codification, but they have chosen unfortunate terms to express it; unfortunate because ambiguous. They have praised the " flexibility " or " elasticity " of the common law. The debate has then turned on the question whether flexibility or elasticity in law is a thing to be desired; and this debate has done much to befog the public mind.

When we say that law is flexible or elastic, we may mean either of two things:

We may mean that its *rules* are so general that the courts have wide discretion in *applying* them; or,

We may mean that the rules themselves are easily modified, or amended.

Elasticity in the first of these senses is not a peculiar attribute of case law as such. It is a peculiar attribute of private law as such, because of the extreme difficulty of formulating any but general rules in this domain. It is mediately and indirectly an attribute of our case law, the common law, because our common law is practically re-

stricted to the field of private law, and precisely to that part
of the field of private law where the formulation of rules
is most difficult. The result of this distinction is obvious.
The enactment of these rules will not lessen their elasticity.
The courts will have quite as free hand in applying them as
before.

Elasticity or flexibility in the second sense, *i.e.*, ease of
amendment, *is* a peculiar attribute of case law. This sort
of flexibility is destroyed by enactment; and it is only in
this sense that codification will make the private law less
flexible.

The whole debate in reference to the advantages or disadvantages of elastic law has been vitiated by the failure to
draw this distinction. And the issue has been further obscured by removing the discussion from its proper field,
the field actually occupied by case law, and arguing the
question, abstractly and at large: Is elasticity of law in
general a desirable thing? It has been extremely easy to
answer this question in the negative. It is not at all desirable that all parts of our law should be elastic. An elastic
criminal law — elastic in either sense of the word — would
be highly objectionable. Rules of criminal law formulated
in so general a way as to leave great discretion to the courts
would be extremely abhorrent to our sense of justice; and
a system of criminal law subjected to constant modification
and amendment would be hardly less so. In general, all
rules based upon and intended to enforce " public policy "
must be phrased with the greatest possible definiteness,
construed with the greatest strictness, and changed only for
great and weighty cause.

Even in the domain of private law *par excellence,* in the
law which looks out for the interests of individuals, there are
matters which can be and must be definitely and *specifically*
regulated. An elastic law of prescription or a flexible law of
bills and notes would subserve nobody's interests. These
and all cognate cases resemble the law of the road; there may
be no particular reason why we should keep to the right hand

rather than the left, but there is an absolute need of agreement. So it is comparatively immaterial how long the period of prescription shall be, or what shall be the form of a valid bill of exchange; but a fixed period is indispensable in the one case, and a fixed form in the other. And such rules, once settled, should not be lightly changed, because of the confusion that will ensue.

But all this discussion is wide of the issue. We may readily admit that elasticity or flexibility is in no sense a desirable thing in those portions of the law which express public policy, or in those matters of law where it is ethically immaterial what the rule be, so there be a rule. But in a great portion of our private law, only general rules can be laid down, and great latitude must be left to the courts in their application; and this will be the case whether the rules are judge-made or statutory. The reason why this part of the law should not be made statutory is that society is perpetually assuming new forms and perpetually in need of new law, and that the new law needed in this field can be furnished more rapidly and more smoothly by the courts than by the legislatures. That the American people really feels this to be true is indicated by the practical cessation, in all our codeless states, of statutory encroachment upon this field of judicial legislation.

In the foregoing discussion I have endeavored to argue the question in the abstract, without reference to existing conditions. I have been reckoning, to some extent, with ideal quantities; *i.e.*, with factors of assumed value. I have assumed a judiciary that embodies the best talent of the legal profession, and is guided by the soundest traditions of English-American jurisprudence; legislatures that represent the best instincts of the people and proceed according to the most approved principles of political science, making only such laws as are needed, and making them carefully and methodically; and codifiers who can and will state accurately the existing rules of our law, and who are able to group them into a scientific system. I have made these assumptions because I have been trying to set forth the absolute and inherent advantages and disadvantages of the common law and of civil codes, of judicial and statutory legislation. In the social sciences, as in mathematics, no result of even relative truth can be obtained except by employing quantities of fixed value. If the quantities are in fact variable, the result must be corrected subsequently by taking account of the variations.

I do not propose to attempt this task. It is an ungrateful one; and the reader can do it for himself as well as I can do it for him. I think he will agree with me that the variation from the ideal standard is least in our judiciary; much less than in our legislatures. I think it a matter of notoriety that the American people is at present much better satisfied with its judges than with its legislators. The best proof of this is that the judges have been let alone, in our older states, for the last half-century. The legislators have not been let alone. Besides the encroachments of the constitution-making power which have been noticed above, and which express the determination of the people to define directly its most vital interests, there is another class of constitutional provisions which have been increasing in number with every constitutional revision, and which express profound distrust of the character and efficiency of the legislatures. What most concerns us here is the attempt to lessen the activity of these bodies. In most of the states the legislatures have been confined to biennial sessions; in thirteen states the number of days is prescribed beyond which they shall not remain in session.[17] All this means, of course, that the people wishes the least possible amount of legislation from its legislatures; and it certainly does *not* look as if the people really desired to transfer to the legislatures the duty of developing the entire private law.

I think the variation from the ideal is greatest in our codifiers. This remark is less invidious than it seems, because

[17] For a complete collection of the constitutional provisions indicating popular distrust of the state legislatures, see " The American Commonwealth," *Political Science Quarterly,* vol. i, pp. 27 *et seq.*

the kind and grade of capacity demanded are higher in the case of the codifier than in that of the ordinary legislator or the judge. The capacity of our codifiers, of course, can be determined only by their work, by the codes that have been adopted and by the codes that are proposed for adoption.

The code which has been most fully investigated is that which was prepared for New York, but which has not been adopted in this state. It has twice been passed by the legislature and vetoed by the governor; it has twice been rejected by the legislature. It is again before the legislature at this moment. Although it has not been adopted by the state for which it was prepared, it has been adopted as the civil code of California.

This code is not an accurate presentation of our common law. The testimony of the lawyers of California, who are living under it, and the testimony of the lawyers of New York, who are afraid that they may have to live under it, agree upon this point.[18] Nor is it scientifically satisfactory in its general plan or in its details. Its general arrangement is based upon that of the code Napoleon; an arrangement which is now regarded, in Europe, as antiquated and unsatisfactory. It reproduces some of the worst features of that code; particularly in its abundance of definitions and rules of interpretation.

That these matters should not be inserted in a code is now a maxim of European codification. The Austrian commissioners appointed to draft a code, in 1772, were instructed to omit everything " which does not belong in the mouth of the lawgiver, but in the lecture room." [19] The judgment of the French jurists of the present day concerning the rules of

---

[18] See among numerous other publications: J. N. Pomeroy (Professor of Municipal Law in the University of California), "The Civil Code in California," in the *West Coast Reporter,* vols. iii and iv, reprinted by the New York City Bar Association, 1885; James C. Carter, *The Proposed Codification of our Common Law,* 1884; The *Annual Reports* of the Special Committee of the New York City Bar Association, 1881–1885, particularly the *Fourth Annual Report,* 1884. See also Sheldon Amos, *An English Code,* pp. 99–107, where the New York code is unsparingly condemned.

[19] Behrend, *Die neueren Privatrechts-Kodifikationen,* S. 370, Anm.; Unger, *Oesterreichisches Privatrecht,* S. 7.

interpretation (of contracts and testaments) and concerning the definitions of the code Napoleon, has been energetically expressed by M. Huc, professor of the code in the law faculty of Toulouse. He stigmatizes them as " senseless rules (*dispositions banales*), which are useless when they are not dangerous, and which, in any case, belong exclusively in the domain of jurisprudence [*la doctrine*] and not in that of the legislator." [20]

The New York codifiers have not only reproduced these " useless if not dangerous " provisions of the code Napoleon; they have outdone the French codifiers by reproducing, in their " maxims," Justinian's *regulae juris,* that title of the Digest which, as all students of mediæval jurisprudence are aware, did more than anything else to confuse the law and make its application uncertain.

But these mistakes are venial in comparison with the great error of trying to force our law into the mould and form of a foreign system; because this cannot be done without modifying its spirit and substance. It seems that other codifiers besides those of New York have committed this error; for Mr. Stimson finds " civil " (*i.e.*, European) law in all our private law codes. This ought to set us thinking. Why do all our codifiers go to France to find a scientific system? Is it not because they are unable to find it at home?

When it was proposed, in 1815, that a civil code should forthwith be constructed for Germany, Savigny objected that German legal science was not sufficiently developed to warrant the undertaking. To-day every German jurist admits that Savigny was right.

In the introduction to this article, I indicated that there were two distinct questions to be answered. I have discussed the first only, *viz.*, the probable effect of codification upon the codifying state. The second, and, in my opinion, the more important question, *viz.*, the effect of the general adoption of

[20] *Le Code civil italien et le Code Napoléon.* 2me ed., Paris, 1868, t, i, p. 14.

state codes upon the general development of American law, will form the subject of a second paper.

When, in this country, we distinguish statutory from common law, we habitually think only of the different sources from which these two bodies of law proceed. The antithesis, in our minds, is between judge-made law and that enacted by legislatures. But (if we leave the federal statutes out of the question) there is another and very important difference. Our state statutes are local law, while the common law, as its name implies, is a national system. This, the political point of view, has been strangely ignored in all recent discussions concerning the advisability and the effect of state codifications.

That this point of view has been neglected is due to a lack of agreement upon the principal premise. It is not uniformly recognized that our common law is a national system. Even in the Supreme Court of the United States it has been said, *obiter*, that there is no national law except the constitution, the treaties and the laws of the United States.[21] Now it is quite true that there is no other *supreme* national law; no other law, that is, which overrides the statutes of the single states. But the law which regularly prevails in the absence of other law, national or local, may properly be called national law, and it is in this sense only that the term is applied to the common law. It is our *subsidiary* national law.

It has also been said, again in the Supreme Court of the United States, that the common law obtains only so far as it has been " adopted by the several states, each for itself." [22] This is not quite true. Under the constitution and laws of the United States lies, as the recognized basis of interpretation, the law which our forefathers brought from England; [23] and in every domain of jurisdiction assigned to the federal

---

[21] Wheaton *vs.* Peters, 8 Peters 591, 657 ff.
[22] Wheaton *vs.* Peters; Smith *vs.* Alabama, 124 U.S. 465, 478.
[23] Smith *vs.* Alabama, *loc. cit.*

judiciary, this law in fact prevails in the absence of opposing statutory law, national or local. In the single states, on the other hand, it is true that the common law obtains only so far as it has been adopted; but the adoption was not dependent upon any legislative act. The English common law lay at the basis of our colonial civilization, and the acts by which the majority of our commonwealths recognized or " adopted " it were simply declaratory. It would no more have ceased to prevail in the absence of such acts than would the English language. Except where its rules are absolutely inapplicable, and except in those parts of the country where it is not a national heritage — where the colonists and all their institutions were French or Spanish, — the English common law, in the absence of opposing statutes, is the law of the land.

The recognition of this fact, that our common law is a national system, is further impeded by the method in which it has been developed since the establishment of our independence, and by the legal theories under which this development has proceeded. Its interpretation — which of course means its development — has been largely entrusted, under our constitutional system, to the state courts; and it has been difficult for the layman, and still more difficult for the lawyer, to conceive that a law interpreted by the judiciaries of nearly forty independent states could remain for more than a century really national. And even in the federal courts, the natural organs for the development of national law, the fact that the law applied is national has been cloaked from the outset under a contrary theory. Barring the cases where the United States courts apply supreme national law, — that is, the constitution, treaties and laws of the United States, — their jurisdiction rests upon the following provision of the constitution:

The judicial power shall extend . . . to all cases affecting ambassadors, other public ministers, and consuls; to all cases of admiralty and maritime jurisdiction; to controversies to which the United States shall be a party; to controversies between two or more states; between a state and citizens of another state; between citizens of different states; between citizens of the same state claiming lands under grants of different states; and between a state, or the citizens thereof, and foreign states, citizens or subjects.[24]

In the exercise of this jurisdiction, the United States courts are controlled by the Judiciary act of 1789, chapter 20, section 34, which provides:

That the *laws of the several states,* except where the constitution, treaties, or statutes of the United States shall otherwise require or provide, shall be regarded as rules of decision in trials at common law in the courts of the United States, in cases where they apply.

In all cases, therefore, where the federal courts obtain jurisdiction under the constitution and laws of the United States, and where no provision of the supreme federal law is applicable, they are obliged first to determine in what state the law governing the case is to be sought, and then to find and apply the law of that state.

But how has the Supreme Court of the United States interpreted this command? It has declared, in an unbroken series of decisions, that if the law governing the case is common law, it (the Supreme Court) is not bound by the interpretation placed upon that law by the courts of any state, but will follow its own judgment. In 1838 Justice Story said:

Questions of a general and commercial nature . . . are not deemed by the courts of the United States to be matters of local law, in which the courts of the United States are positively bound by the decisions of the state courts. They are deemed questions of general commercial jurisprudence, in which every court is at liberty to follow its own opinion.[25]

In 1842 the Supreme Court at Washington declared:

In all the various cases which have hitherto come before us for decision, this court have uniformly supposed, that the true interpretation of the thirty-fourth section limited its ap-

---

[24] The jurisdiction granted by this clause is limited, of course, as far as suits against states are concerned, by the eleventh amendment.

[25] Robinson *vs.* Commercial Insurance Co., 3 Sumner 220, 225.

plication to state law strictly local, that is to say, to the positive statutes of the state, and the construction thereof adopted by the local tribunals. . . . It has never been supposed by us, that the section did apply, or was designed to apply, to questions of a more general nature, not at all dependent upon local statutes, . . . as, for example, to the construction of ordinary contracts or other written instruments, and especially to questions of general commercial law.[26]

These decisions have been followed, in uninterrupted line, by others of like import.[27]   In the construction of a deed conveying land in the state of Maine, the federal court disregarded the views of the supreme court of that state, asserting its right to interpret " matters and language belonging to the common law " as it saw fit.[28]   In the exercise of its equitable jurisdiction,[29] and in its ecclesiastical decisions, it has always maintained equally free hand.   In a case of the latter sort, that of Watson *vs.* Jones,[30] the Supreme Court of the United States had occasion to apply the law of Kentucky; and, finding no statute, overturned the decision of the supreme court of that state, and at the same time departed from the English decisions — thus making absolutely new law.

But *what* law is this — this law which the Supreme Court of the United States creates, changes and destroys at its will?   Is it state law, or is it national law?   In some cases the court seems to avoid the question.   In commercial cases it has more than once declared that the commercial law is " international "; but it does not seem in any such case to have sought its precedents outside of the English and American reports.   In other cases, it has sometimes declared the ques-

---

[26] Swift *vs.* Tyson, 16 Peters 1, 19.

[27] Carpenter *vs.* Providence Insurance Co., 16 Peters 495, 511; Foxcroft *vs.* Mallett, 4 Howard 353, 379; Meade *vs.* Beale, Taney 339, 360; Oates *vs.* National Bank, 100 U.S. 239, 246; Railroad Co. *vs.* National Bank, 102 U.S. 14, 29; Williams *vs.* Suffolk Insurance Co., 3 Sumner 270, 276; Austin *vs.* Miller, 5 McLean 153, 157; Gloucester Insurance Co. *vs.* Younger, 2 Curtis 322, 339; The Brig George, Olcott 89, 101.

[28] Foxcroft *vs.* Mallett, 4 Howard 353, 379.

[29] Neves *vs.* Scott, 13 Howard 272, and cases there cited.

[30] 13 Wallace 679.   For discussion of this case, see Burgess, Religious Associations, *Andover Review*, July 1887.

tion to be one of " general jurisprudence " ; but where this phrase is used, it is not demonstrable that the principles of general jurisprudence resorted to were other than those of the common law. As a rule, however, the court asserts or implies that, in interpreting and applying the common law, it is actually enforcing " the laws of the several states," as the Judiciary act directs. The latest declaration to this effect occurs in the case of Smith *vs.* Alabama, decided January 30, 1888. Mr. Justice Matthews, who delivered the opinion of the court, said:

A determination in a given case of what that [the state] law is may be different in a court of the United States from that which prevails in the judicial tribunals of a particular state. This arises from the circumstance that the courts of the United States, in cases within their jurisdiction, where they are called upon to administer the law of the state in which they sit or by which the transaction is governed, exercise an independent though concurrent jurisdiction, and are required to ascertain and declare the law according to their own judgment. This is illustrated by the case of Railroad Co. *vs.* Lockwood, 17 Wallace 357, where the common law prevailing in the state of New York, in reference to the liability of common carriers for negligence, received a different interpretation from that placed upon it by the judicial tribunals of the state; *but the law as applied was none the less the law of that state*.

It seems clear to me, on the contrary, that the law applied in the case of Railroad Co. *vs.* Lockwood was not the law of New York. According to all legal logic, the interpretation placed upon the law of a state by its highest court is the law of that state; and if a court of Kentucky, or a court of the United States, in pretending to apply a rule of New York law, gives it a different interpretation and effect from that which the highest New York court has given, then neither the Kentucky nor the United States court applies the law of New York. This consideration has been conclusive with the Supreme Court of the United States as far as state

statutes are concerned. When the state law is statutory, the
federal courts recognize the authority of the state interpretation, declaring that a well-settled construction is a local
rule.[31] But the argument is really stronger when the rule
governing a particular question is of judicial origin. A statute
is one thing and its interpretation is another. Different
courts may give diverse interpretations, and maintain in
each case that they are applying the statute. But a rule of
common law exists only in its interpretation; it is nothing
but a series of concurrent decisions. Change its interpretation, and you change the thing.

The theory of the Supreme Court, that in putting its own
interpretation upon common law it is applying state law, is
therefore obviously a legal fiction. But the fiction is a necessary one. It was forced upon the federal courts by the
language of the Judiciary act, which in fact recognizes no
national law except " the constitution, treaties [and] statutes
of the United States." And this fiction is a power. It has
been said that the English Parliament could not make a man
a woman; but it could establish a legal fiction to that effect,
and cause a particular man to be subjected to all legal disabilities which attach themselves to womanhood. The federal courts cannot make their interpretation of the common
law " law *of* the several states "; the logical impossibility
in this case is as complete as the natural in the other; but
they can make their interpretation law *in* the several states,
as far as their jurisdiction extends, and this they have done.

Without this fiction the Supreme Court of the United
States would be reduced to a subordinate and unworthy
position. It would discharge, as against the supreme court
of any single commonwealth, the office of a district court, fol-

[31] Burgess *vs.* Seligman, 107 U. S. 20, 33, and cases there cited; Flash *vs.*
Conn., 109 U.S. 371, 378; Gibson *vs.* Lyon, 115, U.S. 439, 445; Norton
vs. Shelby County, 118 U.S. 425, 439, Hanrick *vs.* Patrick, 119 U.S. 156, 170.
— Such cases as Ohio Insurance Co. *vs.* Debolt, 16 Howard 416, 432; Watson
vs. Tarpley, 18 Howard 517, 520; and Pine Grove *vs.* Talcott, 19 Wallace 666,
677, form no exception to the rule. These decisions rest upon the clause in the
federal constitution forbidding the states to impair the obligation of contract; a prohibition which, in the view of the Supreme Court, extends to
state courts as well as state legislatures.

lowing the decisions of a higher tribunal. It would then be only logical, instead of removing cases from the state courts to the federal courts on writ of error, to give defeated suitors appeal from the Supreme Court at Washington to the supreme court of the state whose law is recognized as determinant of the issue. Without this fiction, again, our common law could hardly have remained what it is, a substantially uniform system. Every student of state reports knows how great an influence the federal interpretation of the common law has exercised upon our state courts; how often a side current of state decisions has been drawn back into the main stream of judicial interpretation by a decision of the supreme federal tribunal. Unchecked by the great authority of this court, the interpretation of the common law in the different states must have been far less consistent. The law of each state would have diverged from that of the others, until the common law of the nation had become a meaningless phrase.

When it is remembered that the Supreme Court has been able to maintain its uniform interpretation of the law only by steadily affirming that the national law which it applies is state law, the paradox is perfect. The court has kept our common law national by ignoring the existence of a national common law. It is one of the cases, not infrequent in legal history, where a legal fiction keeps law in harmony with political verities.

The position taken by the Supreme Court of the United States has necessarily exercised a great influence upon the state courts. They too, while affirming the common law to be state law, have treated it as a national system; [32] they

[32] In Faulkner *vs.* Hart, 82 N. Y. 413, the New York Court of Appeals followed the theory of the federal courts. The law governing the case, it was recognized, was the law prevailing in Massachusetts;; but in Massachusetts the law concerning the point at issue was common law; and in interpreting the common (commercial) law, the New York court declared itself in no wise bound to follow the decisions of the Massachusetts courts. It accordingly decided the case on its own theory of the common law. This, to my mind, involves a recognition of the national character of the common law. The court disclaimed the intention of applying New York law, and undertook to apply the law prevailing in Massachusetts; but it cer-

have always paid great regard, not only to the decisions of the federal courts, but to those rendered in other states; they have always discussed with especial interest those cases where the views held by courts of different commonwealths are found to be in conflict, and they have generally been animated by a sincere desire to bring out of such discords a more perfect harmony. In a word, they have done their best to keep the common law common. This effort is doubtless due, in part, to considerations of public policy. Our judges are well aware that conflicting decisions cause practical inconvenience, embarrassing business and confusing family relations. But another and more subtle influence has made for unity in the development of our judicial law, — I mean the theory of the common law itself concerning the source of its rules. Theoretically, the special rules of the common law are derived from a pre-existing body of general principles, and when a new question arises the answer is to be found by deducing from some recognized principle the required new rule.[33] This conception has great and beneficent results.

---

tainly did not apply Massachusetts law, for the case, it was conceded, would have been decided by the Massachusetts courts in the opposite sense; therefore the common law, in Massachusetts, is something other and something more than Massachusetts law.

[33] In point of fact, the rules of every legal system are ultimately determined by social needs, and the principles (which are nothing but very general rules) are obtained by induction from the (special) rules. But as the work of induction goes on, and the formulation of principles becomes more perfect, new rules can be and are obtained by deduction from accepted principles. In this sense, the theory of the common law is true. But this does not invalidate my assertion that the rules are ultimately determined by social interests; for if the rule obtained by deduction does not work well (*i.e.,* does not correspond to the social necessities which it is designed to meet), it is discarded, and a " positive " rule, accepted *contra tenorem juris* and *propter utilitatem,* is set in its stead. Then the principle is burdened with an exception, and perhaps with a second and a third; until the development of juristic science shows that the principle was wrongly formulated, and so recasts it that all the exceptions become corollaries. In this sense it is perpetually true that the principles themselves are determined by induction. Just as the rules of judge-made law are " working rules," subject to continual amendment, so the principles are " working hypotheses," subject to continual correction — and therefore capable of continuous development.

But the decision of a concrete case, in a court of law, is always a deductive operation. In the simplest cases, the opinion of the court is reducible to a syllogism, of which the major premise contains the rule of law, the minor premise the facts of the case, and the conclusion the decision. In more complicated cases, the judicial reasoning consists of a

Since every case is regarded as a scientific problem, to be solved by logical deduction from established premises, contradictory results awaken a certain impatience. Jurists who differ in their conclusions are eager to detect the cause of the difference, the error in their own reasoning or the fallacy in that of their opponents. The comparison of conflicting decisions thus becomes not merely natural but inevitable; and their discussion is less apt to be barren of result than most controversies, because the disputants commonly admit each other's premises. Even under these conditions, argument will not always produce agreement; but agreement is infinitely easier than it would be if the courts approached new questions as legislators do, and endeavored to solve every problem by a direct appeal to "public policy." Agreement, in fact, has so generally been attained, that, in spite of the limitless possibility of divergence afforded by the number of our states and the independence of their courts, the interpretation of the common law remains fairly uniform throughout the Union.

From the point of view here taken, we have in the United States four great bodies of law:

(1) The constitution, treaties and statutes of the United States;

(2) The constitutions and statutes of the several states;

(3) The common law as interpreted by the federal courts; and

(4) The common law as interpreted by the state courts.

Of these, the first represents strictly national law; and the third and fourth, although in theory local, are really national also. The second, on the other hand, in theory and in fact alike, is simply and strictly local. The order of validity is that in which I have placed them. Each of these bodies of

---

series of syllogisms. When a new rule has to be formulated, a syllogism is employed in which the major premise is one of those broad generalizations which we call principles. When I say that these principles are really obtained by induction, I assert what John Stuart Mill, in his famous discussion of the syllogism, claims to be true of major premises generally; see his *System of Logic*, book ii, ch. iii.

law overrides those which follow, and each is overridden by those which precede. The entire common law is thus at the mercy of our state legislatures. As soon as a state statute seizes the ground previously occupied by a rule of common law, not only are the state courts bound to give it effect, but the federal courts, in applying the law of that state, are bound not merely by the words of the statute but also (as the Supreme Court has regularly declared) by the interpretation placed upon that statute by the highest court of the state. Every state statute which invades the domain of the common law therefore invades and *pro tanto* destroys the subsidiary national law of the land.

Now a code, as the phrase is commonly understood, is intended to supersede the entire common law of the state in which it is enacted. It is intended to make the law of that state wholly statutory. Accordingly, the adoption of such codes in all our states would entirely destroy our subsidiary national law. It may be objected that the intent of the codifier is usually not to change, but to declare, the common law. To this the obvious and immediate answer is, that all the codes that have been adopted, and all that are proposed, do in fact involve changes. But even if this were not the case, and even if we assume, for the sake of argument, the establishment in each of the several states of codes simply declaratory of pre-existing common law, the point of greatest consequence is not touched. The chief question is: What will be the effect of the general adoption of state codes upon the general *development* of our law? For law, it must always be remembered, cannot remain stationary. It must change with the changing form and needs of the society which it rules.

What, in the first place, will be the effect as regards the development of our law by interpretation? As far as the single states are concerned, the inevitable results have been sketched in my previous paper. The effect upon the nation at large, upon the unity of our law, remains to be noticed. Unless the Supreme Court of the United States changes its practice, the construction of all these codes will lie wholly with our state judiciaries.[34] If the Supreme Court adheres to the rule it has heretofore recognized, and follows the construction placed upon each state statute by the highest state court, the controlling influence which the federal judiciary now exercises upon the interpretation of our common law will disappear. And not only will this regulative influence vanish, but another force that has worked for harmony in our state decisions will cease to be felt. From the standpoint of legal science, the interpretation of words is a much lower and less interesting problem than the deduction of rules from principles; and since the construction of our code law in the different states will turn largely upon the exact meaning of words, the state courts will take much less interest in, and pay far less heed to, each other's decisions than is now their custom.

Judicial interpretation, however, will play but an insignificant part in the development of code law. Codification means the substantial transfer of the law-making function, within the domain now occupied by common law, from the federal and state judiciaries to the state legislatures. The question of the development of our law, regarded from the national standpoint, accordingly shapes itself as follows: — How will our state legislatures acquit themselves of this task? Will they show the same comprehension of the needs of the nation, the same disposition to keep its law uniform, which the state judiciaries have manifested? I fear these questions can hardly be answered in the affirmative. Forty-six state and territorial legislatures cannot be expected to work with harmony of purpose and unity of result. There is for them no such regulative central influence as is exercised over our state judiciaries by the Supreme Court of the United States; there is for them no such agreement upon the premises and methods of their action as exists for our state courts in the

[34] It is noticeable that in its more recent decisions the Supreme Court does not say that it is bound to follow the state courts in their construction of state statutes, but that it does this " for the sake of harmony and to avoid confusion." If, therefore, greater confusion would be caused by following conflicting constructions of similar statutes in different states, it seems probable that the court would change its practice.

theory of the common law. The prime aim of the state legislator, be he ever so honest and ever so able, is to serve the
people of his section, to defend their peculiar interests and to
realize their peculiar wants. If by chance he rises above the
needs of his section, he is limited by his office to the consideration of the interests of his state. It is not his duty to take
thought for the American people. These *a priori* conclusions
are confirmed by facts. In those portions of the law of which
our state legislatures have assumed control, there is a lam-
entable and increasing divergence. I have shown in my
previous paper that, in our codeless states, a natural and
unconscious division has been made in the field of legislation;
that the legislators have taken control of all questions which
directly involve a social interest (public law), but have left
to the courts those matters in which the interests affected are
primarily individual (private law).[35] From the standpoint
of the state, this adjustment is satisfactory; from that of the
nation, it is not. There are many questions which fall within
the domain of public law, and of which our state legislators
have assumed control, in which the nation has an interest
higher than that of the state — the interest of unity. Our
state legislators, rightly leaving the great body of our commercial law in the control of the courts, have generally enacted and have largely changed the law of commercial paper
and that of interest and usury; and they have assumed almost
entire control of the law of marriage and divorce.[36] In both
cases they have acted rightly, from their point of view; for
all these subjects involve direct interests. But the result of
their action has been disastrous to the country at large. It is
precisely in commercial law and in the law of marriage and
divorce, that the national need of uniform law is strongest.
Diversity of commercial rules in the several states impedes
and annoys business, for American business pays little heed
to state lines. Conflicting laws of marriage and divorce un-

---

[35] The peculiar sense in which I employ these words, public and private, is explained in my previous paper, p. 122.
[36] See the data furnished by Mr. Stimson, *Political Science Quarterly,*
vol. ii, pp. 117, 118.

settle family relations and undermine the moral basis of society.

The degree of confusion which our laws of marriage and divorce have reached, is a matter of common notoriety. It is possible, for example, that a man married in New York, divorced and re-married in Indiana, shall be the lawful husband of one woman in Indiana, and shall be regarded by the law of New York as the husband of another. By the law of Indiana his status is completely regular; by the law of New York he is a bigamist. He may have a second family of children, who by the law of Indiana are legitimate, but by the law of New York are bastards. It is needless to insist upon these facts, because the matter is already so universally regulated by statute that codification can do no harm. They are instanced here simply to illustrate the tendency of our state legislations to diverge upon matters of national concern.

In the domain of commercial law, the case is different. There is already legislation enough, and enough conflict of legislation, to harass the business of the country. At every meeting of the American Bankers' Association, for example, complaints are made and resolutions passed concerning the diversity of the bankrupt laws and the laws regulating commercial paper in the different states; and committees are regularly appointed to urge upon Congress the necessity of passing a national law of bankruptcy, and other committees to consider the possibility of obtaining more uniform legislation in reference to bills and notes.[37] But in the domain of commercial law, the inroads of the state legislations have been comparatively trifling. In the main, the law of movable property and of contracts is still common law, and its development is still in the hands of our federal and state judiciaries. Here then the general adoption of state codes will work a great change; and if our state legislatures, in assum-

---

[37] The proceedings of the annual conventions of this association are regularly published, and can be obtained from the secretary, 237 Broadway, New York City. It is useless to cite years and pages, because *all* of the recent proceedings that I have examined contain these complaints and resolutions.

ing control of this field, show the same indifference to the business interests of the nation which they have shown to its moral interests in their treatment of the marriage and divorce laws, the results will be, not more serious, for nothing can be more serious than the demoralization of our people, but certainly grave in the extreme.

I think I have maintained the theses with which I opened this discussion: [38] that the ultimate effects of state codification are far more important than those which lie upon the surface; and that the relation of the movement to the general development of our law is vastly more important than its results for good or evil in any single state.

Considering, now, that a number of our states have already adopted complete civil codes, or codes which claim, at least, to cover the entire field of the common law; and considering the pertinacity of the movement in other states, I am tempted to go beyond the original plan of this discussion and endeavor to forecast the ultimate consequences of this threatened denationalization of our law. If my views were the outcome of pure speculation, or the result of a balancing of probabilities, I should not undertake this task. But, on the contrary, they rest upon the experience of other nations, whose legal development, in its earlier stages, is so strikingly analogous to our own that I cannot avoid the conclusion that we are destined to traverse the further stages which they have completed or are completing. Shakespeare has stated very accurately the possibilities and the limitations of historical inference, in affirming that a man who observes " the nature of the times deceased "

> . . . may prophesy,
> *With a near aim, of the main chance of things*
> As yet not come to life, which in their seeds
> And weak beginnings lie intreasuréd.
> Such things become the hatch and brood of time.

[38] See above, p. 52.

IV

The evolution of continental European law, since the sixteenth century, may be summarized, roughly, as follows: general or common law is gradually destroyed by local codes, and these local codes are ultimately replaced by national codes. To comprehend this development, we must start far back of the sixteenth century. We must go back to the overthrow of the West Roman empire, in the fifth century, and follow, at least in its main lines, the movement of European law during the intermediate thousand years.

The conquerors of the Roman empire were barbarians. They swept away, not the rule of Rome only, but its civilization. They did not attempt to maintain and enforce its laws; they lived by their own simple tribal customs. On the other hand, they made no systematic attempt to destroy the Roman law or to force Germanic usages upon the conquered Romans. They suffered these to live by their own law. But in the wreck of the Roman civilization, the Romans had no longer any use for a highly evolved system of jurisprudence. The Roman law survived only as a body of adages and rules — the local custom of separate communities.

In the midst of this general destruction, something — and not a little — was saved by the church. The German conquerors were, or soon became, Christians. They left the organization of the church intact, and suffered it to control its own personnel and to manage its own affairs. It did this, and more. It assumed many state functions, which the rude governments of the middle ages were unable to discharge. It cared for education and dispensed charity. It drew into its domain the entire control of the family relations. It undertook, partly in its own interest, to enforce testaments. It was able to do all this, because it had brought over from the Roman into the mediæval world a well-developed governmental organization. It added to this a complete system of courts, with appeal to Rome. In the exercise of its judicial powers, it developed an extensive body of law — the *jus canonicum*.

The states that arose on the ruins of the empire — if the kingdoms of the Goths, the Burgundians and the Franks can be called states — confined their governmental activity to military affairs and the maintenance of the peace. The popular courts administered the rough justice of the time, which consisted chiefly in the redress of torts. It was not until one of these states conquered and annexed the others and the kings of the Franks became rulers of Christendom, that the legal development of Europe entered upon a new phase. Charlemagne, especially, laid the basis for a development of German usage into European law. He imposed upon the different tribes a body of imperial laws, passed with the consent of the magnates, and a body of equity law developed and enforced by a king's bench and a system of circuit courts. He brought the county courts more fully under central control, and introduced numerous reforms in procedure. But all these innovations perished with the destruction of the Carolingian empire. The kingdoms which established themselves in its place were kingdoms in name only. They were feudalized from top to bottom. The offices of the empire became hereditary fiefs, and the magnates petty princes. Nor did the disintegration of the state stop with the independence of the crown vassals: the sub-vassals fought themselves, and later the cities bought themselves, free from all real control. The development of law became wholly particularistic. Each province, each city, each village and each manor even, evolved usages which, as local custom, overrode any higher law. Besides this local divergence, there arose distinctions of class: one law for the noble, another for the burgher, another for the free peasant and still another for the villain. And across the entire network of local laws and local courts, stretched the independent jurisdiction of the church. This state of things lasted, to fix a rough boundary line, until the latter part of the thirteenth century.

In England, the conditions were quite different. The Norman conquest had given the island a strong monarchy. In England, the Carolingian institutions reappeared: king's bench, circuit courts, local judges appointed by the crown — an orderly and centralized administration of justice. The national common law of England was already in process of development.

On the continent, nothing of the sort was possible. Neither in France, Germany nor Italy, was there any power capable of centralizing justice and creating national law. But European commerce had come to life again and assumed great importance, and the diversity and the resulting uncertainty of law were intolerable. The result was the singular historical phenomenon which we call the " reception " of the Roman civil law. In Justinian's digest the Italian jurists of the twelfth century found a system of law that was adequate to the needs of the new commerce. Schools of Roman law sprang up in Italy, were visited by students from all parts of Europe, and sent out masters and doctors by the hundreds. Returning to their homes, the civil doctors crowded the hereditary expounders of local usage off the judicial bench; under the fostering care of the kings and princes, there appeared a " learned judiciary." The law the doctors had learned was nearly a thousand years old and was written in a dead language, but it was not regarded by them, nor by their countrymen, as foreign law. All authority in Europe was derived ultimately from the Roman empire, and the Roman law was the law of the " sacred predecessors " of the German emperors and the French kings. Thus continental Europe obtained a common commercial law in the *corpus juris civilis*, as it had obtained a common family law in the *corpus juris canonici*. This development was completed, roughly speaking, in the sixteenth century.

It should be noted that both these legal systems, although embodied in what are called codes, are systems of case law. The most important part of Justinian's compilation, the digest or pandects, is essentially a collection of decisions upon stated facts; and most of the imperial constitutions are noth-

ing more. The same is true of the code of canon law compiled by Gratian about 1140, and enlarged by the addition of
later decretals; for the papal decretals were usually decisions
of actual cases. As case law, these codes were treated by the
jurists and the courts with a certain scientific freedom, very
much as our common law is treated by our courts. The *dicta*
of the Roman jurists, emperors and popes were not construed
like statutes. And for this reason again, the courts were
able to develop new law from the old, finding the needed
rules by analogy or deduction, precisely as do our courts.
So there grew up, on the basis of the Justinian digest, a *novus
usus pandectarum;* and the development of law kept pace,
after a fashion, with the needs of society.

It should be noted, again, that these systems were "received" as subsidiary law only. Local law, whether written
or customary, prevailed; and only in its absence was common law applicable. But the civil doctors had little love for
local usage, and demanded clear and complete evidence of
its existence; which was not always easily obtainable. Thus
in Germany the Roman civil law, especially during the period of the reception, overrode and destroyed many rules of
German customary law.

The reception, as I have said, was completed in the sixteenth century. Since that time, this subsidiary common
law, resting upon and developed by judicial decisions, has
been replaced everywhere save in a portion of Germany, and
is in process of being superseded in Germany also, by codes
of a statutory character, enacted by the legislative power.
From these facts it is customary to draw the simple inference
that code law is better than judge-made law. But a careful
study of European codification [39] leaves this apparently obvious inference doubtful, and suggests other — and, I think,
far more important — conclusions.

[39] For the whole movement, but especially for Germany, see Behrend,
" Die neueren Privatrechts-Kodifikationen," in Holtzendorff's *Encyclopädie
der Rechtswissenschaft,* 4. Aufl. (1882). For France in particular, see
Zachariä, *Handbuch des französischen Civilrechts,* Bd. I, §§ 7 ff., and
Schäffner, *Geschichte der Rechtsverfassung in Frankreich,* Bd. IV, S. 304 ff.

In France, the particularistic development of law was checked, after the thirteenth century, by the growing power of the monarchy. The kings became strong enough to make the parliament of Paris a supreme court of appeal for the whole of France, and to control the procedure of the local courts. This judicial centralization gradually lessened the diversity of the local laws, but it came too late to enable the royal courts to develop a common law. In the southern provinces, where a rude form of Roman law had maintained itself, the Justinian law books were received, but only as subsidiary law; they prevailed only when the provincial customs furnished no rule of decision; and the provincial customs were themselves subordinated in the same way to the custom of each locality. In the northern provinces, single institutions and rules of the Roman law were adopted, but the *corpus juris civilis* was not received. The law remained customary. In course of time the customs were all reduced to writing, *i.e.*, codified; at first, in the thirteenth century, by private enterprise; later, in the course of the fifteenth and sixteenth centuries, under royal direction. Royal codification involved many changes or " reformations," largely in the direction of greater unity of law. But more was accomplished in this direction by the royal power of ordinance, which, as the monarchy became more absolute, developed into a general power of legislation. The *Ordonnance civile* of 1667, the *Ordonnance criminelle* of 1670, and the *Ordonnance de commerce* of 1673 were practically codes of civil and criminal procedure and of the law merchant. But at the outbreak of the Revolution, in spite of all these reforms, France was far from possessing unity of law. The *pays du droit écrit* in the south and the *pays coutumiers* in the north had fundamentally different systems: the one was Germanic, with Roman infiltrations; the other Roman, with Germanic excrescences. In

---

For Italy, Huc, *Le Code civil italien et le Code Napoléon* (1868), § 1, and authorities there cited. For Switzerland, de Riedmatten, " Notice sur le mouvement législatif en Suisse, et specialement sur les derniers projets de codification," in the *Bulletin de la Société de legislation comparée,* 1880, pp. 455 *et seq.*

the conquered eastern provinces, the Netherlands and the *terres d'empire,* the legal systems were again divergent. And within these four great divisions were hundreds of codified customs, provincial and local. This state of things was intolerable. Unity of law was one of the popular demands in 1789. The "complaints and grievances" which the delegates of the local estates carried up to the Estates General in that year, were full of protests against this "diversity of customs, which, so to say, makes the subjects of the same realm, and often of the same province, foreigners to each other." It was demanded "that the provinces sacrifice to the nation their particular constitutions, capitulations and treaties," and that "a common law," "a general, uniform, national code," be established for all the realm.[40] The revolutionary assemblies declared, from time to time, in their laws and constitutions, that this should be done; that "a general and uniform code of civil laws" should be established; [41] and the Convention caused a code to be drafted, but rejected the draft because it contained "no new and grand ideas, suitable to the regenerated France." Law was being made and unmade too rapidly to permit codification. It was not until the revolutionary storm had spent its force, and the first consul had established a strong and conservative government, that the desire of the nation could be realized. When Portalis introduced the first sections of the civil code into the *Corps Législatif* in 1803, he indicated, tersely and accurately, the causes which had led to codification, in declaring:

Up to this time the diversity of our customs constituted, in one and the same state, a hundred different states. The law, opposed everywhere to itself, divided the citizens instead of uniting them. This condition of things could not last longer.

And Grenier answered, in the same strain:

[40] *Cahiers des États Generaux:* vol. i, p. 747 (Amiens); vol. 2, p. 524 (Cambrai); vol. ii, p. 593 (Chalons sur Marne); vol. iii, pp. 83, 84 (Vienne); vol. iii, p. 100 (Bayonne); vol. iv, p. 260 (Montreuil sur mer); vol. v, p. 288 (Paris *intra muros*); vol. v, p. 571 (Riom); vol. vi, 230 (Fismes).

[41] L. 16 (24) août, 1790, tit. 2, art. 19; const. 3 (14) sept. 1791, tit. 1 (*in fine*); const. 24 juin, 1793, art. 85.

As regards the diversity of its laws, France was in almost the same state in which Cæsar found it: *Hi omnes linguâ, institutis, legibus inter se differunt.*[42]

Italy, which had given Europe common law, was unable to keep its own law common. Unlike the other nations of Europe, the Italians had not even the semblance of a national organization; and the development of law, whether by judicial decisions or by legislation, was necessarily particularistic. In the kingdom of Naples and Sicily, a civil code based upon the code Napoleon was published in 1819; and the kingdom of Sardinia was governed by a code of its own after 1838. In the other states, the basis of the law was Roman; but the development of this law was not uniform, and the superimposed statute law was of course different in each state. The Italian jurists reckoned four or five "principal systems" of law in the peninsula. As soon as Italy obtained a central government and a national legislature, the Italians gave themselves a national law. The work began in 1860, and the civil code was published in 1865.

The completed reception of the Roman law in Germany, and the beginning of a reaction against its rule, are almost synchronous. Germany had obtained a common law, but it was after all foreign law. Many of its rules seemed unnatural to the German instinct, and were not adapted to the needs of German society. Moreover, the enthusiastic devotion with which its theoretical symmetry inspired the civil doctors had resulted, as we have seen, in the reception of many rules of Roman law at the cost of genuine German law, embodied in unwritten local usage. But organs for the creation of national law were wholly lacking. The empire had been losing ground and the "territories" gaining independence since the thirteenth century. The result of the religious wars in the sixteenth and seventeenth centuries was the definite disintegration of Germany. There were imperial courts;

---

[42] "Code civil ou recueil des lois qui le composent, avec les discours, rapports et opinions" (Paris, 1806), vol. i, pp. 2, 34.

but the more important states obtained exemption from appeal. There was an imperial diet, theoretically capable of legislation; but after passing a criminal code (with great reluctance and with careful reservation of established local usages) in the reign of Charles V, this body lapsed into permanent sterility. In the eighteenth century the empire was a mere shadow, and this shadow was destroyed by the revolutionary wars. In 1815 Germany was reorganized as a confederation of sovereign states — a confederation destitute of executive, judicial or legislative authority.

From the period of the reception, accordingly, the development of the law rested with the single states. In the seventeenth century, collections of local " statutes " began to be made. These were merely rules of German customary law. In the eighteenth century, attempts were made to codify the subsidiary Roman law also, in order to remove uncertainties that had arisen in the practice of the courts. So there came into existence the Prussian (provincial) code of 1721, and the Bavarian code of 1756. In both cases, the common law remained subsidiary to the code. Very different in purpose and character were the Prussian code of 1794, the Austrian code of 1811 and the Saxon code of 1863. These law books endeavored to fuse the subsidiary Roman law and the local German usage; they were really codifications of the entire law of these states. The Prussian code left divergent provincial customs in force; but the Austrian and Saxon codes swept them away. All three abolished the subsidiary common law of Germany. Finally, during the revolutionary wars, the code Napoleon was introduced in the western part of Germany, and it remained in force in Baden and the Prussian Rhine province after the overthrow of the Napoleonic empire.

The abrogation of the " foreign law " was a relief in the codifying states, but the destruction of the common law was felt to be a disadvantage to Germany. The movement for unification of the law, for the creation of a national German law, began early in this century. Thibaut's pamphlet, *On the necessity of a general civil law for Germany* (1814), called forth Savigny's famous reply, *On the vocation of our time for legislation and jurisprudence.* Savigny took the ground that German legal science was not ripe for the undertaking, and also set forth the objections to code law in a way that has never been surpassed. That nothing came of Thibaut's suggestion was due less to the force of Savigny's arguments, than to the fact that the German confederation had no legislative power. Popular dissatisfaction constantly increased, and the popular demand for national law, especially in commercial matters, grew steadily stronger. The German parliament of 1848-9 took measures for the codification of the commercial law; but the revolutionary government did not last long enough to complete the task. The plan was taken up again in 1856, at the suggestion of Bavaria, and a commercial code was actually drafted. The Federal Diet had no power to enact this code; but it was adopted, with slight modifications, in all the single states.

The establishment of the North German confederation in 1867, and of the German empire in 1870, gave Germany a strong federal government. The constitution gave the federal legislature complete control over criminal law, civil and criminal procedure, and commercial law; and in 1869 the commercial code was revised and made federal law, in 1871 a criminal code went into force and in 1877 a code of civil and criminal procedure. In the domain of civil law, the constitution gave to the federal legislature power over obligations only. In the constituent parliament of 1867, an amendment was proposed bringing the entire civil law within the federal competence; but the bill failed to obtain a majority even in the popular branch of the legislature, the Imperial Diet. In 1869 the same amendment was passed by the Diet, but was thrown out by the house of states, the Federal Council. The same thing happened in 1871 and 1872; the Imperial Diet passed the amendment and the Federal Council rejected it. In 1873 the amendment was passed a fourth time by the Imperial Diet, and resolutions in its favor were secured from the legislatures of the two most important states, Prussia and Bavaria. The Federal Council thereupon abandoned its opposition, accepted the amendment, and appointed a commission to draft a German civil code. This commission has been working ever since; with German deliberation, certainly, and, it is to be hoped, with German thoroughness also. The preliminary draft is now completed and will soon be published.

The debates to which this amendment gave rise, both in the imperial and the state legislatures, are full of interest and suggestion. It is pointed out that there are four principal systems of law existing in the empire, namely, the Prussian, French and Saxon codifications and the common law, with an infinite number of local variations. In the Imperial Diet, the National-Liberal deputy Miquel said:

I believe all thoughtful jurists agree that such a state of things cannot continue, now that we have a common German representative body, capable of expressing the will of the whole people; that as a nation we must desire to set in the place of these various codifications a common German law.[43]

In the Bavarian chamber of deputies, the minister of justice, von Fäustle, declared:

We are dealing here, gentlemen, with a domain in which the German efforts toward unity first made themselves felt. . . . While in earlier times, in the main at least, the common law mediated the inner community of the German legal life, it became evident after the dissolution of the German empire that the numerous particularistic developments of law and the efforts of the several states to proceed independently in the establishment of their private law . . . worked harm only. Our legal life and science were thereby deprived of that inner community, the destruction of which was necessarily as prejudicial to the scientific culture of the law as to the satisfaction of the practical needs of the nation.[44]

[43] Verhandlungen des 1. deutschen Reichstags, 2. Session, S. 206 (Oct. 25, 1871).
[44] Speech of Nov. 8, 1873, reprinted in Hirth, *Annalen des deutschen Reichs,* 1874, S. 329 ff.

The opposition in the Imperial Diet, as in the Federal Council, was based on state-rights theories. The leader of the Guelphs, Windhorst, declared that the adoption of the amendment meant the destruction of the federal character of the German union, and the abasement of the German sovereigns to the position of the *Standesherren.* " In twenty-five years," he asserted, " the house of Wittelsbach will hold the position which the house of Hohenlohe holds now." To this the most distinguished of living publicists, Professor Rudolf Gneist, responded:

If I took the federalistic point of view, I should feel bound to support just this proposal, because it establishes the sole condition upon which the independence of the single states in matters of internal administration can be maintained. For the centralization of administration does not arise through uniform legislation, adapted to the situation and to the needs of the time, but through the lack of organs for such legislation, which forces the state to furnish what is needed by the organization of a centralized bureaucracy [durch die Gewalten der Executive des Präfectenthums].[45]

In comparison with the great national movements described above, the legal development of the smaller states of Europe is of slight importance. In many cases, through a natural dislike for legal isolation, these states have adopted codes patterned on those of their greater neighbors, or of the countries with which their commercial relations are most important. But there is one of these smaller countries which is developing, by codification, an independent system of law, and in which the movement is of especial interest because the form of the state, as in Germany, is federal.

The Swiss cantons did not receive the Justinian law when it forced its way into the rest of the empire. The conditions of life were so primitive that the old local usages were amply sufficient. As the confederacy grew in size and its civilization became less simple, no federal law was developed, be-

[45] Verhandlungen des 1. deutschen Reichstags, 4. Session, vol. i, p. 176 (April 2, 1873).

cause the confederation possessed no law-making powers. These resided in the single cantons. Each canton, accordingly, went its own way. Six or seven established codes copied, with more or less modification, from the code Napoleon. About the same number followed the Austrian model. Zurich enacted an independent codification of its own. The rest of the cantons lived by their old customary law, more or less fixed by decisions and more or less modified by legislation. Switzerland thus possessed a variety of legal systems fairly comparable to that which obtains in Germany.

This diversity of legislations produced the usual reaction, a movement toward unity. The obstacle to any thorough reform lay, as in Germany, in the constitution. In 1872 a constitutional amendment was submitted to the people, bringing the whole civil law within the legislative competence of the confederacy; but it failed of adoption. In 1874 a general revision of the constitution took place; and the revised constitution, which was accepted by the people, gave the federal legislature control of marriage, civil status, civil capacity, all matters relating to commerce, transactions concerning movables, literary and artistic property, the prosecution of debt, and bankruptcy. In 1881 federal laws were passed regulating civil capacity and obligations. The law of obligations is practically a code of commercial law in the widest sense, including the law of contracts and that of movable property.

V

The preceding sketch of European codification yields some important results. The movement in Europe to-day is national. Its object is to substitute uniform law for divergent local legislations. The relative merits of case law and statute law have not been and are not in question. The issue, in many cases, is between a single national code and a variety of local codes; in all cases, between national law and local law. And in every case the decision has fallen in favor of national law. From this point of view, the fact that France and Italy have codified their civil law, and that Germany is about to follow their example, is no reason why New York or any other American state should codify. The movements are not analogous, but diametrically opposed. In Europe, the purpose of codification is to obtain common national law; in this country the effect of state codification is to destroy our national common law.

To obtain any analogy to the movement now in progress in our country, we must go back of the European movement of to-day. State codification in the United States falls in line with the codification of the provincial customs of France; with the Neapolitan and Sardinian codifications in Italy; with the Prussian and Saxon codifications in Germany; and with the cantonal codifications of Switzerland. But when we make this comparison, we must remember that in all these countries the local development of law was the result of the non-existence or the atrophy of all central law-making organs. In no case were active and productive central organs deliberately put out of action; in no case was the development of national law deliberately arrested. It has been left to American codifiers to propose this — for the first time in legal history.

It should be remembered, finally, that the whole development of continental European law differs from that of the English law in one fundamental point. The Norman conquest gave England a centralized governmental machinery and made the gradual and organic development of national law possible. The destruction of the Carolingian empire left Europe without law-making organs. Lacking these, no European state was able to develop common national law; and this inability resulted in the general acceptance of foreign law. Accordingly when the nations of Europe worked their way out of feudalism and developed effective governmental organizations, they naturally proceeded to rid themselves of the foreign law by substituting law of their own making. But the only method by which this could be done was codification: local codification, if the law-making power was local; national codification when the legislative power became national.

The agitation for codification in England, to-day, is in line neither with the continental movement nor with the American. It has neither the reasons in its favor which justify national codification in Europe, nor the reasons against it which militate against state codification in this country. The European codes substitute national statutes for local statutes. American codes substitute local statutes for common case law. England, if it codifies, will simply substitute one form of national law for another, statute law for case law.

Finally, the study of the codification movement in Europe gives us strong reason to believe that the ultimate result of the general adoption of state codes in this country will be a transfer of legislative power from the state legislatures to Congress, and the ultimate re-nationalization of our law by federal legislation. Everywhere in Europe the demand for legal unity has been precisely proportioned to the amount of legal diversity. If patriotic impulses have had much to do with the demand for national law, as was notably the case in Italy, it is true on the other hand that the inconveniences and annoyances caused by conflicting local legislations have everywhere been a potent factor in fostering a spirit of national patriotism. All political feelings are the product and expression of social interests.

The history of the movement in Germany and Switzerland is especially suggestive, because in these federal states the proposal to increase the legislative power of the central government encountered prejudices precisely similar to those which exist in the United States. The triumph of the national idea in Germany and Switzerland was not the result of feeling, as in Italy, but of the overwhelming pressure of material interests. From this point of view, any indication in the United States, that the divergence of state legislations is causing people to look to the federal government for relief, becomes of extreme importance. Any proposals to enlarge the legislative powers of Congress by constitutional amendment or change of constitutional interpretation, however sporadic they may be, are symptoms not to be slighted. The divergence of our state laws is causing most trouble, as we have seen, in the matters of marriage and divorce, and of commercial paper. Here, then, we should look for symptoms of an appeal to federal legislation; and here we find such symptoms.

The agitation for more uniform laws of marriage and divorce sometimes culminates in the demand that some association or committee of right-thinking and zealous citizens shall frame such uniform laws, and that sufficient pressure to compel their passage shall be brought to bear upon the several state legislatures. But if uniform laws are desirable, and if the state legislatures, in order that the laws may be uniform, are to be reduced to the position of assenting bodies simply, there seems no reason why their assent should be sought at all, or why the uniform laws should be framed by an irresponsible committee of reformers rather than by the elected representatives of the nation. Accordingly, the more radical demand is heard with increasing frequency — the demand for a constitutional amendment which shall give Congress complete and exclusive control of marriage and divorce. That so conservative a newspaper as *The* (New York) *Sun* favors this solution, is an excellent illustration of the pliancy of political theories under the pressure of social needs.

The conflict of state laws concerning commercial paper, and the annoyances and losses suffered in consequence by the business men of the country, have occasioned much discussion, as has been remarked already, at the annual conventions of the American Bankers' Association. Here again we find that Congress is to give relief; and that Congress is to be enabled to give relief by a more liberal interpretation of the constitution. In 1882 the convention passed the following resolutions:

That the executive committee be directed to ascertain: (1) The laws in the several states in regard to commercial paper, and especially the variations and differences therein. (2) Whether, under the constitutional power given to Congress to "regulate commerce between the several states," it is not competent for Congress to enact laws governing commercial paper drawn in one state upon a party in another, or made in one state and payable in another, so that such laws shall be uniform throughout the nation. (3) Whether it be expedient for Congress to exercise such power if the constitution confers it.

It is an interesting fact that Hamilton thought that this clause of the constitution would cover such legislation.[46] The Supreme Court has construed the word "commerce" more narrowly; but if such a law as the above resolution contemplates were actually passed by Congress, in response to an urgent popular demand, it is not inconceivable that it might be pronounced constitutional.

Whether it be by change of constitutional interpretation or by direct constitutional amendment, there is no doubt, I think, that the nation will find a way to keep its law national. No theory of state rights, no jealousy or fear of centralization, will prevent so practical a people as ours from satisfying its real needs. If the encroachment of state statutes upon common law goes much further, if business relations become as uncertain and confused as marriage relations have become already, the state-rights theory will either disappear or, more probably, change its form. Like all political theories, it has a kernel of truth and expresses a real social interest. In administrative matters, the greatest practical development of local self-rule is not only desirable, but essential to the perpetuity of free government. This will be seen more clearly as our governmental problems become more complex and difficult; and the tendency to decentralize administration will probably result in an increased autonomy of our cities and counties. But it will

---

[46] *Works,* Lodge's edition, vol. iii, p. 204.

be seen, also, that the making of laws concerning matters of national interest is no legitimate function of local government, and that an American citizen is no freer because these laws are made at Albany or Trenton than he would be were they made at Washington.

IV

FOUR GERMAN JURISTS.[1]

BRUNS, WINDSCHEID, JHERING, GNEIST.[2]

OF the jurists under whose personal influence it was my good fortune to be brought during my studies in Germany, four of the most distinguished have since passed away: Bruns in 1880, Windscheid and Jhering in 1892, and Gneist during the past summer. To each of these men I owe debts of the kind that cannot be repaid; and the impulse to describe, however inadequately, their lives and labors springs partly from the feeling that a tribute to the memory of these

[1] Reprinted from the *Political Science Quarterly,* vol. x, no. 4, December, 1895, pp. 664–692; vol. xi, no. 2, June, 1896, pp. 278–309; vol. xii, no. 1, March, 1897, pp. 21–62; vol. xvi, no. 4, December, 1901, pp. 641–679.

[2] Karl Georg Bruns was born at Helmstedt, in Brunswick, February 24, 1816; studied law at Göttingen, Heidelberg and Tübingen; practised for a short time in Brunswick; began to teach at Tübingen in 1839; was advanced to the grade of extraordinary professor in 1844; accepted a call to Rostock as ordinary professor in 1849; went to Halle in 1851; to Tübingen again in 1859; to Berlin in 1861, where he remained until his death, December 10, 1880. His published works were: *Das Recht des Besitzes im Mittelalter und in der Gegenwart* (1848). *Fontes iuris Romani antiqui* (1860; 5th ed. by Mommsen, 1887). *Das Wesen der bona fides bei der Ersitzung* (1872). *Die Besitzklagen des römischen und heutigen Rechts* (1874). *Die Unterschriften in römischen Rechtsurkunden* (1876). *Syrisch-Römisches Rechtsbuch aus dem 5ten Jahrhundert* (1880). To Holtzendorff's *Rechtsencyclopädie* he contributed the important articles on the history of the Roman law and on modern Roman law. Two volumes of essays (*Kleinere Schriften*) were collected in 1882. A sketch of his life and work was published by Degenkolb in 1881.

Rudolf von Jhering was born at Aurich, in East Frisia, August 22, 1818; studied law at Heidelberg, Munich, Göttingen and Berlin; began to teach at Berlin in 1843; accepted calls, as ordinary professor, to Basel, 1845; Rostock, 1846; Kiel, 1849; Giessen, 1852; Vienna, 1868; Göttingen, 1872. Here he remained, declining calls to larger universities, until his death, September 17, 1892. He was ennobled by the Emperor of Austria. His published works were: *Abhandlungen aus dem römischen Recht* (1844). *Civilrechtsfälle ohne Entscheidungen* (1847; 6th ed., 1892). *Geist des römischen Rechts auf den verschiedenen Stufen seiner Entwickelung* (4 vols., 1852–1865; 4th and 5th eds., 1878–1891). *Das Schuldmoment im römischen Privatrecht* (1867). *Ueber den Grund des Besitzesschutzes* (1868; 2d ed., 1869). *Die Jurisprudenz des täglichen Lebens* (1870; 9th ed., 1893). *Der Kampf ums Recht* (1872; 10th ed., 1891). *Der Zweck im Recht* (2 vols., 1877–1883; 3d ed., 1893). *Vermischte Schriften juristischen*

great teachers from some one of their American pupils is a
duty of scholastic piety. But I am also influenced by the
conviction that such a description will be of interest and
value to the readers of this review. The life-work of these
scholars cannot be set forth on purely biographical lines:
to study it involves a study of the movement of German
jurisprudence in the nineteenth century. To understand

Inhalts (1879). *Gesammelte Aufsätze* (3 vols., 1881–1886). *Das Trinkgeld* 1882; 3d ed., 1889). *Scherz und Ernst in der Jurisprudenz* (1885;
4th ed., 1892). *Der Besitzwille: Zugleich eine Kritik der herrschenden
juristischen Methode* (1889). From his literary remains: *Vorgeschichte
der Indo-Europäer* (1894). *Entwickelungsgeschichte des römischen Rechts*:
Einleitung (1894). Sketches of his life and character by de Jonge (1888)
and Merkel in *Jahrbücher für Dogmatik*, vol. xxxii (1893).

Bernhard Josef Hubert Windscheid was born at Düsseldorf, June 26,
1817; studied law at Bonn and Berlin; was employed in the judicial service 1837–1840; began to teach at Bonn in 1840; was appointed extraordinary professor in 1847; accepted a call to Basel the same year as ordinary professor; went to Greifswald in 1852; to Munich in 1857; to
Heidelberg in 1871; to Leipzig in 1874. Further calls to Strasburg, Vienna
and Berlin were declined. From 1874 to 1883 he was a member of the
commission appointed by the German Federal Council to draft a civil code
for the Empire. He died October 26, 1892. His publications were: *Die
Lehre des römischen Rechts von der Voraussetzung* (1850). *Die Actio des
römischen Civilrechts* (1856). *Lehrbuch des Pandektenrechts* (3 vols.,
1862–1867; 6th ed., 1887). *Wille und Willenserklärung* (1878). *Zwei
Fragen aus der Lehre der Verpflichtung wegen ungerechtfertigter Berei-
cherung* (1878).

Rudolf von Gneist was born at Berlin, August 13, 1816; studied law
at Berlin; entered the Prussian judicial service and was advanced, in 1841,
to the position of assistant judge; resigned, on political grounds, in 1850;
was appointed, in 1875, a member of the superior administrative court
(Oberverwaltungsgericht) of Prussia. — In 1848 and 1849 he was a member of the city council of Berlin; in 1858 he was elected to the Prussian
Diet, and was reëlected with unfailing regularity until his withdrawal, a
few years ago, from active political life. From 1867 to 1884 he was a
member of the Imperial Diet also. In 1883 he was appointed a member
of the Prussian Council of State. He was ennobled by the Emperor Frederick III. — His academic career began, at Berlin, in 1839; he was appointed
extraordinary professor in 1844; ordinary professor in 1858; and retained
this position until his death, July 22, 1895. Among his more important
publications were: *Die formellen Verträge des neuern römischen Obligationenrechts* (1845). *Adel und Ritterschaft in England* (1853). *Das heutige
englische Verfassungs- und Verwaltungsrecht* (1857–1863; 3d ed. of Part
I under the title *Das englische Verwaltungsrecht der Gegenwart*, 2 vols.,
1883–1884; 3d ed. of Part II under the title *Selfgovernment, Kommunal-
verfassung und Verwaltungsgerichte in England*, 1871). *Verwaltung, Justiz,
Rechtsweg, Staatsverwaltung und Selbstverwaltung nach englischen und
deutschen Verhältnissen* (1869). *Die preussische Kreisordnung* (1870).
Der Rechtsstaat (1872; 2d ed., 1879); *Gesetz und Budget* (Berlin, 1879);
Englische Verfassungsgeschichte (Berlin, 1882); *Das englische Parlament*
(Berlin, 1886). — Monograph by Walcker, in Hinrichsen's *Deutsche Denker*
(Berlin, 1888); article by Bornhak, *Archiv für öffentliches Recht*, vol. xi,
p. 2 (1895).

their efforts it is necessary to consider the scientific environment in which they grew up, the points of view which they inherited and retained or abandoned, the tendencies which they continued or opposed. To appreciate their influence it is equally necessary to consider the extent to which they furthered the development of their science upon lines already marked out, and the degree in which, by opening new lines of thought and study, they have given to its further progress new impulses and different aims. The problems which have engaged the attention of German jurists during this century are, in large degree, universal problems; and the solutions which they have reached should be of interest to all who care for legal science.

I

The present period of German jurisprudence begins, as far as any historical period can be said to have a distinct beginning, with Savigny,[3] whose treatise on the *Law of Possession* made him famous a dozen years before Bruns (the eldest of·our four) was born, and who closed his career as a teacher just as Bruns, Gneist and Windscheid were beginning theirs. Savigny was the founder of the historical school which is still dominant in modern legal science. Against the conception of " natural " law, universal in its dominion, eternal and unchangeable in its essence, progressive only in the sense that a fuller recognition and more perfect comprehension of its principles may be progressively attained, Savigny set up the conception of law as an historical product of the life of each people or nation, varying according to the national genius, developing in each nation with that nation's entire social development. A large portion of his life was devoted to studying the history of the Roman law, in both the ancient and the mediæval world. The great monument of these investigations is his *History of the Roman Law in the Middle Ages*.

[3] Born 1779; died 1861.

In addition to these historical studies, however, Savigny carried on throughout his life, with rare acuteness of analysis, the labor of resolving the traditional institutions of law into their ultimate juristic elements. With this he combined, and with no little success, the effort to reformulate and refine the synthetic conceptions with which legal science operates. Of these labors in systematic jurisprudence the chief results were incorporated in his unfinished *System of Modern Roman Law.*

An important impulse to the historical investigation of the Roman law had already been given, toward the close of the sixteenth century, by the French jurist Cujacius; and a serious attempt to establish a more logical and coherent system of Roman law had been made about the same time by his countryman Donellus. But the historical impulse was checked in the seventeenth and eighteenth centuries by the predominance of natural-law theories; and in the systematic field the work of the great Dutch jurists on whom the mantle of Donellus fell was more and more directed to the new science of international law. In Germany, still absorbed in the practical labor of assimilating the " foreign laws," civil and canon, and fitting them to its own social conditions, neither Cujacius nor Donellus had found any important following. In this country the new impulses given by Savigny were especially needed, and the seeds sown by him have brought forth an abundant harvest, not in Germany only, but throughout the civilized world.

II

Every effective human impulse, however, is one-sided and provokes a more or less legitimate reaction. Insistence upon one portion of the truth tends to obscure other portions, and these find new exponents and defenders. It was asserted, and not without reason, that Savigny and his immediate followers regarded the evolution of law as an organic social process upon which the individual reason and the individual will have little influence; that they ignored, or at least underrated, the conscious and reflective element in legal development; and they were accused, not without justice, of "quietism" or fatalism. If legal changes, whether made by custom or by legislation, are, as Savigny maintained, merely the expression of slowly ripening popular instincts, then such changes are sure to come when these instincts are sufficiently ripened. To hasten the process may be impossible; it will certainly result in mistakes. Such was, in fact, the feeling of Savigny, who was politically an extreme conservative;[4] and the attitude of his immediate followers toward reformatory legislation was far from sympathetic. It was also asserted, and again with reason, that the historical jurists insisted too much upon the national character of law and ignored its human character. After all, Greeks, Romans and Teutons were, in the first place, men with human feelings, ideas and tendencies; in all the systems of law that have existed or now exist, there is much that is common, and the common element is the most significant. These points of antagonism, or rather these supplementary considerations, gave birth to the so-called philosophical school or, as Thibaut, its leading representative, preferred to call it, the "philosophical-historical" school. A characteristic controversy[5] between Thibaut and Savigny, in which the former advocated and the latter opposed the construction of a civil code for all Germany, brought out most clearly their different attitudes towards legislation. The attempt of Gans, another leader of the philosophical school, to trace the law of inheritance in its "world-historic development,"[6] marked with equal clearness the reaction against the purely national point of view.

---

[4] Compare with the conservatism of Savigny, the historical jurist, that of Burke, who regarded politics preëminently from the historical point of view.

[5] Thibaut, "Ueber die Nothwendigkeit eines allgemeinen bürgerlichen Rechts für Deutschland." Savigny, "Vom Beruf unserer Zeit für Gesetzgebung und Rechtswissenschaft." Both pamphlets appeared in 1814.

[6] Gans, *Römisches Erbrecht in weltgeschichtlicher Entwickelung* (4 vols., 1824–1835).

What is the attitude of German jurists to-day toward these controversies? What, in particular, was the attitude of the jurists who form the subject of our present study? As regards the emphasis laid by the philosophical school upon the human and universal character of law, at least in its fundamental conceptions, Bruns has well said that this led to the development of a purer legal philosophy,

which no longer regards as its task the discovery of an absolute law of nature, but only seeks to recognize, in their universality and necessity, the general conceptions and ideas which attain concrete historical manifestation in the single national systems of law.[7]

He might have added that the philosophical school furnished the theoretical basis for the new comparative science of law, which is still to-day in the earlier stages of a most promising development.

Jhering, who in the first book of his *Spirit of Roman Law* made brilliant use of the comparative method, condemns, in his introduction to that work, the narrow national view taken by the historical school. " Legal science," he says, " is brought down to the plane of territorial jurisprudence. The scientific boundaries coincide in jurisprudence with the political." [8] After emphasizing the interdependence of nations, and pointing out that the legal development of the modern world, or at least of the modern European world, has been substantially a general and not a national movement, he writes:

And however brief, from the point of view of the ages, is the fragment of history thus far unfolded in this new legal epoch, is it not already clear that it is the thought of universality that gives its character and furnishes the key to the present era? It was with a correct instinct for this trend and drift of modern law that the natural-law school proclaimed its doctrine of the universality of law, elevated above time

---

[7] Bruns, " Das heutige römische Recht," in Holtzendorff's *Rechtsen-cyclopädie,* 3d ed. (1877), p. 336.

[8] Jhering, *Geist des römischen Rechts* (3d ed., 1873), vol. i, p. 15.

and place. However little scientific value I may attribute to
the works produced in this field, the *direction* which the natural-law theorists pursued was as decidedly in line with the
peculiar course of modern history as that of the historical
jurists, with their one-sided insistence upon the principle of
nationality, was divergent from it. The law of nature, far
from standing outside of time and ignoring actual conditions,
was in fact but an idealization of existing conditions.[9]

Gneist also declares, in one of his later monographs, that a
further development of legal science can be attained only by
taking up again the natural-law doctrines of the past, and
giving them further development.[10] The monograph itself is
an interesting attempt to sketch in broad lines the development of human law in general, and of modern European law
in particular.

These utterances of men who regarded themselves as followers of Savigny sufficiently indicate that, on this point at
least, the antithesis of the historical and philosophical schools
has disappeared. It is fully recognized that each was right
in its main contention.[11]

As regards the attitude of the two schools towards legislative reform, it is sufficient to point out that there is to-day
no diversity of opinion among German jurists regarding the
desirability of a German code; although, as was pointed out
in a previous article of mine in this review,[12] the question
to-day is not of the superiority of legislation over usage, of
written over unwritten law, but the preference of general
federal law to divergent state laws. It may be added that
nearly all modern German jurists agree with Savigny that
Germany was not ready for codification in 1814.

[9] *Ibid.*, p. 11.
[10] " Dies Vorwärtsschreiten [der Wissenschaft] wird nur in der Wie-
deranknüpfung an die naturrechtlichen Lehren der Vergangenheit liegen
können, und in der Weiterführung derselben." Zur Lehre vom Volksrecht,
Gewohnheitsrecht und Juristenrecht, in *Festgabe für Beseler* (1885).
[11] So Windscheid, also, in his lectures on Pandects, in 1878: " The correctness of both sides is now fully recognized. The antithesis was long
ago surmounted."
[12] " State Statute and Common Law," *Political Science Quarterly,* vol.
iii, pp. 155–160 (March, 1888).

III

Of less interest to science at large than the philosophical reaction, but of more practical consequence to Germany, was the " national " opposition. Savigny and his disciples were attacked by the nationalists not as historical jurists — for the armory of historical jurisprudence furnished the assailants with their best weapons — but as " Romanists," as champions of the Roman law and advocates of its continued supremacy in Germany. The attack came from the " Germanists," the defenders of Teutonic ideas and institutions.

In the sixteenth century, at the period of the completed reception of the Justinianean codes, and for some two centuries afterwards, there were no Germanists in Germany — at least among the jurists. The only protests against the overwhelming triumph of the Roman law, and against the partial destruction of German legal institutions, came from laymen — knights and peasants. The jurists had all been trained in the Roman law, first in Italy and later in the German universities. They were carried away by its cosmopolitan breadth of spirit, its logical symmetry, and above all, by the fact that it furnished ready solution for all the new problems with which German folk-law was clumsily wrestling. To them the native Germanic customs were barbarous and irrational, things in which no intelligent man could take an interest. To their attitude was due not the fact of the " reception," [13] but its completeness. In theory, the Roman law

[13] The prime cause of the reception, not in Germany alone, but throughout Europe, was the change in economic conditions which followed the revival of commerce in the eleventh and twelfth centuries. Social life became more complex, and the simple customs by which the greater part of Europe was governed became inadequate. One of the first results of the commercial revival was the extension of the mercantile law of the Eastern Mediterranean, which was largely Roman or Græco-Roman in its structure, over the new highways of trade — along the coasts of the West Atlantic and of the North and Baltic Seas, and along the great land routes between these seas and the Mediterranean. (*Cf.* Goldschmidt, *System des Handelsrechts,* vol. i.) This body of law, however, was applicable only to traders and to distinctly mercantile transactions. For the rest of the people new law was needed, and the law books of Justinian amply met the need. Where the Roman law was theoretically in force already (*e.g.,* in South France) such rude compilations as the " Breviary of Alaric " were supplanted by the " Corpus Iuris Civilis." In other parts of Europe a true " reception " of the

was received as subsidiary law, to be applied only when the local law furnished no rule.   But the jurists recognized German law only in the form of local custom, and insisted that every such custom was a fact to be pleaded and proved by the party who desired its application.   When it is remembered that questions of fact, as well as questions of law, were decided by the learned judges, themselves doctors of the civil law, the effect of the procedural rule just stated can easily be imagined.   In all parts of Germany the German law was more or less submerged and lost; more in the South and West, less in the North and North-East.[14]

Roman law occurred. In those countries which were not at first touched by the revival of trade, and where simple economic conditions continued to prevail (*e.g.,* in the old cantons of the Swiss Confederacy), the Roman law was not received.

A negative condition of the reception was the inability of the mediæval state to furnish the new law that was needed. Feudalism had so disintegrated political authority that in most parts of Europe there were no organs for the development of national law, whether by legislation or by decisions on appeal. Recourse was therefore had to the older laws of the Roman Empire. Their application was facilitated (not caused) by the general belief that all authority in Europe was ultimately derived from the Roman Empire, and that the Roman Emperors, from Augustus down, were the predecessors of all mediæval rulers. Where this condition of political disintegration did not exist, neither economic changes nor the fiction of " continuous empire " was strong enough to secure the reception of the Roman law. In England, where the Norman conquest had so solidified the state that the King in Parliament could enact statutes for the realm, and the King's courts could develop the *lex terrae* by their decisions, the new law required was worked out on the basis of existing Anglo-Norman customs. In Spain, where the struggles with the Moors had strengthened royal authority, the reception of the Justinianean law books was averted by the publication of a Spanish code, largely influenced by Roman ideas, but still an independent and national system of law. In North France, where in the fourteenth century the royal power was so far increased that procedure could be reformed by royal ordinances, and appeals carried to the King's courts, the Roman law was not received as law but was invoked simply as *ratio scripta* when the customs were silent. Here, as in England, the basis of the legal development remained Teutonic.

In Germany and in the Netherlands the " practical," as distinguished from the " scientific " or theoretical reception of Roman law, was generally synchronous with the appearance of the " learned judiciary," *i.e.,* with the substitution of governmental justice administered by professional lawyers for popular justice administered by lay judges. The conviction that Roman law was applicable and authoritative, and the attempt to apply it, of course hastened this change, and the control of the courts by men trained in the civil law was the decisive element in the practical reception.

[14] In the Saxon lands much of the Teutonic custom was preserved through a private compilation which obtained great authority, the *Sachsenspiegel*. A somewhat similar compilation existed in South Germany, the *Schwabenspiegel*.

Not a few Teutonic ideas and institutions, however, were preserved by putting them, so to speak, into togas and teaching them to talk Latin. They found shelter and recognition in the so-called *novus usus pandectarum,* a collective designation of the changes wrought in the Roman civil law by mediæval practice. Some of these disguised natives of Germany crossed the Alps in the very van of the Roman invasion. They had already received Roman citizenship in the Italian courts. Still others came over in sacerdotal vestments. They had been naturalized at an even earlier period in Kome itself, and figured as canons of Holy Church.[15] After the reception of the foreign laws, and largely in consequence of a popular reaction against them, still other fragments of Teutonic law were preserved in official compilations of " statutes " or local rules of law.

That any community of origin existed between those rules of German law which had found shelter in the canon law, or in the new usage of the *Pandects,* and which were, therefore, common law, and those other rules which had survived the reception as local customs or statutes, was not generally understood until the present century. Not until the eighteenth century were even the various local customs recognized as fragments of an earlier whole.[16] It was through the labors of Carl Friedrich Eichhorn,[17] a contemporary and friend of Savigny, that German law was raised to the rank of an inde-

[15] In Germany, as in Italy, the canon law overrode the civil when the two came in conflict.

[16] In 1643 one Herman Conring, a physician, published a treatise, " De Origine Iuris Germanici," in which the results of later historical investigation were largely anticipated. Curiously enough the treatise was called forth by a current theological controversy. The jurists paid no attention to Conring's work. In the eighteenth century the common origin of the various local customs was discovered by members of the legal profession, and lectures on German law began to be delivered in the universities. This innovation was at first regarded with little favor. The Prussian Chancellor Cocceji, having been charged by Frederick William I with the preparation of a general civil code, submitted for the King's approval, in 1738, a preliminary report concerning the scope and plan of the proposed codification. In this report the chancellor went out of his way to express his contempt for that " imaginary German law which sundry tutors (Privat-Doctores) have taken the liberty to invent." His code was to be based on natural reason. When drafted it turned out to be substantially Roman.

[17] Born 1781; died 1854. His great work was his *Deutsche Staats- und Rechts-geschichte* (1808; 5th ed., 1842–1844).

pendent juristic discipline. For many years now the Germanists have occupied in every university a position fully coördinate with that of the Romanists or Pandectists, and an acquaintance with the history and institutes of German law is as necessary for university degrees and bar examinations as is a knowledge of the Roman law.[18]

Between the leaders of the two schools, the Romanistic and the Germanistic, there was no controversy. Savigny himself, in pleading against immediate codification, had insisted that the different elements of which the existing law of Germany was composed were still imperfectly comprehended, and had urged a thorough historical study of Roman and of German law; and Savigny and Eichhorn coöperated in establishing the *Zeitschrift für geschichtliche Rechtswissenschaft,* which from the outset gave impartial shelter to the fruits of investigation in both fields. But the younger Germanists, with the heat that naturally resulted from their struggle for academic equality, opened an attack upon the Roman law. They disputed the rightfulness of its supremacy. They denied that it had any legitimate place in Germany. Savigny's theory of the national character of law gave them an admirable opening. He had declared, in the introductory article of the first number of the *Zeitschrift,* that the law of a nation was the product " of its innermost nature and its history." " If this be true," said the Germanists, " what justification was there for the reception of the Roman law in the fifteenth and sixteenth centuries? What justification is there for its continued supremacy? Ought it not to be thrust out as an illegitimate interloper, and should not the teachers of the historical school be the first to demand its exile? " Savigny, of course, had an answer. In the evolution of every national law there comes a period when it ceases to be the direct and immediate product of the national consciousness. Its further development falls into the hands of a class, the lawyers, and

---

[18] At least, in theory. Practically, the time devoted by the German law-students to Roman law is at least thrice that given to the German law, and the relative stress laid upon these subjects in the examinations is roughly in the same proportion.

ultimately into the hands of legislators. At the time of the reception the jurists represented the German people, and their reception of Roman law made it German law. To this the Germanists responded that the legal profession might, indeed, represent a nation, as was the case in the development of the ancient Roman law, but that the German jurists of the fifteenth and sixteenth centuries had divested themselves of all national feeling and were no true representatives of Germany.

The national agitation against the Roman law reached its highest point in the forties.[19] The events of 1848 raised new questions, political rather than juristic in character, and the discussion between the Romanists and the Germanists terminated in apparent agreement. It was generally admitted by the Romanists that the way in which the Roman law had been received was unfortunate; that the overturning of established German customs was indefensible. It was conceded by the Germanists, on the other hand, that the reception of the Roman law was not on the whole a misfortune; that the appropriation of this portion of the vast inheritance of the ancient world had greatly enriched modern European civilization.

Jhering justifies the reception of the Roman law in Germany on the broad ground that no nation can attain the highest civilization save by participation in the civilization of the world.

The life of nations is no isolated existence side by side, but, like that of individuals in the state, a common life; a system of reciprocal contact and influence, peaceful and hostile; a giving and taking, borrowing and bestowing; in short, a vast business of exchange that embraces every side of human existence. The same law that governs the physical world exists for the spiritual: life is reception from without and internal assimilation: these are the two basic functions on whose

---

[19] Among the more important contributions to the controversy, on the Germanistic side, were: Kjerulff, *Theorie des gemeinen Civilrechts* (1839); Bluntschli, *Die neuern Rechtschulen der deutschen Juristen* (1841); Beseler, *Volksrecht und Juristenrecht* (1843).

maintenance and balance rest the existence and health of every living organism. To prevent reception from without and condemn the organism to development " from within outwards," is to kill it. That sort of development begins with the corpse.[20]

This vast system of exchange has always included spiritual as well as material goods; and it is from this point of view that he condemns the national standpoint of the historical jurists.

In the ship that brought wares, gods went back. . . . Language, morals, religion, words, ideas, prejudices, faith, superstitions, industry, art, science, — all follow the rule of international communication and influence. And law? Does that alone stand outside of this universal rule of civilization? That is the outcome of the doctrine we are combating, and which we must combat if we are to find a place for the Roman law, — the doctrine of the historical school that law develops purely from within each nation. We are not to introduce juries, because they did not spring up on our native soil; the constitutional form of government is of foreign growth, and therefore to be condemned. . . . The question of the reception of foreign legal institutions is not a question of nationality, but simply one of expediency, of need. No one will fetch a thing from abroad when he has as good or better at home; but only a fool will reject the bark of the cinchona because it did not grow in his vegetable garden.[21]

A warning example of the results of national isolation is afforded by China, " the Don Quixote of the principle of nationality."

The special justification of the reception of the Roman law in mediæval Europe Jhering finds in the supra-national, universal character which the Roman law had already assumed in the first centuries of the Christian era, and in the similar character which its reception has given to modern European law. In this, as in other matters, Rome furnishes the point of communication between the ancient and the modern world;

[20] *Geist des römischen Rechts,* 3d ed., vol. i, pp. 5, 6.
[21] *Geist des römischen Rechts,* 3d ed., vol. i, pp. 8, 9.

and here, as always, Rome stands for the principle of universality as against that of nationality. No one who has read the *Spirit of the Roman Law* can forget the striking sentences with which the book opens.

Thrice has Rome dictated laws to the world, thrice bound the nations together in unity: the first time, while the Roman people still stood in the fullness of its power, in the unity of the state; the second time, when that people had already perished, in the unity of the church; the third time, in consequence of the reception of the Roman law in the middle ages, in the unity of law; the first time by external coercion, by force of arms; the second and third times by force of intellect.

Windscheid goes a step further towards the Germanists. He remarks that Jhering's theories of international exchange and of the supra-national element in law, particularly in the Roman law, are " certainly true. But it does not follow that the peculiar genius of each nation should not in last instance determine whether any thing is or is not properly *its* law." [22]

Bruns also emphasizes the universal side of the Roman law, and seeks to define it.

The significance of the Roman law in the history of the world lies chiefly in the fact that in it was developed the abstract conception of the personal right (*des subjektiven Rechts*), and especially the general and equal attribution to individuals of private-law rights. Herein lies what is called the universal character of the Roman law. This does not mean that the Roman law is eternal and absolute law for all nations and times, or that it alone can satisfy the needs of any modern nation, but that in it an essential and general element of law, which must find place in (and, in a sense, form the basis of) every system of law, was worked out in so complete a way as to furnish all nations and times with a model of theoretical and practical value. [23]

[22] Windscheid, *Pandekten*, § 10, note 4.
[23] Bruns, " Geschichte des römischen Rechts," in Holtzendorff's *Rechtsencyclopädie*, 3d ed., p. 81.

He emphasizes, as does Jhering,[24] the new touch of universality which the Roman law gained by its reception in the
middle ages.

We must guard ourselves carefully against the notion that
what is called modern Roman law is simply that part of the
Roman law that is still in force to-day. In modern Roman
law are embodied the labor, intellectual development and
science of all modern Europe. Modern Roman law is by no
means the actual law of Rome. Its substance from beginning to end is permeated with modern ideas. Its entire form
is, in even higher degree, an essentially modern creation of
the modern mind, in which nearly all nations have participated.[25]

As to the practical inferences, also, to be drawn from these
considerations the jurists have reached substantial agreement. That which is really universal in the Roman law is to
be retained and developed; that which is based upon conditions peculiar to the ancient world, or upon ideas of justice
and expediency that were specifically Roman, is to be rejected. Jhering puts all this in a single phrase which has become famous: " Through the Roman law, but beyond and
above it." [26]

With these declarations of the Romanists the Germanists
seemed satisfied. Their own utterances were not dissimilar.
But the apparent agreement was largely due to the acceptance of a common formula which each party could interpret
and apply as it saw fit. How much of the ancient Roman
law was really universal and how much temporary and national? How far did the practice of the mediæval Italian
and German courts eliminate the antiquated and foreign elements? How far had institutions originally foreign to German instincts become German by adoption? These are questions upon which differences of opinion are perfectly natural;
and given an academic system under which a large number

---

[24] *Geist des römischen Rechts,* vol. i, pp. 10, 11.
[25] Bruns, " Das heutige römische Recht," in *Holtzendorff,* p. 334.
[26] " Durch das römische Recht, aber über dasselbe hinaus." *Geist des
römischen Rechts,* vol. i, p. 14.

of jurists devote their entire time to studying and teaching the Roman law, while another considerable body is wholly immersed in early Teutonic customs and recent German legislation, such differences were certain. But for forty years Germanists and Romanists lived together in peace, or armed neutrality; taught as they thought, and left it to the students to reconcile or choose between their opposite opinions. The publication of the Imperial draft code in 1888 opened the sluice-gates of the academic reservoirs, and in the flood [27] of controversial literature that at once burst forth, the degree of divergence between Romanistic and Germanistic opinions is strikingly disclosed. Not a few of the Romanists are disturbed by the number of uncouth Gothic details that figure in the plans of this new temple of justice, and have hastened to plead for a stricter adherence to classical lines. But their mild protests are drowned in the cries of wrath that issue from the Germanistic camp. "Doctrinaire devotion to scholastic concepts," "contempt for German law and for the popular consciousness of right," — these phrases will serve, without further extracts, to show what passions have been slumbering through the forty years' truce.

But this revival of the old controversy runs beyond the limits of our present theme, for our four jurists took no part in it. Bruns was already dead; Windscheid was restrained from entering into any discussion of the code by the fact that he had been one of the commission of codification; Gneist had long devoted himself entirely to public law and stood aloof from purely private-law controversies. Jhering indeed published a criticism of the code,[28] but his objections had little to do with the national controversy.

IV

The attempt to codify the private law of the empire has given practical importance to-day to the disputes of the Ger-

---

[27] A catalogue of this literature, published by Puttkammer and Mühlbrecht in 1892, contains some six hundred titles.

[28] *Besitzwille*, pp. 470–534.

manists and the Romanists; the codifiers have been obliged
to choose or compromise in numberless cases between opposed views of legal relations; but it may well seem as if the
controversy that raged fifty years ago, when no general codification was in sight, was purely academic. This was not the
case. The Germanists had a practical grievance against
Savigny and his school. The historical researches prosecuted by the latter had clearly shown that the Roman law, as
applied by the German courts, was in many respects a different thing from the Roman law of the *Digest*. Starting
with the theses that it was Roman law that had been received
and that the authentic exposition of the Roman law was to
be found in the law books of Justinian, Savigny and his followers were disposed to treat the modifications introduced
by mediæval practice as aberrations, and the influence of the
school was thrown in favor of a reversion to the law of the
Digest. Their arguments actually changed [29] in many respects the practice of the German courts in the common-law
territories, *i.e.*, in those parts of Germany where the Roman
law had not been superseded by modern codes. Savigny and
his disciples were therefore accused of having added a fresh
injury to the original wrong of the reception by completing
the reception.

[29] This partial revolution of judicial practice was made possible by the
attitude of continental European theory towards judicial practice. The
German jurists, like the French, almost uniformly deny that decisions make
law. In view of the historical facts their attitude seems inexplicable. They
teach that the Roman law was largely developed by "interpretation";
that old German law was developing along the same lines when its growth
was arrested, first by feudal disintegration of judicial authority and then
by the reception of the foreign laws; that the practical reception of the
Justinianean law was accomplished through its acceptance by the "learned
judiciary"; that the Roman law was received as modified by Italian practice, and that it was subjected to further modifications in the German practice, — and yet they do not concede that judicial custom, as such, is law.
They go no further than to admit that the practice of the courts may in
some mysterious way be transmuted into customary law — or rather, that
it might be and perhaps was so transmuted in the middle ages, although
the process is no longer possible to-day. The leading Germanist of the
present day, Brunner, sees and expresses this point clearly. He writes:
"Romanistic theory and practice are still in large degree unable to grasp
the indubitable truth that the results of the practical reception, even where
they rest upon a misunderstanding of the sources of the Roman law, exclude the application of pure Roman law." — "Quellen und Geschichte
des römischen Rechts," in *Holtzendorff* (5th ed., 1890) p. 293.

Here again, since 1848, the Romanists have, to some extent, seen the error of their ways and drawn nearer to the Germanists. Mediæval modifications of the Roman law are no longer dismissed as mistakes due to ignorance. It is recognized that, in many instances, they represent the further development of progressive tendencies revealed in the later Roman jurisprudence and legislation; in other instances, the adaptation of the Roman law to different social and economic conditions; and, in many cases, the acceptance of legitimate or at least defensible Teutonic points of view. The change in the Romanistic attitude was, in no slight degree, the work of Bruns. He was one of the first to make a serious study of mediæval theory and practice in a special field.[30] He selected that field in which Savigny had begun his crusade for pure Roman law — possession. Bruns's *Law of Possession in the Middle Ages and the Present Time,* published in 1848, was not merely a finished presentation of the results of careful research and an important contribution to legal history: it was an explanation and, in some degree, a justification of the changes introduced by the mediæval jurists. Bruns himself, in this as in his subsequent writings on possession, remained, in principle, an adherent of the Roman theory as reformulated by Savigny, — the theory that finds the characteristic element of juristic possession in the intention (*animus*) of the possessor, — and he exhibited little sympathy for such changes in the law as seemed to him irreconcilable with this theory. The same may be said of Windscheid.[31] Jhering, however, in his last important work, *Possessory Intention,* not only gives a sweeping endorsement to nearly all the changes introduced by mediæval courts and modern legislators, but carries his assault upon the Romanistic doctrine back of Savigny. He finds the first false step, to which all subsequent aberrations are due, in a bad reason given by Paulus for a correct statement of positive law.[32]

[30] Savigny's *History of the Roman Law in the Middle Ages* is rather a history of the civil law as an entirety, with especial reference to its literary treatment, than a study of the development of single legal institutions.

[31] *Pandekten,* § 162.   [32] *Besitzwille,* pp. 269–300; 457 *et seq.*

Another valuable bit of research in mediæval legal history is Bruns's study of the presumption of death in case of disappearance, in which he shows how German custom, modified by a verse from the *Psalms* and a dictum from the *Digest* regarding usufruct, produced the rules which have found their way into the principal modern codes.[33]   The chief importance of these investigations, and of other similar studies to which they furnished an incentive, lies in the fact that mediæval legal development was no longer treated with contempt, but was taken seriously and examined critically.

v

We have thus far confined our attention to the controversies aroused by Savigny's historical theory and by the work of the historical school in the Romanistic field.   We have now to note the results of the impulse which he gave in the domain of systematic jurisprudence.   Briefly stated, these results were, in the first place, a tendency to excessive generalization, a gradual and unconscious transfer of juristic labor from the field of legal science proper to that of legal philosophy; and then a reaction towards a more practical jurisprudence.   Jhering was the leader of this reaction.

The power of generalization which the Germans possess in so high a degree is perhaps the chief factor in their scientific triumphs.   Patient research furnishes the material with which science deals, but to make anything of this material it is necessary to discover the principles which underlie and explain — or at least serve to correlate — the facts.   But every marked power carries with it the risk of abuse.   Not only does the love of generalization easily lead to useless abstraction; it is attended by other and more serious perils.   There is the danger of forgetting that the so-called principles of a science are really working hypotheses; that they have been obtained by induction and are to be tested in their application.   There is the impulse to wrest evidence to their support

[33] *Jahrbuch des gemeinen Rechts*, vol. i, p. 5 (1857).

and to ignore or evade such facts as prove intractable.   There is even, with minds of a certain sort, a tendency to ascribe to accepted principles a character of finality — a truth superior to the apparent truth of mere facts.   The more abstract the generalizations, the greater is the harm which such tendencies may entail.

Savigny's own systematic work was not wholly free from these faults, but in his case they were checked by a strong sense of the practical.   He was fundamentally more lawyer than philosopher.   Among his followers, however, some of whom were obviously intended by nature for philosophers rather than for lawyers, the tendency to excessive abstraction and to undue valuation of its results ran riot.   Puchta [34] in particular, the leading Romanist of the middle period between Savigny and the contemporaries of Jhering, carried idealistic jurisprudence to a point not before attained and hardly exceeded since.   To Jhering, in the earlier period of his revolt, Puchta seemed the incarnation of the tendencies against which he had declared war.   At a later period he carried the attack further back and directed it against Savigny, and ultimately, as we have seen, against Paulus.   Even then, however, he remained so far true to his first scientific enmity that he could find nothing worse to say of the Roman judge and jurist than to term him " the Puchta of the ancient world."   He finds in both

the same fanaticism of juristic construction, which in its zeal overlooks the yawning gaps between the points of view adopted and the existing law; . . . the same blind adherence to legal logic, which infers outright that whatever does not suit it is impossible and whatever does is necessary; . . . the same intolerance of the views of others, and even of the rules laid down by the legislator, when they do not coincide with the concepts which these two jurists have arranged to their own satisfaction.   Intellects, both of them, above the common stature; but violent, scientifically despotic natures, implacable doctrinaires.[35]

[34] Born 1798, died 1846.   [35] Jhering, *Besitzwille,* pp. 283, 284.

In their definitions and statements of principles, as in their whole theoretic construction of the law, Puchta and his followers abandoned to a large extent the method of independent induction from purely juristic data, and took their concepts ready-made from the professional philosophers, especially from Hegel. The philosophy of Hegel has influenced German jurisprudence in various ways. It helped to produce the " philosophical " reaction against the national theory of legal development.[36] It has also helped to give German legal theory an individualistic character. Hegel regarded law as a means for the attainment of true liberty; he described the evolution of law as " the development of the idea of freedom "; and he found the essence of individual freedom in the rational freedom of the individual will.

In pronouncing law to be more a system of liberty than a system of restraint, in emphasizing the element of freedom rather than the element of coercion, Hegel was perhaps influenced by the form in which the Roman law has come into the modern world. The only portion of that law which has survived and continued to influence European civilization is the portion which deals with private relations and in particular that which governs property relations. The constitutional, the administrative, and the criminal law of the Roman Empire are as dead as Julius Cæsar; the Roman private law is a living force. In every system of private law there is a wide range of individual autonomy — the state reaches its ends in private law through liberty as distinctly as in criminal law it reaches those ends through restraint — and in no system of private law is the field of individual freedom more generously measured than in the Roman. Add to this the fact that the Roman law — *i.e.,* the Roman private law — has been for centuries the general law of Europe, as compared with which all other law has seemed a mass of local and special rules, and the influence which the private-law point of view has exercised upon European thought in gen-

[36] Gans, the champion of the universal or cosmopolitan point of view, was a disciple of Hegel and edited Hegel's *Philosophy of History*.

eral, and which it may have exercised upon that of Hegel in particular, becomes sufficiently intelligible. These facts again explain the readiness with which the German jurists, especially those of the Romanistic school, have accepted Hegel's one-sided view of law.[37] Lawyers everywhere are apt to regard private law as *the* law, and the Romanist has a better excuse for this tendency than has the English lawyer.

Hegel's position that legal liberty is freedom of will rather than freedom of action or conduct has also some apparent basis in the Roman law. The Roman jurists laid much stress upon *animus, voluntas, etc.* There is, to be sure, nothing to show that the Roman jurists ever thought of will or intention as obtaining legal significance otherwise than through its revelation in word or deed; there is, in fact, evidence that the intention which a man's language or conduct would naturally suggest to others seemed to them much more important than his real intention; but their curt designation of the expressed will and the indicated intention as will and intention simply, and the importance which they ascribed to the individual will in determining legal relations, lend color to Hegel's assumption. The real explanation, however, of his theory that freedom is freedom of will is perhaps to be sought in the fact that he lived under a system of government which tolerated relatively little freedom of conduct.[38] His view of liberty seems as natural a product of governmental absolutism as Kant's theory of the "categorical imperative" in the field of ethics. But whatever its basis, Hegel's theory has

[37] It may, of course, be urged that the prohibitions of the law, the restraints which it imposes, serve to protect individual liberty; but it is equally true that the attribution of rights to the individual operates to the restraint of others. In fact the two modes of regarding law are not antagonistic but complementary.

[38] Perhaps, too, — since the position of a nation in the world at large affects the philosophy of its members, — the weakness of Germany in consequence of its disunity had something to do with Hegel's doctrine of liberty. Heine's remark that the Frenchmen ruled the land, the Englishmen the sea, and the Germans the realm of dreams, seems in point. And perhaps Heine's more famous saying that "the Englishman loves liberty like his lawful wife, the Frenchman like his mistress, and the German like his grandmother," may be construed as a satire upon the Hegelian conception of freedom.

had great success among German lawyers. Their definitions
and statements of principles are almost uniformly dyed in
the Hegelian color. Not only is a legal act — a contractual
promise, for example, or a conveyance — " a declaration of
will," but a right is regularly described as " a power of volition," the protection of possession is justified on the ground
that the law respects " the realized will," — and so on indefinitely.

Against these tendencies in German jurisprudence —
against the over-valuation of abstractions in particular —
Jhering waged incessant war for the last thirty years of his
life. It would have been difficult to find in all Germany a
man better fitted to champion the cause of " practical jurisprudence." He came of that Frisian stock which is still most
closely allied, in temper as in blood, to the English; he was
by race instinct a realist. He possessed, also, in high degree,
the quality of mind that makes the lawyer — the power of
brushing aside the accidents of a problem, and concentrating
his attention upon its essence. He was a master of dialectics,
quick to discern the weakest point in his adversary's logic.
He had both wit and humor, and knew how to use them;
he could make an untenable position manifestly absurd.
Finally, no German of our day has commanded a more brilliant and persuasive style.[39] Its very defects — a certain
diffuseness, a habit of saying the same thing several times
before the exact formulation of the thought is attained —
have their charm; to read him is to listen to the discursive
talk of a full and ready speaker; the personal note, which so
strongly influences a listener, vibrates from the printed page.
These defects, moreover, — if they be defects, — were far
outbalanced by positive excellences. He could make the
most abstract theme concrete, the most technical question
interesting, by his facility of suggestive illustration; and he

---

[39] In recommending to us, his students, Jhering's first book on possession, Windscheid, who disagreed with the author's conclusions, warned
us that we must read the book critically, " because everything of Jhering's
is written with a brilliancy (*Glanz*) and a power of persuasion (*Ueber-
redungskraft*) that are almost irresistible."

had the power of making his ideas current by rounding them into sparkling epigrams. No legal writer of our day, not even Maine, has counted in his public so large a proportion of laymen. Nor was Jhering's public German only; French and Spanish translations of his *Spirit of the Roman Law*, and French versions of several other books and pamphlets gave him a cosmopolitan audience. To English readers, unfortunately, only his *Struggle for Law* is accessible, and the translation of this pamphlet leaves much to be desired.

Into his agitation against abstract jurisprudence,[40] Jhering, by his own account, brought the zeal of a convert. He has more than once described his change of heart; humorously in the anonymous *Confidential Letters*[41] with which he opened the conflict; seriously in the last part of his *Jest and Earnest*,[42] and in the preface to his *Possessory Intention*.[43]

There was a time [he writes] when I accepted Puchta as master and model of the correct juristic method, and when I was so captivated by that method that I was capable of going beyond my model. . . . That in the legislative embodiment [of legal theories] any other consideration were to be regarded except the desirability of *a priori* logical construction, I did not then dream; and I still remember how low an opinion I held of my friends among the practising lawyers who could not appreciate the coercive force of my ideas and deductions. . . . But then [about 1860] came the revulsion; not from within, but through external influences; through active intercourse with practitioners — an intercourse which I have always sought, cherished and turned to my advantage; through the occasions for practical activity on my own part which were afforded by appeals to the faculty[44] and requests

[40] Other terms employed by Jhering are "speculative," "scholastic," "formalistic" jurisprudence, and *die Begriffsjurisprudenz*.
[41] "Vertrauliche Briefe über die heutige Jurisprudenz," published 1860–1866 in the *Preussische* (later *Deutsche*) *Gerichtszeitung*; reprinted in *Scherz und Ernst* (1885).
[42] *Scherz und Ernst*, pp. 338, 339.
[43] *Besitzwille*, pp. ix, x.
[44] The mediæval practice of referring cases to the law faculties continued through the middle of this century.

to furnish opinions — occasions which not infrequently led me to recoil in terror from the application of theories that I had previously defended; and last, but not in least part, through the moot-court,[45] which I have held all my life, and which I regard as one of the most valuable correctives for the teacher himself against unsound theoretic views.[46]

A convert naturally exaggerates the sinfulness of his unregenerate years, and Jhering's self-accusation must be taken with more than a grain of salt. In the context of the passage just cited he instances, besides his earliest work,[47] published in 1844, sundry treatises which he had begun to write but had left unpublished and unfinished, and his opening essay in the first volume of the *Year-Books*,[48] — a periodical which he and the Germanist von Gerber started in 1857. In this essay, as in the third installment of his *Spirit of the Roman Law*,[49] which was written at nearly the same time, Jhering exalted the function of the " higher " or " productive " jurisprudence; but whether this was the same thing as the abstract jurisprudence which he began to combat three years afterwards, and whether, in his later work, he ever really abandoned the problems which he had set himself in 1857, may well be questioned. As to the unpublished treatises, we must take his word for their unpractical character; but the fact that they were not completed is an argument for Jhering as defendant, not for Jhering as *advocatus diaboli*. For the rest it may be said that his great work on the *Spirit of the Roman Law*, of which the major part was written between 1850 and 1860, does not impress a foreign reader as either abstract or unpractical; and the same may be said of his most important single contribution to " productive " jurisprudence, the theory of the negative interest

---

[45] *" Pandectenpracticum "* — an exercise in applying Roman law to concrete cases, real or hypothetical. " Moot-court " is in so far an inexact translation as the forms of judicial procedure are not usually observed in these *Practica*.

[46] *Scherz und Ernst, loc. cit.*

[47] *Abhandlungen aus dem römischen Recht.*

[48] *Jahrbücher für Dogmatik* — still published under the title *Jhering's Jahrbücher.*

[49] *Geist des römischen Rechts*, Theil 2, Abth. 2 (3d ed.), pp. 357–389.

of contract, which first saw the light in 1860 [50] but was undoubtedly worked out at an earlier date. It may be added that his theory of possessory intention, set forth in his last important fulmination against " formalistic " jurisprudence in 1889, had taken preliminary form in his mind, and had been orally communicated to others, as early as 1846.[51]

There can be no question, however, that about 1860 Jhering became strongly convinced, as he afterwards expressed it, that

a change must take place in our Romanistic theory. . . . It must abandon the delusion that it is a system of legal mathematics, without any higher aim than a correct reckoning with conceptions.[52]

He opened his attack, in the *Confidential Letters,* with a humorous sketch of the beauties of the new jurisprudence. He proceeded to show, in the case of a young theorist just plunged into practice, the unjust and absurd results to which the logical application of accepted general principles would lead. In the later letters he undertook to lay bare some of the causes of the aberrations of legal science. These he found partly in the divorce of practice and theory, partly in the system of legal instruction and examinations, but principally in the custom of requiring that every aspirant to a German professorship shall legitimate himself by producing something new in the way of theory. In Romanistic jurisprudence, he, explains, this is practically impossible. The grapes have been trodden for centuries. The only way to get any more wine out of the dry mass is to pour on water before pressing again, and fortify the product with alcohol and sugar.

The proportion in which these ingredients are added differs with the individual taste of the manufacturer. In most cases water preponderates. One jurist has experimented with alcohol alone; but without his observing it, a good deal of water is said to have run in with his *Spirit.*[53]

[50] *Jahrbücher,* vol. iv, pp. 16 *et seq.*   [52] *Scherz und Ernst,* pp. 341, 342.
[51] *Besitzwille,* preface, p. vi.   [53] *Scherz und Ernst,* p. 110.

This allusion to his own work, with other bits of similar self-persiflage, was of course inserted to mislead those who were seeking to identify the author of the letters. The extent to which his purpose necessitated ridicule of particular writers made the preservation of the secret seem especially desirable. He continues:

There have come into my hands, within a few days, various writings of one Dr. Asher, tutor in Heidelberg, — invaluable contributions, which, with sundry others, I shall use in one of my future letters. But I appeal to you: how can this man, in spite of the incredible ingenuity he displays, get away from the fact that Cujacius lived three centuries before him and took the best ideas off in advance? Had he been born then, and Cujacius in our time, he would very likely have been Cujacius, and Cujacius Dr. Asher. It all depends on the first chance at the press. It is all very well to say that if no new and sensible view is possible, it is better to take one already provided; but you do not understand the situation. Better a senseless view for one's self alone than a reasonable opinion in common with others.[54]

He concludes with a proposal that tutors be released from the necessity of publishing books. He finds in the Roman law a suggestion of a mode in which this reform might be brought about without ostensibly abandoning the rule. He finds there also a precedent for the lenient judgment of tutorial productions.

In Rome, as is well known, the rule existed from the time of Augustus that whoever desired to take by testament must show a certain number of children: *liberi* were the condition of *capacitas*. Persons, however, to whom the emperor was well disposed, escaped this trouble by obtaining the *ius liberorum;* the children were legally presumed or simply waived. Among others, Diana of Ephesus, who as goddess of chastity could not with propriety be held to the observance of the law, was thus invested with capacity. The importance attached in Rome to physical fruitfulness we attach to intel-

[54] *Ibid.,* p. 111.

lectual productivity: there it was " no inheritance without *liberi*"; here it is " no professorship without *libri*." [55]

He therefore proposes that, as soon as law tutors indicate an intention to print,

a *ius librorum* should be granted them, *i.e.,* they should be made professors just as if they had published the necessary books. Even now, in many universities, the requirement of books is not taken very strictly: there is the same leniency in judging them which the Romans observed in the matter of children, and which is set forth in the *Digest* in a way so humane and so applicable to the question before us, that I cannot refrain from printing the whole passage.

D. 50, 16, 135. " Quaeret aliquis, si portentosum vel monstrosum vel debilem mulier ediderit vel qualem visu vel vagitu novum, non humanae figurae, sed alterius, magis animalis quam hominis, partum, an, quia enixa est, prodesse ei debeat? Et magis est, ut haec quoque parentibus prosint: *nec enim est quod eis imputetur, quae qualiter potuerunt, statutis obtemperaverunt,* neque id quod fataliter accessit, matri damnum iniungere debet."

Freely adapted to the case in point: " When tutors have done the best they can to observe the statutes of the university, why should they be held responsible because, by ill hap, the books they have brought forth are not normal literary productions but monstrosities, or exhibit such debility of mind as not to seem viable? They have at least brought something into the world, and that should be reckoned to their credit." The granting of the *ius librorum* and the professorship should of course be made conditional on an undertaking not to publish the book submitted, or at least not to publish it for a term of years, say the classical nine years — *nonum prematur in annum.* The safest course would be to commit it to the custody of the law faculty. After the lapse of nine years and the attainment of the professorship, the author would hardly insist on publication. He would probably thank God that a wise paternal government had preserved him from an over-hasty literary venture.[56]

[55] *Scherz und Ernst* p. 113.   [56] *Scherz und Ernst,* pp. 113, 114.

This is not only very good fooling: there is good sense back of it.

A more serious attack upon the current tendencies in German jurisprudence was made in the concluding sections of his fourth installment of the *Spirit of the Roman Law*. These contained a strong argument against " the over-valuation of the logical element in law," [57] and an attempt to re-formulate the conception of a right.[58] " If a right is a power of willing," he inquired, " how is it that infants and lunatics have rights? " To this the orthodox responded that " the right does not exist through the fact that volition is exercised, that a will is expressed, but through the fact that an exercise of will is permitted, that a will may be expressed." [59] Jhering promptly seized this as an admission that, under the definition, it is the guardian and not the infant or lunatic who has the right, since it is the former whom the law " permits to will." Jhering's own definition of the right is " a legally protected interest." The interest is the " kernel "; the legal protection, by right of action, is the " shell." We speak of a right as appertaining to the infant or lunatic, and not to the guardian, because the interest is not with the latter, but with the former. So in the case of the fictitious or juristic person; the interests of an incorporated stock-company, for example, are those of the stockholders; the conception of juristic personality in the corporation is simply a device for explaining its power to sue. The construction, according to this formula, of the " foundation," when property is held together for some religious, educational or charitable purpose, gave Jhering more trouble; but with the courage of his convictions he here vested the interest — and therefore the right — in the public at large.

It is to be regretted that neither Jhering nor his adversaries were acquainted with the English law of trusts. They would there have found a full recognition of the element of interest, for which Jhering was contending, and they would also have

---

[57] *Geist des römischen Rechts,* Theil 3, Abth. 1, pp. 308, 316.
[58] *Ibid,* pp. 317–354.   [59] Windscheid, *Pandekten,* § 37, n. 2.

found that English law, in distinguishing the legal from the equitable right, has always attributed the latter to the person who has the interest, and the former to the person who has the power. They might well have ended by admitting that these two elements exist in every right, and that the two are separable. Such a termination of the controversy would have left to the adherents of the dominant theory the right to insist that the really juristic element is the power, and to Jhering the credit of having called attention to that element which German theory had previously ignored.

Although no such consensus has been attained, Jhering's arguments have had considerable influence. Some jurists have accepted his definition; others, like Bruns,[60] have attempted to weave into the sacred Hegelian formula a recognition of the interest which underlies the right.

Jhering's next attack upon "abstract" legal theory was directed against the current explanation of the protection accorded by Roman law to the possessor as such, whether the possession be rightful or wrongful, honest or dishonest.[61] The German literature of this century on the law of possession is very extensive: when, in 1889, Jhering returned to this field, his second book[62] was at least the thirtieth treatise on possession that had appeared since Savigny's — doctor dissertations and review articles not included. The English literature can show, within the same period, but one important work on this branch of the law.[63] Why the German mind has been so fascinated — not to say possessed — by this subject is a curious question. In his *Possessory Inten-*

---

[60] "Die subjektiven Rechte sind die Befugnisse, die den einzelnen Subjekten dem objectiven Rechte nach zustehen. Sie bestehen im Allgemeinen in der vom objectiven Rechte anerkannten und geschützten *Freiheit* der Einzelnen in Verfolgung ihrer Lebens*interessen.*" Bruns, in *Holtzendorff*, 3d ed., p. 352. — "Freedom" is still there; but "will" has disappeared, and "interest" has won a footing! Further on it appears that freedom has become freedom of action: "Möglichkeit zum *Handeln.*"

[61] Grund des Besitzesschutzes (1868). First published in *Jhering's Jahrbücher*.

[62] Besitzwille (1889). A third and less technical treatise on the subject is to be found in Jhering's article, "Besitz," *Handwörterbuch der Staatswissenschaften* (1890–1892), vol. ii; reprinted in *Jhering's Jahrbücher*, 1893, pp. 41–98.

[63] Pollock and Wright, *Possession in the Common Law* (Oxford, 1888).

tion Jhering hazards the conjecture that it is the imperfect juristic development of the doctrine that attracts the constructive jurist. Possession is inarticulate, " the mollusk of legal institutions "; it is so " soft and flexible " that the jurist can make of it what he wishes; it is " a rubber figure." [64] Here Jhering is less happy than usual in his similes. The *corpus* of possession, the power of control, is a matter of fact; the law of possession, has grown up about this hard central fact; and the constructive jurist is attracted not by the ease with which this legal institution can be moulded into logical form, but, on the contrary, by the resistance which it offers to his processes.

There is, however, a good bit of truth in Jhering's statement that the doctrine is imperfectly developed. It was imperfectly developed *in the Roman law,* as is shown by the sweeping changes introduced by mediæval practice and modern legislation. Whether the protection of possession at Rome originally represented the natural reaction of civilized society against the assertion of rights by force, or began in the protection accorded to the occupants of the public lands,[65] the Roman law was steadily working towards a broader principle than the discouragement of self-help, or the defense of the established state of things. In the light of the modern European development, and of the independent but similar results reached in the English law, the goal toward which Roman law was tending seems to be the protection of possession under any sort of title against every other title that is no better than that of the possessor, with the premise that naked possession is itself a title. " Every sort of possessor," says Paulus, " by the very fact that he is possessor,

---

[64] *Besitzwille,* pp. 284, 285.

[65] The occupants or possessors of *ager publicus* were legally mere tenants at will, holding at the sufferance of the state. In practice their holdings were permanent, were capable of conveyance and devise, and passed to the heirs *ab intestato*. Niebuhr, *Römische Geschichte,* vol. ii, pp. 150 *et seq.;* Marquardt, *Römische Verwaltung,* vol. i, p. 155; vol. ii, pp. 98 *et seq.* Niebuhr first suggested that the possessory interdicts were devised for their protection. Dernburg, *Entwickelung und Begriff des juristischen Besitzes* (1883), has given an elaborate development to Niebuhr's idea. Against Dernburg, Jhering, *Besitzwille,* p. 124.

has more right than one who does not possess " ; and Ulpian illustrates this statement by saying that the robber who, being asked why he possesses, will only answer, " Because I possess," and will not pretend that he has any color of title, possesses " by title of possession." [66]   The principle of relativity of title is recognized in the *actio Publiciana* and in *condictio possessionis,* for in neither of these actions has the plaintiff to show a good title, but in the first only a color of title, and in the second only that possession has passed from him to the defendant *sine causa;* and in both actions the defendant wins if he can show a title as good as the plaintiff's. The same principle is partially recognized even in the possessory interdicts, in that the possessor who has obtained possession by force or stealth or revocable permission (*aut vi clam aut precario*) has legal relief, in case of arbitrary encroachment or annoyance, against every adversary except the person whom he has ejected, or by whose permission he holds.

But the principle is not fully worked out.   The possessory remedies are not granted to all possessors.   They are granted to the possessor who thinks himself owner, and to the possessor who knows that he is not.   They are granted to the holders of life estates and of perpetual leaseholds, *i.e.,* to all persons holding under such titles.   They are granted even to the person " in possession " of a right of way.   They are granted to the pledgee in possession and to the stakeholder.[67] They are denied to the ordinary lessee and to the ordinary bailee.   Lessees and bailees have not even the relative protection accorded to the tenant-at-will, who is protected against every one except his grantor.   Lessees and bailees are mere " natural " possessors, or, as the modern writers call them, " detentors."   They have not " juristic " possession.

[66] " Qualiscumque enim possessor hoc ipso quod possessor est plus iuris habet quam ille qui non possidet." D. 43, 17, 2.   " Pro possessore vero possidet praedo, qui interrogatus cur possideat, responsurus sit ' quia possideo ' nec contendet se heredem vel per mendacium, nec ullam causam possessionis possit dicere." D. 5, 3, 11, § 1, 12, 13 pr.

[67] *Sequester:* person with whom property is deposited pending determination of its ownership.

If disturbed or ejected by the lessor or bailor, they have no
action except for breach of contract. If disturbed or ejected
by others, they must look for protection to the persons for
whom they were holding.

In the interdict procedure, moreover, the principle of
relativity of right is only faintly developed; the dominant
idea seems to be the discouragement of self-help. To this
idea, it seems, is to be attributed the exclusion of the so-called
exceptiones petitoriae, i.e., the barring of all plea of right on
the part of the defendant. When the possessor seeks relief against arbitrary encroachment, or other disturbance,
the defendant cannot allege ownership or any other substantive right; he can only plead that the plaintiff's possession, as against him, the defendant, is " faulty," because the
plaintiff has derived possession from him *aut vi aut clam aut
precario.* When the plaintiff seeks relief against a forcible
ejectment, even this defense is barred. He who has been forcibly ejected is to be restored *because* he has been forcibly
ejected. That he had previously ejected his adversary is immaterial; his adversary should have appealed to the law for
relief.[68]

Leaving the realm of Roman law and entering that of
Roman theory, it should be noted that the Roman jurists
declared that possession is acquired and held *animo et corpore.* To be possessor, one must intend to possess; he must
have the *animus possidendi;* and he must also have the *corpus;* that is, he must be in control. When possession is held
for us by others, — slaves, children or free agents, — we possess *animo nostro, corpore alieno.* Paulus utilizes the *animus*
theory to explain the denial of possessory remedies to lessees
and bailees. Since these persons intend to hold for the lessor
or bailor, and not for themselves, they are not legally possessors.

---

[68] So in the Justinianean law. In the *Edictum perpetuum* of Hadrian
this rule applied only where the second ejectment was accomplished by
"armed force"—"hominibus coactis armatisve." The ejected possessor
had the right to use ordinary force for the recovery of possession. *Cf.* Lenel,
Edictum perpetuum, § 245.

Starting with these rules of the Roman law and these *dicta* of the Roman jurists, the German jurisprudence of our century has striven to discover the essential nature of that " juristic " possession which the law protects, and the fundamental idea which underlies the protection. It is not wonderful that the task has been found arduous. To an outsider it seems a trifle singular that so many lawyers should have employed their time in such a quest. Why not admit that the Roman distinction between " possession " and mere " detention " is historical, and to some extent arbitrary, and that the protection accorded to possession rests on more than one basis. The answer is, I think, that philosophy instinctively seeks, even in the case of social institutions, a single central idea, a simple and comprehensive explanation, and that the German jurists are nothing if not philosophical.

Savigny found the central idea of juristic possession in the *animus domini,* the intention of holding against all the world. The lessee or bailee, as Paulus had already said, is not a possessor, because he is holding for the lessor or the bailor. It is, of course, true that the pledgee and the stakeholder and the tenant at will, who have no *animus domini,* have the possessory actions; but these are anomalies. The ground for the protection of possession Savigny found in the fact that all violence (*Gewaltthätigkeit*) is illegal. This expression leaves it unclear whether he regarded disturbance of possession as illegal because it is an offense against the public order, or because it is an invasion of a private right. Other passages in his treatise indicate that he leaned to the latter theory. The right invaded is not the right of possession, for possession is a fact, not a right; [69] it is the freedom of the person that is attacked, and the protection given to the possessor is " a protection of the personality." Gans gave to this idea a strictly Hegelian expression, asserting that " the will *an sich* is something substantial, something to be pro-

---

[69] This is Windscheid's interpretation of Savigny's position. Savigny himself says (*Besitz,* p. 44) that " possession is at the same time a fact and a right," but qualifies this statement immediately by explaining that it is a fact in its essence, but resembles a right in its results.

tected," and that " the particular will has to yield only to the higher universal will." In various shadings this explanation has been generally accepted; and the central idea of posses- sion, and the ground of its protection, have thus been brought into most satisfactory harmony. The decisive element in possession is the will, and possession is protected because the law respects " the realized will." So Windschied explains that the distinction between the different kinds of possession " depends upon the possessor's state of mind " ; and that " that possession which is associated with the will to have the thing for one's self, which is the realization of the will to appropriate the thing," is legally protected because " the will which has made itself actually valid in this possession is as such, without regard to the rightfulness of its content, worth just as much as any other single will which aims to bring the thing under its control." [70]   Similarly Bruns:

Power without will is no more possession than will without power. . . .   Will and power must cover each other; the will must go as far as the power, and *vice versa;* and since he alone really wills to control who wills this for himself, and not as mere representative of another, therefore he alone is pos- sessor who wills to have the thing completely for himself. . . .

If in the institutions of positive law we see the revelation (*Erscheinung*) of the universal idea of right, and if, accord- ingly, we seek for such a revelation in this matter of posses- sion, we are instinctively led to the universal right of human personality and liberty, and thus to the principle that the personal will to control, which is realized in possession, needs, as such, to yield to no other will, but only to the law and the forms of law. . . .   The basis of the protection of posses- sion lies in the right of the personal possessory will *an sich.*[71]

In his *Basis of the Protection of Possession* Jhering puffed away with a breath these philosophic mists.   Will, he de-

[70] Windscheid, *Pandekten,* § 148.   In justice to Windscheid it should be added that under this philosophical drapery stands the defensible legal idea that disturbance and invasion of possession are *torts.*   This is also Savigny's theory.   But Bruns expressly rejects it, falling back on philosophy pure and simple.
[71] Bruns, " Das heutige römische Recht," in *Holtzendorff,* 3d ed., pp. 380, 381.   In his *Recht des Besitzes,* § 58, Bruns declares that the will is in its nature free and every coercion of the will is a wrong.

clared, is undoubtedly the *vis agens* in the whole field of private law, but only in so far as it is exercised within legal limits. If the " realized will " is entitled to respect and protection, why does the law compel the person who has forcibly ejected a prior possessor to restore possession and pay damages? It is not true, in law, that one will is as good as another; in some cases the law recognizes and protects the " realized will," in other cases it discountenances and nullifies it. Why the law does this cannot be determined by invoking the right of the will *an sich*.[72]

After classifying the various theories, and subjecting them to a searching and in many cases destructive criticism, Jhering advances his own explanation. Possession is protected for the sake and in the interest of property, of ownership. The owner is regularly possessor; [73] and whenever this is the case the maintenance of his position as possessor is a much simpler matter than the maintenance of his position as owner. As possessor he is spared the proof of his right; he is protected against encroachment, against every sort of disturbance and annoyance, upon his showing that he is in possession. If ejected, he is put back upon his showing that he was in possession and has been ousted without process of law. Possession is the strongest outwork of the fortress of ownership; and the protection of possession is a necessary complement to the protection of ownership. Of course the better protection thus accorded to owners enures to the advantage of non-owners in possession. That is the price which property has to pay for the advantages it secures in the protection of possession; but the advantages are cheap at the price.

The two chief points in Jhering's theory — facilitation of proof in possessory actions and probable ownership of the possessor — were too self-evident to be new. No practicing lawyer, of any time or race, could fail to appreciate the procedural advantage of resting on possession, and avoiding the

[72] *Cf.* Stahl, *Philosophie des Rechts*, 5th ed. (1878), vol. ii, p. 304; and Dernburg, *Pandekten* (1888), § 170.

[73] Either because he holds the property himself, or because a tenant or bailee holds it for him.

probatio diabolica of title; from this point of view possession, as the English lawyers say, is " nine points of the law." The presumptive ownership of the possessor was suggested by Placentinus (of Bologna and Montpellier) in the twelfth century, and in the nineteenth Gans momentarily abandoned the contemplation of *Wille an sich* to point out that honest possession was at least incipient ownership, perfectible by prescription. The combination of these points of view, however, was original with Jhering, and the formulation of the theory was all his own.

If Jhering had contented himself with presenting this view of possession as *an* explanation of the rules of Roman law, it is hard to see how anybody could have taken issue with him. But, like all his countrymen of this century, he was looking for *the* explanation, the basis (*Grund*) of the Roman law of possession.[74] He had rejected other excellent theories, such as the repressal of self-help, the maintenance of public order, *etc.*, because they do not account for all the rules of the law. His opponents, therefore, hastened to point out that his theory does not explain why, in possessory proceedings, the defendant is not allowed to plead title. If the law of possession is based on the interest of the owner, it is quite logical, they declared, to spare him the proof of title when he appears as plaintiff, but quite illogical to deprive him of the opportunity of proving title when he appears as defendant. Jhering had anticipated this objection, and had tried to meet it in his book; but his explanation is far from satisfactory.

Twenty years later, in 1889, Jhering attacked the theory that the intention to maintain control against all the world, the will to hold like an owner (*animus domini*) is the characteristic element in " juristic " possession — the element which distinguishes such possession from the merely " natural " possession of the lessee or bailee. Against this theory, which he terms the " will theory," or " subjective

---

[74] Although he had previously recognized, in a general way, that it is sometimes impossible to find a single principle at the basis of a legal institution, and that a given institution may be " according to its primary plan absolutely dual." *Geist des römischen Rechts*, 3d ed., part ii, div. i, p. 355.

theory," he set up and defended an " objective theory," which may be summarized as follows. The intention of possessing is of course essential to possession, but the intention of possessing for one's self is not essential.[75] The denial of the possessory remedies to lessees and bailees is an arbitrary rule, and its explanation is to be found in the economic and legal development of the Roman state.[76] The Roman tenant farmer (*colonus*) was far more dependent upon his landlord, far more completely under the landlord's surveillance and control, than the modern agricultural lessee. The Roman peasant-proprietor, in Republican times, leased but a part of his property, and landlord and tenant cultivated side by side. When land was given by large proprietors for really independent cultivation, it was given *precario*. Similar conditions prevailed in the earlier leases of dwellings: the tenant (*inquilinus*) took only a part of the house; the remainder was occupied by the landlord. It was natural, in both cases, that the landlord was regarded as the possessor, and that the tenant looked to him for protection against disturbance. This was but a slight extension of the authority of the head of the house, the *paterfamilias*. At first he possessed through the agency of his children and slaves; later he possessed through tenants. Children and slaves had only natural possession; tenants have the same. The extension of this rule to bailees seemed a logical necessity. It did little harm, because the protection of possession by the interdicts was much less important in the case of chattels than in the case of real property.[77] Paulus's assertion that lessees and bailees do not possess *ad interdicta* because they do not possess for themselves but for others, simply represents his effort to find a juristic explanation for the established rules of the

---

[75] The Roman jurists spoke only of the *animus possidendi*, or *possidentis*. The phrases *animus domini, animus dominantis, animus rem sibi habendi*, are mediæval or modern. Only the second phrase, *animus dominantis*, has any basis in the ancient texts; it is a translation of the Byzantine ψυχὴ δεσπόζοντος found in Theophilus's paraphrase of the Institutes, and in the Basilica.

[76] *Besitzwille*, ch. viii.

[77] To sustain an action of theft, or an action for recovery *ex contractu* of things loaned by him, *etc.*, the bailee had need neither of title nor of " juristic " possession.

law. As a piece of juristic construction it is far from admirable. It put a novel meaning into the familiar *animus possidentis;* and it failed to account for the well-established rules which gave the protection of the interdicts to the tenant-at-will, to the pledgee, and to the stakeholder. But in spite of its unsatisfactory character, this explanation of Paulus has been repeated ever since, and has become the basis of the modern theory of juristic possession.[78]

Jhering subjects the " will theory " and his own theory to a series of " tests " — historical, procedural, political and didactic. The most interesting of these (after the historical), and the one that throws most light upon the substantive law, is the " procedural test." [79] The " will theory," which grants or denies the possessory remedies according to the *animus* of the possessor, logically requires that the plaintiff in a possessory suit should allege and prove his *animus dominantis*. But to hold a plaintiff to prove his state of mind is absurd. All that can be required is that he should produce *indicia* of his state of mind, *i.e.*, facts which lead to the presumption that he has been possessing for himself. The most important fact of this sort is the title under which he came into possession — his *causa possidendi*. Accordingly, many authorities have held that the plaintiff must at least show a *causa possidendi* which indicates an intention to hold for himself, *e.g.*, inheritance, devise, purchase or gift. But the ejector and the thief are entitled, by Roman law, to possessory actions. Was it required in Roman practice that such plaintiffs should allege and prove violent ejectment or theft? The Roman practice, Jhering maintains, like that which generally prevails in the modern world, required of the plaintiff no proof save of his corporeal possession.[80] If

[78] *Besitzwille,* ch. xiii.

[79] *Besitzwille,* ch. ix. It seems clear that it was the failure of the " subjective theory " to stand the test of procedure that first led Jhering to question its truth. In the fourth of his " Confidential Letters," printed in 1863, he describes an imaginary suit for protection on the ground of possession which a young practitioner tries to carry through on the basis of Savigny's theory, with a result most disastrous to his client. *Scherz und Ernst,* pp. 63 *et seq.*

[80] For Roman practice there is no direct evidence; but the assertion of Paulus, *Sententiae,* 5, 11, § 2, that to prove *delivery* it is necessary only to

the plaintiff held by force or stealth, or permission from his adversary, it was incumbent on the adversary to allege and prove this. If he held by lease or bailment, it was probably incumbent upon the defendant to allege and prove this. Such at least is the rational mode of distributing the burden of proof.[81] In a rational system of pleading, therefore, *animus* plays no rôle whatever. It never appears.

If this is true, Jhering argues, is it not absurd to make will or intention the criterion of possession in our statement of substantive law? The true statement of the law is that natural possession as such is protected; that the corporeal possessor has not merely the right of self-defense, but the peculiar remedies given to the possessor. In two cases, however, the Roman law withdraws this protection; it refuses the possessory interdicts to lessees and bailees, not because they have the intention of holding for others, but because they are lessees or bailees. Their actual intention is of no consequence whatever; if they decide to hold for themselves, or for third parties, their change of mind has no effect upon their legal position, or upon that of the lessors or bailors for whom they originally agreed to hold. " No one," said the Roman jurists, " can change for himself his *causa possessionis.* " [82]

Between the ruling "subjective theory" and his own "objective theory" there is, as Jhering recognizes, an intermediate opinion, which distinguishes juristic from natural possession by the *animus* or intention of the possessor, but which treats the actual will of the possessor as irrelevant. It attributes to him the " typical " will which a man in his position, with his *causa possessionis*, ought to have, and refuses to consider whether he has any other will. As Jhering

---

prove corporeal possession, makes in favor of Jhering's contention. So, I think, does D. 5, 3, 11, § 1 *et seq.* cited above (p. 141).

[81] So in the French law. *Code Civil,* art. 2230: " On est toujours présumé posséder pour soi et à titre de propriétaire, s'il n'est prouvé qu'on a commencé à posséder pour un autre." " An article," Jhering characteristically remarks, " that in my eyes is of more importance for practical life than all that the literature of this whole century has produced regarding the distinction between possession and detention." *Besitzwille,* p. 168.

[82] *Digest,* 41, 2, 19, § 1.

points out, this theory really abandons will as the criterion of juristic possession, and substitutes positive legal rule. The typical will with which it operates is a mere legal fiction.[83]

To complete this sketch of Jhering's position on the legal topic which has most largely occupied the attention of German jurists in this century, it should be added that in opposition to the Roman, as well as to the dominant modern view, he asserted that possession is not a mere fact, nor merely a " legal relation," but a right.[84] Possession is unquestionably an interest, and possession is undoubtedly protected; and having defined a right as " a legally protected interest," Jhering was logically constrained to admit possession to the category of rights. To most jurists this deductive test of his definition must seem a proof that the definition is at fault. A " right " that figures in legal procedure only so long as the question of right is not raised, is surely a right of a very singular sort. In his *Possessory Intention* Jhering adheres to his earlier statement as far as juristic possession is concerned, but abandons the ground in the case of natural possession, which he declares to be only a "legal relation." [85] But since he maintains that even the natural possessor enjoys some protection, and that natural possession and juristic possession differ solely in the degree of protection accorded by the law, we obtain, from his premises, this result: a right is an interest which enjoys *a certain degree* of legal protection. What degree is necessary is left to every one to settle for himself.[86]

---

[83] *Besitzwille,* pp. 15–20. Of all the representatives of the " causal theory," Dernburg, perhaps, comes nearest to Jhering's position. He writes in his *Pandekten* (2d ed., 1888), § 179: " The will to possess for one's self . . . is to be deduced from the situation (*Sachlage*). It results particularly from the ground — the *causa* — on which possession is taken. He who takes as owner or pledgee is juristic possessor; he who takes as lessee or agent is not juristic possessor." But further back, in § 172: " Possessory relations constitute juristic possession only when the purpose of the possessor is to possess for himself, and when this purpose enjoys the recognition of the state."

[84] *Geist des römischen Rechts,* 3d ed., part iii, div. 1, pp. 351 *et seq.;* " Der Besitz," in Jhering's *Jahrbücher,* 1893, pp. 63 *et seq.*

[85] *Besitzwille,* pp. 50, 51.

[86] In *Besitzwille, loc. cit.,* there is also a curious reversion to the will theory, discarded twenty years before in his *Besitzesschutz.* While the pro-

The principal conclusions which Jhering reached in his *Possessory Intention* seem to me sound; but, for my present purpose, the proportion of truth in this book and in his *Protection of Possession* is of less interest than the point of view which his readers were compelled to take and the kind of considerations which were urged upon them. Before Jhering wrote, the discussion of the law of possession had been conducted in the most abstract fashion. Very little consideration had been given to the practical operation of the rules; and in the search for the principle beneath them, it had apparently not been recognized that the social effect of the rules might furnish a useful clue. In the first of these books he shifted the discussion from the plane of the abstract and ideal to that of the concrete and practical; and to one who had been ballooning through space in the company of the earlier writers — I speak from experience — the descent was jarringly sudden. To the mundane American mind the shock was slight, and its results exhilarating; but to Jhering's metaphysical countrymen it was obviously severe. With some of them, as with Keats's Endymion, the "first touch of the earth went nigh to kill."

For nine years after the appearance of his *Protection of Possession*, from 1868 to 1877, Jhering published but two small books — a collection of questions for discussion in moot-court,[87] and the famous *Struggle for Law*.[88] The cause of this relative reticence, on the part of a man whose mind was as active and whose temperament was as communicative as his, was his absorption in a task for which he felt and confessed himself inadequately prepared — the formulation of a philosophy of law. He was preparing the first volume of *Zweck im Recht* — a title which I cannot translate literally, because the English language has no precise equivalent for *Zweck*. *Teleology of Law* may serve as a para-

---

tection of juristic possession is still based on the interests of owners, the protection of natural possession is based on regard for "the realized will." And yet the only difference between juristic and natural possession is the amount of protection!

[87] *Jurisprudenz des täglichen Lebens* (1870).
[88] *Kampf ums Recht* (1872).

phrase. The *Struggle for Law* was primarily a large chip thrown out from his workshop — a special theme encountered, examined and dismissed into print — while he was elaborating his general doctrine.[89]

At an early stage of his campaign against what seemed to him the aberrations of German legal science, Jhering had become convinced that the cause of these aberrations was the general acceptance of a false philosophy. In dealing with the question of rights, in the last installment of his *Spirit of Roman Law,* he had discovered, as he believed, the basis of a true legal philosophy. Private rights exist primarily for the protection of private interests; but these private interests are themselves protected because they are at the same time public interests. All law exists for the furtherance of social ends, and "the end [*Zweck*] is the creator of the entire law." This, however, is true not only of law, but of morality, of social custom or usage, of etiquette, and even of fashion. The whole social life is governed by rules which are intended to subserve social ends; and these rules, worked out in social life and enforced by social pressure, constitute the system of social order. That which distinguishes social rules from mere social practice or habit [*Gewohnheit*] is their imperative character, the fact that society insists upon their observance, and inflicts upon those who disregard them pains and penalties. That which distinguishes the legal rule from the rule of morals or fashion is the nature of the sanction. The legal rule is enforced by "mechanical" or "external" coercion; behind it stands, in the last instance, the physical force of the community, and this force is directly exercised, in case of necessity, upon the person or the property of the individual. In early society this physical coercion is "unorganized": it appears as lynch-law, clan feud, self-help of the wronged party. In international law, at the present day, the physical coercion is applied in an analogous manner; but early law and modern international law are rightly designated as law, because, in last instance, the

[89] As the author points out in *Zweck im Recht,* 2d ed., vol. i, p. 75.

mechanical sanction comes into play. Within the modern
state, of course, the application of physical coercion is reserved to the state and its governmental organs, and national
law has thus become the body of rules enforced by the state.
Rules of morals, of social usage, of fashion, *etc.*, are enforced
by purely "psychological" or "internal" coercion. The
sanctions are those of public opinion — disapproval, ridicule,
contempt, ostracism. The field of manners and morals and
of the "psychological" sanction is of course much wider than
that of law; it includes nearly all the field of law, and a vast
outlying territory. Of the way in which the legal and the
purely social sanctions supplement each other, he writes:

> The advantage of mechanical coercion by the state lies in
> the certainty of its operation: where it is applicable, it
> attains what it is meant to attain. But it is not applicable
> everywhere, and therein lies its incompleteness. It is too
> unwieldly, too clumsy, to give effect to all the norms which
> society recognizes as necessary. . . . The advantage of
> psychological coercion by society lies in the fact that there is
> no relation of social life from which its influence is excluded.
> It forces its way in everywhere, like the air — into the inner
> chambers of the house and up to the steps of the throne, into
> regions where the mechanical sanction fails of all effect. Its
> weakness lies in the uncertainty of its operation: the moral
> judgment of society, of public opinion can be defied, but not
> the arm of the state.[90]

It will be seen that Jhering's conception of law is analogous
to that of the English positivists; but it is by no means
identical with theirs. Rules of modern national law, he
declares, are *ordinarily* established by the state; [91] they
are commands (*Imperative*) of the state; but it is not their
enunciation by state authority, but their enforcement by state
power that makes them legal rules. "The circumstance,"
he says, "that the state authority declares a rule does not
give it the character of a legal rule, but only the circumstance

[90] *Zweck im Recht*, 2d ed., vol. ii, pp. 182, 183.
[91] *Ibid.*, vol. i, p. 331.

that the state binds its organs to execute the rule by external coercion." [92] In his definition of law from the teleological point of view, the declaration of legal rules by state authority is not included. " Law is the totality of the conditions of existence of society that are assured by means of external coercion through the power of the state." [93] With the rejection, as a criterion of law, of the formulation of its rules by the state, disappears of course the difficulty which the English positivists encounter in bringing customary law under their definition.[94] And with the assertion that execution of law by the state is not essential to the conception of law in the widest sense, provided its rules are actually enforced by mechanical or external coercion, disappears also as we have noted, the difficulty of including primitive national law and modern international law in the category of law.

It was not against the English positivists, however, that Jhering was defining his position, but against the German idealists. To these law is simply the expression of will — of God or of society or of the state; and the rights accorded to individuals are recognitions of the liberty of the individual will, which is " in itself " free. Primarily — and this is what gave the book its name — Jhering insisted on going behind the will and considering the motive. This, he declares, is always something to be attained, an end(*Zweck*). Law is a

---

[92] *Ibid.*, vol. i, p. 337. " Rules that cannot be enforced by him who sets them up are not rules of law." *Ibid.*, vol. i, p. 318. Puchta (*Pandekten*, § 11, note g) had declared that where the legislator has abolished popular custom as a source of law, the result is only to deprive it of its operation upon the judge. It continues to exist as law, only the judge does not apply it. To this Jhering responds: " We might as well say that when fire is put out with water, it is still fire, only it doesn't burn." He shrewdly adds that what led Puchta astray, was the possibility of voluntary obedience to certain rules within a certain circle. " If this is enough to give the rules the character of legal rules, then the rules of a prohibited association must be regarded as legal rules." *Ibid.*, vol. i, p. 322.

[93] " Recht ist der Inbegriff der mittelst äussern Zwanges durch die Staatsgewalt gesicherten Lebensbedingungen der Gesellschaft." *Ibid.*, vol. i, p. 511.

[94] It is precisely because customary law still exists that Jhering qualifies with an " ordinarily " his statement that the rules of law are established by the state. See *loc. cit.* (vol. i, p. 331), note 2.

means to the ends of society; rights are means to individual ends; neither law nor rights are intelligible unless we consider, in the case of every rule of law, the social end, and in the case of every right, the personal end. But from the social point of view the individual end is simply a means to securing social ends; and neither personal rights nor their limitations can be fully comprehended from any other than the social point of view. Private rights exist only because there is a large domain of social life in which egoism, in pursuing its own ends, realizes the ends of society. It is only in this domain, where the individual interest harmonizes with the social interest, that private rights exist; and they are exposed to limitation at the point where egoism menaces or even thwarts a social interest. Jhering illustrates this point by examining the social function of contract and that of private property, and by indicating the limitations which the law imposes upon freedom of contract and upon the employment and disposition of private property.[95]

The *Teleology,* however, is more than a system of legal philosophy; it is a system of sociology.[96] It deals not only with law, but with economics, politics and ethics. Ethics, as Jhering insists, is neither a part of psychology and the twin sister of logic, nor a part of theology and the twin sister of dogmatics. It is a part of social science, and the twin sister of jurisprudence, of economics and of politics.[97] All morality — the recognition of what is moral, and the will to do it — is an historical product, the outcome of the life of man in society. The rules of ethics are no more absolute and eternal than those of law: moral rules, like legal rules, subserve the interests of society, and these interests vary according to the character of the social organization and its stage of development.

[95] *Zweck im Recht*, vol. i, pp. 264–291, 516, 518–534.
[96] "In its present form," Jhering wrote later, "the work ought really to be entitled: *The Teleological System of the Moral Order of the World.*" *Besitzwille*, preface, p. x. [97] *Zweck im Recht*, vol. ii, p. 125.

The theory, of course, is not new. It seemed new to Jhering, when he was working it out in his own mind, because he was imperfectly acquainted with the literature of ethics. He had found nothing akin to his view except in the writings of the English utilitarians — some of which, notably those of Bentham, of Mill and of Spencer, had been translated into German and were thus accessible to him; and he differed from the English utilitarians in that he could not accept the happiness or welfare of the individual as the basis of morals.[98] To Jhering the social interest is the sole basis; and society, he declares repeatedly, cannot be constructed from the point of view of the individual.[99] When, however, after the appearance of the first edition of his second volume, a Roman Catholic ecclesiastic showed that Thomas Aquinas had clearly set forth both the social utility theory and the relativity of " practical " truth,[100] Jhering was visibly taken aback. In his second edition he admitted, with admirable frankness, not only the prior enunciation of his theories by " that great intellect," but also the inexcusable character of his own ignorance. He adds, however, that the modern philosophers and the Protestant theologians are more to blame than he, a jurist.

I ask myself, with astonishment, how was it possible that such truths, once uttered, should have been so completely forgotten in our Protestant science? From what aberrations it might have saved itself, had it taken these utterances to heart! I, for my part, would perhaps have left this whole book unwritten, if I had known of them.[101]

[98] Spencer's *Data of Ethics* was not, I think, accessible to Jhering when he wrote the second volume of *Zweck im Recht*. Jhering had before him such earlier writings of Spencer's as *Social Statics*. In the *Data of Ethics* more stress is laid upon social utility, but even in this work ethical rules seem to be the result of a compromise between social and egoistic interests.

[99] *Zweck im Recht*, vol. i, p. 537; vol. ii, pp. 170 *et seq.*

[100] Jhering quotes: " Firmiter nihil constat per rationem practicam, nisi per ordinationem ad ultimum finem, qui est bonum commune. . . . In speculativis est eadem veritas apud omnes, in operativis autem non est eadem veritas vel rectitudo practica apud omnes. . . . Humanae rationi naturale esse videtur, ut gradatim ab imperfecto ad perfectum veniat. . . . Ratio humana mutabilis est et imperfecta, et ideo eius lex mutabilis est. . . . Finis humanae legis est utilitas hominum." *Zweck im Recht*, 2d ed., vol. ii, p. 161, note 2. [101] *Ibid.*, p. 161.

This apologetic outburst should be taken with more than a grain of allowance. These ideas seemed to Jhering of fundamental importance; had he known them to be Thomasian, it would probably have seemed to him his duty, so long as they had lost their influence on modern German thought, to reannounce them. Jhering had a just pride in his originality; but the desire of personal recognition was not the only motive that led him to write.

The most serious defect in his sociology, it seems to me, is that, in spite of his constant condemnation of the individualistic point of view, he has by no means wholly emancipated himself from it. He not only starts with the purely egoistic individual and works towards the socially minded man,— which is perhaps legitimate as a matter of pure dialectics, — but he constantly assumes that individual egoism is historically antecedent to all social evolution. That absolutely unhistorical being, "the natural man," who lived outside of all social bonds, recognized no social imperatives, sought only the attainment of his immediate selfish ends, is constantly assumed to be the real primitive man. Society apparently starts as a mere aggregation of such egoists, who coax and club each other into the pursuit of social ends.[102]

It is a result of this initial error that he obviously believes [103] that the pressure of society upon the individual has been increasing through the course of human history, and is likely to increase. On this point the studies of the modern sociologists and the researches of the younger school of legal historians [104] are pointing to a directly contrary conclu-

[102] In his third volume, which was never written, Jhering intended to discuss the topics "sense of duty," "love" and "ethical self-assertion"; and he indicated the position which he proposed to take by saying: "I, too, come finally to the result that the individual is to carry morality within himself as the law of himself, and that in acting morally he only asserts himself: but I come to that point, I do not start from it." *Ibid.*, vol. ii, p. 102.

[103] But indicates his reluctance to believe, in a way that shows his instinctive good sense. *Ibid.*, vol. i, pp. 513 *et seq.*

[104] It has long been a commonplace of the writers upon Greek and Roman history that the absorption or "merger," to use a legal phrase, of the individual in the *civitas* was something so different from our modern conceptions as to be difficult to realize; but we have cherished the idea that a much higher degree of personal independence existed among our Teutonic ancestors. On this point the leading German legal historian of our day expresses a

sion. Man appears in history as a mere constituent particle in a horde: it is the horde that feels and wills and acts, carrying the individual with it like a drop of water in a wave. As society develops higher and more complex forms of organization, the demands of society upon the individual increase, indeed, in number and variety, — and it is this fact probably that has led Jhering and many others astray, — but at the same time the intensity of the social pressure as a whole is progressively diminished.[105] Personal freedom increases, and with it the sense of individuality. In last analysis individualism itself, as we understand it to-day, is the product of social evolution, and the freedom of the individual is not the starting-point, but the goal of human development. In this phase the Hegelian statement that the development of law is " the development of the idea of freedom," however it has been misconceived and misapplied, has in it a profound truth.

The contrary theory — that social evolution must have started with the purely egoistic " natural man " — nevertheless so dominated Jhering's thought that it determined the structure of his whole book. The question that he sets himself is: How is the individual brought into the service of so-

---

directly contrary opinion. " A prominent characteristic of early Teutonic law is the inflexible strictness with which it subjects the single person to the dominant social relations, and the single legal issue to the views of the whole social body. The individualistic character that is not commonly attributed to our earliest law, is wholly lacking. More than in later times is the individual fettered to the will and the usages of the various associations in which he moves. . . . The visionary ideal of Teutonic liberty in the primeval forest applied in fact only to the outlawed and outlandish men who were excluded from the circle of tribal companionship. . . . It is not the liberty of the individual, but the equality of all free partakers of the law that is peculiar to the earliest Teutonic system. This equality, however, could be maintained only by the high degree of coercion exercised upon the individual — a coercion, to be sure, which, if consciously felt at all, was scarcely felt as hardship or constraint, because the individual, as an integral part of the community, was dominated by its manner of regarding things." Brunner, *Deutsche Rechtsgeschichte* (1887), vol. i, pp. 111, 121.

[105] To appreciate the truth of this paradox — that increasing variety of social demands is perfectly compatible with an increase of personal freedom — we need not go so far afield as do the historical sociologists. We see the same thing when we compare life in a small modern village with life in a great city. In the village the demands of the social life are fewer, and yet the social pressure, the restraining and coercive power of local sentiment, is greater than in the city. City life makes more demands upon the individual, and yet it leaves him really and consciously freer.

ciety and induced to minister to its ends? His answer, so far as it is developed in the two volumes of which the work consists, is: Reward and coercion. Reward plays its chief rôle in economic life, and the long chapter [106] which deals with this subject is mainly devoted to economics. He apparently assumes that the development of commerce precedes the development of law and the state, and that the state is preceded by voluntary association for common ends. Coercion is then taken up, and first the " mechanical " coercion which is exercised by law. In the second volume he goes over into morals, developing his " historical-social " theory, and dealing *in extenso* with social usages which we are not accustomed to regard as either moral or immoral, but to which society constrains obedience by " psychological " coercion. The latter half of the volume is devoted wholly to manners — the last third (two hundred and forty pages) to courtesy (*Höflichkeit*). The motive that led Jhering into this apparently remote field was the desire to demonstrate that all " social imperatives " — fashion, manners, morals and law — are adapted to social ends and subserve the " conditions of existence of society." To prove this for law alone seemed to him an imperfect solution of the problem. In spite of much serious thought, much keen analysis and many amusing divagations, this portion of the book is hard to read; and the foreigner is impressed, as his countrymen have been, with the feeling that the devotion of several of Jhering's best years to the study of social manners was a regrettable waste of energy. Whether Jhering himself felt this, or recognized only the fact that for the first time he had not " scored " either with his colleagues or with the public, the result was the same. He wisely abandoned the attempt to complete his " teleological system of the moral order of the world " — if carried out on the scale set in his second volume, its completion would have necessitated not merely a third but probably a tenth volume — and returned to legal investigations. One separate book was thrown off in connection with his

[106] Vol. i, ch. vii, pp. 93–233.

labors on the second volume of the *Teleology of Law,* as the *Struggle for Law* had been thrown off while he was writing the first volume.   This dealt with " fees " — not lawyers' fees, however, or even professional fees in general, but *Trinkgelder.*[107]   It attained the moderate success (for Jhering) of a third edition, as did ultimately the *Teleology;* but it met with even greater professional disapprobation than the second volume of the larger work.

Reading the *Teleology* again, as I have done for the purposes of this article, I am struck with the fact that the digressions are the most readable parts of the book.   So long as Jhering clings to the main thread of his argument, he is almost tedious — a proof if one were needed, how far he had strayed from his proper field.   In his excursions, however, he is invariably interesting.   So, for example, in his eloquent protest against *laisser-faire* in the law of contracts; [108] so in his discussion of the difference between wages and governmental salaries, where, after pointing out that salaries are not based, like wages, on the value of the service, since the state pays only partly in cash and the rest in honor, he adds that the corrective is found in " the rich wife," [109] who represents the partial conversion of the honor into cash; so in his denunciation of joint-stock companies, or rather of the absence of control over these companies which marked their first appearance in Germany, and led to the same abuses there as in other countries; [110] so in his vehement attack upon the jury as an institution that formerly subserved important ends, but has outlived its usefulness; [111] so in his demonstration of the advantages of a strict criminal code to the criminals themselves, since popular justice is far more cruel than the most Draconian system administered by government — an admirable text for a sermon on the significance of lynch-justice in our own country; [112] so in his analysis of the principle that underlies the prevention of cruelty to animals,

---

[107] *Das Trinkgeld,* 1882; 3d ed., 1889.
[108] *Zweck im Recht,* vol. i, pp. 132–140.
[109] *Zweck im Recht,* vol. i, pp. 200, 201.
[110] *Ibid.,* vol. i, pp. 220–225.
[111] *Ibid.,* vol. i, pp. 408–420.
[112] *Ibid.,* vol. i, p. 461.

where he shows that the purpose of such laws is purely social, that they are made for the sake of man, and that to explain them by attributing rights to animals would logically constrain us all to become not only anti-vivisectionists, but vegetarians.[113] Quite in his best vein is the exhortation addressed, in the second volume, to students of ethics, not merely to investigate their problem historically, but to start with comparative philology and mythology, since these are " the oldest and most trustworthy witnesses as to primitive popular views of morality."

The two together may be described as the palæontology of ethics. In the deeds of the gods, in all that they permitted themselves and were able to permit themselves without forfeiting in the eyes of the people their claim to veneration, there is preserved for us the most ancient judgment of humanity as to what is morally permissible. . . . The gods are the petrified types of the prehistoric moral man.[114]

Not, perhaps, the most valuable, but certainly the most amusing pages in this volume are devoted to the teleology of fashion (*die Mode*). Fashion expresses, to him, the supposed interest of a social class — the class which commonly calls itself " society." It represents the constant effort of this class to distinguish itself externally from the common herd.[115] In these days of democratic equality, of improved manufacturing processes and of facile and rapid production, the imitative herd presses so closely upon its betters that these are unable to maintain any semblance of differentiation otherwise than by constant change. All that they can do is to keep a little ahead of their pursuers. Hence, the rapid changes of modern fashion.

---

[113] *Ibid.*, vol. ii, pp. 141–144. Incidentally this argument shows how shallow is Macaulay's famous fling at the motive which actuated the Puritans in suppressing bear-baiting. The Puritans were quite right.

[114] *Ibid.*, vol. ii, p. 126.

[115] *Zweck im Recht*, vol. ii, pp. 230–241. Substantially the same theory was set forth a number of years ago in an editorial in the New York *Evening Post* on the question " Shall a Dude wear White Gaiters? " The identity of the theory will scarcely justify a suspicion of plagiarism: it was undoubtedly a case of the attainment of the same truth by independent thinkers.

But to revert to more serious matters. It is refreshing, in these over-sentimental days, to see the social value of force so fully recognized and so courageously proclaimed as we find it in this work. All law, all right, Jhering maintains, are based historically upon triumphant force: they are " the policy of force." Law is thus at first the mere servant of power. But " at the moment that power calls in law to announce its commands, it opens its house to justice, and the reaction of law upon power begins. For law brings with it as inseparable comrades order and equality." [116] But not even in the hghest civilization does law become lord of power. " Power, if need be, can exist without law: it has proved that it can. But law without power is an empty name." [117] To-day, when we speak of the reign of law, we think of power as merely the servant of law; " but at times the relation is reversed; power casts off its obedience to law and itself sets up a new law." Organized power revolts against law in the *coup d'état;* unorganized power, in the revolution.

It is easy for legal theory to condemn these acts; but these disturbances ought to lead our theorists to take a different view of the normal state of things. Law is not the supreme good: it is not itself an end, but merely means to an end: the end is the existence of society. If society cannot exist under the established legal order, and if the law itself is unable to find a remedy, power intervenes and does what is demanded.[118]

In case of necessity the law itself permits the individual to do with impunity what under other circumstances would be criminal. To meet exceptional emergencies, exceptional powers are constitutionally accorded to most governments: the proclamation of a dictatorship or of martial law, the suspension of existing law, the establishment of provisional law by executive ordinance, *etc.* These are " safety-valves which permit the power of the state to deal with crises legally."

[116] *Ibid.*, vol. i, p. 353.   [117] *Ibid.*, vol. i, p. 253.
[118] *Zweck im Recht,* vol. i, p. 250.

But the *coup d'état* and the revolution are no longer on legal ground: the law cannot license them without stultifying itself; from the legal point of view they are simply to be condemned. . . . But higher than law stands life; and if in fact the situation is such as is here presupposed, if there is a case of necessity that narrows the issue to law or life, there can be no doubt as to the decision — power sacrifices law and preserves life. . . . Our judgment concerning such acts is determined by their success. Appeal is taken from the legal forum which condemns them to the tribunal of history. This has always been deemed by all people the higher, the supreme instance, and the judgment that is here rendered is final and decisive.[119]

That private rights have their historic basis in successful force, Jhering had asserted five years before (1872) in his *Struggle for Law.* He had also shown that the value attached by society to a legal rule, or by the individual to a legal right, is exactly proportionate to the importance of the social or individual interest which the law secures. But the central thought in the *Struggle for Law* is the duty of the individual to assert and enforce his rights, not only for the sake of his own manhood but for the sake of society. It is a lay sermon addressed to the conscience of his readers. Like most books that make an impression, the *Struggle for Law* is one-sided. In spite of the care with which Jhering confines his argument to cases where something more than money is at stake, — to cases where submission to wrong is sacrifice of personal dignity and of social interests, — the book impresses the reader as a *laus litium,* a panegyric upon quarrelsomeness. But, however one-sided, the book is substantially true; and the side of truth which is here turned to the reader is one that the modern man needs to have shown him. To this fact and to the warmth and eloquence with which the duty of resentment and litigation is presented, the *Struggle for Law* owes its phenomenal success. In 1880 it had been

[119] *Ibid.,* vol. i, pp. 251, 252.

translated into fourteen other languages,[120] and in 1891 it reached its tenth German edition.

The *Struggle for Law*, if widely read, was also widely criticised; nor did Jhering's critics confine themselves to his main theme. The position taken by him on minor points invited and aroused controversy. No part of the book attracted more attention, nor did any arouse more dissent, than his discussion of the case of Shylock *vs.* Antonio in *The Merchant of Venice*. Jhering asserted that the decision of Bellario-Portia was unjust. The plaintiff should have been thrown out of court because his contract for a pound of Venetian flesh was immoral. But if this was not possible at Venetian law, — and of course the poet was free to make the law of Venice such as suited his dramatic purpose, — Shylock should have had his pound of flesh. He should have been allowed to take a trifle more, if the excess was due to a pardonable error of judgment; he could certainly take as much less as he chose; and he was entitled to as much blood as would naturally flow in the course of the operation. It was grossly unjust first to recognize the validity of his contract and the lawfulness of his claim, and then to avoid the contract and defeat the claim by such wretched, pettifogging technicalities as those to which the court resorted — technicalities which the crude and formalistic code of the XII Tables, in providing for the distribution (*in partes secare*) of the body of the delinquent debtor among his creditors, seems to have intended to bar by the clause: "*Si plus minusve secuerint, sine fraude esto.*" [121]

It is not difficult to see how Jhering was led to take this position. He was insisting upon the solidarity of law and right — upon the necessity, for the maintenance of law, of the enforcement of private rights; and nowhere in literature was a more energetic expression of this idea to be found than that which Shakspere put into the mouth of Shylock:

> This pound of flesh, which I demand of him,
> Is dearly bought, is mine, and I will have it.

[120] *Kampf ums Recht*, preface to sixth edition.
[121] *Ibid.*, 6th ed., pp. 58, 59.

If you deny me, fie upon your law!
There is no force in the decrees of Venice.

Jhering was also exalting the duty of the individual to assert
his rights; and nowhere in history or fiction could he find
a person more bent upon this course than Shylock. But in
order to make of Shylock a proper champion, it was absolutely necessary to insist that he was in the right. In order
to make of him a sympathetic figure, Jhering has to go
further, and to import into Shakspere's comedy the essentially modern view that Shylock is the type of his wronged
and flouted race, " of the mediæval Jew, that social pariah,
who cried in vain for law."

The tremendous tragedy of his fate does not lie in the
fact that law is denied him, but in the fact that he, a Jew of
the middle ages, has faith in the law — one may say, just
as if he were a Christian — a faith in the law that is firm
as a rock, that nothing can cause to waver, and that the
judge himself strengthens, until the catastrophe breaks upon
him like a thunderbolt, shaking him out of his dream and
teaching him that he is nothing but the outlawed Jew of
the middle ages, who gets his right in being swindled out
of it.[122]

Jhering's view of this case has met with little sympathy.
It has been criticised both from the literary and the legal
point of view. Of the many answers that have been made
by lawyers, I single out for mention that of Kohler.[123] He
agrees with Jhering that the decision is technically indefensible, but maintains that it is nevertheless just. It is simply

---

[122] *Kampf ums Recht,* 6th ed., p. 59.

[123] Kohler, *Shakespeare vor dem Forum der Jurisprudenz* (1883), pp.
3 *et seq.,* 71 *et seq.* This is a curious book, too little known to English
readers. The author has gained the conviction by " prolonged juristic and
æsthetic studies " that the English poet possessed " an almost superhuman
power of intuition," by virtue of which he was able to penetrate " the most
secret recesses of legal history, as of history in general." He discusses *The
Merchant of Venice* from the point of view of the law of debt, *Measure for
Measure* from that of *desuetudo* and pardon. Hamlet depicts the conflict
between the custom of blood revenge and the more advanced morality which
leaves vengeance to God and penalty to the state. A closing section is devoted to the legal material in the other plays. In the book as a whole there
is a great deal more law than Shakspere, and a vast if somewhat heterogeneous collection of information about early law in general.

a case of a correct decision on wrong grounds. Such decisions, he urges, are especially common where the development of the law has been outstripped by the development of ethics. That was the case, clearly, in the Venice of Shakspere's imagination. The harsh law of debt, which subjected the delinquent debtor completely to the power of his creditor, was still law, but it no longer corresponded to the contemporary sense of right. Shylock, in attempting to utilize the law for purposes of vengeance, brought the antithesis between the law and the moral sense of the community to distinct consciousness, and placed upon the old rules a strain that they could no longer bear. They give way, and a new and milder law appears — not yet clearly formulated; attained, indeed, by false reasoning and untenable distinction; but capable of logical formulation in the further process of judicial interpretation.

To an outsider, this explanation of Kohler's seems so thoroughly in the line of Jhering's own thought as revealed in many passages of his legal-historical writings, that one is tempted to wonder whether Jhering would not have accepted it if the *Struggle for Law* had been written by a third person. Since, however, the position assailed by Kohler was his own and not another's, he came to its defense in a note appended to his seventh edition, in which he carried the war into the enemy's country, and made merry with Kohler and his methods of studying legal history. To this counter-attack, Kohler responded, with a *Nachwort* which, I believe, was the last word in this controversy. In this characteristically academic interchange of incivilities, the only fresh point brought out was Jhering's insistence that a definite and complete judgment had been rendered in Shylock's favor before any information was given him touching the consequences of a miscalculation in weight or of incidental blood-letting, — that his right was not denied in the judgment, but frustrated when it came to the execution of judgment, — while Kohler insisted that the utterances of Portia, from " A pound of that same merchant's flesh is thine "[1] to

" Thou diest, and all thy goods are confiscate," constitute a single original and integral judgment. One cannot help wondering what the poet would have made of this entire controversy: whether he would have been more surprised at learning that *The Merchant of Venice* was a tragedy, as Jhering asserts, or at being informed by Kohler that he had divined all the subtle modes in which progressive views of ethics obtain recognition in the application of law.

It was Jhering's original plan to conclude his *Teleology* (after he should have worked through the fields of manners and morals) with a detailed demonstration of the value of his point of view for the comprehension of law, both as regards its general principles and its more important institutions. His *Possessory Intention,* as he explains in the preface,[124] represents a partial realization of this broader plan: it is an expanded section of the projected final chapter of the *Teleology.* That is the significance of its sub-title: *Also a Criticism of the Dominant Juristic Method.*

For twenty years (1868–1888) Jhering had devoted his best energies to the task of elaborating and illustrating his philosophy of law. The work in which he undertook to develop his system was indeed left unfinished, but the system itself was clearly set forth. Against the will as the source of law and of rights he had set the goal of the will, the end to be attained. Against the individual interest he had set, as the creator of the whole social order, the social interest. Against the theory of the historical school, which treated all legal development as a process not merely organic but largely unconscious, he had insisted on the reflective and conscious character of legal progress, even in its early stages. He had not, however, fallen into the error of asserting that all law is consciously created to attain ends distinctly discerned: the ends which society strives to realize are not all " subjective," *i.e.*, consciously formulated; " objective " ends play a great part.

It is not easy for men of English blood and traditions to

[124] *Besitzwille,* pp. x, xi.

realize the necessity of the task which Jhering had undertaken. The point of view which we naturally take was
expressed, a year or so after the appearance of the first
volume of the *Teleology of Law,* by an American fellow-
student in Göttingen. "Is it not odd," he said to me,
"that Jhering should be writing a big book to prove what
no English or American lawyer would dispute?" A few
months earlier, however, I had received striking evidence that
what is self-evident to an Anglo-Saxon is not necessarily
self-evident to a German. I had had a conversation at
Berlin with an elderly German friend—a judge, for many
years, of the highest Prussian appellate court. This gentleman had shown a kindly interest in my studies and plans,
and to him I spoke of my intention to spend the following
semester at Göttingen, for the sake of hearing Jhering. "For
heaven's sake," said the judge, "don't do it. Jhering will
mix you all up. His *Geist* was a clever book, but his *Zweck*
is all nonsense [*dummes Zeug*]."

During the years devoted to his *Teleology* and to the
books that branched out from that main stem, Jhering did not
devote all his leisure to fighting philosophy with philosophy.
He recurred more than once to his earlier and more con-
genial mode of attack—*ridendo dicere verum.* The author-
ship of the *Confidential Letters* had ceased to be a secret, and
a second series had been solicited and promised as early as
1872. In 1880 Jhering redeemed his pledge in a series of
"feuilleton" articles, as he himself described them, which
were published at Vienna in the *Juristische Blätter* under the
running title: *Chats of a Romanist.*[125] These essays dealt
entirely with questions of Roman legal history; and while
the practical point of view, the consideration of the "end"
subserved, is constantly utilized for the better understanding
of the rules discussed, the *Chats* are more akin to Jhering's
Spirit of the Roman Law than to his *Teleology;* they rather
form a part of his constructive work in legal history than

---

[125] *Plaudereien eines Romanisten.* Reprinted in *Scherz und Ernst* (1885),
pp. 121–243.

of his polemic against abstract jurisprudence. But when, after the appearance of the second volume of the *Teleology,* he was urged to republish both the *Letters* and the *Chats,* he rounded them into a book — *Jest and Earnest* — by adding new matter,[126] in which he returned to the theme of the *Letters.* Employing the time-honored machinery of the dream, Jhering depicts himself as a newly disembodied spirit, transported by the double title of Romanist and theorist to " the juristic heaven of concepts." This lies far beyond the solar system, in outer darkness. " The sun," his guide informs him, " is the source of all life, but concepts cannot accommodate themselves to life: they need a world of their own in which they may exist for themselves solely, remote from all contact with life." The obscurity of this heaven is no disadvantage to the theorist: " even on earth his eyes have been trained to see in the dark." Candidates for admission must first pass through quarantine for the removal of any trace of earthly air, and they receive, if necessary, a draught from a spring whose waters efface all earthly points of view, — but Jhering is assured that " very few who apply for admission here find it necessary to make use of it." The applicants come chiefly from Germany, and thence only of late years: Puchta was the first. They are for the most part Romanists, but Germanists and criminalists are also received, " provided they share with the Romanists their faith in the sovereignty of concepts." Professors preponderate, but there are also " members of your Imperial Diet and your Houses of Deputies, whose belief that the world is ruled by abstract principles has remained, thank God, unshaken by your Bismarck." An examination is required for admission: it is indispensable that the candidate show " capacity to construct a legal institution purely from the texts or from the abstract concept, without any consideration of its real practical significance." Savigny very nearly failed: he was admitted, however, on the strength of his essay on possession,

---

[126] Im juristischen Begriffshimmel, ein Phantasiebild. — Wieder auf Erden, — wie soll es besser werden? — *Scherz und Ernst,* pp. 247–383.

and because, by opposing codification, he had aided in maintaining Roman law in Germany. Arndts and Wächter were both rejected: Wächter's mind " moved always in the lower region of the practical " ; and although Arndts had based his *Pandects* on Puchta, " he had made too many concessions to the needs of practical life at the cost of pure theory."

Before attempting the examination, Jhering finds that it is admissible to inspect the abode of the theorists, and of this opportunity he gladly avails himself. He examines the palæstra, or field for gymnastic exercises in construing, interpreting, *etc.;* the legal-historical academy, where defective inscriptions and corrupt texts are " restored " ; the museum of pure concepts (which has no doors, and to enter it is necessary *mit dem Kopf gegen die Wand zu rennen*) ; and the pathological cabinet, which displays these same concepts as they have been defaced and distorted on earth from the days of the Roman jurists down, through considerations of expediency. In the examination of these and other objects of interest, and in conversation with his guide and other blessed spirits, Jhering finds full opportunity to satirize his abstract contemporaries and their theories. Convincing himself, before long, that he does not belong in this heaven, Jhering finds that two other localities are open to him — the heaven of the legal philosophers, where reason takes the place of abstract ideas, and the heaven of the practitioners. The former is the abode of the advocates of natural-law doctrines; and the information which Jhering receives concerning the examination held there and the confession of faith exacted of all applicants shows him that he cannot hope for admission to that paradise. He decides, accordingly, upon the heaven of the practitioners, and is conducted thither. As he knocks at the gate, he awakes.

In a closing section, from which I have already made citations,[127] Jhering discusses seriously the evil results of an over-abstract jurisprudence, its causes and its remedies. The

---

[127] *Political Science Quarterly,* vol x, pp. 687 (December, 1895), *et seq. Supra,* pp. 133 *et seq.*

chief cause he finds in an undue separation of theory and practice. His remedies are: that the university teachers of law be required first to pass a number of years in the practical work of the courts, as assessors; that the case system of instruction be more largely employed in the universities, and that participation in the *Practica* be required of the students; that in the state examinations less stress be laid upon written themes and more upon the oral examination, and that in the latter more weight be attached to the solution of concrete cases. He is speaking, of course, of the state examinations for admission to the judicial service and to the bar, not of the academic examination for the doctorate. Two changes suggested by others he emphatically disapproves. The law professors are not to combine practice with instruction, nor is the three-year course of academic study to be lengthened. Three years, he thinks, are enough if properly employed.

Of the justification of Jhering's crusade against abstract jurisprudence — of the necessity of such a reaction in Germany as he strove to produce — I have already spoken. The tendency to undue abstraction was of course at no time universal: there were contemporaries of Jhering as practical as he himself could desire, and among them were professors (like Eck) who strove always to impress their students with the importance of the practical point of view. But the tendency which Jhering combated was certainly dominant, and Jhering made himself the most prominent champion of the opposite movement.

Of the effect of his opposition it is hard to form a definite judgment. That German legal science is to-day more practical than it was thirty years ago, no one who has followed its development ever so cursorily can for a moment question. But how far this change is due to Jhering's efforts, and how far it is due to the pressure of practical legislative problems in the new German Empire, is a question on which it would be rash to express an opinion.

VI

Before Jhering opened his attack upon abstract jurisprudence, he had acquired a reputation that extended far beyond the boundaries of the fatherland by his great work upon the *Spirit of the Roman Law in the Different Stages of its Development*. As a study of the evolution of the Roman law, the work may be regarded as a product of the impulse to historical investigation given by Savigny, and in the catalogues of the booksellers it is usually ranged among the works on Roman legal history; but in its spirit and method this book represented, as we have already noted,[128] a reaction against the purely national view of legal evolution held by Savigny and his school, and it bore little resemblance, in its general plan or in its details, to any previous history of the Roman law.

It emphasized the universal side of legal evolution, and found the significance of the Roman law in the great place which that law occupies in the legal history of the world. It discarded the periods commonly recognized by writers on Roman legal history, and substituted three " stages ": the pre-Roman or Indo-European, the national Roman, and the universal Roman.[129] In the first volume (Introduction and Book I), Jhering undertook to show what the Romans brought with them into their separate national life. In the remainder of the work he meant to show what they made of their heritage, and with what rich interest they gave it back to the world. In the three additional volumes which he completed he carried out but a small portion of the original scheme. He did not even finish his second " book " on the " specific Roman system " (*ius civile*). Its first " section " (*Abschnitt*), on the " general characteristics of the system," extended through the whole of the second and third volumes [130] and nearly through the fourth volume.[131] Its second

---

[128] *Political Science Quarterly,* vol. x, pp. 669, 675–678. *Supra,* pp. 115, 121–124.

[129] *Geist des römischen Rechts,* vol. i, pp. 81–85.

[130] Designated as part II, divs. 1 and 2.   [131] Part III, div. 1.

" section," which was to deal with the special rights recognized in the older private law, was carried only so far as was necessary to complete the discussion of the general conception of a right,[132] and there the work stopped. As we have already seen,[133] the examination of this special question carried him out of legal history into legal philosophy and eventually into sociology. The *Spirit of the Roman Law* was left unfinished that he might write his *Teleology of Law*, and this, in its turn, so grew upon his hands that it was never finished.

The proposed third book of the *Spirit of the Roman Law*, which was to have treated of the development, by the Romans, of a general system of private law for the entire ancient world (*ius gentium*), and in which the characteristics of this universal law were to have been examined, was accordingly never begun — a fact which no admirers of Jhering can more keenly regret than those whose privilege it was to hear his lectures upon Roman legal history at Göttingen, and who therefore know, in part at least, how fresh and suggestive would have been his treatment of this period.

The *Spirit of the Roman Law* is a work so much better known than any of his other writings (except, perhaps, his *Struggle for Law*), and so much has been written about it, that it is hardly needful to do more than indicate in what respects it marked an epoch in legal historiography. It was one of the first important attempts to apply to the study of legal evolution the method of comparison. In describing the " original elements " of the Roman law he thus gave the world a treatise on primitive law in general. In describing the Roman conceptions of liberty and equality, and the way in which these were realized in the national law, the comparison with other systems was so employed as to make this second volume an important contribution to the philosophy of law. The discussion, in the following volumes, of the technique of the Roman law and the methods of the early

---

[132] Cf. *Political Science Quarterly*, vol. x, pp. 691, 692. *Supra*, pp. 134, 135.
[133] *Ibid.*, vol. xi, p. 290. *Supra*, pp. 151, 152.

Roman jurists broadened, in like manner, into a discussion of the function and the methods of all technical jurisprudence. The problems which he set before himself in his *Teleology* are not more universal, nor are they treated in any broader way, than those which engrossed him in the earlier work.

The point of view from which the work was written and the method employed make it unique among histories of the Roman law. All that is peculiarly national in the Roman law — all that is not found in other systems and cannot be utilized for comparison — had for Jhering but a secondary interest. Numerous facts that are set forth in the briefest compendiums of Roman legal history are therefore not even alluded to in these four volumes. These facts appear in the ordinary compendium because they facilitate the comprehension of the law books of Justinian; they were ignored by Jhering because the matters they illuminate are not matters of universal human interest. The ordinary legal historian, as Jhering himself said, regards history as the handmaid of dogmatics.[134] Jhering's mode of writing legal history, as Windscheid indicated years afterwards in his inaugural address as rector of Leipzig University, takes the subject out of legal science in the strict and usual sense, and makes it culture-history.

It is of interest to compare Jhering's work in primitive law in the first volume of the *Spirit* with the independent and nearly contemporaneous work of Henry Sumner Maine. Both of these men used the comparative method, and both wrote from the point of view of the social historian rather than from that of the legal historian. Both worked with a narrower basis of induction — with less knowledge of primitive law — than their successors in the same field, and the theories of each have been largely modified by later investigations; but both possessed a literary gift, a charm of style,

---

[134] *Geist des römischen Rechts,* vol. i, p. 59, note. *Cf. Entwicklungsgeschichte des römischen Rechts* (1894), " Einleitung," p. 9: legal history is " the Cinderella in the house of the law, tolerated there only because she carries wood and water for the household."

that won for them a wider circle of readers than any of their successors have yet obtained.

Of early Roman law Maine knew something, but far less than did Jhering. Of Hindoo law Jhering knew far less than did Maine. Of English law Jhering knew little: I do not think that he read English with any ease. But through the labors of the Germanists Jhering had at his command a knowledge of early Teutonic law, of which the English law is but a transplanted shoot, that far outweighed Maine's advantage in his knowledge of early English law. In reality, then, the only advantage that Maine had over Jhering was his greater knowledge of the laws of India. And it may be seriously questioned whether, for the study of Indo-European beginnings, this was not really a disadvantage. Maine clearly believed that the customs and conceptions revealed in the oldest literature of India were, if not precisely primitive, at least more primitive and closer to the common starting-point of the Indo-European peoples than the earliest known customs and conceptions of the Teutons or Slavs. We are inclined to think to-day that the reverse is true — that the social relations of the Hindoos, at the moment at which their institutions first become clear to us, had developed along lines largely foreign to the oldest Aryan life; and that their civilization had become far more complex and artificial than that of the wandering ancestors of the great European nations. It was the influence of the Hindoo law that led Maine to assert the really primitive character of that household organization which he found in India and also in early Rome — an assertion now questioned by the majority of investigators — and to develop the entire political organization of the Indo-European peoples, the whole sacerdotal system, the administration of criminal and civil justice and the resultant formulation of criminal and civil law, gradually and smoothly, without break or jar of innovation, from the one fact of the household authority of the *paterfamilias*.

Jhering apparently assumed the primitive character of *manus*-marriage, agnatic relationship and *patria potestas*, —

certainly, that these institutions were firmly established when the separate national existence of the Romans began,[135] — but he ascribed no such wide-reaching results as did Maine to the headship of the primitive house. To Jhering nothing in the earliest Roman state was modeled on the family save the *gens*. The *curiae* were military divisions constructed by the king. Kingship was not an outgrowth of family or clan, but a new thing superimposed upon the *gentes* by stress of foreign war. Kingship had built the new state of the royal period upon the partial wreck of the gentile state. Criminal law, to Jhering, began as lynch law: it was the vengeance taken by the whole people for an injury to the whole people. In its further development king and priests coöperated. The king first punished infractions of military discipline, and became gradually a keeper of the peace, because internal peace was necessary for successful foreign war. The priests slew the wrongdoer or drove him out of the city when his wrong was regarded as a sin. They slew or expelled him because otherwise the wrath of the gods would be visited upon the whole people. Over ordinary private disputes neither king nor priest, in Jhering's opinion, had originally any jurisdiction. The wronged party, or the wronged household, righted itself by self-help. If the wrong was obvious, if the right invaded was clear, self-help was regularly effective, because the wronged party had the sympathy and support of the community. Where the wrong was questionable because the right was unclear, self-help was inadequate. It was necessary, in such cases, that all doubt should be dissipated. At this point the civil jurisdiction of the king or the priest came in, but not at once, nor because of any original right of king or priest to interfere. There were various methods by which the parties settled their own disputes. One of these was arbitration; and out of the practice of referring disputes to king or priest grew gradually the right of priest and king to exercise jurisdiction over disputants.

[135] Bernhöft, *Staat und Recht der römischen Königszeit* (Stuttgart, 1882), believes that these were patrician institutions, not originally shared by the plebeians.

This last point is perhaps doubtful; but that Jhering's picture of early society is, as a whole, far truer than Maine's, will hardly be questioned by any one who has followed the later investigations in this field; and where the conjectures of the one writer or the other have been neither substantiated nor disproved, Jhering's theories seem to me to be at least better working hypotheses than Maine's.

As regards the power of the two writers to attain and formulate generalizations of the widest sort — to grasp and state the laws of legal evolution itself — Jhering was unquestionably superior. Maine's most famous single generalization, that the progress of human society is from status to contract, is but a partial expression of the rule laid down by Jhering, that law begins as a system of one-sided and unlimited powers, and gradually becomes a system of jural relations with limited powers and definite duties on each side.

Jhering's greater success in reconstructing the remote past of European civilization was partly due to the fact that early German customs were really more primitive than those indicated in the oldest literature of India. But it was also due in large part to an extraordinarily quick and sympathetic imagination. He thought himself or *felt* himself back into primitive life until it all became as real to him as the life of a little German university town in the nineteenth century under a wise and kindly bureaucracy. It may be questioned whether the earlier conditions, as they took body in his fancy, did not grow more attractive to him than those by which he was surrounded. It is certain, I think, that if he had never depicted, first to himself and then to his readers, the beauties of self-help as he did in the first volume of his *Spirit,* he would never have written the *Struggle for Law*.

In the *Spirit,* the evolution of law is regarded, primarily at least, as a psychological process. To comprehend it, the student must reconstruct for himself not merely the social environment but also the social mind of the people and period with which he is concerned. And this Jhering continually strove to do. Other students of legal history have made use of myths, language, symbols, *etc.*, to help them in the reconstruction of early institutions, but few have used these aids just as Jhering did. He has put his method in a sentence. He declares that "the unuttered thoughts" that underlie a legal institution

have not infrequently obtained a veiled and mysterious but pregnant expression in myths, in etymology or in symbols. *At times the genius of the people makes a confession in the dreaming state that we should never have lured from it in its waking moments.*[136]

In opposition to many legal historians, however, Jhering was not inclined to regard all legal development, even in primitive society, as an unconscious process. Even primitive men may agree, from motives of policy, to establish a novel institution or to observe a new rule. We have seen that in some matters in which Maine assumed evolution without conscious innovation, Jhering assumed changes which, if his explanation be true, must have been in large degree reflective.

It is interesting, again, to compare Jhering's explanation of early Roman institutions with those given by another brilliant and suggestive writer, Fustel de Coulanges. In *The Ancient City*, religion is treated as the creator of the whole legal order. Institutions and customs appear to be produced by religious beliefs. Now Jhering in no wise underrated, I think, the extraordinary influence of religion in early law; but to him religion was obviously a power that sanctions rather than a power that creates. Institutions came into existence, rules are established, because they are of social advantage. Once established, they come to be regarded as divine; and standing under the protection of the gods, they enjoy the tremendous sanction of religious fear. Religious ideas may easily affect the form of legal institutions, but rarely their substance. Religious ideas may modify the operation of a rule, and may often keep it alive after the social reason which justified it has ceased to exist; but reli-

[136] *Geist des römischen Rechts*, vol. i, p. 46.

gion alone, has rarely created important rules of conduct, nor does religion originally endorse such rules without regard to their social utility. The gods are not so unreasonable.[137]

In the remaining portions of the *Spirit of the Roman Law,* in which Jhering dealt with the specific national law of Rome as partially formulated in the Twelve Tables and as developed by the older Republican jurists, less use was made of the comparative method. The legal system that he most needed for purposes of comparison, the legal system that bears the closest relation in its spirit and in its methods to the Roman *ius civile,* is the English common law before it was modified by the equitable jurisdiction of the English chancellors. What little Jhering knew of this law had shown him its similarity to the Roman national law — a similarity that is less of substance than of method, and is due to the fact that the two systems represented the same stage of legal evolution. Jhering felt, and was never weary of declaring, that the hard-headed, unimaginative, technical English common-lawyers were far more like the jurists of the Roman republic than are the modern civilians of continental Europe. But he knew too little of the English law to make much use of it. When his work shall be translated into English, it is devoutly to be hoped that the translation may be made by some one familiar with English legal history, and may be copiously annotated with references to the English common law.

When the subject permitted it, however, — when, for example, he was discussing the general problems of legal equality and personal liberty, as a prelude to an examination of the solutions which these problems found in the older Roman law; and when he was considering the value of technical forms of action and rigid forms of contract, *etc.,* before de-

---

[137] In his *Vorgeschichte der Indoeuropäer,* Jhering devoted several pages (64–71) to a criticism of the theories of Fustel de Coulanges. It is, of course, in the family organization that the connection between religion (ancestor-worship) and law is closest; and even here, according to Jhering, "the *sacra* do not determine the constitution of the family; on the contrary, the latter determines the former."

scribing the forms of the *ius civile*, — Jhering drew constantly upon modern European law; and even in the description of the Roman institutions and forms, modern law, if not directly available for illustrative purposes, was utilized for purposes of contrast.

In speaking of Jhering's change of attitude between 1857 and 1860 — a change which he himself described as an *Umschwung* — and of his new zeal, manifested after 1860, for "practical" jurisprudence, I have already indicated, in a previous paper,[138] that Jhering's earlier work was by no means so unpractical as his own descriptions of his conversion imply. Throughout the *Spirit of the Roman Law*, from the discussion of the "physiology" of law in the first volume to the paragraphs on "juristic economy" in the last,[139] there is constant insistence upon the practical purpose and the practical operation of legal institutions and rules — upon the relation of law to life. What Professor Max Müller has said of Jhering's work in legal history is as true of the first volume of the *Spirit of the Roman Law*, published in 1852, as of the work upon the prehistoric institutions of the Indo-Europeans, published after Jhering's death.

It was the leading principle of all his brilliant researches to discover in everything that has become formal its original substance, in what seems unmeaning its true purpose, in what is irrational its original *raison d'être*.[140]

And in the later volumes of the *Spirit* there are whole chapters, notably those upon legal forms, that might have been written for the *Teleology of Law*.

When the last installment of the *Spirit* was published, in 1865, Jhering had become engrossed in his polemic against abstract jurisprudence, and for many years he published but one other work upon legal history. This was *The Element of Fault in Roman Private Law*.[141] It is a study of the mode

---

[138] *Political Science Quarterly*, vol. x, pp. 687, 688. *Supra*, pp. 133, 134.
[139] *Geist des römischen Rechts*, vol. i, pp. 48–58; vol. iv, pp. 236–301.
[140] *Cosmopolis*, September, 1896.
[141] *Das Schuldmoment im römischen Privatrecht* (1867). Reprinted in *Vermischte Schriften juristischen Inhalts* (1879).

in which society gradually differentiates the malicious from the accidental injury, the willful invasion of a right from the honest interference of the person who believes himself to be in the right. As in the *Spirit*, the method of treatment is comparative: various systems of primitive law are examined to show that early society punishes the overt act without regard to the mental attitude of the actor. It is a study, further, of the gradual elaboration and refinement, in the Roman law, of the conception of fault, down to the final differentiation of malice from negligence, and of gross from ordinary negligence. Incidentally, it is an important contribution to the history of remedies, showing the priority of actions of tort in many relations that are ultimately regarded as contractual.[142] It should be added, as a supplement, to any translation that may be made of the *Spirit*. It is, in fact, a chapter of the unfinished third part of that work.

In the *Chats of a Romanist*, published in 1880, Jhering returned, as we have already noted,[143] to the field of Roman legal history; and in his *Possessory Intention* (1889) there are two chapters, the seventh and the eighth, that are purely historical [144] and that rank with the best parts of the *Spirit*. But through all the later years of his life it was the completion of the *Teleology* rather than the continuation of his historical work that Jhering had really at heart.[145] He had undertaken, however, to write the history of the Roman law for Binding's *Systematic Handbook of German Jurisprudence*,[146] and after the completion of his *Possessory Intention* he addressed himself, at the age of seventy-one, to the fulfillment of this promise. It was his intention to begin, as in the *Spirit of the Roman Law*, with a description of the Indo-European institutions which the ancestors of the Romans brought with them into Italy, but this was to be a mere sketch, much briefer than the first book of the *Spirit*. Like

---

[142] *Vermischte Schriften*, pp. 187 *et seq.*
[143] *Political Science Quarterly*, vol. xi, pp. 306, 307. *Supra*, pp. 168, 169.
[144] *Ibid.*, pp. 285, 286. *Supra*, pp. 146, 147.
[145] *Vorgeschichte der Indoeuropäer*, Vorwort des Herausgebers.
[146] " Systematic Library " would be a more descriptive title, since the plan provides for forty-seven volumes by twenty-eight different jurists.

every other task that Jhering took in hand, this grew rapidly
to unforeseen proportions. Nearly forty years had elapsed
since the first volume of the *Spirit* was written, more than
twenty since the last edition of that volume was printed.
Philological research had thrown much new light upon the
civilization of the primitive Aryans. The common heritage
of the Indo-Europeans had shrunk under investigation: the
Aryans had been thrown back upon a lower plane of social
development than had been previously assigned them. Many
institutions and customs that seem common to all the European members of the family were obviously developed
after their separation from the original stock. What then
were the conditions under which these changes were wrought
— changes that have differentiated the European man from
his Asiatic kinsman? Such was the question that primarily
forced itself upon Jhering's mind. But then came further
questions. What were the influences that differentiated the
Greeks from the Romans? What were the influences that
differentiated these nations from the other peoples of the European branch, and gave them a lead of more than a thousand
years in the march of civilization? Was it simply the different character of the countries in which each people settled
— the influence of topography, climate, *etc.?* Or was it the
earlier contact of the Greeks and Italians with the civilized
peoples whom they found on the other side of the Mediterranean — the Egyptians and the Phœnicians? What was
the origin and what the character of the Semitic civilization?
The result of all these queries, which it was impossible for a
scholar of Jhering's temperament to brush aside, was, as his
literary executor, Victor Ehrenberg, tells us,[147] that he devoted the last two years of his life (1890–1892) to the study
of the Babylonian civilization, and that the very last thing
that he wrote was a criticism of Renan's explanation of the
difference between the Aryan and the Semite.[148]

Of the promised history of Roman law there were found

[147] *Vorgeschichte der Indoeuropäer,* Vorwort des Herausgebers.
[148] *Ibid.,* pp. 288–305.

among Jhering's papers only the beginnings — an introduction on the task and method of legal historiography, and a chapter on the organization of the early Roman household. These were published under the title which Jhering had selected, *History of the Evolution of the Roman Law.*[149]   In his description of the Roman household, as in all his writings upon Roman history, there is something new.   In this case it is his identification of *familia,* in the oldest texts, with *res mancipi,* and *pecunia* with *res nec mancipi.*   The introduction is of special interest: it gives Jhering's latest views not only as regards the way in which legal history should be written, but as regards the way in which law itself is evolved. Legal history, he says, should not be merely descriptive; it should not content itself with telling what happened, what changes occurred; it should discover the reason, the " why," of the facts described, and the forces that underlie and determine the changes.   Nor should legal history content itself with this alone: it should show the causal relation between antecedent and subsequent facts, how changes begot other changes, — it should be a history of the evolution of law.   As such, legal history has a right to exist for itself, as an independent science.   It should emancipate itself from the idea of practical utility to the lawyer.

In seeking to discover the influences which make and modify law, the historian should turn his attention first to the facts of social life.   He will find that all law is begotten by social necessities.   These necessities are first perceived by the most enlightened members of the community, and it is through their influence upon the mass that new institutions are established, new rules recognized.   Law is made, even in early society, by the conscious action of the natural leaders among men, as a path is broken through the wilderness.   The line of conduct which they have laid out is followed by the mass and becomes customary, as the path opened by the pioneer becomes a trodden way.

The theory of Savigny and his followers that law is an

[149] *Entwicklungsgeschichte des römischen Rechts* (1894).

emanation of the popular mind, an expression of the popular sense of right,[150] is no explanation of the genesis of law. It is an abandonment of the attempt to discover any explanation. Moreover, the theory has no warrant in history. The popular sense of right is not anterior to law: it is begotten of law. Even the most advanced thinkers regularly regard that which is legal in their day as rightful, — Plato himself so regarded slavery, — and the masses are incapable of any other view. If at any time the popular sense of right seems to emancipate itself from law and to produce changes in the law, — which only happens when civilization and law have reached a relatively high stage of development, — what occurs is usually this: a few men, who stand above their fellows, have discerned social needs or interests to which the people are blind. These few gradually open the eyes of a majority of the people, or at least of a number sufficient to secure a change in the law; but it is not until the change has been made and the new law has long been established that the feeling of its justice becomes universal. This is the history, for example, of the abolition of slavery, of the abandonment of torture in criminal procedure, of the disappearance from the statute books of laws against witchcraft.

When this is not true, when a new sense of right appears to develop and a change of the law is demanded on grounds of right, we notice that the demand comes from a special class, — that the cause of the demand is an interest, an injury to be avoided or an advantage to be secured; and that the feeling that the demand is just is really derived from the existing law. When the peasant demanded protection against animals preserved for the chase, he asked only that the protection which the law already gave to property should not be withheld from his property. When inventors and authors demanded protection, they asked only that the right of the laborer to the product of his labor, already recognized in the case of others, should be recognized in theirs also.

---

[150] Sense of right (*Rechsgefühl*) should not be confounded by the English reader with moral sense (*das sittliche Gefühl*). It is the sense of right in those matters with which law has to do; it is the sense of justice or of equity, the jural instinct.

If, then, the popular sense of justice is derived from the established legal order, it is absurd, Jhering argues, to make that sense the creator of the legal order.

Against the doctrine of the unconscious growth of law, I for my part assert, to express it for the nonce in all bluntness, the doctrine of its conscious making. The law is not an efflux of the sense of right, discharging its creative function naïvely under obscure impulse — that mysterious process which would cut off (and deliver the legal historian from) further investigation; it is, on the contrary, the work of human purpose and calculation, exerting themselves in every stage of social development to find what is suitable. The history of law is the history of human thought in reference to the practical realization of the conditions of existence of the human community. In this sense all the law on earth has been *made,* and if it seems to have grown of itself, it is because in many instances insight into the making is denied us.[151]

In examining Jhering's first historical work we noted the beginning of a reaction against Savigny's theory of the unconscious development of legal custom,[152] and here we have the opposite theory set forth, as Jhering himself says, " in all bluntness." It will be observed that there are open links in the chain of argument. We may admit that the general sense of justice is commonly in accord with the law, that a different and more advanced sense of justice is rarely to be found even among the best and wisest men, that law influences through education the sense of justice, that the child " inhales," as Jhering says, the spirit of the law; but after making all these concessions we are not obliged to admit that the sense of justice is altogether the product of the law. With an equally careful choice of illustrations it would be easy to construct an equally plausible argument for the opposite contention. The truth seems to be that the sense of justice and the law, developing side by side, exercise a reflex

---

[151] *Entwicklungsgeschichte des römischen Rechts, Einleitung,* p. 28.
[152] Above, p. 178. Also in *Zweck im Recht.* See *Political Science Quarterly,* vol. xi, pp. 305, 306. *Supra,* pp. 167, 168.

influence each upon the other, that each is partly the product and partly the producer of the other; and this truth Jhering himself has set forth in his *Teleology*. In the development of the sense of justice, he says, "the objective and the subjective, the internal and the external, stand in the closest relation of reflex influence, each reciprocally conditioning and furthering the other." [153]

It will be noted also that in asserting that law is not the product of the general sense of justice, but the product of social interests, Jhering has treated the latter supposition as necessarily excluding the former, and has assumed that if law be the product of social interests it must be the product of conscious purpose, of calculation. But it is possible to maintain that the general sense of justice is itself the product of social interests, keenly felt without being consciously formulated. And in fact this is a theory of the evolution of the sense of right which Jhering himself held, and which he constantly applied both in his historical and philosophical writings. In his *Teleology* it is not only the sense of right in jural relations that is thus accounted for, but also the sense of right in matters of morality, and even the sense of propriety in social intercourse. [154]

Such self-contradictions are not infrequent with Jhering, and he himself in a characteristic passage of his *Jest and Earnest* explains and, we almost say, justifies them:

But, you ask, do I seriously mean this? Honestly, no. When it is a question of doing justice to the different sides of one and the same institution, it is my habit to think myself into the side which I am at the moment treating with a complete, deliberate and conscious one-sidedness — to fall in love with it, I might say, as if it were the only side worth considering. When the other sides have their turn, I act in the same way; their predecessor is then wholly forgotten, as is not uncommon when it is a question of falling in love; and so I am sure that none of them will receive less than its due. [155]

[153] *Zweck im Recht*, vol. i, p. 379.
[154] *Political Science Quarterly*, vol. xi, pp. 291 *et seq. Supra*, pp. 152 *et seq.*
[155] *Scherz und Ernst* in *der Jurisprudenz*, p. 187.

The self-imposed task which had drawn Jhering away from his promised history of Roman law, the examination of the beginnings of Indo-European and Semitic civilization, had been brought, at the moment of his death, much nearer to completion; and the *Prehistoric Development of the Indo-Europeans*,[156] which his executor published before the fragment of the *History of the Evolution of the Roman Law* was given to the world, makes a good-sized volume. The first book treats of the Aryans in their original home and of the grade of civilization which they had attained; the third, fourth and fifth books deal respectively with their exodus, their wanderings and their " second home." These books are either completed or so far completed as clearly to indicate the author's conclusions. The second book, which describes the civilization developed at Babylon and its transmission to the Mediterranean peoples, is also practically completed, and is nearly as long as all the others. Only the last section of this book, which was to set forth and compare the racial characteristics of the Aryans and the Semites, is unfinished. The sixth and seventh books, which were to explain the origin of and the differences between the European nations, are entirely wanting.

What are Jhering's conclusions — or hypotheses — on all these matters, and how were they reached? To me, at least, the first question is the less interesting of the two. Jhering regards the Aryans as a purely pastoral people, without knowledge of agriculture, of architecture or of the working of metals. As they were an inland people — Jhering holds to the theory that they lived on the northern slope of the Himalayas in the modern Hindoo-Koosh — and as they were secluded by high mountain ranges from intercourse with other peoples, they were also ignorant of navigation and had developed no commerce. The Babylonians, on the other hand, had developed agriculture, architecture and manufactures some 3500 years before the Christian era. They

---

[156] *Vorgeschichte der Indoeuropäer*, Leipzig, 1894.

had ships not only upon their great rivers, but on the Indian Ocean.

The Aryans had the patriarchal type of household: if at any very early period they had lived under the system of mother-right, they had outgrown it before the beginning of the migrations. They had reached no political organization higher than that of the tribe. The Babylonians, however, owing to their invention of bricks and to the consequent development of architecture and of city life, had reached a high stage of political organization.

The Aryan law was extremely rudimentary. From the juristic point of view the Aryans had no law, for with them law, morals and religion were wholly undifferentiated. The Babylonians, on the other hand, had a highly developed law, particularly as regarded commercial transactions. Of their law merchant, Jhering says:

The Babylonian legal documents enable us to construct a clear picture of their commercial and monetary transactions. It yields in no respect to that displayed to us by the Roman law at its highest point of development in the first centuries of the Empire. I know no legal concept, no legal act of that system that does not find its counterpart among the Babylonians. In addition to those that are a matter of course, — sale, in which we find the Roman rule that the risk passes to the vendee with the conclusion of the contract, and hiring, in which subhiring also appears, and loan at interest,— there are found in the Babylonian law interest for default, conventional penalty, assignment of claims and assumption of liability, the order to pay, set-off, releases, commission on purchase, the contract of partnership, the contract recognizing debt and the abstract [157] promise to pay, suretyship and pledge, *antichresis* even and the pledging of pledges; and

---

[157] " Abstract," because the reason (*causa*) for the promise is disregarded and the defenses admissible in the case of ordinary contracts are excluded. The abstract contract of the Roman law was the *stipulatio*. The abstract contract of the English common law was the promise under seal. The chief abstract promises of modern law occur in the case of negotiable instruments.

there occur transactions of a subtlety that would do credit to the trickiest modern usurer.[158]

Through its commerce the influence of Babylon extended eastward to India and westward to the Mediterranean. It was from Babylon that the Egyptians and the Phœnicians derived their civilization.

Increase of population drove repeated swarms of Aryans from their Asiatic home. In their wanderings they developed the type of military organization with which all the European nations started, and the military leadership which grew into the later European kingship. On the march was also developed that peculiar type of priesthood which we find in ancient Rome — priests who are experts in certain matters of especial moment to the migrating hordes. A further result of the migration was the development of monogamy. The chief result, however, was a gradual metamorphosis of racial character. Each exodus implied the selection of the most enterprising and courageous: centuries of migration secured the survival of the fittest, and transformed the indolent and unpractical Aryan into the energetic and matter-of-fact European.

The repeated migrations left no Aryans between the original home and the plains of modern Russia. If any tarried, they were unable to maintain themselves. The first rest-ing-place, the " second home " of the wanderers, was in southern Russia and Bessarabia. Here they lived for cen-turies, and here they learned from the earlier inhabitants the art of tilling the soil. The conquered aborigines were not reduced to slavery; serfdom was invented. The use of ma-nure was not yet known, and therefore in the course of cen-turies new exoduses became necessary. Then the work of natural selection began afresh, with the result of differentiat-

---

[158] *Vorgeschichte der Indoeuropäer*, pp. 257, 258. Jhering also describes to the Babylonians the invention of *foenus nauticum*, the maritime loan (" bottomry bond ") in which the claim of the lender perishes with the ship, and in which the rate of interest is correspondingly high (*pretium periculi*). — *Ibid.*, pp. 242 *et seq.*

ing Greeks, Latins, Celts, Germans, *etc.*, from the Slavs, who remained in the " second home," and of whom, as compared with the other European nations, Jhering had a very poor opinion. What were the influences that differentiated these other European nations, was to have been set forth in the unwritten sixth book. We have hints that the explanation was to have been found partly in the position, soil and climate of their final abodes, partly in their earlier or later contact with the Semitic civilization of the Mediterranean. It was Jhering's theory that all differences in national type are due, in the last analysis, to external conditions and influences. This he termed the theory of " historical causality."

What are the data on which Jhering based this daring reconstruction of the forgotten beginnings of civilization? As regards Babylon, we have the bricks with their inscriptions.[159] In that city the brick took the place of wood, metal, parchment or papyrus as writing material. Myths, legends and history were made eternal by fire; contracts were made binding by burning them. The permanence and the comparative worthlessness of the material have preserved the inscriptions. These Jhering used with a certain independence. He could not control the translations given by the Assyriologists, but he could interpret them. A historical document is open to the interpretation of every historian. A legal document is more easily interpreted by a jurist than by a philologist; and if the jurist be also a legal historian, familiar with the various stages of legal evolution, his interpretation carries greater weight than that of the philologist. But Jhering went behind the Babylonian civilization at the period of the inscriptions, and endeavored to explain its genesis. His starting-point was the character of the country. Its great alluvial plains were destitute of stone and scantly furnished with wood. The Aryans, who had plenty of wood, never got beyond it. With the Babylonians, necessity was the mother of an all-important invention, that

---

[159] The collection of which Jhering makes most use is that of Oppert et Ménant, Documents juridiques de l'Assyrie et de Chaldée (Paris, 1877).

of the brick. The great navigable rivers led to another invention, that of the ship. From the brick and the ship Jhering deduced the entire Babylonian civilization. His construction is, of course, wholly hypothetical. His hypotheses are sometimes fanciful, usually plausible, often almost convincing. In every case he ended by convincing himself at least. It may have been so; it must have been so; it was so — is a sequence that fairly represents his mental process. That it all was as he had pictured it, he was at the last so thoroughly assured as to declare that Babylonian history — by which terms he designated his own hypothetical reconstruction of that history — was of especial interest and value because it so perfectly exemplified the theory of " historical causality," [160] — this theory being the initial hypothesis upon which the whole reconstruction was based.

In the rest of his journey into *Vorgeschichte* — in visiting the first and second homes of the ancestors of the European and in following their migrations — Jhering has nothing beneath his feet that is nearly so solid as the bricks of Babylon. The data are words, symbols, rites, customs, institutions; the evidence, as lawyers say, is circumstantial, that is, the proof is inferential. As in the *Spirit of the Roman Law*, he utilizes the results attained by the philologists; and Professor Max Müller tells us that the authorities upon which Jhering has chiefly relied are good authorities. [161] As in the *Spirit*, he has utilized institutional material to corroborate, interpret, qualify and supplement the material furnished by the philologists. He has made far more use than in the earlier work of religious institutions, rites and symbols. A large part of the book is devoted to a study of Roman religious antiquities, in which he finds reminiscences of the exodus from the Asiatic home and reproductions of the customs of the migratory period. In none of his writings has he made more fascinating use of the historical imagina-

---

[161] Article cited above (*Cosmopolis*, September, 1896).
[160] *Vorgeschichte der Indoeuropäer*, pp. 270, 271.

tion than in his explanation of the *ver sacrum*,[162] of the priestly colleges and of the auspices.[163] He explains what seems inexplicable; he accounts for things that all other students of Roman antiquities have dismissed as irrational superstitions; and as he accounts for them, they become in their origin completely rational.

Far more clearly than in his earlier books is here revealed his theory of the relation of religion to custom. Religious faith does not create customs: these are originally expressions of social utilities. But old customs become hallowed by time, and they are preserved as religious observances long after their reason for existence has disappeared. They are "superstitions" in what is perhaps the strict etymological meaning of the word, that is, things left over. For the historian of civilization religious forms have thus the same worth that fossils possess for the biologist.

Whatever opinion be held of the value of Jhering's *Indo-Europeans,* no one will deny that it is an extraordinary work for a septuagenarian to conceive and so nearly to execute. That a man of so advanced an age should have attacked such problems, that he should have brought to their solution such quickness and fecundity of imagination, that, at the very last, he should have thrown himself with such energy into a field of investigation so remote from all his previous studies as Assyriology — all this bears witness to an exceptional intellectual vitality. Jhering was of those whom the gods love, for, though full of years, he yet died young.

In our review of Jhering's life work we have seen him dropping one task after another, and leaving each unfinished; hurrying from legal history into legal philosophy, and from legal philosophy into sociology; taking up legal history again at the close of his life, only again to abandon it and to devote his last energies to the history of civilization. And yet there was a single impulse behind all his efforts and a con-

---

[162] *Vorgeschichte der Indoeuropäer*, pp. 309 *et seq.*
[163] *Ibid.*, pp. 425 *et seq.*

tinuity in all his work. What interested him above all things, what occupied him always, from whatever side the problem was approached, was the evolution of law as an integral part of civilization. And his work is in no proper sense unfinished; he has found a solution for his problem; law is explained from its crudest beginnings to its latest and most refined development as the expression of social utilities. The thought is, for our time, one of fundamental importance. Developed as Jhering developed it, particularly in his *Teleology,* it contains the corrective for the aberrations of socialistic theory; for it derives from socialistic premises the justification of individualism.

VII

The legal reader (if any legal reader has had the patience to follow me thus far) may begin to wonder whether, in Germany, jurisprudence means simply legal history and legal philosophy; and whether, because of the national yearning to get to the bottom of every subject, however abysmal its depths may be, the tendency of German legal history and philosophy is to eliminate the legal element and to become mere subdivisions of universal history and of pure philosophy. If any such impression has been created, it is doubtless because, in these essays, I have thus far emphasized the more general tendencies of German legal science, and have dwelt especially upon that side of the work of our four jurists which seems to me of most general interest. It is of Jhering, too, that I have thus far had most to say; and Jhering made more frequent and more extended excursions into neighboring fields than any of his fellow jurists. Jhering himself, however, was primarily a jurist, and devoted the greater part of his restless energy to labors which even an American lawyer would recognize as legal. The work of Windscheid and of Bruns was wholly legal. That of Gneist, as we shall see, was partly political, but in the main legal. All these men — apart from their work as instructors, of which I shall speak later — made important contributions to the better comprehension of existing law, and each of them influenced, in greater or less measure, the development of the new law which German imperial legislation has produced during the past thirty years.

To vindicate Jhering's character as a practical lawyer, it should first be noted that he was consulted in sundry cases of great importance, and wrote admirable opinions.[164] His *Year Books* were established for the scientific discussion of modern legal problems; and to this journal, during the thirty-five years of his editorship, he made constant and important contributions. In its pages first appeared, as we have already noted, his treatise on the protection of possession. Among the topics that he discussed were *periculum rei* in sale, joint obligations, limitations on property rights in the interest of neighbors, and protection against the malicious invasion of rights — all of them sufficiently practical themes. These and other contributions to the *Year Books* are reprinted in his three volumes of *Collected Essays*.

In these essays it was his constant effort to find the principles that underlie the positive rules of the law. In the heat of the battle against abstract jurisprudence he often spoke as if principles were the bane of the law; and at the close of his life, in the introduction to his unfinished *History of the Evolution of the Roman Law,* he wrote:

A rude age has one priceless advantage over an age of higher development: *it is not yet acquainted with any principles.*[165]

But in this instance, as in so many others, Jhering's utterances must be read in the light of his immediate purpose. Like all good preachers, he had most to say about the sins to which his hearers were prone, and to enhance their blackness he was capable of blanching those opposite sins to

---

[164] Some of the more important will be found in his *Vermischte Schriften* (1879) and *Gesammelte Aufsätze* (1881–1886).

[165] *Entwicklungsgeschichte des römischen Rechts,* p. 17. The italics are Jhering's.

which they had no leaning. Had he lived in a land where the average lawyer cared only for the rule, and not for the reason; where fictions and presumptions were commonly accepted as final legal truths and estoppel stopped all scientific inquiry, he would have denounced such disregard of principles as vehemently as he denounced the ideolatry of the Germans. In his *Possessory Intention* he remarks that " the nature of the case is invoked only by him who does not really know how to justify his views " ; [166] and in another passage he declares that the establishment of a legal presumption, in order to escape the objectionable results of a recognized principle,

is, in my eyes, simply escaping from an *impasse* into which we have strayed by our own fault by climbing over roofs or walls. When we find ourselves in an *impasse*, it proves that we have missed the right road, and the moral is that we must turn back and try to find it.[167]

Jhering's real quarrel was with that purely deductive jurisprudence which treats as absolute and final truths the principles heretofore commonly recognized. " Principles," he said, " are not written in the stars, nor have they fallen from the skies; man makes them for himself." [168] If they do not correspond to the existing rules of positive law, or if rules deduced from them do not subserve the interests of society, the principles, he held, must be remade; and Jhering was in no wise disposed to shirk this task. Among his contributions to constructive jurisprudence, that which has obtained most general recognition is his theory of the " negative interest of contract." [169]

The problem is this: A person supposes, and under the circumstances is entitled to suppose, that he has a contract. Under this supposition he incurs expenses, or he neglects or

---

[166] *Besitzwille*, p. 206, note.   [167] *Ibid.*, pp. 17, 18.   [168] *Ibid.*, p. 504.
[169] Culpa in contrahendo, oder Schadensersatz bei nichtigen oder nicht zur Perfektion gelangten Verträgen. — *Jahrbücher für die Dogmatik*, vol. iv, pp. 1–112. The essay is reprinted in *Gesammelte Aufsätze*.

refuses to make another contract, and in consequence of this neglect or refusal he suffers loss or lets an assured profit escape him. It turns out that, owing to circumstances for which he is in no wise responsible, of which he was not aware and could not be expected to be aware, he has no contract. What remedy can the law give him?

The problem arises, as Jhering pointed out, in many different classes of cases. The contract may be invalid because the other party is by law incapable of binding himself. It may be invalid because the thing which the other party has undertaken to do is impossible. Or it may be that the other party to the contract has made a mistake such as the law permits him to plead — a mistake that is excusable and of such importance that but for the mistake he would not have made the declaration, whether of offer or acceptance, which he has made. Or a mistake has occurred in the transmission of the declaration, whether by messenger or by telegraph.[170] In some of these cases [171] the Roman law treats the contract as void, while the English law makes it voidable only; but under either view the party who has taken at its face value the declaration made or sent to him, who was justified in so taking it, and who has suffered damage by reason of his confidence, seems to have no remedy on the contract.

Has he any other remedy? In one case he undoubtely has, namely, in the case of fraud or misrepresentation on the part of his antagonist. If, however, no fraud or misrepresentation can be shown, — and in some of the cases above set forth this is excluded by hypothesis, — the dominant German theory, before Jhering's essay was published, gave him no claim for damages.[172] In some modern decisions, how-

---

[170] In the case of telegraphic mistakes the German jurists are forced to decide whether the resultant damage shall fall upon the sender or the addressee, because the telegraphs are governmental, and the government will not pay.

[171] Other cases discussed by Jhering are here omitted, either because they are peculiar to the Roman law, or because they are of minor importance.

[172] After Jhering had elaborated his theory, he discovered that it had been substantially anticipated by Richelmann, *Der Einfluss des Irrthums auf*

ever, and in some of the modern codes, Jhering found a
claim for damages sporadically recognized — recognized,
that is, in some of the cases in which he believed it should
be recognized. Damages, when allowed, were sometimes
measured by the interest which the party had in securing
the performance of the contract. This, Jhering maintained,
was going too far. In other cases only such damages were
allowed as the party suffered by reason of his justifiable
belief that he had a contract. This Jhering declared to be
the correct solution. The party in question should have no
claim either for the performance of the contract or for damages for non-performance; for to allow either claim would
be to recognize the invalid contract as valid. What should be
accorded him is a claim to be put in as good a position as
if he had never been led to suppose that he had a contract.
This, as contrasted with the " positive interest " in performance, Jhering termed " negative interest." [173]

In one class of cases Jhering was able to show that this
claim for negative interest was recognized by the Roman
jurists, namely, in cases where a contract of sale was void
because its performance was objectively impossible. Where,
for example, a person unwittingly bought land that was
sacred, or religious, or the property of the people, Modestinus
declared that " although the purchase does not hold, yet
the purchaser will have an action on the purchase against
the vendor to recover damages for being misled " — " *quod
interfuit eius ne deciperetur.*" [174]

Neither in the *Digest,* nor in the modern codes in which
Jhering found the rule for which he is pleading practically

Verträge (Hanover, 1837). Richelmann, however, had not so presented it
as to make any impression on his contemporaries.

[173] " Interest "— *quod actoris interest,* the difference it makes to the
plaintiff — is the older European term for damages, including both *damnum
emergens,* positive loss, and *lucrum cessans,* failure to gain. In the French
law we have the phrase *dommages-intérêts.* In the new German code,
Interesse designates the measure of damages; damages recovered are *Schadensersatz.*

[174] *Digest,* 18, 1, fr. 62, § 1. *Cf.* Inst. 3, 23, § 5. See also *Digest,* 11, 7,
fr. 8, § 1, and 18, 4, frs. 8, 9. The passages cited, as Jhering shows, cannot
be explained on the supposition that the vendor knew and concealed the
impossibility.

recognized, was the reason for the rule set forth; nor did he find it satisfactorily enunciated in any of the modern decisions. According to his theory, the claim for negative interest is based upon the negligence (*culpa*) of the antagonist. In the case mentioned in the *Digest,* as he urges,

the vendor contracts without being personally able to furnish the requisites of the validity of the contract, and through the false semblance of contract he misleads the other party.[175]

It is true that there is usually, at Roman as at English law, no liability for negligence except in contractual relations. The contractual duty to exercise proper care does not, however, begin with the *conclusion,* but with the *concluding* of the contract. In contracting,

the first and most general obligation assumed is this: to exercise in the act of contracting itself the requisite *diligentia.* Not merely existing contractual relations, but such also as are coming into existence, must be brought under the protection of the rules regarding negligence.[176]

This point of view gave the essay its title, "*Culpa in contrahendo.*" In the essay itself, however, there are indications that this construction was not wholly satisfactory to its author. In some of the cases in which he desired to hold a party liable for negative interest, it is impossible to show any real negligence; and Jhering, admitting this, fell back upon a presumption of negligence.[177] This, according to his own declaration,[178] is tantamount to abandoning the search for "the right road."

That he should have clung to this theory is the more singular because in other passages of the original essay he clearly develops a different and more tenable construction. He tells us that the party to whom an apparently good declaration comes should not be required, in order to protect himself,

---

[175] *Jahrbücher für Dogmatik,* vol. iv, p. 41.
[176] *Ibid.,* p. 42.
[177] *Ibid.,* p. 36.
[178] *Supra,* p. 43.

to exact an express warranty of the absence of negligence or, more particularly, of the existence of the legal requisites of contract. The law can and should spare him this trouble by reading into the act of contracting itself *the tacit assumption of such a warranty [die stillschweigende Uebernahme dieser Garantie]*. In extra-contractual relations no one can demand from another the warranty of the trustworthiness and truth of his utterances and communications. . . . In contractual intercourse, on the contrary, in which just these utterances are intended to acquire binding force, he can look to the other party to determine whether they are well founded; he himself, as a rule, is not in a position to make any such investigation. In concluding the contract with him, the other party *warrants [garantirt]* to him the satisfactory result of such an investigation. . . . Whether he assures him in words or by his act that he is in a position to conclude this particular contract, can make no difference: *this assurance [Versicherung] lies in the act of contracting itself.*[179]

Jhering's rule of negative interest has found very general acceptance,[180] both among German writers and in German legislation. It has found a place in almost every compendium of modern Roman law. The new German civil code recognizes it in the cases where contracts are voidable because of the mistake of the other party or because of mistake in the transmission of a declaration, and in the cases where contracts are void because their object is impossible or illegal.[181] Many of his colleagues, however, have chosen to

---

[179] *Jahrbücher, loc. cit.*, pp. 42, 43. The italics are mine.

[180] Except in the case where the invalidity of the contract is due to the lack of capacity of the other party. Jhering himself was not quite sure of this case. — *Ibid.*, pp. 57 *et seq.*

[181] The German code also recognizes the negative interest of contract in one case in which Jhering declared that it should not be recognized. § 93 reads: " A declaration not seriously intended, which is made in the expectation that the lack of serious intention will not fail to be perceived, is void; " and § 97 gives to the other party, if he failed to perceive, and under the circumstances could not be expected to perceive, the lack of serious intention, a claim for negative interest. Jhering, in his essay (p. 74), took the very sensible ground that when a declaration is made jocosely, the joke, under the circumstances, must either be one that other persons are bound to see, or one that they are not bound to see. In the former case, no one ought to

base the rule on the theory of implied warranty, and not on
the theory of *culpa in contrahendo*.[182] In Jhering's view
the action for negative interest is contractual; the contract,
though invalid for every other purpose, is upheld for this.[183]
On the theory of implied warranty, the action is not on
the contract, but on the separate warranty involved in the
act of contracting.

---

have any claim, even for negative interest; in the latter case, the joker should
not be allowed to plead his humorous intention.

The sections of the code which refer to negative interest are the following:

" § 97. If a declaration of will is null according to § 93 [lack of serious
intention], or is avoided on the basis of §§ 94, 95 [mistake as to the content
of the declaration, absence of intention to make a declaration of such content,
mistake as to essential qualities of the person or the thing, mistake in the
transmission of a declaration], he who made the declaration is liable, in case
it was addressed to a particular person, to this person, in other cases to every
third person, for the damages which such person suffers by reason of his
reliance on the validity of the declaration; but not beyond the amount of
the interest which such person has in the validity of the declaration.

" The liability for damages does not arise if the person who suffers
damage knew the cause of the nullity or voidability, or failed to know it in
consequence of negligence (was bound to know it). In the case of § 95, the
liability for damages is also excluded if the incorrectness of the transmission
is owing to an unavoidable cause [*höhere Gewalt*]."

" § 259. A contract looking to an impossible performance is null.

" If in concluding the contract the one party knew or was bound to
know the impossibility of performance, he is liable for the damages which the
other party suffers by reason of his reliance on the validity of the contract,
but not beyond the amount of the interest which such party has in the
validity of the contract. The liability for damages does not arise if the other
party knew or was bound to know the impossibility.

" The provisions of clause 2 will have suitable application in case the
promised performance is only partially impossible, and the contract is valid
as regards its possible part, or in case one of several performances alter-
natively [*wahlweise*] promised is impossible."

" § 261. If a contract is in conflict with a legal prohibition, the provisions
of § 259, clauses 2, 3, . . . will have suitable application."

The limitation, in the above paragraphs, of the negative interest to the
amount that might be claimed, were the contract valid, for its non-performance, is reasonable and necessary. Suppose, for example, that a vendor,
thinking himself bound, refuses a better offer; is he to claim the profit which
the acceptance of such offer would have given him? Without the limitation
in the above paragraphs he would be entitled to do so.

The above citations are from the revised draft — Entwurf, *Zweite Lesung*.
The text of the code as adopted is not before me, but it is understood that
few changes were made.

[182] *Cf.* Windscheid, *Pandekten*, vol. ii, § 307, n. 5. *Contra* Vangerow,
Pandekten, vol. i, § 109, and Dernburg, *Pandekten*, vol. ii, § 10, n. 10, who
are satisfied with the theory of negligence. In the first draft of the German
civil code, §§ 97, 345, liability was expressly based on negligence (*Fahrläs-
sigkeit*), but this is not the case in § 97 of the revised draft, cited above.

[183] This appears to have been the view taken by Modestinus, in *Digest* 18,
1, fr. 62, § 1, *ex empto experietur;* but compare Ulpian's *quasi ex empto,*
Digest 11, 7, fr. 8, § 1.

Another portion of the new civil code reveals the influence of Jhering's theories. The first draft of that code appeared in 1888, while he was writing his *Possessory Intention*, and he subjected the section on possession (§§ 797–825) to a searching criticism.[184] The codifiers had maintained, formally at least, the Roman distinction between purely physical control or detention (*Inhabung*) and possession (*Besitz*) ; and in accordance with the dominant theory,[185] the distinctive element in possession was declared to be " the intention of the holder to hold the thing as his own." Possession was therefore excluded, and only detention recognized, in three cases: (1) Where one cannot hold the thing as his own, because it is incapable of being owned; (2) Where one cannot hold the thing as his own, because it is a part of another thing and incapable of separate ownership; and (3) Where the thing is held for another. With the first of these cases Jhering made merry:

Things in which no ownership is possible — of what things are we here to think? I know of none, and I have sought in vain for any in the motives accompanying the draft. For the Roman law, the rule, . . . where there is no ownership, there there is no possession, had practical reality, for the Romans recognized things in which ownership was not possible (*res extra commercium*) ; but what has the rule to do with us? It might be reversed without making the least difference. The Roman category is retained, but there is nothing to put in it. It is an empty druggist's jar, left standing after a change in the official pharmacopœia, although the article for which the label calls is no longer kept in stock.[186]

As regards the second and third cases Jhering pointed out that, according to §§ 814 *et seq.* of the draft, the detentor was to have all the rights of a possessor except as against the possessor of the entire thing (*e.g.*, a building) of which he

---

[184] *Besitzwille*, ch. xix, pp. 470–534.
[185] *Political Science Quarterly*, vol. xi, pp. 282, 283, 285. *Supra*, pp. 143, 144, 146.
[186] *Besitzwille*, pp. 472, 473.

holds a part (*e.g.*, a suite of rooms), or the possessor for whom and in whose name he holds. Why then, Jhering urged, is he not called possessor? Why keep up the distinction of names when the possessor and the detentor have been substantially assimilated?

In the second draft this suggestion was followed. The detentor (*Inhaber*) has disappeared, and with him has disappeared the requirement of the *animus rem sibi habendi* for the possessor(*Besitzer*). Of the Roman possessor but one trace is left. The last paragraph of the section (§ 793) declares that " he who possesses a thing as belonging to him, is *Eigenbesitzer*." This old friend with a new face, who thus makes his entrance just as the curtain drops upon possession, reappears later when the stage is set for prescription; and in this scene he plays the leading part.

Another and more practical criticism upon this section of the code turned upon the protection which it gave to the detentor who holds for another against the person for whom he holds. He was authorized to meet arbitrary disturbance or an attempted ouster with force. He was authorized, if forcibly deprived of a movable, to employ force for its immediate recovery; if forcibly ejected from real property or ousted in his absence, to resume control by force (§ 815). This protection, said Jhering, is all very well in the case of the person who has borrowed or hired from me a horse, or has leased from me a house or an apartment; but how about household servants and other employees? How about agents? If I wish to turn my butler out of the room he occupies in my house, or if I wish to prevent a messenger whom I have hired from making off with a parcel instead of delivering it, must I appeal to the courts? If I lend an opera glass to a person sitting by me in the theatre, and he refuses to give it back, may I not take it? And if I take it from him by force, is he to be permitted to use force for its immediate recovery? [187]

Here again the second draft puts things straight. After

[187] *Besitzwille*, pp. 503 *et seq.*

defining possession as "actual power" (*thatsächliche Gewalt*) over the thing, without any allusion to the intention with which this power is exercised, the code continues:

§778. If any one exercises the actual power over a thing for another person in that person's household or business affairs, or in any other relation by virtue of which he has to follow that person's instructions in reference to the thing, that person only is possessor.

Here then the Roman "natural possession" reappears, and in very much the same relations in which Jhering asserted, by virtue of his reconstructive imagination, that it originated.[188] This natural possessor of § 778 has only those natural rights of self-defense and self-help which are requisite to protect the property entrusted to him against third persons (§ 782). On the other hand, all those who hold for or in the name of another, but in relations other than those indicated in § 778, are possessors, with full possessory rights even against those for whom or in whose names they hold. If they are to be derived of possession, it must be by process of law. In this class we find, as at Roman law, the usufructuary and the pledgee, and also the lessee, to whom the Roman law was so unfair (§ 790).[189]

Considering the attention which German writers have devoted to this subject,[190] and the care with which the first draft of the code was worked out, the section on possession was surprisingly bad. In the second draft, the same section is admirable, both in substance and in expression. The credit for the improvement is largely due to Jhering.[191]

[188] *Ibid.*, ch. viii. *Cf. Political Science Quarterly*, vol. xi, pp. 285, 286.

[189] Those also for whom possession is held have possessory rights against third persons: they have "mediate" or constructive possession.

[190] *Cf. Political Science Quarterly*, vol. xi, p. 278.

[191] Credit for inducing a more practical consideration of the whole subject is also due to Count Piniński, *Der Thatbestand des Sachbesitzerwerbs* (Leipzig, 1885). Great credit — as much, perhaps, as can be claimed for Jhering — is due, as regards the improvement of the section in the code, to Gierke, who had anticipated in Schmoller's *Jahrbuch für Gesetzgebung, etc.*, vol. xii, 3, pp. 74 *et seq.*, many of Jhering's criticisms. Credit is doubtless due to others; but when there was such a deluge of criticism as was poured upon every part of the first draft, it is not possible to do justice to all the critics.

Windscheid's chief contributions to constructive jurisprudence were his theories of the "claim" and of the "presupposition." Claim (*Anspruch*) he defined as the personal incidence of the right.[192] Real rights, that is, rights in things, are, he explained, primarily powers over the things themselves; but they have personal incidence also. They run against every one, carrying with them a claim for noninterference. When a claim of this character is infringed, when some one interferes with the dominion of him to whom the right pertains, the claim assumes the form of a right of action. Personal rights, on the other hand, have for their primary object the acts or forbearances of particular persons. They exist only in their personal incidence: they are simply claims. If what is claimed be an act, the claim is, from the start, a right of action. If what is claimed be a forbearance, there is no right of action until he whose duty it is to forbear violates this duty.

The Romans used the word *actio* to describe, not merely the appeal to the courts, nor merely the power of appealing to the courts, but the right itself in its personal incidence. They often used *actio* and *ius* as equivalent terms. The distinction between actions *in personam* and actions *in rem* is really a distinction between personal and real rights according to their primary or immediate incidence. In the concrete sense all actions are against persons. Windscheid found in German law no term to express the personal incidence of the right, whether immediate or mediate, and he proposed to use *Anspruch* in this sense.

So far the matter is one of terminology merely, but Windscheid went further. Because of failure to discriminate between the different meanings of *actio*, courts and legislatures, he maintained, have come to treat as merely procedural, as connected with remedial law only, rules and institutions that in reality belong to substantive law. The most important case of this sort is the *praescriptio temporis*

---

[192] "Die persönliche Richtung des Rechts." — *Die Actio des römischen Civilrechts vom Standpunkte des heutigen Rechts* (Düsseldorf, 1856). See also *Pandekten,* vol. i, § 43.

in its application to actions. According to Windscheid, it is
not the suit merely, but the claim, that is prescribed; and
the whole subject should be treated under the caption " prescription of claims," not under that of " prescription of suits."
According to his construction, prescription begins to run
as soon as the claim exists and is " unsatisfied." Prescription is interrupted, not only by bringing suit, but by any
distinct exercise of the right against the person of incidence. The prescription of the " real claim " (*actio in rem*)
leaves the right intact, because the prescribed claim is
but an expression or manifestation of the right; but the
prescription of a personal claim (*actio in personam*) destroys the right, because the right is nothing but claim.
To translate this latter conclusion into the terms of English law: the limitation of an action for the recovery of
debt, or of an action for damages for breach of contract,
does not merely bar the remedy, but destroys the right.

Windscheid's theory has not obtained general or unqualified acceptance among his colleagues. Brinz[193] declared that he could not think of a claim without a particular
person against whom the claim was directed. Thon[194] pronounced the theory of a claim against the world to be as
idle as it is misleading. Their criticism touches Windscheid's
" real claim " which runs against everybody, and is, I think,
sound. According to Windscheid's own definition no " real
claim " should be recognized until the right has found a
really personal incidence. It is, however, mere juggling
with words to say in the same breath that my right to be
paid one hundred dollars on B's note has " personal incidence " against B, and that my right to the control and
enjoyment of my back yard in New York has " personal
incidence " against every citizen of the United States. Accordingly, the majority of the German jurists who have
accepted Windscheid's word, give to the *Anspruch* a narrower
and more definite meaning, and recognize no " real claim "

---

[193] *Pandekten,* vol. i, p. 252; cited by Dernburg, *Pandekten,* vol. i, § 39,
n. 5.   [194] *Rechtsnorm,* p. 159; cited by Dernburg, *Ibid.*

except against the person who has interfered with the control and enjoyment of the thing.[195] Thus construed, the " claim " becomes practically equivalent to the English " right of action " in its broader sense.[196]

Windscheid's conclusions touching prescription of actions are unaffected by this question of the construction of his own definition. In fact, they harmonize better with the construction which makes his claim equivalent to the English right of action than with his own construction; for his " real claim " is not subject to prescription until it is " unsatisfied," and it is perfectly satisfied so long as there is no interference with the substantive right. As soon as this interference comes, however, there is a right of action. His theory of limitation may accordingly be stated as follows: It is not actions that are limited, but rights of action. If the English courts accepted this theory, they would be obliged to hold, as he does, that when an action for the recovery of debt is barred, the debt is extinguished. Their contrary decisions are based upon the theory that statutes of limitation operate only as a bar to suits. In this matter, again, there is, among German jurists, no general and complete acceptance of Windscheid's views.[197]

In the new German code the term *Anspruch* is very freely used. It is defined in § 161 as " the right to require from another an act or forbearance " — " *ein Thun oder Unterlassen.*" It is everywhere employed in this broad sense: it is practically the substantive form of the verb " require " (*verlangen*). In the law of things it is not always a claim against a particular person.[198] In the law of obligations it plays a subsidiary part: the primary claim is termed *Forderung,* while other claims are commonly described as *Ansprü-*

---

[195] Windscheid himself is inconsistent in his own construction. If the " claim " of an owner for forbearance runs against all the world, and if limitation of the action is destruction of the " claim," then the limitation of an action on trespass extinguishes the owner's claim against all the world, and he can bring no action on anybody's trespass.

[196] For a criticism of Windscheid's theory on other grounds, see Jhering, *Besitzwille,* p. 520, and Dernburg, *Pandekten,* vol. i, § 39 *in fine* (pp. 87, 88).

[197] See Dernburg, *Pandekten,* vol. i, § 145, pp. 335, 336; § 150, p. 346.

[198] See §§ 803 *et seq.*

che. Forderung is clearly a species of the genus *Anspruch*.[199]
The section on prescription [200] speaks throughout of the
prescription of *Ansprüche;* the German word for action,
Klage, occurs only in the paragraphs relating to the interruption of prescription by bringing suit. The whole
section is drafted in substantial harmony with Winscheid's
theory.

In his doctrine of " presupposition " [201] Windscheid endeavored to show that several distinct institutions of the
Roman law were merely different expressions of one idea,
and that numerous rules, not previously brought into relation with each other, were all corollaries of one general
principle. The character and range of these rules may be
indicated by a few examples. A man buys a brass vase supposing it to be of gold, or clothes that have been renovated,
supposing them to be new; the vendor labors under the same
mistake; the sale may be rescinded, or the difference in value
recovered.[202] A testator has named as his heir a person
whom he supposed to be his son; it is shown that this person
is not his son; the testament may be overturned.[203] A
person has paid what he supposed to be money owed; it
turns out that nothing was owed, or not so much; he recovers
the money paid, or the excess, with the *condictio indebiti.*[204]
A person has paid money which he supposes that he will owe;
and it turns out that he does not owe it — *e.g.,* he has paid
rent in advance, and the house he has leased burns down;
he recovers the money.[205] A person pays money that a slave
may be manumitted; the slave is not freed; he recovers on
the *condictio ob causam dati.*[206] A man gives presents to
the girl to whom he is betrothed; the engagement is broken
by her or her parents; he recovers the presents on the *condic-*

---

[199] So Windscheid, *Pandekten,* vol. ii, § 250.
[200] *Verjährung,* §§ 161–190.
[201] *Die Lehre des römischen Rechts von der Voraussetzung* (Düsseldorf,
1850), and *Pandekten,* vol i, §§ 97–100; vol. ii, § 423; vol. iii, §§ 556, 636.
[202] *Digest,* 18, 1, fr. 45. As to the question of a warranty, see Windscheid,
Voraussetzung, p. 116. He assumes that there was no warranty.
[203] Cod., 6, 23, c. 5; *Digest,* 37, 10, fr. 1, § 11.
[204] *Digest,* 12, 6 *passim.*
[205] *Digest,* 19, 2, fr. 19, § 6.   [206] *Digest,* 12, 4, fr. 3, § 2.

tio ob causam dati.[207] A testator makes a bequest of land to
a municipality, with the request that the annual income be
expended upon public games; no games are celebrated for
four consecutive years; the testator's heir can recover the
mesne profits.[208] In cases analogous to this last, the Roman
jurists also recognized a right to obtain performances. They
held that a legacy with such a charge annexed could be held
back until the legatee gave security for performance of the
charge; and that, where a gift was made *inter vivos* with such
a charge annexed, the donor or his heir could sue for its
fulfillment.

According to Windscheid, the principle that underlies these
and other analogous cases is as follows: He who has made a
declaration of will (done a legal act) [209] in the belief that a
certain state of things, actual or legal, existed in the past
or exists in the present, or in the expectation that a certain
state of things, actual or legal, will exist in the future, and
who would not have willed (acted) as he did but for such
belief or expectation, has willed (acted) under a " presupposition," and has imposed upon the operation of his
will (acted) a limitation that is analogous to a condition.[210]
The presupposition is " an undeveloped condition." In
case of the failure of the presupposition — in case the belief
was erroneous; in case the assumption, although originally
correct, becomes incorrect; in case the expectation is not
realized — the person who has assumed obligation has a
defense, and the person who has parted with anything has
an action for recovery; or if the person is dead, the same
defense and the same action pertain to his representative
(heir or executor). If the presupposition was that the
party benefited by the act was to do anything, there is
also a claim for specific performance. In the case of acts

---

[207] Cod., 5, 3, c. 15.   [208] *Digest*, 33, 2, fr. 17.

[209] This and the following parentheses are inserted to aid the English
reader in translating Windscheid's formula from the realm of will to the
realm of its external manifestation in conduct, with which alone the law has
to do.

[210] The presupposition, according to Windscheid, may also be negative —
that a certain fact or legal relation did not, does not, or will not exist.

mortis causa, the above rules are unqualified. In the case of acts *inter vivos,* they obtain only when the presupposition was indicated, expressly or by implication, to the other party — only when, in other words, he perceived or should have perceived that the act would not have been done but for the belief or expectation in which it was done.

On its face this construction has merits. The separate doctrines of mistake in motive [211] and of charge (*modus*), and at least a large part of the doctrine of unjust enrichment, are brought under one cover. On more careful examination, however, the question arises whether anything is gained by this achievement. Does Windscheid's rather cumbrous theory make the application of the rules more easy? Does it make their application more certain? The Roman doctrines are clear cut; there is little difficulty in applying them. In contemplating Windscheid's doctrine, on the contrary, we are conscious of a vagueness of outline, and we are not sure how it would work out in practice. If we concede its merits as a bit of legal science, can we call it a good piece of legal art? [212] On all these points there is much difference of opinion among German jurists. Not a few of Windscheid's colleagues have accepted it,[213] and it has obtained some recognition in the courts.[214] Other jurists have rejected it.[215] In the first draft of the German code it found partial recognition.[216] In the second draft it has completely vanished.

[211] Savigny's distinction between mistake that excludes consent (" fundamental mistake," Pollock terms it) and mistake in the motive is generally accepted by German jurists, and Pollock (*Principles of Contract,* p. 393) pronounces it applicable to English law.

[212] To the distinction between the two Jhering has given classic expression.— Geist des römischen Rechts, 3d ed., part ii, div, ii, pp 323, 324.

[213] Rudorff, Bähr, Unger, Brinz and others; cited by Windscheid, *Pandekten,* vol. i. § 97, note 1.

[214] Citations from Seuffert's *Archiv für Entscheidungen,* in Windscheid, *Ibid.*

[215] Voigt, *Die Condictiones ob Causam* (1862), pp. 515-523, cited by Windscheid, *Ibid.* Dernburg, *Pandekten,* vol. i, § 116, finds that really heterogeneous matters are brought by Windscheid under one category, and that his presupposition cannot take the place of the concrete and definite constructions of the Romans.

[216] In the first draft the commissioners put the *condictio ob causam* under the heading *Voraussetzung* (§§ 742 *et seq.*), and stated the rules of

The effect produced by these special doctrines, claim and presupposition, was trifling compared with the influence which Windscheid exercised upon theory, practice and legislation at large, through his great work on *Pandects*.[217] The title, it may be well to explain, signifies a detailed presentation of the rules of modern Roman law. As the Roman law, in the absence of contrary custom or legislation, is the general law of Germany, and as the newer codes, for the most part, are based upon Roman law, the German who lectures or writes upon Pandects lectures or writes upon the private law of Germany as a whole. The Germanist, who describes those institutions of Teutonic law that survived the reception of the Roman law and notes the modifications introduced by modern German legislation, simply adds a number of details to the picture drawn by the Pandectist.

In every German university there are regularly two Pandectists, and many of these publish their Pandects. Of all these Pandectists Windscheid was for a generation the most popular. In his lectures he counted his hearers by hundreds where the majority of his colleagues counted theirs by tens, and his book enjoyed a corresponding vogue. It was the book which must be studied, whatever other books were read or left unread. It was the *vade mecum* of the referendary and of the assessor. It was constantly cited by the advocate and consulted by the judge.

----

the Roman law in accordance with Windscheid's theory. They declared also that testamentary dispositions and inheritance contracts might be attacked because of failure of presupposition (§§ 1781 *et seq.*, 1948 *et seq.*); and they based the claim for recovery of gifts after dissolution of an engagement to marry on the presumption of a presupposition (§ 1229). In all these cases, however, they limited the term to the expectation of future events or future legal results; and in connection with the *condictio ob causam* they declined to admit recovery on the ground of an erroneous supposition as to past or present circumstances, because this would open the door to numerous attacks upon contracts because of mistake in motive (*Motive zu dem Entwurfe,* vol. ii, p. 843). In other portions of the draft, however, they used the term presupposition for a determinant supposition as to past or present circumstances: *cf.* § 290, cl. 4; § 667, cl. 2; § 684, cl. 2. In treating of *modus* or charge (*Auflage*) (§§ 448, 1757, 1886 *et seq.*), they avoided the term presupposition entirely; and in *Motive,* vol. i, p. 249, they explained that the doctrine of presupposition as a general category of the self-limitation of the operation of legal acts was not sufficiently developed to make its employment safe (*unbedenklich*) in legislation.

[217] *Lehrbuch des Pandektenrechts.* Three vols.. 1862–1870. Seventh ed., 1891.

The book has, of course, striking merits, or it could have had no such success. It has proportion: the space allotted to the various subjects is determined by a sound sense of their relative importance. Each section is carefully thought out, and — a rarer excellence — the bearing of each section upon the others is thought out with equal care. Each institution is regarded in its relation to other institutions. The whole book hangs together: it is really systematic. The style is concise and clear. The vocabulary is German. Windscheid was a purist, and coined many German expressions to take the place of the customary Latin terms.

The most remarkable and most admirable part of the book is the footnotes. They constitute by far its greater part: they fill, at a rough estimate, two-thirds of the space, and contain more than four-fifths of the matter. In them, as I can testify from long use, every significant passage of the *Corpus Iuris* — every passage, at least, that has any relevancy to modern life — is somewhere cited. If there is serious doubt as to its interpretation, the doubt is noted and Windscheid's interpretation is briefly indicated. Wherever it seems necessary, reference is made to books, brochures or articles in which the passage is more fully discussed. Modern German decisions are not neglected; they are at least more frequently cited than in any other German work of the same kind. The notes serve also as an index to the German literature, from Savigny down, including not a little of the periodical literature. They are, however, much more than an index: it is hardly saying too much to call them a digest. All important controversies are noted; the chief arguments on all sides are stated (it is a poor controversy in Germany that has only two sides); and the prevalent opinion is fairly indicated, whether it happens to be the author's opinion or not. For the German literature of the Roman law in this century — barring the purely historical writings — Windscheid has done what Accursius did for the glossators. It is no wonder that his book became a new " standard gloss " in the German administration of civil justice.

The faults of the book — the extremely abstract statement

of principles and even of rules, the over-valuation of deductive results, the undue stress laid upon the psychical processes of the individual and the useless subtlety displayed in their analysis — these faults, I think, rather increased than diminished the influence of the work; for in his defects as in his excellences Windscheid fairly represented the jurisprudence of Germany in the nineteenth century. A few very practical young men, most of them Jhering's converts, accused Windscheid of being a " post-glossator," which meant that, in their opinion, he represented the scholastic tendencies of European jurisprudence in the fourteenth and fifteenth centuries; but the great majority of his contemporaries were in full sympathy with his views and methods.

The first draft of the German civil code gave striking evidence of the hold which Windscheid's *Pandects* had gained in German practice. The great majority of the commissioners were not theorists, but practitioners; not pupils of Windscheid, but his contemporaries; and yet, when the code was published in 1888, the remark that was most often heard — I speak as a witness on the spot — was, " It is pure Windscheid." [218] In this remark there was, of course, no little exaggeration. Much that was designated as Windscheid was simply Roman; much was really Savigny-Puchta-Windscheid, or modern Romanistic theory. Uttered by a Germanist, the remark usually meant that the code contained too little German law. As the code was studied, moreover, it was found that in employing Windscheid's terms the codifiers had not always followed Windscheid's construction. But, allowing for all exaggeration, the remark remains an extraordinary tribute to Windscheid.

In the second draft the amount of pure Roman law was ap-

[218] Windscheid was himself a member of the commission — one of the two " theorists " — but his direct and personal influence cannot have been decisive. Apart from the fact that he was but one among eleven, it should be noted that he was not charged with the preliminary draft of any part of the code; and that in the general discussion which continued from October, 1881, through December, 1887, Windscheid participated for the first two years only. In October, 1883, he was recalled by the Saxon government to his professorial duties at Leipzig, and was obliged to resign from the commission.

preciably diminished, and the quantity of " pure Windscheid " was lessened in more than the same proportion; but in spite of these changes, the civil law of Germany will bear, possibly for centuries, as legible an impress of the labors of the Leipzig professor as that which the work of Pothier, professor at Orléans, has left upon the civil code of France.

Bruns was a less prolific writer than Jhering or Gneist, and he published no work of such importance as Windscheid's *Pandects*. His earliest and his latest writings, like Jhering's, were historical.[219] The line of research which he opened in his *Law of Possession in the Middle Ages* was carried further in an essay on prior possession [220] and in a book on *The Possessory Actions of the Roman and the Modern Law*.[221] The fact that he deplored many of the changes in the law of possession which were effected in mediæval practice, and that, like Savigny, he preferred the Roman rules, did not neutralize the weightier fact that he showed these changes to be steps in a process of development and not a mere series of misconceptions. His bias did not prevent him from interpreting the Roman rules in a sense more liberal than Savigny's; nor did it prevent others from using the data furnished by him as a basis for conclusions divergent from his own. It was thus that his *Law of Possession*, as has been noted in a previous article,[222] helped to produce a reaction against Savigny's revival of pure Roman law. It should be added that the book was characterized by a freer employment of the comparative method than was at all usual in the middle of the century. In 1880, the year of Bruns's death, appeared his *Syrian-Roman Law Book of the Fifth Century*. This work was the product of philological and juristic collaboration: in the establishment of the text and in the translation Bruns obtained the assistance of Eduard Sachau. The commentary, however,

---

[219] He was also, for many years, an editor of the *Zeitschrift für Rechtsgeschichte*.

[220] " Der ältere Besitz und das Possessorium Ordinarium," in *Jahrbuch des gemeinen deutschen Rechts*, vol. iv, p. 1 (1860).

[221] *Die Besitzklagen des römischen und des heutigen Rechts* (1874).

[222] *Political Science Quarterly*, vol. x, p. 681. *Supra*, p. 127.

in which the significance of this provincial compilation of Roman law was for the first time clearly brought out, was Bruns's own. The importance of the *Syrian Law Book* lies, as he showed, in the evidence it gives of the variety of provincial systems that existed in the Roman empire,[223] of the resistance which they opposed to codification, and of the connection between the legislation of Justinian, in the sixth century, and the older customs.

Bruns's historical investigations, unlike Jhering's, were prosecuted solely for the purpose of making the existing law more intelligible. Legal history, in his opinion, ought to be " the handmaid of dogmatics." Like Windscheid, moreover, he devoted the greater part of his energy to the direct study of modern Roman law. Had he lived a few years longer in that vigorous health which was his till within a few days of his death, he also would have published his Pandects. He had begun the book.[224] As it is, the only permanent record of this portion of his life-work, apart from his minor essays, is found in the article on " The Roman Law of To-day," which he contributed to Holtzendorff's *Encyclopædia of Jurisprudence;* and it is by this and the preceding article on " The History and Sources of the Roman Law "[225] that Bruns is best known to the " cultured public " of Germany — including in the phrase that class of lawyers, numerous even in Germany, who lack the time or the energy to follow such minute researches as those by which Bruns won his scientific reputation. These are not such articles as the title " encyclopædia " naturally suggests to English readers. They are of such length that, printed as we print law books, the systematic article alone would make a volume of the same size as Maine's *Ancient Law,* and the two articles, a volume nearly

---

[223] Mitteis, *Reichsrecht und Volksrecht in den östlichen Provinzen des römischen Kaiserreichs* (1892), p. 30, declares that Bruns underrated the importance of the non-Roman elements in the Syrian Law Book.

[224] Degenkolb, *Karl Georg Bruns* (1881), p. 6.

[225] " Geschichte und Quellen des römischen Rechts," *Encyclopädie der Rechtswissenschaft,* 3d ed. (1877), pp. 77–129; " Das heutige römische Recht," *Ibid.,* pp. 333–477. In later editions the historical article is revised by Professor Pernice and the systematic article by Professor Eck, both of the Berlin University.

as large as Holland's *Jurisprudence*. They are not mere statements of the dominant views and theories: they present, in compact form, the results of original research by an investigator of exceptional insight and the conclusions of a singularly sane and well-balanced judgment. I know no better sketch of the development of Roman law than that which is given in the first of these articles. It is legal history in the strict sense, not culture history; but it is planned and written on broad lines. The second and longer article, on the modern Roman law, was greatly admired by Bruns's colleagues. Windscheid always urged his hearers to study it; Goldschmidt pronounced it " classic." [226] It is the universal side of Roman law that is emphasized throughout, and the article is more truly a book on general jurisprudence than many larger works that bear this title. I know no better exposition of private law from the Hegelian point of view.

VIII

The jurists whose work has been examined in the preceding papers of this series [227] confined themselves, in the main, to teaching and writing. Gneist's activities were more varied: he was at once professor, author, judge and politician, and in each of these callings he attained distinct eminence. He taught at the University of Berlin for forty-six years, and during this period his lectures were attended by nearly fifty thousand students.[228] He wrote almost as many books, pamphlets and articles as Bruns, Windscheid and Jhering together,[229] and his writings brought him recognition as the first publicist of Germany, if not of the Continent.[230] He

---

[226] *Zeitschrift für Handelsrecht*, vol. xxvi, p. 338.

[227] *Political Science Quarterly*, vol. x, p. 664; vol. xi, p. 278; vol. xii, p. 21.

[228] In 1886, when Gneist had completed his forty-seventh year of academic service, the records of the University showed that more than forty thousand students had subscribed for his courses. (Walcker, *Rudolph von Gneist*, p. 11.) In February, 1888, Gneist was appointed instructor of the present Emperor (then Prince) William in constitutional and administrative law.

[229] A list of the chief publications of each of the four jurists was given in *Political Science Quarterly*, vol. x, pp. 664, 665. *Supra*, pp. 110, 111.

[230] The esteem in which Gneist was held by his professional brethren is indicated by the fact that he was for twenty years president of the German Bar Association. — *Walcker*, p. 12.

held judicial office for nearly thirty years; he was a member during the last two decades of his life of the highest administrative court of Prussia; and during his last twelve years he sat also in the Prussian Privy Council. He took an active part in Prussian and German politics; he was a member, for more than thirty years, of the Prussian Chamber of Deputies and for seventeen years of the Imperial Diet also; and he was recognized as a leader of the right wing of the Liberal party.

Like Bruns, Windscheid and Jhering, Gneist began teaching and writing in the field of Roman private law. He offered the customary Romanistic courses at the University, and he published in 1845 a work, which is still regarded as valuable, upon " The Formal Contracts of Modern Roman Law."[231] But a lively interest in public problems and a strong desire to aid in solving them were already drawing him out of private life and away from private law. He belonged, both on the father's side and on the mother's,[232] to that official class which for more than a century had been the only political class in Prussia; and the conditions of the period (1840–48) were such as to excite political interest among all educated men. The rhetorical phrases of Frederick William IV upon his accession to the throne had fired the public imagination and had aroused hopes of the establishment of constitutional government. The acts and omissions of the king during the following eight years converted the elation of expectancy into the anger of disappointment. During these years Gneist added to his Romanistic courses lectures on criminal law and procedure, in no wise confining himself to the exposition of existing law, but insisting on the necessity of its reform: advocating, in particular, public and controversial as against secret and inquisitorial procedure, and decision by the verdict of an independent jury. These were,

---

[231] *Die formellen Verträge des neueren römischen Obligationenrechts.* In 1858 he published a pamphlet dealing with a special question in the same field, " De causae probatione stipulatoris," and also a Syntagma of the Institutes of Gaius and of Justinian.

[232] *Cf. Walcker*, pp. 9, 10.

at the time, political questions, and their discussion involved or, at least, facilitated the discussion of many other political questions.[233] Gneist's next publications were the outcome of these courses of lectures: they treated of duels and of juries.[234]

Immediately before the disturbances of 1848 and the establishment of constitutional government, Gneist entered political life at the only point then open, by seeking and obtaining election to the municipal assembly of Berlin. In 1848 and in 1849 he stood for election to the Prussian National Assembly and to its successor, the Prussian Chamber of Deputies; but in both cases he was defeated by the Radical candidate.[235] In the movements of 1848 and 1849 he accordingly participated only in the modest positions of municipal assemblyman and member of the civic militia, which, however, gave him opportunity to exercise a moderating influence at several decisive moments.[236] The only immediate literary result of these experiences was a description of the conditions that obtained in Berlin during the revolution.[237]

At this time, as indeed throughout his life, Gneist was a moderate Liberal. The central article of the Liberal program was the demand for constitutional government, which meant representative government created by popular elections, after the English fashion. But the imitation, in France and other European countries, of English parliamentary institutions had not yielded the desired and anticipated results. Wherever continental constitutionalism had established government by party, the outcome had been partisan government. Instead of securing the liberty of the individual, it had merely substituted for the arbitrary rule of the crown the equally ar-

[233] *Cf.* Bornhak, " Rudolph von Gneist," *Archiv für öffentliches Recht,* vol. xi, 2, p. i.

[234] *Der Zweikampf und die germanische Ehre,* 1848; *Bildung der Geschworenengerichte,* 1849.

[235] *Walcker,* p. 12; *Bornhak,* p ii. Gneist's statement that he declined a summons to the national assemblies of that time (*History of the English Constitution,* Author's Preface, p. iv), although it apparently refers to the years 1848 and 1849, must actually refer to the years immediately following.

[236] *Bornhak,* p. ii.

[237] *Berliner Zustände von März* 1848 *zu März* 1849.

bitrary rule of changing ministries. Instead of securing
peaceful progress, it seemed to beget an alternating series of
executive usurpations and popular revolutions. So now
again, in due course, the Revolution of 1848 was followed, in
France, by the *Coup d'État* and the Second Empire; in Prussia, by a period of reaction, guided and utilized by the landed
aristocracy. As long as these experiments and failures were
confined to Latin Europe, German writers were at no loss
for a theory that should exculpate constitutionalism; but
when similar phenomena revealed themselves in Germany, it
became clear that the constitutional theory must be re-
examined.

To this task Gneist addressed himself, withdrawing from
active political life [238] and abandoning his judicial career.[239]
As a pupil of Savigny and a faithful adherent of the historical
school, he of course went back of continental constitutionalism to its English prototype and proceeded to study the English constitution in its historical development. Some of the
preliminary results were given to the public in a paper read
before the Berlin Scientific Union in March, 1853, which was
expanded, by the addition of notes, into a pamphlet of a hundred pages, *Nobility and Gentry in England*.[240] At this time
Gneist had already convinced himself that the English constitution could not be comprehended or explained apart from
the English system of administration, and to the study of this
system he devoted the next three years of his life. Much of
this work he afterwards declared was like an excursion
through a primeval forest.[241] The administrative law was
the unknown part of the English law; in fact, the English

[238] He made no further attempt to enter political life until 1859. *Cf.
supra*, p. 217, note 235.

[239] His resignation of his judicial office in 1850 was primarily a protest
against the reactionary policy of the Prussian government. If it had not
been offered then, it certainly would have been offered later; for a man of
Gneist's character and opinions could not have submitted to the influence
which the administration exercised upon the judiciary during the period of
reaction (in 1850–1858) and the period of conflict (1862–1866). He re-
sumed his judicial career in 1875.

[240] *Adel und Ritterschaft in England.*

[241] *History of the English Constitution*, Preface, p. v; *Verwaltungsrecht*,
vol, ii, p. v.

lawyers had not even a name for it. English historians had not yet brought out the facts necessary to elucidate its development. Blackstone, a century before, had blazed a path into the wilderness, but Freeman and Stubbs had not yet cut roads, and Gneist was obliged to struggle through " the chaos of disconnected antiquarian matter piled up around Blackstone's commentaries," the English statutes and Parliamentary reports and the decisions of the English courts.[242] The result of these pioneer labors was Gneist's *magnum opus*, his *English Constitutional and Administrative Law*. It first appeared in two volumes, in 1857 and 1860, and was ultimately expanded into four volumes of nearly three thousand pages, published between 1871 and 1884.[243] Printed in the form in which our less rugged branch of the Teutonic family handles its solid literature, the number of pages and of volumes would be doubled.

Gneist claimed that he had solved the problem which he had undertaken to solve, that he had discovered why parliamentary government worked well in England and badly or

[242] *Ibid.; Verwaltung, Justiz, etc.,* Vorwort, p. 6; *Rechtsstaat,* pp. 258, 259.

[243] The first part of the work, " Geschichte und heutige Gestalt der Aemter in England," 1857, was expanded in 1867 into two volumes, entitled *Das englische Verwaltungsrecht,* of which the first volume gave the history and the second the modern law. This was again expanded into three volumes: *Englische Verfassungsgeschichte,* 1882, and *Das englische Verwaltungsrecht der Gegenwart,* Allgemeiner Theil, 1883; Besonderer Theil, 1884. *Das englische Parliament in seinen tausendjährigen Wandlungen,* 1886, covers to a large extent, but in a more popular way, the same field as the *Englische Verfassungsgeschichte.* Only these two historical volumes have been translated into English. The *History of the English Constitution,* translated by Ashworth, was published in two volumes in 1886 (2d ed., 1890). The *History of the English Parliament* has been twice translated, by Shee and by Keane, and each of these translations has run through several editions. Gneist read the proof of Keane's translation.

The second part of the original work, " Die heutige englische Communalverfassung und Communalverwaltung oder das System des Selfgovernment," 1860, was expanded in 1863 into two volumes, and appeared in its third and final edition in 1871 in one volume, under the title *Selfgovernment, Communalverfassung und Verwaltungsgerichte in England.* Of this part there is a French translation: *Constitution communale de l'Angleterre, traduit par Hippert,* 5 vols., 1868–1870.

A condensation of the entire treatise into an article (which, however, would make a very respectable English octavo volume) may be found in Holtzendorff's *Encyclopädie der Rechtswissenschaft* (5th ed., 1890), pp. 1377–1478.

not at all on the Continent. He found the solution, not wholly in the differences between the Teutonic and the Latin peoples, and not at all in any difference between the English and the German peoples, but in certain political and legal institutions which had been developed in England, but were lacking in Latin Europe and were only imperfectly developed in Germany. There were differences, he recognized, between the Teutonic and the Latin peoples, — differences which made the establishment of constitutional government among the latter more difficult, — but these differences, he believed, were largely the result of their different institutions. In its administrative and judicial institutions especially England had solved the chief problems of public law — " problems which had made Germany doubt and France despair " — as adequately as Rome had solved the chief problems of private law.[244] The trouble with continental constitutionalism was that English public law had been received only in part, and that the part which had been ignored was the necessary basis of the part that had been selected.

These convictions gave to Gneist's literary work, from 1857 on, a propagandist character. He did not advocate a general imitation of English institutions; he maintained that in many respects the Prussian institutions were better than the English. He did not advocate the simple transfer to his own country of any English institution, for he recognized that every nation must develop its policy along its own lines. He advocated the recognition and acceptance of the principles which he found embodied in certain English institutions and the development, in accordance with those principles, of equivalent Prussian and German institutions. In this way, he believed, it would be possible to organize a German constitutional state which should improve upon the English model. In the first edition of his *English Constitutional and Administrative Law* the missionary spirit was clearly discernible: he emphasized throughout the differences between English and continental institutions and the points in which

[244] *Verwaltung, Justiz, etc.*, p 3; *Verwaltungsrecht*, p. 4.

the former were superior. In the last edition of the *Administrative Law* he added to the title the words "in comparison with the German administrative systems." During the thirty-six intervening years he published several books and many pamphlets and articles which were simply longer or shorter tracts for the dissemination of sound constitutional theories. In 1864, in an article of a hundred pages on the *Representative System in England*,[245] he made a first attempt to popularize his views. In 1869 he published, for the benefit of the legal and official classes, an elaborate comparison between the English, French and German administrative and judicial systems; and since nearly every subsection on Prussian conditions concluded with suggestions *de lege ferenda*, the work presented a complete program of reform. In spite of its uncouth title, *Administration, Justice, Recourse to the Courts, Central Administration and Self-government*,[246] the book reached the classes for which it was written; and when, ten years later, Gneist assured us, his students, — not naïvely, but with an admirable detachment of his public from his private personality, — that this book had "made an epoch," he did not exaggerate its importance. Another attempt to influence German legal opinion was made by him in 1871, in an address of welcome delivered on behalf of the Berlin Juristic Society to the legal members of the first German Parliament. This address was published in 1872, under the title of the *Jural State*.[247] In special studies, moreover, regarding city and county government, public schools, taxation, the budget, the organization of the bar, judicial procedure and the powers of the courts,[248] — studies published,

---

[245] "Das Repräsentativsystem in England," in Haxthausen, *Das Constitutionelle Princip*, vol. ii, pp. 87–180.

[246] I translate only a part. The full title is: *Verwaltung, Justiz, Rechtsweg, Staatsverwaltung und Selbstverwaltung nach englischen und deutschen Verhältnissen.*

[247] *Der Rechtsstaat und die Verwaltungsgerichte in Deutschland.* A second enlarged edition appeared in 1879. There is an Italian translation by del Artom, *Lo Stato secondo il diritto*, 1885.

[248] For example: "Das englische Grundsteuersystem" (an advance instalment of his *Englische Communalverfassung*), 1859; *Soll der Richter auch über die Frage zu befinden haben, ob ein Gesetz verfassungsmässig zu Stande gekommen?* 1863; *Budget und Gesetz, nach dem konstitutionellen*

as a rule, when the topics treated were under legislative consideration, — Gneist drew upon the reservoir of political wisdom which he had found walled up within the English public law, and sent its vivifying waters trickling over the arid fields of the German *Polizeistaat*.

In this mass of scientific and controversial literature there is an amount of repetition that is very wearisome to the reader of to-day — repetition not only of facts and conclusions, which was inevitable under the circumstances, but of words and phrases also. Gneist, however, would have deemed it a waste of time to search for different ways of saying the same thing. If he found it necessary to describe again occurrences or tendencies which he had described before, he did it in the same words as before; and when he had settled on the phrase which to him best expressed a certain idea, he used it not only to the end of the chapter but to the end of his life. He was preaching to a nation a political gospel, line upon line, precept upon precept, and simple iteration deepened the impression without blurring it. No collection of his miscellaneous writings has been made, nor is it likely that posterity will demand one; but selections from these writings are preserved in condensed and imperative form in the laws of Prussia and in those of the German Empire.

The character of Gneist's writings makes it easy, in spite of their great volume, to disengage the principal political ideas which they contain; but to make these ideas completely intelligible to English or American readers it is necessary, in many cases, either to abandon Gneist's form of statement, at the risk of failing to give full expression to his thought, or to explain the peculiar sense which he attached to certain words and phrases — a sense so different from that in which we

---

Staatsrecht Englands, 1867; *Freie Advocatur, die erste Forderung aller Justizreform in Preussen*, 1867; *Die Selbstverwaltung der Volksschule*, 1869; *Die preussische Kreisordnung*, 1870; *Vier Fragen zur deutschen Strafprocessordnung*, 1874; *Ueber den Entwurf einer deutschen Strafprocessordnung*, 1876; *Zur Steuerreform in Preussen*, 1878; *Gesetz und Budget, constitutionelle Streitfragen aus der preussischen Ministerkrisis*, 1879; *Zur Verwaltungsreform und Rechtspflege in Preussen*, 1880; *Die preussische Finanzreform durch Regulirung der Germeindesteuern*, 1881.

commonly employ them as to make his language, to other than German readers, obscure or even misleading. When, for example, he described certain tendencies in a nation as " social," he did not mean that they made for the good of the nation, but the opposite: they were tendencies which we should describe as anti-social. Neither did he mean that they were socialistic; on the contrary, the tendencies which he reprehended as social were, in most cases, tendencies of the property-holding classes. Behind his use of the words " society " (*Gesellschaft*) and " social " (*gesellschaftlich*) lay a whole system of social philosophy.

This system was not of his own making. For a German, Gneist was not much of a philosopher. His aims were highly practical, and his close touch with life as a judge and a politician checked, in his case, that tendency to the overvaluation of abstract concepts which was so common in Germany in the nineteenth century. Regarding " philosophic constructions " in public law he occasionally used language as disrespectful as that employed by Jhering regarding similar constructions in private law. The constructions, however, which Gneist disliked were those of the older natural-law type. Constructions that were, or seemed to be, based upon " positive knowledge of things " [249] — constructions, especially, that were derived from the study of history — were as attractive to him as to the other members of the German historical school. In the writings of Lorenz Stein he found a social philosophy which appealed to him and which he thenceforth used. It was from Stein's point of view that he originally approached the study of English constitutional history, [250] and to the end of his life he expressed his political ideas in Stein's phrases.[251]

[249] *History of the English Constitution*, Preface, p. iv.
[250] *Cf. Adel und Ritterschaft*, p. 55; *Der Rechtsstaat*, p. 333; *History of the English Constitution*, Preface, p. iv. *Cf.* also Gneist's letter to Stein, published in Haimerl's *Oesterreichische Vierteljahresschrift für Rechts- und Staatswissenschaften*, vol. xviii, " Literaturblatt," p. 56.
[251] *Die nationale Rechtsidee von den Ständen und das preussische Dreiklassenwahlsystem*, 1894, *passim*. The English reader will find an elaborate restatement of Stein's theories in the first portion of Gneist's *English Parliament*.

For this reason, and also because of its intrinsic interest, Stein's system deserves a somewhat careful examination.

IX

Stein's social philosophy was elaborately set forth in 1850, in his *History of the Social Movement in France*,[252] a study of the French revolutions from 1789 to his own time. The value which the author attached to concepts is indicated by his remark that " the knowledge of human things differs from other knowledge in that the single facts have no value if they be not comprehended in the unity of a concept." [253] His concept of the state is thoroughly Hegelian: the state is " the community (*Gemeinschaft*) manifesting itself in its personality as will and act." [254] The state, however, is not the only form in which the community manifests itself; in its economic organization it possesses " an equally solid, equally vast and equally powerful organic unity," [255] and this unity is society (*Gesellschaft*). Stein's state and Stein's society are in perpetual conflict, because they represent opposing principles. The principle of the state is to secure the highest possible development — *i.e.*, the greatest possible wealth, power and intelligence — of all its individual members, because the degree of development attained by its members is the measure of the development attained by the state itself. The state must desire, further, that each of its members participate in forming its will, both on its own account, because the sum of human insight is always greater than the greatest insight of any individual, and on account of the individual, because of the educating and elevating influence of political liberty. The principle of the state, therefore, demands prog-

---

[252] *Geschichte der socialen Bewegung in Frankreich von 1789 bis auf unsere Zeiten.* The work consists of three volumes with separate titles: I. " Der Begriff der Gesellschaft und die sociale Geschichte der französischen Revolution bis zum Jahre 1830." II. " Die industrielle Gesellschaft: der Socialismus und Communismus Frankreichs von 1830 bis 1848." III. " Das Königthum, die Republik, und die Souveränetät der französischen Gesellschaft seit der Februarrevolution 1848." A second edition, from which I quote, was published in 1855.   [254] *Ibid.*, p. xv.
[253] *Begriff der Gesellschaft*, p. xii.   [255] *Ibid.*, p. xxviii.

ress through liberty towards equality; and in pure theory, as Stein recognized, the democratic republic is the ideal form of the state.[256]

Stein's society, *i.e.*, the community in its economic organization, exhibits tendencies precisely contrary to those of the state. Property, which is at once the product of labor and the basis of further production by labor, invariably concentrates itself in the hands of a part of the community; and those members of the community who have only labor power become dependent on those who have property. Family and inheritance perpetuate this inequality and divide society into more or less permanent classes; and the propertied class strives, more or less consciously, to perpetuate and increase its own power and the dependence of the laboring class. Class interest is the active principle of society, and its necessary tendency is through inequality toward the destruction of liberty.

What now is the course and what is the outcome of this conflict of tendencies, or, to use Stein's own language, of this antithesis of principles? As soon as we descend from the airy region of concepts and consider actual conditions, the field of conflict is shifted and the character of the conflict is changed. The conflict is not fought out between state and society; for the state, regarded as an organization independent of society, is "a pure concept." [257] No such state has ever existed. The actual state is always based on society, and it is always controlled by society. This control is inevitable, because the state can will and act only through individuals, and every individual brings with him into his activity as legislator or administrator the views and tendencies of his social class. More precisely, the control of the state by society is its control by the propertied class, because in this class is chiefly to be found the ability required for public office. This rule of the propertied class, however, is not inconsistent with the principle of the state. That principle

---

[256] *Das Königthum, die Republik, etc.*, pp. 133 *et seq.*
[257] *Begriff der Gesellschaft*, p. xlviii.

does not require the abolition of the social order, but only the effort to raise the dependent and unfree into independence and freedom. What is distinctly contrary to the principle of the state is the misuse of the power of the state by the propertied class to perpetuate the dependence of the laboring class and to make it impossible for members of that class to struggle up into the ruling class. To this misuse of political power, however, the ruling propertied class is always prone. It not only denies to those who have no property any active participation in the state, but it shapes law and administers government in its own interest.

Changes in the organization of the state, whether they are accomplished by reform or by revolution, are always the result of a want of correspondence between the political and the economic organization of the community. They are caused by the fact that those who have wealth, and are thus socially independent, are excluded from participation in the state. When the change is accomplished by revolution, the holders of new wealth commonly secure the aid of the laboring class by preaching liberty and equality; but in the end this class is excluded, as before, from political power. Without social (*i.e.*, economic) independence, political liberty is impossible.

In the actual world, accordingly, the conflict for liberty must be waged in society; and the prize aimed at must be, not liberty for all, which is unattainable, but the chance of liberty. The principle of the state shrinks to the modest demand that the possibility of acquiring property and influence in the state shall be kept open for the laboring and subject class. But how is even this end to be realized, when its realization involves the sacrifice, by the propertied and ruling class, of a part, at least, of its class interests? It is hinted, early in the discussion, that the solution is to be found in a principle higher than that of the state or that of society — in the principle of the community. In Stein's philosophy the community is the higher unity which comprehends both state and society; and while the tendency of the state is toward the independence of all its members, and that of society towards the dependence of the majority of its members, the principle of the community is the interdependence of all its members.[258] If labor is dependent on property, property in turn is dependent on labor. Property yields income only through the coöperation of labor. Harmonious coöperation cannot be secured if the members of the laboring class work without hope of bettering their position. It is, accordingly, in the interest of property that labor shall yield to the laborer something more than the mere necessities of existence. This higher interest, it must be admitted, is seldom recognized by the propertied class, because the immediate and obvious interest of this class lies in the exploitation of the laboring class. Its members, however, may be somewhat enlightened by agitation; and social reforms that are really in its own interest, as well as in that of the laboring class, may be carried through by legislation. This is where the state comes in again, and particularly the state with a king at it head. The hereditary king stands above society and is therefore in a better position than any other human being to conduct reform movements to a successful issue; and if the king undertakes this task, monarchy, even in a constitutional state, may preserve something of the substance of political power.[259]

Stein's society, the reader will note, is as pure a concept as his state. It is an abstraction, like the " economic man " ; it is, in fact, the sum of all the members of the community considered as economic beings. Such an abstraction is perfectly legitimate. It may be a useful counter in our social reckoning. Its usefulness, however, depends upon the way in which it is used. The use made by Stein of this particular abstraction is to discover the tendency of economic society. This society is studied in action, and particularly in its action upon the state. As soon, however, as its action is

[258] " Das für einander Vorhandensein der Einzelnen in der Vielheit ist die Gemeinschaft." — *Begriff der Gesellschaft*, p. xiv.

[259] *Begriff der Gesellschaft*, pp. xxxvii, xxxviii; *Das Königthum, die Republik, etc.*, pp. 45–49.

examined, we perceive that it is never the whole body that
acts: it is always a class, and usually the propertied class.
To term the interests and tendencies of this class "social"
is inexact and confusing, because it suggests that they are
the interests and tendencies of the entire body. Stein not
only does this, he goes further: he actually accepts this
self-suggestion. Because the chief interest of the dominant
propertied class, which is domination, tends to prevail over
the chief interest of the dependent laboring class, which is
independence, the interest of the former class, disguised
under the generic term "class interest," [260] is declared to
be "the active principle" of economic society; and the result of the conflicting interests and tendencies of the two
classes, *viz.*, the increasing dependence of the laboring class,
is declared to be the tendency of that society. In other
words, a tendency which manifests itself *in* economic society
is presented as a tendency *of* that society. This is hardly
worthy of a philosopher who has undertaken to comprehend
the facts of human life "in the unity of a concept," since it
is in fact from the duality of his concept [261] that his results
are derived.

This criticism, however, touches the form rather than
the essence of Stein's theory. Stripped of its philosophical
trappings, his theory gives us, primarily, an estimate of the
tendencies of man as an economic being acting in an economic
organization, *viz.*, the class. The theory, however, does

---

[260] *Cf. Begriff der Gesellschaft,* pp. xl, xli.

[261] It is singular that Stein should not have perceived that he was
using the word "society" in two senses, for the double meaning with which
he charged it involved him in contradictions. His society is distinguished
from his state in that the state is personal, while society is impersonal; in
that the state has a will, while society has none. But in one passage we are
told that both state and society "will definite ends" ("wollen ein Be-
stimmtes"—*Begriff der Gesellschaft,* p. xxxiii); and in another passage—
that in which the principle of society is first formulated (p. xxxviii)—the
question is put: "How can that which is impersonal have a principle of
action?" and this question is begged by the answer that society acts through
individuals. Stein here forgot that he had said the same of the state,—
that it acts only through individuals,—and he failed to answer the question he had just proposed, which was really: "How can the economic organization determine the direction of its action, *i.e.,* how can it will?" The
explanation of these contradictions is, of course, that when he speaks of society as willing or acting, he is thinking of the dominant class.

not stop here. It considers also the tendencies of man as a citizen, acting in the state; and it takes into account, however slightly and inadequately they are presented, the tendencies of man as a moral being, acting in the community. Finally, the theory indicates, not formally in any one passage but by assertion and implication in many passages, the resultant of all these different tendencies; and this is the triumph, all along the line, of the economic side of human nature. The propertied class, which is dominant not only in the economic organization of the community but also in its political organization, does not feel or think or act politically or morally, but always economically. It rules in the state but it does not consider the ends of the state. It is the only factor that counts in the community, but even as a portion of the community it is unaffected by sympathy or conscience or any other moral influence, except when the line of conduct supported by such feelings happens to coincide with its own ultimate interests. The theory assumes the prepotency of economic interests in determining the conduct of the individual, and derives from this assumption the supremacy of the interests of property in society, state and community.

Gneist constantly used Stein's phrases and never, to my knowledge, wrote or spoke of Stein's system with anything but approval; but he made significant additions which rendered his own system much less one-sided. To the political and economic organizations of the community he always added the ecclesiastical. The Christian church is a makeweight against the undue power of wealth; like the state, it makes for liberty and equality and resists the exploitation of the poor. It does this, at least, as long as it is true to its mission.[262] Like the state, the church is liable to be captured and controlled by society, *i.e.*, by property interests; but this is a pathological, not a normal, condition; and when

---

[262] *Rechtsstaat*, pp. 5–13; *Eigenart des preussischen Staats*, p. 6; *History of the English Constitution*, vol. i, pp. 84, 104; vol. ii, pp. 699, 700; *Stände und Wahlsystem*, pp. 15 *et seq.*

it occurs, there is likely to be a reformation.[263]   The same is true of the state; it is not normally controlled by property interests.   In Gneist's theory, as in Stein's, it is natural that the propertied classes shall rule in the state; but, according to Gneist, it does not follow that they shall rule the state itself, making its power subserve their economic interests. If they do this, there is likely to be a reassertion of the idea and of the power of the state.   In Gneist's system church and state stand over against society as independent factors, influenced indeed by the social basis on which they rest, but themselves influencing society and, in case of need, building their social bases anew.[264]   The church educates men to morality; the state trains them to political consciousness.   Both deal, in their work, with instincts quite as deeply rooted in human nature as are the economic instincts.   Gneist's writings differ greatly from Stein's in the value ascribed to duty as a motive.   In Stein's book moral considerations are rarely mentioned; and when they are mentioned, they are presented as the cloak of class interests. To Gneist, duty was as imperative as it was to his countryman Kant, and he assumed that it appealed in a similar way to his fellows.[265]

There are other points of difference on which I can only touch.   In Stein's system, no special place is made for the educated class.   " Spiritual goods " are recognized, but they are treated merely as means for obtaining material goods; and it is assumed that, as soon as the clergy and the other professional classes acquire property, their sentiments and tendencies become substantially identical with those of landholders and capitalists.   In Gneist's writings, much greater

---

[263] Gneist accounted for the Protestant Reformation in this way. — *Rechtsstaat*, p. 100; *Eigenart des preussischen Staats*, pp 8, 9; *Stände und Wahlsytem*, pp. 46 *et seq.*, 174 *et seq.*

[264] See, especially, *Stände und Wahlsystem*, pp. 15, 170.

[265] " In the coarsest man, deep sunk in selfishness and materialism, we often see an unexpected awakening of sympathy and conscience and a return to the fulfillment of human duties. — *Rechtsstaat*, p. 328.   *Cf. Stände und Wahlsystem*, pp. 12–16.   When Freund (*Thaten und Namen*, p. 20) asserts that Gneist regards men as slaves of purely egoistic motives, he is misled by Gneist's uncritical use of Stein's phrases.

importance is attached to the educated class. Not only is the clergy treated as something more and something other than a section of the propertied class, but the same view is taken of the professional officials of the state and of the professional classes generally. Finally, while there are in Stein's system but two really important classes, the Haves and Have-nots, in Gneist's books there is discernible, between wealth and poverty, a middle class, and to this class is attached something of the importance usually attributed to it by writers on politics.

X

Of all the additions which Gneist made to Stein's theory, that on which he most insisted is the power of the state to make men political — to imbue them, as he expressed it, with the " consciousness of the state " or, more simply, with " practical knowledge of the state and the right feeling for it." [266] It is able to do this by holding them to the personal performance of public duties. If it so shapes its institutions as to draw into its service all of its citizens who are capable of serving it, it will succeed in educating to its ends not individuals only but whole classes. If it distributes the burdens of its service according to the capacity of its citizens to bear them, the heaviest burdens will fall upon property. If it gives political power to those who bear its burdens in proportion to the burdens borne, it will intrust governmental authority chiefly to the propertied classes. These, however, under such a system, do not rule as propertied classes; they rule by right of service.[267] They may misuse their power, at times, to promote the interests of

---

[266] *History of the English Constitution*, vol. ii, p. 438.

[267] According to Gneist, the propertied classes have never obtained power in the state by their wealth merely, nor even by the superior intelligence that is commonly associated with wealth. They have always had to earn power by service, and ordinarily they have served for generations before their position in the state has obtained legal recognition. They may indeed retain the power thus acquired for generations after they have ceased to serve; but sooner or later the state will be so reconstructed as again to apportion power according to service, rights according to duties. *Cf. Eigenart des preussischen Staats*, p. 14.

the classes to which they belong, but they will not do so in the long run, for by the habitual performance of public duties they are trained to " right feeling." This is Gneist's " harmony of state and society " ; and this, and not conflict, is the normal relation between his society and his state.

It follows that social classes are. not, as Stein maintained, purely economic products. In harnessing them into its service the state modifies not merely their instincts and aims, but their structure. In England, for example, as Gneist pointed out in his first work on English constitutional development,[268] the country gentry and the burgesses were brought together by the state into a single class, the Commons; and this he pronounced the most striking event in English history. The organization of society by the state and for the state is not only possible, it is necessary; and the chief problem of the modern state is to find the proper organization (*Ordnung*) of modern industrial society.

It follows, again, that in a properly organized state parties are not social, as Stein regarded them, but political; that they do not represent conflicting class interests, but divergent views concerning public policy. The appearance of purely social parties is a symptom of disease in the body politic; it indicates the necessity, to use Gneist's own phrase, of a " recombination (*Wiederverbindung*) of state and society," *i.e.*, a readjustment of services and powers, duties and rights.

As a means of educating men to right views of the state and the right feeling for it, nothing, in Gneist's opinion, can take the place of habitual personal service [269] — not the press, nor meetings, nor any other expression of so-called public opinion, nor even frequent elections. The press can only reproduce and emphasize, for each social class or group, its own thoughts, which are the expression of its own interests. Public meetings bring together only those who are already

---

[268] *Adel und Ritterschaft*, pp. 32–34.

[269] " For the individual who confronts the state without responsible and personal activity in the service, the ego is the central point of the commonwealth. The existence of coördinate rights, views and interests is ignored." —*Verwaltung, Justiz, etc.*, p. 115.

in sympathy and agreement.[270] In a community untrained
by public service, what is called public opinion is only class
opinion; there is no public opinion. A semblance of public
opinion may be created by concealing inconsistent views
and divergent tendencies under platform phrases; [271] but
when the attempt is made to translate these phrases into
facts, it becomes evident that they represent no " energetic
total will." [272] Voting has no intrinsic educational value:
" never in all the centuries have mere elections produced
political sense or capacity for public activity." [273] Election
is essentially a social device, a method by which groups of
men associated for common purposes find agents to do their
will. It is the method, for example, by which the
joint-stock company organizes itself and obtains officers. To
the citizen whose public activity is confined to paying taxes
and voting at elections, the state may well seem a larger
joint-stock company. There is nothing in the mere process
of voting

to enlighten men as to the difference between voluntary
associations and political unions — between associations for
what one can do and wishes to do, and unions for what one
ought to do and must do. . . . For every people that is
relieved of the burdens of direct and personal public activity,
there is an empty space between the state and the individual — a void that is not to be filled by the reflection of
individuals, nor by the interchange of thoughts in speech or
writing, nor by the combination of these thoughts into
philosophic systems.[274]

What Gneist most admired in the English polity and was
most eager to see imitated in his own country was the way
in which England had utilized the services of the propertied
classes in country and local government: the landed gentry
acting as county magistrates, the yeomen and burgesses

[270] *Ibid.*, p. 60.
[271] *Ibid.*, *Vorwort*, p. vii; *Repräsentativsystem*, p. 166; *Rechtsstaat*,
pp. 241, 245.
[272] *Repräsentativsystem*, p. 158.
[273] *Ibid.*, p. 161.
[274] *Ibid.*, p. 160.

serving on juries and filling the parish offices and both meeting periodically at quarter sessions. The administration which they conducted — as it existed in the days before the first Reform Bill and still exists in part — Gneist termed " self-government," because the officials were not sent in by the central government but were selected from among the people of the locality, and because they did their work in an independent way with little intervention on the part of the ordinary courts and no interference on the part of the the central administration. He was careful not to describe the system as " local " self-government, for he was especially anxious to have it understood that the functions intrusted to it were not solely or even mainly local. English self-government, he insisted, had never been anything but a branch of the general adminstration of the state.

The county, borough and parish authorities are not empowered to develop and shape a local militia system, a local administration of justice, a local poor relief and local taxes, according to their own judgment and the local interests: all that they do is to discharge as officers and organs of the state the duties of the state as determined by law.[275]

Logically accordant, in Gneist's view, with this relation was the fact that the authorities of county and parish government were appointed, not elected; that the acceptance of office was compulsory, and that service was unpaid. All classes served the state according to the measure of their capacity because it was their duty. In the " honorary office " (*Ehrenamt*) Gneist saw the fullest and final expression of the just relation between wealth and service and between service and power. Election and voluntary and paid service were to him " social principles " ; appointment and compulsory and unpaid service, political principles.

Gneist admired English self-government, further, because it was government according to law and thus constituted the firm substructure of the " jural state." Bit by bit, as he

[275] *Repräsentativsystem*, p. 153.

pointed out, all the details of local administration that were capable of legal regulation had been regulated by acts of Parliament, until by the patient labor of centuries England had obtained the most complete and most minutely detailed administrative law in the world. Hand in hand with this development went the transformation of the local offices into " jurisdictions." As the duties of the county authorities came to consist more and more in the application of written laws, these authorities became more and more judicial in their character. As police magistrates, the justices of the peace were judicial officers from the outset; but they were also charged with many administrative duties. In the discharge of these duties, in so far at least as their discharge affected the private rights of individuals, the procedure of the justices was surrounded more and more with the guaranties of judicial procedure: it was made formal, public and controversial. The most important result of this transformation was the protection of the individual against the misuse of administrative power; but a secondary result was an increase in the educational efficacy of self-government. All public service is of educational value, but the highest value attaches to service in the administration of the law, whether as juror or justice, because such service develops the sense of fair play.[276]

[276] Some of Gneist's German critics have accused him of idealizing the English justices of the peace — of ascribing to them a freedom from class prejudice and a spirit of fairness which they did not possess. They have cited statements made by English writers, conveying a much less favourable judgment regarding these magistrates. *Cf. Bornhak*, p. xvii, citing Macaulay; also Freund, *Thaten und Namen*, p. 16, note 2. Gneist, however, instituted no comparison, as do these writers, between the English justices of the peace and the salaried professional judges either of England or of other countries. He compared their administration of police justice, from the fourteenth century to the nineteenth, with the manorial jurisdiction exercised simultaneously by the great landed proprietors on the continent, and he found it incomparably fairer and less oppressive. He compared them as administrators with the paid officials who conducted the local administration in France and in Germany in the eighteenth and nineteenth centuries, and he conceded that they did not always do their work as efficiently; but this disadvantage was more than counterbalanced, in his opinion, by their independence, which made it difficult to use them as instruments of party policy. He compared, above all, the class to which they belonged with the landed aristocracies of France and Germany; and he found in the English gentry a sympathy with other classes, both in country and in town, a desire

In all administration there is necessarily a wide field of discretion; and not all the functions intrusted to English county and parish authorities were susceptible of detailed legal regulation. In English self-government guaranties against the abuse of discretionary powers were sought (and, as Gneist believed, found) in the social position of the justices of the peace, in the sense of fairness developed in what was practically a life tenure of a quasi-judicial position and in the principle of joint action in all matters of importance.

The result of this whole development was decentralization of the most admirable sort: not decentralization of legislation, which is autonomy, but decentralization of administration. Under the laws enacted by Parliament and interpreted by the ordinary courts, English county and local government was practically self-controlling. The ordinary courts retained jurisdiction in questions of law; but in questions of fact and in matters of discretion the decisions of the justices of the peace in quarter sessions were final. The crown and its ministers ceased to interfere at all with the course of county and local administration, and Parliament ceased to intervene otherwise than by legislation. The local independence thus established was historically the result of the fact that the county authorities were socially independent by reason of their rank and wealth, and politically independent because they received no pay. The man who works without pay will commonly work in his own way or not at all. To these elements of strength must be added what Gneist called the "collegial" organization of the justices of the peace, *i.e.*, their constant association with each other at sessions and in boards, and the resultant *esprit de corps*.

It was on this system of self-government, as Gneist constantly insisted, that the whole parliamentary system of

---

for even-handed justice to all, high and low, a respect for law and a sense of duty to the community, which he did not find developed to anything like the same degree among the seigneurs of France or the Junkers of Prussia.

government in England rested. Representation in Parliament was not granted to persons inhabiting a certain arbitrarily defined district; it was granted to neighborhoods organized for self-government. Parliamentary suffrage was not given to individuals as a natural right; it was given to those who discharged political duties. It was not given to property as such; the possession of property imposed duties of service, and the duty of service carried with it electoral right. Constituencies associated in self-government and educated by continual personal service, members of Parliament trained for the state by lifelong service in honorary offices, a people fitted for self-government in gross by self-government in detail — these were the elements that made parliamentary government possible; and parliamentary government, which is of course party government, was shielded against the sins which most easily beset it by the fact that the whole sphere of internal government was practically removed from ministerial control. These views of the character and the significance of English self-government so pervade all Gneist's writings that any selection of particular citations is at once difficult and unnecessary. One striking passage, however, deserves notice.

In the English administrative organism it is the intermediate structure of self-government which gives to the whole tension and life and to the single parts political independence. As it proceeded out of absolutism, so English administration would revert to the absolute form if the activity of the higher and middle classes in the self-administration of state functions should be brought to an end. After taking out this intermediate structure nothing would be left but a bureaucratized police-state.[277]

[277] *Verwaltung, Justiz, etc.*, p. 91. It may be noted that Gneist attributed the capacity of the American people for self-government to the institutions which the colonists brought with them from England, and particularly to the fact that American administration is so largely conducted by the people and not turned over to professional officials. Of our political capacity Gneist had a high opinion, founded largely, as he once told me, on his observation of his American students in the fifties. At that time he had in his lectures a considerable number of students from the South as well as from the North, and he repeatedly contrived to get them together at his own

The changes in this system that began in 1832 with the
first Reform Bill and have continued to our day were, in
Gneist's opinion, ill-advised and unfortunate. He recognized
fully that the accumulation of new wealth unrepresented in
Parliament necessitated a reform of the suffrage, but he disapproved of the innovation by which suffrage was made to
depend upon a naked property qualification, without corresponding duties of personal service.[278] He recognized
fully that some parts of the English internal administration
had worked badly; but he believed that the defects could
have been remedied without abandoning the principle of the
compulsory unpaid services of the propertied classes. The
occupation of the field of local government by a host of
professional paid officials and the extension of central administrative control that accompanied this invasion, meant
to him the passing of that old England that he admired.
The collection of men untrained by personal service into
elected councils which had only appointing, tax-voting and
supervisory functions, and which could not intelligently exercise the latter functions because of their lack of practical
experience — this was to him not self-government. The
movement seemed to him an overrunning of the state by
society.[279]

---

house and to set them to discussing the slavery question. In these discussions he was much struck by the fairness and good temper shown on
both sides. In his later writings he expressed a less favorable judgment regarding the development of our institutions.

[278] He believed that the difficult problem of the suffrage — a problem
especially difficult in the cities — could have been solved by introducing the
Prussian three-class system, making the members of the first two classes
(those who pay two-thirds of the total direct taxes) liable not only to jury
duty but to compulsory service in " honorary offices," and causing the members of the third class to elect representatives who should be charged with jury
duty and bound to accept communal offices. Suffrage, according to his suggestion, should then be given to all the members of the first two classes and to
the elected representatives of the third. (*Verwaltung, Justiz, etc.*, pp. 124,
125.) He also proposed the modification in the same sense of the three-class
system in Prussia — a system which he disliked because it made suffrage independent of service and distributed voting power simply according to the
amount of taxes paid. (*Ibid.*, p. 131.) He came back to this subject twenty-
five years later in his *Stände und Wahlsystem.*

[279] For a study of both the old system and the new, *cf.* Goodnow,
" Local Government in England " and " The English Local Government
Bill," *Political Science Quarterly,* vol. ii, p. 638; vol. iii, p. 311. For Gneist's
latest utterances on the subject, see *Stände und Wahlsystem,* pp. 149–169.

With the political philosophy which was developed to justify and further these changes he had no patience. Instead of basing power on service and regarding all political powers as duties, *i.e.*, as trusts, it treated these powers, suffrage and eligibility to office alike, as human rights based upon interests. The only logical outcome of this view, he declared, was universal suffrage — not manhood suffrage merely, but a vote, personally or through a guardian, for every man, woman and child in the nation, not excluding lunatics, paupers and criminals, since all of these had interests to protect. The interests of the inmates of asylums, workhouses and prisons, he dryly added, were of all the most urgent, because most directly affected by government. Gneist found the fullest and most lucid expression of the new political philosophy in Mill's *Representative Government,* and in criticising this book he clearly formulated his own antagonistic views.[280] He maintained that the only logical outcome of Mill's theories was the Napoleonic constitution, and that this was " the universal constitutional idea of the new industrial society." [281]

Gneist was not the only person of his generation who had found the chief defect of continental constitutionalism in the centralization of governmental power. De Tocqueville had expressed similar views and had urged decentralization, and so had other writers in other countries. But Gneist was the first to set forth the true character of English self-government and to show clearly what it was not: not local autonomy, which dissolves the state into a multitude of petty republics; not a descending series of provincial, departmental and local councils, equally incapable of conducting administration and of exercising any real control over the current administration conducted by professional officials; not manorial jurisdiction, associated with landed property. All these arrangements had been called self-government, and their respective advocates had imagined that their systems were

---

[280] First in *Repräsentativsystem,* pp. 160, 161; more fully in *Verwaltung, Justiz, etc.,* pp. 52–60.
[281] *Ibid.,* p. 60.

at least akin to the English. Gneist's writings, Bornhak [282] tells us, put a stop to all these partisan appeals to English precedents.

XI

What Gneist really thought of parliamentary government as developed in England, whether he considered it on the whole a good thing or a bad thing, is to be read rather between the lines of his writings than in the form of direct statement.[283] He attributed the establishment of parliamentary government to the folly of the Stuarts, and he would probably have assented to the statement that, if England had possessed, during the last three centuries, a dynasty as capable and intelligent as the Hohenzollerns, parliamentary government would have been neither possible nor desirable.

That he did not desire the establishment of parliamentary government in Prussia or in Germany until a thorough system of self-government in the localities should have trained the people for public life, is made clear in all his writings. His experience in public life could have led him to no other view. Germany has not yet developed the first requisite for party government; it has no parties. It has only fractions, which often dissolve and recombine like the color in a kaleidoscope. The instinct for party organization and the recognition of the necessity of party discipline are almost wholly wanting.[284] He would doubtless have conceded that the organization of strong parties, capable of assuming rule, could not be expected until there should be a prospect that, if organized, they would have a chance to rule; but he would

---

[282] *Loc. cit.*, pp. iv, v, vi.

[283] A fair statement of the advantages and disadvantages of parliamentary government is to be found in Gneist's article in *Holtzendorff*, pp. 1454–1456.

[284] Of this defect Gneist was at times irritably conscious. During the passage through the Imperial Diet of the protective Tariff Bill of 1879, I asked him one evening how his party had voted that afternoon on the second reading of the measure. "Fifty-one for and fifty against," he replied, and added: "That is a pretty party. The hundred might as well have hired cabs and driven about the *Thiergarten*."

still have insisted that the parties would be social, rather than political, until self-government in the localities had done its perfect work.

Gneist's assertion that parliamentary government was impracticable without self-government in the localities did not, however, by any means imply that he regarded parliamentary government as even a distant goal of Liberal effort in his own country.[285] Many of his utterances indicate, on the contrary, that he assigned to monarchy permanent political functions. Like Lorenz Stein, he pronounced hereditary monarchy the purest expression of the state, because it raises the state above society. History, in his interpretation, shows that the bases of free states have always been laid by lawgivers invested with dictatorial or monarchic powers. It was so in the ancient world; it was so again in mediæval Europe. It by no means follows, however, that after the bases of the state have been established monarchy becomes superfluous. Great changes in the distribution of wealth and the resultant rearrangement of the social classes will always necessitate the readjustment of political and social relations, the "recombination of state and society." An elective assembly cannot do this work, for elective assemblies, particularly at such periods, represent interests; and the state cannot be built on a basis of interests: it must always be reconstructed, as it was originally constructed, on the basis of duties. The Norman monarchy laid the foundations of the English free state; the Parliaments of the nineteenth century undermined them. Prussian monarchy not only built the old Prussian state, but it also laid, in 1808, the bases for the new Prussia and the new Germany. It was to the Prussian monarchy that Gneist looked for the realization of his program of political reforms, because this program required the imposition of duties from which society would shrink; and it was the Prussian monarchy, as he after-

---

[285] He went furthest in his *Stände und Wahlsystem*, p. 271, claiming that the reformed Prussia possesses the firm bases "on which a House of Commons may develop into the highest council of the crown with a position of increasing power." This, however, does not mean parliamentary supremacy.

wards declared, that had carried these reforms to a successful issue.[286]

One reason why Gneist had comparatively little to say
regarding the question here raised — the question which
exists in republics, as well as in monarchies, and which we
usually describe to-day as that of the relative superiority of
presidential, as compared with cabinet, government — was
doubtless that many of his friends in the Liberal party in
fact looked forward (as Bismarck always said they did)
to the establishment of parliamentary control over the crown,
not merely in legislation and in finance but in every branch
of administration, and that Gneist, as a good politician, desired to live, so far as possible, in harmony with his party
associates. As it was, he was quite at odds with most of
them concerning the financial powers of Parliament and the
doctrine of ministerial responsibility. To them the power
of the legislature to vote appropriations seemed a power to
prevent the government from spending a penny of revenue
without the authorization of the legislature and a means
of making the ministers responsible to the legislature.
Gneist showed, again and again, that the English House
of Commons, in making appropriations, had never attempted
to deal with anything more than a certain " mobile part "
of the governmental expenditures; that expenditures authorized by law must be made, according to the English
theory, until the law was changed; and that the refusal of
subsidies to a mediæval king was a very different thing
from an attempt to bring all the necessary work of the
modern state to a standstill.[287] He drew a sharp distinction between the political responsibility of ministers to the
legislature, which meant that system of parliamentary
government for which neither Germany nor Prussia was prepared, and their legal responsibility, which meant that they

[286] *Cf. History of the English Constitution,* vol. i, p.16; *Repräsentativsystem,* p. 158; " Eigenart des preussischen Staats, *passim;* " *Rechtsstaat,*
pp. 278, 279; *Holtzendorff,* p. 1465.

[287] *Budget und Gesetz,* 1867; *Gesetz und Budget,* 1879; *Rechtstaat,* p. 343.

ought to be amenable to legal procedure in case they should violate the law.

The chief reason, however, for Gneist's relative silence regarding the abstract desirability of parliamentary government was, doubtless, that constitutional problems were to him of less interest than administrative problems. To him, as to many jurists, political liberty seemed less important than legal liberty, *i.e.*, the protection of the personal and property rights of the individual. These forms of liberty, of course, are not only distinct in theory, they are also separable in fact. Legal liberty may be effectively protected under governments of the absolute type, as was the case under the Antonines in the second century and under the Hohenzollerns in the eighteenth; it may, on the other hand, be trampled under foot by governments as popular in their constitution as was that of the French Convention. Legal liberty, as Gneist was never weary of insisting, is a thing that depends mainly on the kind and degree of control to which the administration is subjected, because the chief points of collision between government and private interests occur in the field of administration. The control must in first instance be legal, *i.e.*, the law must declare what the officers of administration may do and what they may not do. It must in second instance be judicial. The most admirably devised bills of rights will be vain things, and even detailed legal provisions intended to carry out the principles formulated in such bills of rights will be of uncertain efficacy, if the interpretation and enforcement of the law is left to administrative officers acting simply as administrative officers. The interpretation and enforcement of the law must be intrusted to authorities whose position and tenure make them independent of the administration and whose forms of procedure and decision are judicial. The ordinary courts, if properly constituted, are of course such authorities; but they are not the only possible authorities of the kind. Officers of the administration who are intrusted with judicial functions, whose procedure is judicial in its form and who enjoy the same independence against the central administration that is conferred upon the ordinary courts, become judicial officers, and permanent boards composed of such officers, become courts. To what extent the interpretation of the law shall be left with the ordinary courts, to what extent it shall be intrusted to administrative courts — in other words, just how the judicial control of the administration shall be divided between these two classes of courts — is a secondary question, a question in the main of expediency.[288] The chief thing is that the courts, whether ordinary or administrative, shall be really independent, and that they shall be intrusted with the powers necessary to protect individual rights against administrative power. Any state in which the rights of the individual are thus safeguarded against the administration by proper laws, interpreted and enforced by independent judicial authorities, is what Gneist calls a " jural state."

To us, on this side of the ocean, it seems that we have gone a step further. The jural state protects the individual against the misuse of administrative power; our constitutional state (a term to which we have given an entirely new meaning) seeks to protect the individual against the misuse of legislative power. Gneist, however, thought that this devise of ours — safeguarding private rights by constitutional provisions and intrusting the enforcement of these provisions to the courts — was indeed a fair substitute for the conservative influences of monarchy and aristocracy, but that the inflexibility of our constitutional law unduly hampered legislation.[289]

The state that is not jural — the state in which, on the contrary, the protection of private rights is subordinated to considerations of public policy — is termed by Gneist " welfare-state." Of this sort of state he found a typical

---

[288] *Cf.* Goodnow, " The Executive and the Courts," *Political Science Quarterly*, vol. i, p. 533.
[289] *Soll der Richter, etc.*, p. 23.

example in France. The French failure to realize the jural
state was ascribed by him in part to the national temper.
When a great public end is to be gained, it is hard for a
Frenchman to understand why such little things as private
rights should be regarded, or why the courts should be permitted to impede the realization of the general will and the
promotion of the general welfare. In this they are true to
the Latin tradition which has always subjected *iurisdictio*
to *imperium*.[290] The French point of view, however, is not
peculiar to France; it is the natural social point of view.
It is shared by every society that has not been educated
by personal service to political consciousness. The French
temper is largely ascribable to the defective character of
French institutions, and the defects in these institutions are
explained by the history of the French state. The French
monarchy did not harness the ruling classes of the feudal
period into the service of the state. It did not impose
upon them governmental duties, but simply thrust them
aside or bought them off with privileges; and it secured
the performance of the necessary functions of the state by
hiring soldiers, judges and administrators. In restoring
and perfecting the administrative system of the old monarchy, Napoleon acted completely in accordance with the
will of the sovereign people, who knew no other mode of
governing.[291] When, in the nineteenth century, the attempt
was made to combine parliamentary government with this
bureaucratic administration, private rights were exposed to
greater perils than had menaced them under the old monarchy or under the dictatorship of Napoleon. The power
of the centralized administration began to be used, not simply
to carry out the purposes of the state, but to further the interests of parties, to reward the faithful, to punish the dis-
affected and, above all, to carry elections. For the protection
of private rights France possessed, indeed, a highly developed
system of courts. Even under the Second Empire, the or-

---

[290] *Verwaltung, Justiz, etc.*, p. 180.
[291] *Verwaltung, Justiz, etc.*, p. 181.

dinary courts were apparently independent of the administration, since the tenure and pay of the judges were secured
by law; but the administration placed these judges where
it pleased, transferred them, not simply from one court to
another, but also from one section or chamber to another,
and thus controlled the composition of the chambers by
which special classes of cases were tried. In criminal procedure, moreover, where conflicts between private rights
and public or party interests occur more frequently than in
civil procedure, prosecution was in the hands of officials
appointed and removed by the government; the preliminary investigation was conducted by a judge designated by
the government; the bench that tried the accused was a
bench constructed by the government, and the jury was a
" committee of persons enjoying the confidence of the prefect." Certain precedents and considerations of decency
restrained the government in the use of its power over the
judiciary, but it was precisely when the abuse of this power
was most dangerous that these safeguards became ineffective.[292]

The French administrative courts are admirably devised
" to secure continuity of practice in the administrative field."
They afford also a high degree of protection to property
rights. In the Council of State, which is the highest administrative tribunal, the forms of judicial determination are
scrupulously observed. The personnel, however, of the administrative courts and the composition of the section of the
Council of State by which controversies are decided are controlled by the ministry. In opposition to England practice,
it is, moreover, the administration that raises all questions of
competence between the civil and the administrative courts:
cases are not removed from the administrative jurisdiction

[292] *Verwaltung, Justiz, etc.*, pp. 181, 182. Gneist's criticism of the
French judicial system was well founded for the Second Empire; but the
conditions were not so bad between 1820 and 1852, and in the present
republic the courts and the juries have again been made independent of the
administration. *Cf.* Flourens, *Organisation judiciare et administrative de la
France*, 1814–1875.

to the ordinary courts, but *vice versa*. Jurisdiction in questions of public law is almost wholly withdrawn from the ordinary courts and vested in the administrative courts. All this is in accordance with the principle of the separation of powers and secures " the independence of the executive branch." But the independence thus secured is practically supremacy.[293] The chief defect, however, in the French polity, as Gneist always insisted, is the lack, in the localities, of that self-government which not only makes internal administration independent of changing majorities and ministries but also trains the people to the right feeling for the state.[294]

Gneist's categories of the jural and the welfare state may be criticised on the ground that the distinction which they represent is not absolute, but relative. Every civilized state is more or less jural, and every civilized state is more or less a welfare state: the difference between the two classes consists in the predominance of one or the other tendency. In his distinction there is, nevertheless, an element of universal and permanent truth. If we substitute for his jural state our constitutional state, which to us is simply his jural state raised to a higher power, his welfare state remains the expression of the opposite tendency; and the chief problem which the rule of our insular territories has forced upon us may be expressed in the terms of this antithesis. We are face to face with the question whether we, like the Romans, shall subordinate law-finding to empire. Fortunately for us, the decision, which is not yet rendered, rests not with the administration nor with Congress, but in the first instance with our highest court of justice and in the second instance with a people who, if Gneist's judgment was not mistaken, possess in a fair degree the jural consciousness.

[293] *Verwaltung, Justiz, etc.*, pp. 182–184.

[294] *Cf. Rechtsstaat*, pp. 158–190. The decentralizing movement which was under way when Gneist published the second edition of the *Rechtsstaat*, and which has since been carried further, has not established what Gneist called self-government. The existing French system resembles that newer system of English local government which he regarded as an abandonment of self-government.

XII

In 1859 Gneist reëntered active political life as a member of the Prussian Chamber of Deputies, and in 1867 he became a member of the newly created Imperial Diet also. Reëlected with unfailing regularity for many years to both bodies, he was henceforth in a position to urge more effectively the reforms he had at heart. During the first seven years of his parliamentary life, however, the Prussian government and the deputies were not in such harmony as to make reform legislation possible. It was a time of internal conflict, during which the king reorganized the Prussian army in defiance of a hostile majority in the Chamber, and his ministry collected and disbursed the revenues of the state without parliamentary authorization. It was also a time of external conflict, during which the German question was solved by the expulsion of Austria from the German confederation and the establishment of a new federal state under Prussian hegemony. In the internal conflict Gneist took an active part, opposing as resolutely as any of his Liberal associates the unconstitutional acts of the ministry, but filing from time to time separate dissenting opinions, in the form of speeches and pamphlets, to explain the grounds of his opposition. He did not fully share, as we have seen, the prevailing Liberal opinions regarding the financial powers of a parliamentary body; and he preferred to base his opposition to the ministry on the ground that in enlarging the army without the consent of the Chamber they were modifying by ordinance the conditions established by law. When Bismarck solved the German question, — a result at which Gneist was as much surprised as any of his Liberal associates,— Gneist went with the more moderate portion of his party into the new National Liberal party, which accepted Bismarck's generous terms of peace and acted in general concert with him for the next twelve years. Much as he came to admire the great chancellor, Gneist could never quite forget the bitterness of the years of conflict:

and he always maintained — I have heard him assert it
in the lecture room — that Bismarck solved the German
question only because, in his contest with the Prussian
Chamber, he had been forced into an *impasse* from which
nothing but a successful foreign war could extricate him.

With the termination of the conflict and the establishment
of harmonious relations between the Liberals and the
government began a period of great legislative activity,
in which Gneist took an important and, in some instances, a
decisive part. His chief aim, of course, was the reform
of Prussian local government. This problem was simplified,
in his view, by the fact that the leading principles of self-
government, as he understood them, had already been introduced into the government of the Prussian cities by the
famous ordinance of 1808. Its author, Baron Stein, was
himself familiar with English local government and had
appreciated its essential features; and in the ordinance of
1808 he had given the cities an independent administration
based on the compulsory and unpaid service of non-professional officials. The problem, in Gneist's opinion, was,
therefore, to extend Stein's system of city government, with
such modifications as might be required, to the open country.
At the outset, however, hardly any one else viewed the matter in this way. Every one was in favor of self-government in the localities, but there were great differences of
opinion as to the meaning to be attached to the phrase.
The Conservative party demanded the maintenance and
extension of the manorial police system, which still survived in the eastern provinces. The Liberals generally desired the maintenance of professional service under a popular control, to be exercised by elected councils of the French
type. The Prussian bureaucrats themselves desired to go
on governing with much less interference on the part of the
ministry. Gneist, however, found as early as 1868 a supporter whose single voice was easily worth the opinion of
any one of these groups — the Prussian minister president.
A memorial drafted by Gneist in the summer of that year

was presented by Bismarck to the ministry; [295] and although at the outset Gneist's plans found no other supporter, a bill abolishing manorial jurisdiction and creating a system of what we should call county and local government was gradually worked out, and this bill, after three years of discussion, became law in 1872.[296] It was first put into force in the eastern provinces of Prussia and then gradually extended with modifications to other provinces. Further laws passed in 1875 and 1876 reorganized the provincial administration on similar lines. Except that election was made to play a larger part than Gneist desired in the creation of the local and provincial authorities, and that the system was made more complex 'than he wished, these laws substantially realized his chief aims. They certainly represent a serious attempt to draw the well-to-do classes into the service of the state and to give them, through compulsory service, that political training which Gneist believed could be obtained in no other way. They represent also a serious attempt to make local government independent of central bureaucratic control.[297]

These laws provided at the same time for a reorganization and reform of administrative jurisdiction substantially in accordance with Gneist's ideas. As late as the beginning of the nineteenth century the Prussian administrative system was organized in a manner that gave very substantial protection to private rights; but the Stein-Hardenberg reforms and later laws based on French parliamentary theories so increased the power of the Prussian ministry as greatly to weaken the independence of the lower administrative instances; and, in consequence of the abolition of the Council of State, the final interpretation of law in administrative

---

[295] *Rechtsstaat*, p 359. The substance of this memorial was published by Gneist in 1870, under the title, *Die preussische Kreisordnung.* *Cf.* Gneist, "Les Reformes Administratives en Prusse," in the *Revue Générale de Droit, etc.* (Bucharest), vol i, p. 251. For the history of the reform see also his *Verwaltungsreform in Preussen* (1880) and *Stände und Wahlsystem*, pp. 208–215. [296] Kreisordnung, von Dec. 13, 1872.

[297] For details of the reform, *cf.* Goodnow, "Local Government in Prussia," *Political Science Quarterly*, vol. iv, p. 648; vol. v, p. 124.

questions was placed wholly in the hands of the ministers. In connection with the reform of local and provincial government, from 1872 to 1876, administrative courts were organized in which the non-professional elements, the " honorary officers," have the controlling voice; and for final decision of all cases involving the interpretation of public law, and not falling within the competence of the ordinary courts, a superior administrative court was established at Berlin, with the same guaranties of independence and impartiality that exist in the case of the ordinary courts. Of this new court Gneist was very properly made a member.

To the control of the administration by law, Gneist regarded it as essential that the ordinary courts should have power to disregard an ordinance which trenched upon the field of law; and it was, in his opinion, one of the chief defects of the Prussian constitution that, in accordance with the Latin theory and in imitation of constitutions of the French type, it withheld this power from the judiciary. This mistake, however, was not repeated in the imperial constitution; and in Prussia the attribution of this power to the superior administrative court substantially remedied the evil, since the decision was taken out of the hands of the ministry and intrusted to a judicial body. It was essential, again, in Gneist's opinion, to the legal control of the administration that officials by whose acts or laches private persons had suffered in person or in purse should be subject to the ordinary processes of law — not, of course, on account of injudicious exercise of their discretionary powers, but for acts beyond their competence or for neglect of their legal duties. In Prussia and in other German states, the liability of officials to civil suits and to criminal prosecutions had been unduly limited by laws passed during the first six decades of the nineteenth century. By imperial legislation, adopted in 1877, all these limitations are annulled or rendered innocuous.[298] At the same time, the administrative " monopoly of criminal prosecution," which

[298] *Einführungsgesetz zum Gerichtsverfassungsgesetze,* § 11.

Gneist had frequently reprehended, was modified by the imperial code of criminal procedure, which provides that, if the public prosecutor refuses to act, the injured party may apply to the highest state court or, in cases falling within the competence of the Imperial Court, to that tribunal, and that the court may order the prosecution of the alleged offender.[299]

It avails little to subject the administration by law to judicial control, if the judiciary is in law or in fact controlled by the administration. In Prussia, as Gneist repeatedly pointed out, the judiciary had been subjected, since 1851, to a ministerial control that really destroyed its independence. Not only had the Napoleonic device been introduced, by which the minister of justice placed judges where he pleased and formed the chambers into which the higher courts were divided, but the judges had also (again in imitation of the French practice) been made subject to disciplinary proceedings conducted by the administration; and the powers thus conferred upon the ministry had been employed, during the Conservative reaction and during the period of conflict, with a disregard of decency unexampled in France.[300] The return of such conditions was made impossible, and the independence of the judiciary was secured against all assaults, by the imperial law of judicial organization passed in 1877. In addition to the ordinary guaranties of judicial tenure and salary, it is provided in this law that judges may not even be retired on partial or full salary except under the conditions established by law or with their own consent, and that without their own consent they may not be transferred from one post to another, even when the transfer is a promotion. It is further provided that, while the number of chambers or senates in the state courts and in the Imperial Court is to be determined by the respective ministers of justice and by the imperial chancellor, the composition of these divisions and the

---

[299] *Strafprocessordnung*, §§ 169–173.
[300] *Verwaltung, Justiz, etc.*, pp. 184 *et seq.; Freie Advocatur*, pp. 29–49.

distribution of business among them shall be determined by the courts themselves.[301]

Gneist had always maintained that by instinct and temper his countrymen were as well fitted as the English for self-government and the jural state. He had repeatedly demonstrated that the institutions of German absolute monarchy had never been as purely bureaucratic as those of France and that the idea of subjecting administration to law had never been permanently obscured. With the reforms above indicated, he felt that the chief bases of the jural state were securely laid.

There were, however, two things that still troubled him — two places in which the jural state was incomplete, both in Prussia and in the empire. Neither the ministers nor the army were subjected to due legal control. The ministers of the Prussian crown and the chancellor of the empire are declared, by express constitutional provisions, to be responsible; but neither in the Prussian nor in the imperial constitution, nor in any law, is it indicated to whom they are responsible or what their responsibility really signifies. Bismarck always declared that the Prussian ministers were responsible to the king, and the imperial chancellor to the emperor; and if the word be taken to mean politically responsible, his statement is true. Gneist took the word to mean legally responsible; and argued that if a minister or the chancellor violated the law, he ought to be impeached and tried. In the absence, however, of any law determining who may impeach and what tribunal shall try, he conceded that nothing could be done.[302] There the matter still rests alike in Prussia and in the empire: the constitutional provision, in each case, remains what Gneist called it — a *lex imperfecta.*

---

[301] *Gerichtsverfassungsgesetz,* §§ 8, 61–68, 133.

[302] In *Verwaltung, Justiz, etc.,* p. 219, he expressed the opinion *de lege ferenda* for Prussia that the Chamber of Deputies should be intrusted with the impeachment, but that a special tribunal should be established for the trial, since the Herrenhaus was not the right sort of upper house for such cases.

The second open place in the German jural state is what Gneist described as " the practical exemption of the military authorities from legal control " and " the consequences drawn from the fiction of ' a military class.' " " Conditions," he pleaded, " should not persist in which the life, health, freedom and property of the people are placed in the hands of the military authorities without legal protection or judicial control." The idea should be abandoned that the army officers form a separate class, and their special forum should be abolished, at least in the case of ordinary crimes. Courts of honor he pronounced unnecessary; the ordinary military courts can dismiss an officer for conduct unbecoming a gentleman. " The English aristocracy is certainly not insensible to the real point of honor." [303] It is not likely that Gneist expected to witness these reforms; but they remain, for all that, permanent demands of the German Liberal program, and they are sure to be realized in time.

Law books, like all other technical works, become antiquated. Of their contents so much as is permanently true reappears, often without acknowledgment or even recollection of its first presentation, in a series of sequent treatises, each of which, in its time, is up to date, and each of which, after its time, passes into oblivion. This fate will probably be shared by Gneist's great work on the English constitution.

The literature of reform is even more ephemeral. The more successful it is, the sooner it ceases to find readers. The names, indeed, of successful advocates of important reforms are often preserved in history; but even in this matter there is an element of luck. Gneist's part in the work of establishing self-government in Prussia is the more likely to be under-estimated because the reforms of 1872–76 will be viewed, and rightly viewed, as the completion of the reform of 1808. Baron Stein will receive, in history,

[303] *Verwaltung, Justiz, etc.,* pp. 258 *et seq.; Verwaltungsrecht,* pp. 571–576.

the credit of initiating the movement, Prince Bismarck that of completing it. In history the eminent results in any movement stand out with increasing clearness as they recede further into the past; but as they recede, they also draw nearer to each other, and the intervals shrink until sixty or seventy years in which nothing of consequence occurred seem as a day. It will therefore hardly be stated or even remembered by future historians that the origin and the meaning of Stein's reforms had to a great extent passed out of the consciousness of Gneist's generation; that in the middle of the nineteenth century the bases of municipal self-government which Stein had laid had been seriously weakened by unwise legislation; or that, for many years, Gneist was the only prominent advocate of the principles on which the reforms of 1808 were based.

Gneist's best title to remembrance will probably be found in his political doctrines. Had he possessed, as a writer, that indefinable quality which we call style, — a quality which often gives a long lease of life to a book that contains no ideas, and which causes a book that does contain ideas to be read for centuries, — he might have written a *Jural State* or some such book which would have made him one of the immortals. He would then not merely have been remembered as one of the most prominent representatives of the nineteenth century reaction against the exaggerated individualism of the time: he would have had a place forever among the great political teachers: for no man ever saw more clearly, felt more strongly or declared more insistently than he that states rest not on rights, but on duties, and that the citizen is not born, but trained; and these are permanent and fundamental truths that need to be reiterated to every generation.

V

ROMAN LAW IN AMERICAN LAW SCHOOLS [1]

SHOULD the Roman law be included in an American scheme of legal education? If so, should it be treated as an optional, an elective, or a required study? And if required, how much should be required? The answer to the third question may be postponed until the first two questions are answered. These every man will answer according to the theory which he holds, consciously or unconsciously, regarding the purpose of legal education.

I

One tenable theory of the function of a law school — a theory which seems to be held by the majority of American law teachers — is that such a school exists simply for the purpose of training lawyers. By lawyers the adherents of this view mean practitioners in the field of private law, men who are to give advice upon legal questions that affect the persons or the pockets of their clients and who are to fight their clients' battles, if battles there must be, in the courts of justice. The education that is needed is partly informational. The graduate of a law school, the candidate for admission to the bar, cannot be expected to know all the rules obtaining in every department of private law, but he should know the leading and well-settled rules in each department, and he should know where to go for information upon minuter matters. A more important part of his training is that which deals with method. He has to learn how to handle the original matter of the law. He must learn the art of construing statutes, and the degree of possible difference between a broad and a narrow construction. He must learn the deeper mysteries of interpreting decisions, so that

[1] Reprinted from the *American Law Register and Review*, vol. 45, no. 3, March, 1897, pp. 175–186.

he may marshal precedents skilfully upon the side which he represents and may destroy by " distinction " the precedents similarly marshalled by his opponent.

Given this theory of a legal education, it is easy to show that knowledge of the Roman law may be useful, but its study can hardly be shown to be needful. Its purely informational value is not great. In most portions of the Anglo-American private law there is more or less Roman law, ancient or mediæval, civil or canon. In some portions there is a great deal of Roman law. It is interesting to know whence the rules of the English law have been derived, but such knowledge is by no means necessary. Where the exact scope and significance of the English rule is disputed, it may be of practical use to show how the rule was interpreted by the great Roman jurists or by the mediæval civilians or canonists. Once in a while a case may be won in this way, but once in a while a case may be won by a knowledge of chemistry or of mechanics. These are, in practice, *casus rariores*. It may be urged, and with truth, that the process of drawing new rules, where new rules are needed, from the apparently inexhaustible storehouse of Roman jurisprudence has by no means ceased. Even within the last hundred years it has been discovered by English courts that old debts can be extinguished by substituting new ones: *Tatlock* v. *Harris*, 3 Durnford and East, T. R. 174; and that where action is brought against a surety he can set-off a sum owed by the plaintiff not to himself, the surety, but to his principal, the original debtor: *Bechervaise* v. *Lewis*, 7 C. P. 372; and in each case the decision was drawn directly from the Roman law. These, however, are now *casus rarissimi*. As the English law has grown more complete, the tendency to borrow rules from the Roman law has steadily diminished, and the practice is more likely to become extinct than to increase.

In cases involving conflicts of law the informational value of the Roman law is more considerable. With the increasing movements of persons and property across national frontiers, and with the rapid and unprecedented development of international commerce, the cases have greatly multiplied in which foreign law — really foreign law, I mean, not the law of a sister state — determines the decision of the American courts. To the lawyer who has no acquaintance with Roman law, the legal vocabulary of continental Europe and Latin-America is a stumbing-block and the text of their laws is a snare. This practical problem, however, is apparently to be solved by a further specialization of law business. A few lawyers will devote themselves to the study of foreign law, and to these the others will turn for help when help is needed. It may be urged that these specialists should have a chance to prepare themselves for their work in our law schools, and this may be regarded as a valid argument for introducing courses in Roman law, at least in the more important law schools of the East. This argument, however, calls for nothing more than elective courses. It does not justify the introduction of Roman law as a required study. It is no more needful to make every graduate an expert in foreign law than to make every graduate an expert in patent law. And if elective courses are introduced for the benefit of the few students who may wish to make a specialty of foreign law, more stress should be laid on the modified Roman law of modern Europe than upon the law of Justinian's days.

A stronger plea may perhaps be made for the study of Roman jurisprudence as a part of the law student's training in method. In the lax or rigid construction of statutes, and in the determination of the exact value of previous rulings as precedents, the Romans were assuredly not inferior to the acutest of the moderns. They handled statutes in particular with more freedom than do our lawyers — with somewhat of the same freedom with which our greatest lawyers have handled our federal and state constitutions. But these arts can also be learned from English and American cases; and from the point of view of the intending practitioner, they can best be learned by studying cases in which are set forth the arguments of counsel. For this element in legal training the Roman law offers no exact equivalent. The greatest jurists of the Empire, whose responses and opinions form the bulk of the *Digest*, had been drawn into the service of the state, and their responses are not briefs, but decisions. Dissenting opinions have in some cases been preserved, with reasons for the dissent, but not arguments of counsel. In the accepted opinions and in those which were not accepted, the controlling influence was, of course, the interest of society at large, and not the advantage of any individual; and in so far the *Digest* furnishes better training for a judge than for a practitioner.

It may, of course, be said that our law schools in educating practitioners educate some who will be judges; and if it be admitted that a broader training, or a training in any way different from that required by a barrister, is needed by a judge, then it must be admitted that the theory of legal education upon which our discussion has thus far been based, is an imperfect theory even from the practical point of view. But the advocates of the technical, or trade-school theory, do not concede the necessity of a different training for the judicial office. They take things as they are, and base their theory upon the established Anglo-American custom. It has long been usual, both in England and in America, to take the judges from the bar, and therefore the law school may be content to train good barristers. If special qualifications are needed in the judicial office, they presumably come with the ermine. All this is thoroughly Anglo-Saxon, and in accordance with the old German saying: "To whom God gives an office, to him He gives understanding also."

II

There is, however, a second possible view of the function of legal education, and of late years there are signs that this view is beginning to gain wider acceptance. The old and sound tradition is reviving that law is not a trade, but a profession; and by a profession is meant not merely a trade that requires more than the average breadth of mental grasp and an uncommon subtlety of discrimination, but something else and something more. By a profession is meant a calling that subserves the interests of society as well as the interests of individuals, and that places, or should place, social welfare above individual advantage. There is no basis for the honor traditionally accorded to the professions as compared with the trades except the recognition and expectation of social service. There is no other reason for the endowment of professional schools, or for the maintenance of professional schools by an endowed university. If society pays part of the cost of a man's education, it is because it expects to recover its outlay through that man's services. What the services are which society expects from its lawyers, what the duties are which it imposes, is clear enough. The legal profession is custodian of the most important element of social life — the body of rules which are necessary to the existence and progress of society, and to which, accordingly, society constrains obedience through the strong arm of political power. Nor is our profession simply custodian of the law which society has created; it shapes the new law which the constantly changing needs of social life require. This great service, and the duties it entails, cannot be thrown off upon the shoulders of the judges and the legislators. Apart from the fact that the majority of our legislators and all of our higher judges come from the bar, it is impossible that these should do their work in the best way without the sympathy and support of the bar.

From this point of view, the problem of legal education is far less simple than it appears to the advocates of a purely technical training. Private law — the law of family and of property — cannot be divorced from public law. It can be thoroughly comprehended only in its relation to public law. This relation is not one of independent co-existence, but of organic interdependence. Each supplements and modifies the other. Hence the necessity of introducing into the curriculum of our law schools far more international, constitutional and administrative law than has heretofore found place there. Hence the necessity of giving to constitutional law, as taught in our schools, a different and a wider meaning. Constitutional law should not be taken to signify merely the protection of individuals and their property against governmental encroachment; it should be taken in its legitimate sense, as including the organization of our entire political system.

Nor can law be really understood by studying it simply as it is to-day. We really comprehend things only when we know how they have come into existence and how they have grown to their present form. To the lawyer, as a professional man, some knowledge of the history of our law is absolutely essential. It is one of the great merits of the case system that it gives glimpses of the evolution of legal rules. But general courses in English legal history, which shall show the development not merely of this or that legal institution but of the law as a whole, are greatly needed.

Nor can the law be really understood, as it should be understood by those who are its makers and its guardians, by studying law alone. It can be really understood only in its relation to ethics, politics and economics. Unless the law student has been thoroughly grounded in these subjects before he begins his law studies — and how few of our American law students are thus grounded! — these matters also must find some place in the scheme of legal education.

At present it is only in a few of our larger universities that any attempt is made to meet these needs. At such universities there have been established, side by side with the law schools, schools of political science or graduate courses in the political sciences; and courses in history, public law, economics, etc., have been thrown open to the law students, in some cases as optional courses only, in some cases and to some extent as elective courses leading to the law degree. This solution of the problem is inadequate. In all our law schools, even in those that are associated with our greatest universities, the traditions of the technical school are still dominant among the students themselves. To most of them law means private law; public law is politics. To most of them history, ethics and economics seem matters as remote from law as are geology, theology or *belles-lettres*. At the same time the work of the law schools has been growing more and more minute and intensive in the field of private law; and in spite of the extension of the law course from two years to three, the pace of the work has been quickened. Under the optional system, therefore, hardly any of the law students can make use of the new opportunities extended to them; and even under the elective system the number who strive to broaden their education is comparatively small.

Judging from European tendencies, this method of dealing with the problem of professional education in law is probably destined to prove a temporary and transitional method. On the continent of Europe public law has long constituted a required part of the legal education, and of recent years courses in economics are beginning to be required.

But what of the Roman law? Are its claims stronger in the professional school than in the technical school? They are certainly stronger, but not even from this point of view are they imperative. When the history of English law is studied, we find the influence of Roman law, civil and canon, increasing as we go backward. To the lawyer who studies English legal history as an investigator, with the intent of increasing our stock of knowledge, a considerable acquaintance with ancient and mediæval Roman law is necessary. But to the lawyer who studies English legal history merely to gain a better comprehension of the existing Anglo-American law, the Roman law, however useful, is not necessary. The same statement must be made as regards the study of public law, and as regards the study of economics and of ethics. To the historical investigator in these fields, some knowledge of Roman law is, I think, necessary. To the ordinary student it is of advantage, but it is not necessary. In public law, in economics, and in ethics, the elements derived from the Roman civilization have been so largely assimilated and transmuted that the ordinary student can get the results of the historical process without going back to its beginnings.

From the point of view of professional education, accordingly, the demand for elective courses in Roman law is stronger than from the point of view of technical education; but it is still a demand for elective courses only, and not for a required course.

III

A third view of law and of legal education — a view which all our teachers of law accept in theory, but which many of them disregard in practice — is that law is not a trade merely, nor a profession merely, but a science, and that legal education should be scientific. This view is not wholly incompatible with the theory that law schools exist simply to produce practitioners in the field of private law, for the training given in private law may be more or less scientific. Much less is this view incompatible with the theory that law is a profession, and that social duties of the greatest importance rest upon the bar. It has always been felt instinctively that the true professional spirit — the spirit of public service — is most fully developed among men who regard the subject-matter of their profession as a science; and it is the testimony of the world's experience that such men serve society most gladly and most effectively in laboring for the advancement of their chosen sciences. From the scientific point of view, also, there is the strongest reason for including in the legal curriculum legal history, public law, economics, and ethics; for every true science studies and presents its material in the light of its development and in its relations to allied sciences.

But every true science employs a method of which the technical and professional schools make little use. This method is comparison. It is preëminently *the* scientific method; without the employment of the comparative method, no body of knowledge regarding the facts of the physical world or the facts of social life can take rank as a science.

In considering law from the technical and professional points of view, we have considered it as a national system. We have considered Anglo-American law alone. But law, though primarily a national product, is also a human product. Social organization is always fundamentally the same among peoples standing on the same plane of social evolution. Many of its basic facts are constant throughout the course of human history. Many of the problems with which English and American lawyers have to deal are problems with which the Roman jurists dealt; all of them are problems with which the jurists of modern Europe are dealing. Nor is law human in this sense only — that the problems confronted and the conditions of their solution are everywhere similar — but also in the sense that its development has been human. There is, and there will some day be written, a history of law; and the particular development of Roman law and of English law will first be wholly intelligible when each is regarded as a stage in the development of the law of the world.

A professor in one of our university law schools was accustomed, as I have been told, to open his first lecture by declaring that it was not his intention to treat of the law of England, or of the law of the United States, or of the law of his own commonwealth, but of law. This announcement, of course, exaggerated purposely the point which he desired to emphasize; but it will serve to illustrate the point which I am trying to make. A science of English law or of Anglo-American law is as inconceivable as a science of Anglo-American ethics or economics. It is, indeed, as unthinkable as a science of American physics, or mechanics.

It follows that, for the scientific study of law, some knowledge of the Roman law is absolutely necessary; for the civilized world is ruled to-day by two great systems of private law, the English and the Roman, and as soon as the student, who is to employ the comparative method, emerges from the English law, he plunges into Roman law.

From the purely scientific point of view, moreover, the

study of the Roman law, ancient and modern, is more important than the study of the English law. The latter, as far as it is an independent product, is the product of a shorter period of conscious, reflective development — a period that covers scarcely one-third of the centuries that have been consumed in the development of the modern Roman law. The English law, again, is the product of the genius of a single highly-gifted race. The Roman law of to-day is the product of the coöperation of all the other races that have helped to make general history. Even in the ancient world the institutions and customs of all the Mediterranean peoples were fused by a process of selection that was partly automatic and partly reflective, into the universal law, the *ius gentium* of the Roman empire; and in the scientific elaboration of this law Romans, Greeks, Semites, Gauls and Spaniards labored side by side. In Mediæval Europe a new element was added to this already cosmopolitan law by the introduction of Teutonic institutions and ideas; and in the further scientific development of this wider *ius gentium* all the modern nations of continental Europe have had a share.

If an example be needed to demonstrate the scientific value of Roman law to the English jurist, it is only necessary to compare the jurisprudence of Bentham and Austin, itself not uninfluenced by the " dust of the Roman jurisprudence " which they had half consciously inhaled, with the jurisprudence of Holland and Pollock, vitalized by a deeper inspiration of living Roman law.

IV

I have examined the questions proposed in the light of what seem to me the three possible theories of legal education. Which of these theories, now, shall we accept as the true theory? For me, each has its justification, and each should obtain at least partial recognition. The American law school must train practitioners — that is, indeed, its primary purpose — and it should so train them that they may earn a livelihood, for this is the immediate end which nearly all men must set before themselves. But it should not content itself with this. It should strive to make of all its graduates professional men, imbued with the spirit of public service and fitted to discharge the duties which our social organization and our national custom impose upon the legal profession. And it should strive to imbue all of them with the scientific spirit, not merely because the scientific spirit brings with it the professional spirit in its highest and purest form, but for the sake of legal science itself, of which our law schools should be the great and general reservoir. And besides awakening in the minds of all of its students, as far as this is possible, the scientific spirit, the law school should provide a special training for the chosen few who are able and willing to devote their lives to the investigation of legal history and jurisprudence. This our university law schools, at least, should do; for a university that contents itself with the preservation of the inherited capital of science, and makes no provision for its increase, is a university only in name.

If this view be accepted, I think it must be recognized that some knowledge of Roman law should be required from every candidate for a law degree; and that advanced elective courses should be established in European legal history and modern European law for the few who desire to devote themselves to the widening of the borders of legal science.

If the preceding discussion be viewed by any reader as a brief for the Roman law, he will wholly mistake the spirit in which it has been written. Had I undertaken to plead, as an advocate, for the study of Roman law in American law schools, I should have claimed far more, and conceded much less. I have striven to take a judicial rather than a partisan view of the claims of the Roman law, and in all doubtful points I have charged rather against than in favor of claims which my prejudices would lead me to support.

V

The question remains to be considered, how the Roman law should be studied. To answer this question we must consider what are the most valuable portions of that law — the portions that constitute a permanent contribution to legal science.

The most valuable portion of the Roman law is incontestably the private law. The whole doctrine of private rights was first clearly worked out by the Romans, and these rights were formulated with a sharpness of outline which no Teutonic system of law has ever equalled. In the Roman private law special stress should be laid upon the law of things, and upon that of contractual and quasi-contractual obligations. The law of testaments should be noticed, but with less detail. Roman succession *ab intestato* deserves little attention. It is of even less scientific value than the order of succession in the code Napoléon. Both are arbitrary things, but the latter is of more interest *de lege ferenda*.

The Roman law of personal status and of the family relations should be relegated, for the most part, to the limbo of legal antiquities. To the American law student the legal status of the *Latini Iuniani* is of less consequence than that of the German *liti;* and the doctrine of *peculium quasi-castrense* is more remote from our modern life than the matrimonial property law of the early Suabians. Of all this portion of the Roman law so much only is needed as may be necessary to understand cases in the *Digest* which deal with property rights or obligations, but which turn in part upon the relation of husband and wife, father and son, or master and slave. And, perhaps, even so much had better be taught incidentally, in discussing the cases, than set forth dogmatically in a course on the *Institutes*.

It is the great fault of the attempts now making to introduce the study of the Roman law in England and in America that too much time is devoted to the *Institutes* of Justinian, and too little, if any, to the *Digest*. The latter is a vast re-

pository of case-law, from which a judicious instructor can
select matter of permanent value.   The former is an attempt to set forth dogmatically, in brief compass, the legal
rules which were of chief importance in the sixth century.
It includes, therefore, much that is of purely antiquarian
interest.   In England, where the *Institutes* are now a required study, the vice of the system shows itself clearly in
the cram-books.   In Chamier's *Manual*, for example, the
student can learn something about the freedmen who were
treated like Latins, and about the *peculium quasi-castrense;*
but the law of contractual obligations is condensed into
thirty-six small pages of heavily-leaded large type, and, as
far as I can discover, no hint is given that obligations were
assigned by the Romans, as by Englishmen, by making the
assignee an attorney in his own interest.

However brief the time that can be devoted to a required
course of Roman law in an American law school — and the
minimum that could possibly be of any use would be three
hours a week for four months — at least half of this time, in
my opinion, should be devoted to cases from the *Digest* —
cases similar in their nature and, as far as possible, in the
conditions given for their decision, to the cases with which
we have to deal to-day.   So taught, Roman law should interest the most narrowly utilitarian of students, and to those
who have a spark of the scientific temper it should open
new vistas of thought and a wider mental horizon.

VI

CUSTOMARY LAW.[1]

I

Roman, Mediæval and Modern Theories.

At the time when the Roman law had reached its highest development, when the supreme power of interpretation was vested in a personal sovereign, the emperor, and when such changes as seemed desirable and could not well be made by interpretation could be and were made by imperial enactments, the Roman jurists and the emperors themselves asserted that law was established by custom as well as by legislation. They treated these two sources of law as equal in potency: they recognized that law, whether of customary or of legislative origin, might be changed either by legislation or by custom.[2] Even written law, they declared, might be superseded by a contrary custom, or disappear in consequence of non-user: " enactments," Julian wrote, " are abrogated by desuetude." [3] The jurists who expressed these opinions were not closet thinkers, but were actively engaged, as judges and as members of the imperial council, in the administration of justice and in the drafting of laws.

Neither in the Roman juristic literature nor in the imperial constitutions do we find any dissent from these doctrines. The only qualification anywhere hinted occurs in an imperial rescript of the fourth century, in which it is declared that custom is not to prevail against the spirit and purpose of the law as a whole, or against imperial legisla-

---

[1] The first part of this essay is reprinted from the *Political Science Quarterly*, vol. xviii, no. 2, June, 1903, pp. 256–281. The remainder is from manuscript.

[2] *Digest* 1, 3, fr. 32–40. *Cf. Inst.* 1, 2 § 9, and *Cod.* 8, 52 (53).

[3] *Digest* 1, 3, fr. 32, § 1, Cf. *Inst.* 1, 2, § 11, and 4, 4, § 7; *Cod.* 6, 51, c. unica, pr.; *Nov.* 89, c. 15.

tion.[4] If this passage be construed to apply to custom in general, it becomes wholly inconsistent with the dicta of the imperial jurists and with other utterances of the emperors themselves. It probably refers to local customs; and the principle which it affirms applies equally to local custom and to local legislation. In a state in which lawmaking power is centralized, no form of local law can prevail against general law.[5]

The Roman doctrines regarding customary law were neither challenged nor doubted in the middle ages; but, as far as secular land was concerned, the qualification which we have just noted disappeared. The mediæval European idea of the relation of local and general law was precisely opposite to the Roman imperial idea. According to the mediæval idea, the local law of the manor, village or city, whether written or unwritten, prevailed against the law of the province, and the law of the province prevailed against the law of the realm. This idea squared with the political facts, at least after the disruption of the empire of Charles the Great; and it began to disappear only when the political facts changed — when, first in England, later on the Continent, the hands of the kings were so strengthened that they were able to establish national states.

As far, indeed, as ecclesiastical law was concerned, the church upheld the Roman idea. It asserted that neither local nor provincial nor national law or custom, whether secular or ecclesiastical, could displace the general law of Christendom.[6] It made significant reservations, however,

---

[4] *Cod.* 8, 52 (53), c. 2: " Consuetudinis ususque longaevi non vilis auctoritas est, verum non usque adeo sui valitura momento, ut aut rationem vincat aut legem." *Cf. Nov.* 134, c. 1, *in fine; Decr. Grat.*, dist. 11, c. 4, and *Decretal. Greg. IX.* 1, 4, c. 11. Ratio iuris (and, often; ratio alone) is something narrower and more definite than reason. Ratio legis is the intent or purpose of a particular law; ratio iuris the tendency of the law in general. See Heumann, *Handlexikon zu den Quellen des römischen Rechts,* " Ratio " (5) and passages there cited.

[5] So Windscheid, *Pandekten,* vol. i, § 16, n. 5; § 18, n. 2. For other explanations, see Vangerow, *Pandekten,* vol. i, § 16, note. Dernburg, *Pandekten,* vol. i, § 28, n. 5, rejects all explanations offered, and assumes a flat contradiction.

[6] *Decr. Grat.,* dist. 11, c. 1–3, 11; dist. 12, c. 1, 2. *Decretal. Greg. IX,* 1, 4, c. 3, 4, 5, 7. *Sexti Decretal.,* 1, 4, c. 1. 2. *Extrav. comm.,* 1, 1, c. unica.

which facilitated compromise. If neither the unity of the Christian faith nor the necessary discipline of the Christian Church were impaired or imperilled, not only might national councils adopt rules varying from those of Rome, but a contrary custom in a locality might be pleaded against the general laws of the church;[7] and even in the absence of any such positive legislation or custom, it was sometimes inquired whether the general rule established by the church had ever been " accepted "[8]— a practice which led to Gratian's broad assertion that " laws are instituted when they are promulgated; confirmed, when they are approved by the custom of those who observe them." [9]

Apart from this question of the relation between general and local law, the mediæval theory was identical with that of the Roman jurisprudence. Any different theory would have been singularly inconsistent with the legal situation. Not only were the customs of manors, of cities and of provinces recognized as law; there were also general European customs. Decisions made in Lombardy were cited in all the feudal courts of Europe; judgments rendered at Pisa, at Barcelona and at Oléron enjoyed an equally wide authority in questions of commercial and maritime law. Class custom was law not only for merchants, but also for artisans and peasants; and in certain matters (particularly in family law) the same authority was ascribed to the customs of different religious confessions. The destructive force of desuetude was recognized, not only as against custom but as against written law. Even legislators, in affirming the validity of older collections of written laws, sometimes added the significant limitation, " as far as these are still in use." [10]

After the close of the middle ages, a different theory prevailed. Legislation was exalted above custom: it was denied that written law could lose its force through desuetude or be displaced by contrary custom; it was even

---

[7] *Decr. Grat.*, dist. 11, c. 6, 8; dist. 12, c. 3, 4, 6–11. *Decretal. Greg. IX*, 1, 4, c. 8. *Sexti Decretal.*, 1, 4, c. 3. *Cf.* Maitland, *Canon Law in England*, p. 10, n. 3, 4.
[9] *Decr. Grat.*, dist. 4, c. 3.
[8] *Cf.* Maitland. *op. cit.*, pp. 31, 32.
[10] *E.g.*, Leyes de Toro (1505) 1.

denied that custom was or could be law otherwise than by the express or implied consent of the legislator.[11] The development, or at least the general acceptance, of these views was closely associated with political changes which were taking place at the close of the middle ages, and with legal changes which were beginning at that period and which have been completed in our own time. On the Continent, the modern national state obtained its political organization in the absolute monarchy; the monarch was regarded as sovereign; [12] and to admit that his actions could be restrained or his commands invalidated by custom was to deny his sovereignty and make his power merely governmental.[13] Within each national state common law was needed, and on the Continent this could be developed only by legislation. The transition from feudal to democratic society required sweeping legal reforms, and these could be made only by enactments.

In some of these matters the English political and legal development was altogether different from that of the Continent; in others an analogous development took place, but

[11] Some of the Roman jurists had already attempted to assimilate custom to enacted law by treating each as an expression of the will of the sovereign people. *Cf.* Julian, in *Digest* 1, 3, fr. 32 § 1: "Nam cum ipsae leges nulla alia ex causa nos teneant, quam quod iudicio populi receptae sunt, merito et ea, quae sine ullo scripto populus probavit, tenebunt omnes; nam quid interest suffragio populus voluntatem suam declaret an rebus ipsis et factis?" *Cf.* also *Hermogenian, eod. tit.*, fr. 35; "velut tacita civium conventio." But the conclusions drawn from this doctrine of popular sovereignty were opposite to those which have been drawn in modern times from the attribution of sovereignty to the legislator. In the sentence which immediately follows that above cited, Julian says: "Quare rectissime etiam illud receptum est, ut leges non solum suffragio legislatoris, sed etiam tacito consensu omnium per desuetudinem abrogentur."

[12] The common impression that the reception of the law-books of Justinian contributed to the development of the theory of princely sovereignty is, of course, quite correct; for in the later imperial constitutions there are clear assertions of the divine right of the prince: terrestrial majesty is derived by delegation from celestial majesty. In Justinian's *Digest* sovereignty is with the people; in his *Institutes* the imperium et potestas of the prince are derived from the people; in his *Codex* the emperors claim to rule iure divino.

[13] Burgess, *Political Science and Constitutional Law*, vol. i. pp. 66, 93, 127, maintains that the authority of the absolute monarch was only governmental. He describes the absolute monarchies of Western Europe as democratic states with monarchic governments. His theory is thus identical with the juristic theory of the Roman principate.

not by any means an identical development. Even a brief comparison will show, I think, that while the new [14] theories were a natural product of Continental conditions, they represented in England either fruitless protest or unnecessary imitation.

In England, governmental power had been centralized three or four centuries earlier than in any other modern European state; and in the period in which absolute monarchy was giving national organization to Spain and to France, the English national state was strong enough to tolerate the transfer of governmental power from the crown to the king in Parliament. In the reaction towards absolutism, however, which followed the disorders of the seventeenth century, the new theories found a classical formulation in the *Leviathan*. Hobbes declared that all law proceeded from the sovereign, and that custom was law only by his allowance.[15] He fully recognized that sovereignty might be vested in an assembly of aristocrats or in a popular assembly,[16] but he regarded monarchic sovereignty as the best organization of the state, and he asserted that in England sovereignty was in the king.[17] In England, naturally enough, his theory was not generally accepted until it was fully recognized that sovereignty was elsewhere than in the king.

A second great difference between England and the Continent, at the close of the middle ages, was that England had what no Continental state possessed, a supreme " custom of the realm," developed by the decisions of the royal courts, and continually readapted by reinterpretation to the changing needs of English social life. On the Continent, where the central governments of the single states were too weak

---

[14] It is hardly necessary, but it is perhaps prudent, to say that the word " new " is used relatively.   [15] *Leviathan*, ch. 26.

[16] Hobbes's secure title to fame rests on the fact that he formulated a theory of sovereignty which is applicable to every form of state, although, like all mediæval and nearly all modern thinkers, he confused state and sovereignty with government and governmental power. His great service to jurisprudence lies in the drawing of a sharp distinction between natural and positive law.   [17] *Ibid.*, ch. 18, 19, 22.

to furnish national law, either by legislation or by a controlling central interpretation, a different development had taken
place. At the close of the middle ages nearly all the Continental law was either less than national or more than
national: it was either local or European. To the ecclesiastical law, the feudal law and the law merchant, all of which
were European systems, had been added, by the reception of the law books of Justinian, the Roman civil law.
The acceptance of all this common European law did not,
however, solve the problem of furnishing common law to
each state; for most of this European law, and notably the
Roman civil law, had subsidiary force only: it was applicable only in cases for which neither provincial nor local custom nor city law supplied a rule. To get rid at once of
European law and of local law — to substitute national law
for European law, and to make this national law the supreme
law of each country, overriding the various provincial and
local laws — the modern European states were obliged to
resort to legislation.

On the Continent, moreover, even before the close of
the middle ages, the word custom had come to be nearly
synonymous with local law. Nearly all the common European law had been reduced to written form; and although
neither the Roman civil law nor the canon law had been
put into purely statutory form, although the *Digest* and half
of the *Codex* of Justinian and a great part of the canon law
consisted of digested decisions, all this European law was
regarded as enacted law. In a measure the same was true of
the standard compilations of the feudal law and of the law
merchant. On the other hand, the reduction of local customs to written form did not generally bring about any
such change of view or of nomenclature. Even when the
customs of provinces and localities were unified, they were
still termed customs. In becoming synonymous with local
custom, customary law was identified with particularism.
And since the local customs had not continued to adapt themselves to the changing needs of even the smaller areas which

they governed, customary law was largely identified with outgrown law.[18]   Under these circumstances it is not surprising that customary law came to be regarded with hostility and contempt.

It is significant in view of this great difference between Continental and English conditions, that Hobbes displayed no such hostility to custom as existed on the Continent, and no such prejudice against judge-made law as was later manifested by Bentham.   Hobbes was obliged to insist that custom was law only by the king's tolerance, because Parliament had invoked the political custom of the realm against the attempts of the Stuarts to expand prerogative.   He left, however, a wide area for the judge-made common law by declaring general customs and unwritten law to be " natural law." [19]   He maintained, indeed, that the sovereign had the sole power of interpreting natural law, and that nothing that the sovereign did not recognize was law; but this power of interpretation was of course regularly exercised by the king's judges.   These, he significantly declared, were not mere judges; they were more like the

[18] For a single example, take the report of the French royal commissioners who revised the Coutume of Normandy. (The old Coutume was a private compilation made in the fourteenth century: the revised Coutume was promulgated by Henry III in 1577.)   In their procès verbal the commissioners explain that the provisions of the old Coutume were in a large measure " hors d'usage et peu ou point entendus des habitans du pays."   And this was the end of a body of customary law which in the eleventh century was perhaps the most advanced in Europe; which had retained more than any other the institutions of the Frankish empire, and from which much of the English common law had been derived.   Among the institutions " out of use and not understood " was the jury in its half-developed Norman form.   Brunner, "Quellen des normannischen Rechts," in Holtzendorff, *Encyclopädie*, 5 ed., p. 328.   It seems to be well established that law cannot develop beyond a certain point in a limited area.   It must then expand, like the law of the Roman city; or borrow, like the law of the Swiss cantons; or perish through arrest of development.

[19] " If an unwritten law, in all the provinces of a dominion, shall be generally observed, . . . that law can be no other but a law of nature."   " Civil and natural law are not different kinds, but different parts of the law: whereof one part, being written, is called civil, the other, unwritten, natural." *Leviathan*, ch. 26.   Taking this last utterance in connection with his famous remark that natural laws are not properly laws, his attitude seems contradictory.   His own theory, however, requires the conclusion that in so far as the sovereign recognizes and enforces natural law, it becomes (although still unwritten) positive law; and it is doubtless of such natural law only that he is thinking when he recognizes it as part of the law and not different in kind.

Roman jurisconsults.[20] It is clear, I think, that Hobbes regarded interpretation as a mode of legislation; and so far from showing any desire to restrict judicial law-finding, he maintained that the royal judges should pay less regard to precedents.[21]

On the Continent, common law (*i.e.*, national law) could be established only by legislation; for when princely government became strong enough to centralize the administration of justice, the diversities of local and class law were too great to be interpreted away. Consequently, during the past three centuries, and particularly during the nineteenth century, the Continental European states have legislated to an extent unprecedented in legal history. They have attempted to cover the whole field of legal relations with codes, and to make these codes so complete as to leave no room for the survival of the European and local systems against which they were waging war. This movement began in France with the great ordinances of Louis XIV, regulating commerce and civil and criminal procedure; and it has gone on throughout Europe till the present day.[22] It has recently been completed in Germany, and is on the eve of completion in Switzerland, where the cantons have been as autonomous as were the German territories or the mediæval provinces of France.[23]

In the midst of this process came the revolutions of the eighteenth and nineteenth centuries. The reorganization of government on a more or less popular basis was secured by legislation: in all the states of Western and Central

---

[20] *Ibid.*

[21] " No man's error becomes his own law, nor obliges him to persist in it. Neither, for the same reason, becomes it a law to other judges, though sworn to follow it." *Ibid.*

[22] *Cf.* " State Statute and Common Law," *Political Science Quarterly,* vol. iii, pp. 153 *et seq.*

[23] German imperial legislation has left considerable legislative power with the states, but not in the field of private law. It is already evident that a similar solution will be attained in Switzerland. In Spain the civil code leaves the laws of several important provinces in force, and has only subsidiary application; and in the dual monarchies of Austria-Hungary and Sweden-Norway dual legal systems exist; but in all the other states of Europe the law has been made uniform by the adoption of general codes of supreme validity.

Europe the unwritten law was replaced by written constitutions. The limitation of princely power, like its development, was attained by overriding customary law of the highest order of validity, constitutional custom; and the theory which was brought forward to justify the later movement, like that adduced in support of the earlier, was of necessity a theory of sovereignty. Hobbes's argument that a seeming grant of powers of sovereignty by the sovereign is void, " for, when he has granted all he can, if we grant back the sovereignty all is restored," [24] was substantially reproduced in the revolutionary assertion that the rights of the people are " imprescriptible." What here concerns us is that in each case the legality of the earlier political custom was impugned, and that in consequence all customary law was in a measure discredited.

The development of the English constitution, which has been accomplished with few abrupt changes, has never required in any such degree the discrediting and delegalizing of earlier custom. Constitutional statutes have been passed from time to time, but much of the fundamental law has remained unwritten. It has held its own against absolutist tendencies, whether these were royalistic or democratic. Hobbes's denial of the validity of the custom of the constitution was never generally accepted; parliamentary government is carried on to-day with the machinery and in the form of government by the crown. No such prejudice against political custom as arose in the Continental monarchies has ever existed in England, because for centuries the custom of the constitution has been identified with the limitation of governmental power and the protection of popular rights.

Modern Continental legislation, finally, has had yet another incentive and has attained another end. The older customary law, reflecting the social conditions of the middle ages, was an unequal law. By legislation class privileges have been abolished; disabilities of birth and creed have

[24] *Leviathan,* ch. 18.

been removed; equal law has been established. These reforms, which have at once marked and secured the transition
from feudal-aristocratic society to modern democratic society, were in part accomplished by special enactments. They
did not require the revision and codification of the whole law.
To a large extent, however, the new rules that were required
were worked out in the great national codes of civil and criminal law and procedure. Here we have an additional reason
for the Continental antipathy to customary law. To the
people of the eighteenth and even to those of the nineteenth
century, customary law connoted not only particularism and
an inconvenient diversity of local rules, but also inequality,
with privileges for the few and disabilities for the many.

Here for the first time, in considering legislation as an
agency of social reform, we find an analogy between Continental and English development, and a reason for English
dissatisfaction with the custom of the realm as interpreted
and developed by the English courts. The analogy, indeed,
is not complete, nor does the reason seem to amount to a
justification. In England the development of class privileges had been restrained by the early centralization of law-
finding: the common law was not only common to all England but to all Englishmen. The transition from feudal
to democratic society began earlier in England than in
any Continental kingdom,[25] and some of the necessary
changes in the law were made by judicial modification of
the common law, others by acts of Parliament. In the
eighteenth century the English law contained less mediæval
débris than the legal systems of the Continent. It contained
enough, however, to make Bentham's attitude comprehensi-
ble. Rapid and sweeping reforms of the law, such as he
rightly desired, could be made only by legislation. It was
not necessary for the realization of his practical aims that
judges should cease to find law; but it is quite intelligible
that the inability of the judges to find the sort of law he

[25] Not earlier than in the Continental cities, but earlier than in any
system of territorial law upon the Continent.

wanted should have blinded him to their usefulness as law-finders, and should have led him to regard legislation as the normal mode of making law. For the rest, he and the other English utilitarians seem to have been much influenced by Continental tendencies,[26] and the analytical theory took its final form without adequate analysis of the conditions which had produced those tendencies. Not perceiving that the Continental states were codifying in order to obtain what England already possessed, a national law, they assumed that codification was the natural goal of all legal development. If we say that English analytical jurisprudence began with Hobbes and ended with Bentham and Austin, we may say that it began with a defence of royal absolutism, which England had already repudiated, and that it ended in a demand for general codification, which neither England nor any of the people that have inherited the English common law have thus far recognized as necessary.

This review of conditions and theories, and of their inter-working during the past four centuries, would be incomplete without a word regarding natural-law doctrines. These ancient theories, which had little more than speculative interest in the middle ages, became of great importance in the seventeenth and eighteenth centuries. The assertions of Cicero and of Thomas Aquinas that laws contrary to natural law were not truly laws, that they were the corruption of law — these assertions became dynamic when the interpretation of natural law passed from the church and the princes to the people, *i.e.*, to any one who chose to set himself up as a natural lawyer, and whose assertions gained popular approval. The fundamental principles of the new law which was required in the transition from princely to popular

---

[26] The ideas and tendencies which we associate with Bentham's name were dominant in Europe in the later decades of the eighteenth century. Bentham's ideal of a code which was to determine every possible legal controversy, and leave no loop-hole for the making of law by judicial decisions, was the ideal, for example, of the authors of the Prussian Code of 1794. See "State Statute and Common Law," *Political Science Quarterly*, vol. ii, pp. 108, 109, n. *Supra*, p. 56, n.

government and from feudal to modern society were proclaimed as natural law in the seventeenth and eighteenth centuries; and the assertion that these principles were already law did much to hasten their acceptance. Words are forces; and to say that the particular arrangements and rules which one desires are law is a much more effective mode of agitation than to say that they ought to be law. The revolutionary natural lawyers said both: " Are and ought to be " was the natural-law formula. In this way the natural-law doctrines gave to the revolutions what seemed a legal basis; and they made the legislation in which the results of revolution were embodied seem merely declaratory.[27] But before natural law can be applied, it requires something more than declaration, it must be worked out in its details by judicial construction or by legislation; [28] and the revolutionists and reformers naturally adopted the more rapid method of statutory construction. Theoretically, the natural-law school was sharply distinguished from the positivist or analytical school, since the latter denied that natural law was law at all. But when the English successors of Hobbes had become dissatisfied with the custom of the realm and desired legislative reforms, and the natural lawyers were hastening to transform all their natural law into positive law, the tendencies of the two schools became indistinguishable. It has been shrewdly remarked that English utilitarianism was really a natural-law system; and in fact Bentham and the natural-law writers had an equally firm faith in the power of reason (*i.e.*, their reason) to find the right solution of all social problems, and an equally poor opinion of the results of the thought and experience of antecedent generations. The attitude of the natural lawyers

[27] The declaratory form was typical. As the American Colonies had declared in 1776 that they not only ought to be but were already independent, so the first French attempt to define the fundamental rights of the individual took the form, not, as in England, of a bill but of a declaration. In the United States, where natural-law theories have survived longer than in Europe, the declaratory form has not infrequently been used in the nineteenth century.

[28] " The law of nature . . . is become of all laws the most obscure, and has consequently the greatest need of able interpreters." *Leviathan,* ch. 26.

and of the English utilitarians toward historical law in general and customary law in particular was thus practically identical. Both disliked custom and regarded it as something anomalous.

With the reaction against the revolutions came a scientific reaction against natural-law theories. The leaders in the new movement were accused, and not without ground, of being reactionaries in politics and obstructionists in the matter of social reform; but the fundamental tenets of historical jurisprudence were soon accepted by liberals and reformers (perhaps because the natural-law propaganda had substantially accomplished its ends) and the historical school became dominant. With the acceptance of the historical point of view in England there has come also a reaction against the analytical school. The historical jurists have done much to rehabilitate customary law. They maintain that custom, so far as it is observed and enforced, is really law, whether its rules agree with the views of natural lawyers or not. As against the analytical jurists they assert that much law has existed, and some law still exists, which cannot be traced to the direct or indirect command of any determinate sovereign. Nevertheless, the historical jurists do not generally attribute to custom any such constant efficiency as was apparently attributed to it by the Roman jurists. Custom, in their view, is the chief source of early law, but it plays no important part in making late or highly developed law. The dominant opinion, not merely of English but also of Continental jurists, is expressed by Pollock: " Except in matters outside the scope of positive law, the formation of custom belongs to an archaic stage of legal history." [29]

In considering this remark and similar utterances of other modern writers, two things are to be noted. To English and to Continental jurists alike, modern custom means local custom. On the Continent this is natural

[29] *First Book of Jurisprudence*, p. 265. German jurists would hardly indorse the word " archaic," but most of them would accept the word " past."

enough: European custom had been reduced to written form long before it was displaced by national codes, and, except in the political field, no national customs had developed. A body of what we should call judge-made law is now rapidly growing up about the new national codes, but this is not generally regarded as law: it is merely " interpretation." [30] In England, where a custom of the realm has existed for several centuries, where this custom has been only partially replaced by acts of Parliament, and where it is still developing, as it has always developed, from precedent to precedent, the restricted use of the word custom is less easily explicable.   If the English common law is not the general English custom, what is it? We are sometimes told that it is a scientific development of the ancient customs of the realm.   This indisputable statement does not directly answer the question with which we are here concerned; but taken in connection with the repudiation of the Hobbes-Austin theory, that judge-made law is a sort of legislation, and with the refusal to describe judge-made law as customary law it seems to imply that there is a third species of law which rests neither on legislation, nor on custom, but on " science." [31]

It is to be noted, in the second place, that those who describe custom as a vanishing form of law exclude or ignore some portions at least of public law. Some jurists seem to deny the legal character of those rules that are not enforced through courts of justice, thus excluding a considerable part of international, of constitutional, and even of administrative law. The majority of modern jurists, especially on the Continent, declare that all public law, including inter-

---

[30] In Germany, indeed, judicial usage (*Gerichtsgebrauch, Praxis*) is beginning to be recognized as customary law (*Gewohnheitsrecht*). The newer theories on this point will be noted later.

[31] The term " scientific law," which was employed by Savigny, is familiar on the Continent; but in the Continental theory scientific law is not positive law until it is incorporated in legislation cr becomes customary law by the general acquiescence of the community. The present controversy in Germany, to which allusion is made in the preceding note, turns on the question whether judicial custom, as such, is positive law or whether it becomes positive law only by force of popular custom.

national law, is really law; but in discussing the sources of modern law (as indeed generally in framing their systems of jurisprudence) they seem to be thinking of private law only.

If an attempt to determine the nature of customary law, and to indicate what place it occupies in the modern civilized world, were to lead us into, and leave us in, a quarrel over the meaning of the words " law" and " custom," it would be of questionable advantage to prosecute any such inquiry. If, however, it can be shown that archaic custom and modern public law, local custom, class custom and modern judge-made law, exhibit in their development and in their character similarities so great as to justify their inclusion under a single term; if it can be shown that, even at the present time and among the most highly civilized nations, legal rules are coming into existence without legislation, by processes analogous to those through which customary law has always been produced; and that, as long as human society, as we know it, continues to exist, a very appreciable quantity of such rules will inevitably be produced by such processes, — if these things can be shown, the question of nomenclature becomes one of secondary importance. And even if the result of the inquiry be simply a reaffirmation of the substantial truth of the Roman view that all law is produced either by custom or by legislation, and that custom and legislation are factors of equal potency, even this result may perhaps be regarded as a contribution to legal theory.

Archaic Custom

The resemblance between the mode in which early customary law is developed and the mode in which late unwritten law is produced has been obscured by the German historical jurists. They describe early custom as " popular usage " (*Volksgebrauch*), and the law of which it constitutes so large a part as " popular law " (*Volksrecht*); and they contrast this popular law, as such, with the " official law " (*ius honorarium, Amtsrecht*) which is imposed, at a later period, by governmental power. Both of these forms of law are further contrasted with legislation. The element of truth in these contrasts will occupy us later: what now concerns us is the sense in which early customary law is described as popular. We find that these jurists generally assume and frequently assert that such law emanates directly from the people at large. Some of them hold that it is established by the spontaneous acts and forbearances of the people. Others assert that the conduct of the people supplies only the visible manifestation of the popular law, and that this law exists, antecedent to any such manifestation, in the " jural consciousness " (*Rechtsbewusstsein*) of the people.[32]

These assumptions and assertions are, I think, untenable. Whether the so-called jural consciousness is really a spontaneous popular development is a question which we may leave to sociologists: it does not directly concern lawyers, for the simple reason that the content of this jural consciousness is not law. The jural consciousness is what we call, in English, the sense of justice or sense of equity. It is a mixture of ethical sentiment and of a more or less clear perception of social utilities, applied to matters which we regard to-day as matters of law. It may exercise a controlling influence upon the making of law; it is perhaps the source of the majority of those rules of conduct which ultimately become legal rules; [33] but it contains nothing more than law " in the making," or, as a German might express it, *werdendes Recht.* The error in the German assumption that the content of the *Rechtsbewusstsein* is law is concealed, and the assumption itself is probably caused, by the ambiguity of the word *Recht,* which (like the words *ius, droit, diritto* and *derecho*) may mean either ethical right

[32] *Cf.* Vangerow, *Pandekten,* § 14. References to the German literature *ibid.,* § 13.

[33] Jhering denies the priority of the jural consciousness, and declares it to be a product of positive law. See his *Entwickelungsgeschichte des römischen Rechts,* Einleitung. *Cf. Political Science Quarterly,* vol. xii, pp. 32 *et seq. Supra,* p. 184 *et seq.*

in the abstract or a concrete legal right or law in the abstract.

The assertion that customary law is established by the spontaneous acts and forbearances of the people at large is more plausible. It must be remembered, however, that social habits are not necessarily legal customs; that not every rule of conduct is a rule of law. In case of doubt, we must inquire whether the observance of the rule is secured by any sort of penalty for non-observance, and if so, by what sort of penalty. If the violation of a rule entails ridicule or contempt, unpopularity or general detestation, and nothing more, the rule is not what we should call a legal rule. If the violation of the rule is believed to bring upon the offender divine displeasure, and if it brings nothing more, the rule is still not a legal rule. If, however, the man who has awakened the popular or divine resentment is thrust out of the community or sacrificed to the gods, we have what may be called a legal sanction. In general, if the violation of a rule entails a penalty which affects the person or the property of the offender, if the violator is fined or flogged or mutilated or slain or enslaved or banished, then we may say that a really legal sanction stands behind the rule and that the rule is undoubtedly legal.

The beginnings of law in the proper sense are, therefore, to be found at the point at which the infliction of penalties affecting the property or the person begins to be assured; and if it be affirmed that any rule of early law is really popular in its origin, it must be shown that the people at large, and not a priest or a king, inflicts or secures the infliction of the penalty which is attached to the violation of the rule; for if it be a priest or king who takes the initiative, it is probable that the sanction which makes the rule a legal rule proceeded originally from the priesthood or the kingship. And if we wish to go to the bottom of the question, we must further inquire, even when we find the people inflicting penalty or securing its infliction, whether the popular action is spontaneous or results from obedience to a priest or a king; for in the latter case it is the priest or king who is really making a precedent and shaping the customary law of the community.

In early criminal law there is much evidence of what seems to be spontaneous popular action. Some offences are so clearly injurious to the whole community that they awaken a spontaneous popular reaction, and the offender is lynched or expelled from clan and tribe. We commonly find, however, that it is the priests who declare whether this rough justice is pleasing to the gods. We find also that popular justice is limited to a small class of offences. In a larger number of instances, priests or kings inflict penalty or secure its infliction.

In early society, the range of criminal law is comparatively limited. Many acts which are regarded later as offences against the peace and welfare of the community are viewed as private wrongs simply; and those wrongs are redressed by self-help, *i.e.*, by the act of the injured person or kinship-group. An attack upon the person, physical or moral, justifies not only self-defence but counter-attack. Wounding justifies retaliation; insult, revenge. When a man is slain, it is the right and duty of his kinsfolk to exact blood-vengeance. Similarly, an attack upon possession justifies not only defensive but aggressive action; the person who has been robbed of wife or child or cow may summon his kinsmen and try to recover the stolen property, with something to boot by way of satisfaction to his outraged feelings. In all these cases self-defence may be carried to the point of slaying the assailant. Recovery and vengeance may reach that point, if the offender resist.

If, however, the offender and his kinsfolk be permitted in turn to avenge themselves; if, in particular, the kinsmen of a slain murderer or thief be permitted by the community to take vengeance for his blood — and there is evidence, particularly in early Germanic tradition, that this was at one time permitted — the so-called right of self-help is no right at all, nor is self-help a legal sanction. Even if the act of reprisal be approved by the community, and the act of counter-reprisal disapproved, the right of self-help has not developed beyond the stage of moral right as long as the community remains passive. To make it legal right, the feelings of the community must express themselves in deeds. There is no true right of self-help until the community begins to protect its exercise by defending the persons who exercise it This means the intervention of other and neutral kinship-groups to restrain the kinsmen of the original offender from seeking vengeance for his punishment. Now, in the history of every tribal community there was, of course, in connection with each group or class of wrongs, an occasion on which such an intervention first took place; and because it was unprecedented, it is hardly likely that it was spontaneous and irreflective. It may well have occurred at the exhortation of a tribal priest or chieftain. If it did occur spontaneously, as the result of a slowly ripened popular sense of justice or of expediency, there must have been no little discussion afterward, among the leading men of the tribe, of the question whether the intervention was rightful. Only by virtue of a general agreement on this point could the action of the neutral groups come to be regarded as a precedent for tribal intervention in future cases of like character; and only when the intervention had become a regular practice could the legal rule take form that the slain offender is rightfully slain, and that no vengeance or compensation is to be exacted for his blood.[34] Such a development cannot properly be termed spontaneous.

If, again, we consider early forms of legal acts — *e.g.*, forms of conveyance and of contract — which date from the period of self-help, and which constitute another great branch of early customary law, we are struck with the evidence of reflective construction which they bear on their very face. At a time when only such rights as were perfectly clear

---

[34] XII Tables, viii, 12: " iure caesus." In the Anglo-Saxon laws, the slain offender is to lie " ungylde "; in the Frankish laws " absque compositione." *Cf.* Brunner, *Deutsche Rechtsgeschichte*, vol i, pp. 157, 158.

were at all likely to receive recognition and effective protection, these forms aimed to make rights clear, not only by calling in witnesses but also by giving to these witnesses visible as well as verbal demonstration of the nature and content of the act. Hence, the constant use of symbols. These symbols were apparently connected, in many cases, with ancient superstitions; but the peculiarly expressive symbols which we find, for example, in early Roman and in early German law, give ample evidence of a reflective selection and adaptation.

Through forms of conveyance and contract and through the development of remedial law, not a little substantive law took shape even in the period of self-help. In many instances we find traces of innovations and of ingenious adaptations of old customs to new uses — innovations and adaptations which could hardly have been made in the jural consciousness. Take, for example, in family law, the transition from mother-right and uterine kinship to father-right and agnatic kinship; and consider the later restrictions placed upon the power of the husband who has bought and owns his wife — restrictions by which an unlimited property right became a limited power over a free person. Take, in property law, the extension of the right of following and punishing a thief until it became a process for recovering things even where no theft could be shown (*furtum nec manifestum, Anefang*), with the resultant development of property rights which, in German law, became all more or less independent, and which in Roman law became almost wholly independent of possession. Take self-pledge, which, as a form of obligation, appears very early and seems very natural, and consider what it implies. It means that title to a thing can be held without holding possession, and that this possibility has been utilized first to create mortgage, and then through mortgage of the promisor's person to create obligation.[35] These are but a few of the illustrations that

---

[35] Nexum in the oldest Roman law was clearly a fiducia of the debtor's person.

may be drawn from archaic custom, and that lead us to doubt its spontaneous popular development.

Early usage, like all usage, is simply persistence in lines of conduct marked out by the practice of the past. Such usage however is not yet law. If the observance of a social practice has been and is absolutely uniform and uninterrupted, if no living man remembers or has heard of any violation of the usage, and if there is no tradition as to the results which should attach to its violation, the rule by which the community is living is not a legal custom. It may be a rule of conduct of the highest importance, but it is not law. It cannot become law until it has been violated. Then for the first time the community is forced to decide whether the breach of usage shall be punished by any sort of physical coercion, or, if it has already been punished, whether the person or persons who have inflicted the punishment are to be punished in turn or protected. This decision is a legal precedent: it takes the broken rule out of the debatable domain of usage, and assigns it provisionally either to the domain of morals or to that of law.[36] If it be decided that punishment is rightful, and if this decision be followed in later controversies, a legal rule is established.

The earliest customary law is thus the observance of legal precedents; and these precedents, as in modern law, are established by decisions. These decisions, multitudes of which must have been made before right of jurisdiction over controversies had been vested in any single persons or bodies of persons, were, in a sense, decisions of the whole community; but they were really made by those persons whose position or age and familiarity with the customary law commanded deference if not obedience. The community as a whole might approve or reject a decision proposed, but the initiative, the formulation of the decision, rested with a few natural leaders of the community; usually, it would

---

[36] That the rule found is regarded as having always existed is a fiction which the English and American courts maintain in all their law-finding to the present day. In early society it is a very natural view, for the usage existed before it was found to be a legal custom.

seem, with the priests. Whether the decision first reached on a novel question should determine the attitude of the community in future controversies, depended again mainly on the attitude of these earliest law-finders; and as concordant decisions hardened into customary law, it was not popular custom but the custom of the law-finders that made the law. All that the people contributed was the custom of acquiescence. The expression, in clear and memorable sayings, of the rules implied in the decisions — an achievement which to primitive men seemed a real law-making, and which perhaps first cleared the way for legislation — this was again the work of these leaders of progress and breakers of new paths.

Savigny, who is chiefly responsible for the rather mystical theory of the really popular development of early custom, has taught us that, as soon as social relations become at all complex, a select body of lawyers appears and takes the development of the law out of the hands of the people. In fact, however, we have yet to discover, in history or in the uncivilized world of to-day, a community possessing anything that can fairly be called law, even in its rudest form, without discovering at the same time traces of a select few who both make and interpret the precedents which constitute the law. The popular traditions, found almost everywhere, which base the ancient customs of the people on the decrees of some great law-giver, probably contain more truth than the historical jurists are wont to admit. Romulus and Numa may never have existed, Moses may have been in no greater degree the author of the Jewish law than Alfred was the maker of Saxon or Rollo of Norman customs; but these and other legendary law-givers may be regarded as composite mythographs, each representing a long series of forgotten law-finders.

German Tribal Law and Roman City Law

When we pass from the period of unorganized law-finding to the period in which jurisdiction is vested in determinate authorities, *i.e.*, in courts, we find that the customary law consists of the rules recognized in these courts. We find, also, that the progressive re-formulation of these rules in judgments is the work of a few men who are especially familiar with the legal traditions of the community, which are the residuum of forgotten precedents, and with the comparatively recent precedents of which a distinct memory still survives.

The old German court was indeed a popular court: it was attended by all the freemen, and its judgments were not valid without their approval. The judgments, however, were actually found by one or more " wise men " or " advisers " or " law-speakers." Their " wisdom " or declaration of the law seems to have been regarded as authoritative: among many tribes " wisdom " means law.[37] Among some tribes the judgment, as formulated by these judgment-finders, was submitted to the people for approval by the king or prince who presided over the court; among other tribes it was submitted by the law-finders themselves at the request of the presiding king or prince, or on the demand of the plaintiff. The ordinary freemen who stood around (the *Umstand*) [38] simply approved the proposed judgment: they gave the " full word " (*Vollwort.*) [39]

In early Roman history there is no trace of any such popular court, except as an appellate court in criminal cases; and if Roman tradition may be trusted, this exception was not a survival but an innovation. The ordinary criminal court at Rome was apparently the court of the king himself, or of magistrates appointed by him; and judgment was rendered by the king or the magistrates without any popular coöperation. Of the Roman civil courts in the royal period we know next to nothing: there are traditions of a royal administration of justice, and there are evidences of pontif-

[37] So in the Old High German, the Gothic, and the Old Saxon. *Cf.* Brunner, *Deutsche Rechtsgeschichte,* vol. i, p. 110.

[38] The law-finders, like the presiding official, were seated. If there were several, they sat on a bench.

[39] Termed, by Tacitus, auctoritas. The previous formulation of the judgment is indicated by the word consilium. *Cf.* Brunner, *op. cit.*, vol. i, p. 154.

ical jurisdiction. The civil court of the Roman Republic was a composite thing: pleadings took place before a magistrate, but the case was sent for decision to one or more *iudices*. These *iudices* were not necessarily learned in the law, and when they were confronted with legal questions of any difficulty they were guided by the opinions of jurists. In the Roman jurists of the republican period we have something corresponding to the German law-speakers, but in a higher stage of development. The jurists of the royal and early republican periods were the pontifices. In the later Republic the jurists were laymen, and their authority, which was extra-legal, rested on popular recognition of their learning and acumen.[40] This popular recognition, however, was of course based in each case on the opinion of the juristic class itself. That these jurists really controlled the decision of the unlearned *iudices* on all legal questions cannot be doubted. They also, and they alone, kept record of the opinions rendered in connection with decisions and determined the authority of such opinions. An opinion which was generally regarded by them as unsound was promptly overruled. Only the opinions which they approved (*sententiae receptae*) possessed legal authority. These jurists also devised forms of legal acts, and through their control of judgments they secured the recognition of the forms which they had devised. That they were actually the makers of the old Roman civil law was fully recognized by their successors, the imperial jurists. That they exercised this law-making power, however, only through their control of decisions is self-evident.

The earliest compilations of Roman and of Germanic customary law — the Twelve Tables, the Leges of the different German tribes, and the Dooms of the Anglo-Saxons — are statements of the legal tradition established by de-

---

[40] The position which the jurists held at Rome was very different from that of modern lawyers; they did not plead cases (this was left to the orators), and they gave legal advice gratuitously. In a sense, they were rewarded by the community at large, for their services recommended them to political office.

cisions. In the Twelve Tables — which, although a thousand years older than the German Leges, represent appreciably later law — the digesting of decisions into rules has gone so far that the abstract, imperative form of statement predominates; but even in the Twelve Tables we find many rules stated in the conditional form which is proper to caselaw. We find a conditional clause setting forth facts, and a concluding clause laying down the rule.[41] In the German Leges the casuistic, conditional form is much more general. Some of the Leges are little more than collections of " wisdoms," *i.e.*, of answers given to specific questions by the regular law-finders. In the composition of these Leges we find king, wise men and people playing precisely the same parts as in an ordinary judgment: the wise men stated the law at the king's request, the king submitted the statement to the people, and the people give their " full word " or approval.[42]

The imperfect differentiation of law-finding and law-making, which we have noted in early society, persists even when law has emerged from its archaic stage. The Latin *ius* like the Spanish *fuero* designates both the court and the law. Among the Germans, as we have seen, a proposed law, like a proposed judgment, is a " wisdom." The Anglo-Saxon termed both laws and proposals " dooms." There is also much resemblance between the forms of judgment and those of legislation. In early German legislation, as we have seen, the same persons, king, advisers, and people, act in the same way as in rendering judgments.[43] In the Roman popular assembly, acting as centuries, later in the English Parliament, we find, conversely, that the machinery and procedure of legislation were employed to secure the condemnation or

[41] *E.g.*, viii, 12: "If he has committed theft by night, and if he has slain him, let him be (regarded as) rightfully slain; " and viii, 24: " if he has let the javelin slip from his hand rather than hurled it, let him supply a ram (for sacrifice)."

[42] Brunner, *Deutsche Rechtsgeschichte,* vol i, p. 110.

[43] In the old High German glosses, "eosago " (law-speaker) is sometimes translated " legislator " and sometimes " iudex." Brunner, *op. cit.,* vol. i, p. 150, n. 33. The scabini of the Carolingian period were also described as " legum latores." *Ibid.,* vol ii, p. 224.

acquittal of the person charged with crime (*irrogatio poenae,* bill of attainder). The early German relation between the two is probably the more primitive. Probably there were judgments before there was legislation, and the earliest legislation which was not purely declaratory was essentially a judgment rendered in advance on a question which seemed likely to arise frequently in the future. In early legislation another idea is indeed discernible, the idea of compact or agreement.[44] It is, however, not improbable that the same idea underlies the earliest termination of controversies by judgments.

Before going further, two questions should be answered. First, in what sense is such early law as we have been examining popular? The adjective may be used in either of two senses. It may be used to indicate that the law really proceeded from the people as such, or to indicate that the agencies which produced it were popular as distinguished from governmental. Early legislation, among both the Romans and the Germans, involved indeed the coöperation of the people, but the only direct influence which the people could exercise was negative. They had no initiative, no power of amendment; they had simply to say yes or no. They could prevent legislation, but they could not frame it or directly influence its framing. As regards the far more important mass of law which was established and developed by judgments, the German people played the same negative part as in legislation; while the Roman people, except in criminal procedure, played no part at all. Neither the written nor the unwritten law, then, proceeded from the people as such. When, however, we inquire whether the agencies that really produced the law were or were not governmental, we must distinguish. In Roman legislation the formulation of a bill seems to have been purely governmental: there is no evidence

---

[44] Some of the German Leges are described as "pacts"; others begin "it is agreed." The Roman jurists always based the force of law on the consent of the people; and the Roman form of legislation, like the old German, was contractual; the king or magistrate proposed, the people assented.

that Roman jurists were asked to propose rogations, as the German wise men were asked to suggest wisdoms or dooms. Among both peoples, however, the formulation of judgments, as far as any question of law was involved, was non-governmental. The real makers of early German law as of early Roman law, as far as these systems were developed by judgments, were the experts, the wise men, the jurists; and these were not governmental agents. The term popular, in the sense of non-governmental, may therefore be applied both to the legal customs of our German ancestors and to the unwritten law of the Roman Republic.

The second question is whether this early law which we have been examining, in so far as it was developed not by legislation but by judgments, can fairly be termed customary. It is generally recognized that the law set forth in the Twelve Tables, like that embodied in the German Leges, was of this character; but the law that was developed at Rome between the publication of the Tables and the reform of the civil law by the prætors is not usually described as customary law. In the Roman official theory, indeed, all the jurist-law of the republican period was merely interpretation of the Tables. This theory was strained nearly to the breaking point, as similar theories have often been strained in later times; but it was persistently maintained until the imperial period.

Postponing for the present the general question of the relation of interpretation to law-making, we need only observe that in Rome, before the close of the republican period, the civil law had attained dimensions very disproportionate to the basis on which it nominally rested; that this development had been accomplished by the responses or decisions of the jurists; that no single response or decision was regarded as law, except as it was received as correct by the general opinion of the profession and was followed in actual judgments. It was, then, by the custom of the law-finders that the Roman civil law was built up, just as German custom was built up centuries later; and it is not easy to see why German tribal law should be termed customary while the appellation is withheld from Roman city law.

II

In a preceding article [45] it was asserted that customary law, as distinguished from mere usage, has always been developed by decisions, and that decisions have always been determined by a relatively small number of persons. In the earlier stages of legal development decisions may indeed be rendered, apparently, by the entire community. The people must at least acquiesce in a proposed decision; and they must often lend active aid to make the decision effective. The attitude of the community, however, even in the earliest periods, seems to be determined by a few law-finders; at least, these law-finders determine the form and scope of each decision; and it is by their persistent custom that the rules of early law are determined. Among the Romans and among the Germanic peoples the earliest law-finders seem to have been priests. In the Roman Republic the law-finding power of the priests passed to secular jurists; in the Germanic tribes, after their conversion to Christianity, it passed to secular law-speakers. Neither Roman jurists nor Germanic law-speakers rendered judgments which were immediately capable of execution; but the Roman *iudices* and the German folk-moots regularly took their law from these law-finders. Law-finding was " popular " only in the sense that it was not yet governmental.

In the Frankish Empire there was a tendency, even in the popular courts, towards governmental law-finding. The Frankish counts apparently selected the " advisers " (*rachineburgi*) who proposed the judgments,[46] and in the Frankish and Franco-Roman territories of his empire, Charles the Great caused permanent judgment finders (*scabini*) to be appointed — not more, apparently, than a dozen to a county.[47] With this change, the law-finding became in a sense govern-

---

[45] *Supra*, pp. 289, 290.
[46] Brunner, *Deutsche Rechtsgeschichte,* vol. i, p. 150.
[47] *Ibid.,* vol. ii, p. 223.

mental, since the law-finders no longer became such by virtue of general opinion and by a sort of natural selection, but were governmental appointees. After the disruption of the Frankish Empire, however, the office of *scabinus* was regularly associated with a particular estate or holding, and conditions arose which will be discussed later under the head of local and class custom.

ENGLISH COMMON LAW

In England, thanks to the Norman Conquest, the administration of justice was centralized at a far earlier period than on the Continent; but justice was not, and is not to-day in any English-speaking country, so completely governmentalized, if the expression may be permitted, as in the Roman Empire or in the modern states of Continental Europe. Almost simultaneously with the establishment and organization of the English royal courts there developed a new form of popular coöperation. Out of the Carolingian inquest grew the Norman jury of proof and, finally, the English jury of verdict. In criminal cases, as has been well settled since the reign of Charles II, the jury is judge of the law as well as the facts; *i.e.*, law-finding is or may be non-governmental. In civil cases, on the other hand, the jury has theoretically no voice in finding the law. It must take the law from the judge, and if it fails to do so its verdict may be set aside. Since, however, verdicts are set aside only in extreme cases, the decisions of civil juries may largely affect the practical working of the law. On the whole, however, the instruction or charge of the judge is decisive as far as questions of law are concerned, not merely in civil but also in criminal cases. It should be noted, further, that the verdicts of juries have never been regarded as precedents in England any more than the decisions of *iudices* were regarded as precedents at Rome. The instructions which the judges give to the juries, and which are approved by the court of highest instance, are alone regarded as establishing precedents, just as the opinions expressed by the Roman jurists and approved by the general opinion of their fellows constituted the only precedents recognized in Roman law. Hobbes was quite right when he asserted that the English royal judges were jurisconsults rather than judges. That the English royal courts made the English common law is a fact seldom seriously questioned. The orthodox judicial theory, indeed, has always affirmed the contrary. The English judges have always affirmed that they were not making law but finding it by " interpretation." They began by interpreting Saxon and Norman customs; they went on by interpreting the interpretation. When a rule could not be found elsewhere, it was sought in the nature of the case or in natural reason or in the general principles of jurisprudence or even in the Roman law; but however far afield the courts went in their search, and however great the range of selection which they gave themselves, the rule which they applied was in theory always found and not made. The making of law belonged to Parliament. This theory is not, however, now taken very seriously even by the courts, and English and American writers generally discard it. The facts that English common law has never had any existence except in decisions; that by decisions it has been developed in historical times from scanty beginnings into a great and complex system; that by decisions its rules have continually been modified and frequently overruled, — these facts have been more cogent to the average mind than any official theory. Although English common law has frequently been styled " the custom of the realm " [48] it is not now usual to call it customary law. It has always rested, however, like all the customary or unwritten law we have been examining, upon the persistent practice or custom of the law-finders.

It is, however, frequently asserted, by those who frankly recognize the law-making power of judicial decisions, that each decision in which an old rule is modified or a new rule is laid down makes law; that it is not the current of decisions

[48] *Cf.* Pollock, *First Book of Jurisprudence,* pp. 239–243.

or judicial practice that determines unwritten law any more than it is legislative practice that determines the written law. Under this theory, of course, English common law could not properly be termed customary law. The discussion of this point will be deferred until we come to consider the general relation that exists between law and the interpretation of law.

Official Law or Equity

The Roman distinction between citizen's law (*ius civile*) and official law (*ius honorarium*) and the equivalent German distinction between *Volksrecht* and *Amtsrecht* do not correspond with the distinction which I have attempted to draw between non-governmental and governmental law-finding. The substitution of governmental for popular agencies in ordinary law-finding usually involves no abrupt breach with the past. The Roman imperial courts, the English royal courts and the courts of modern continental Europe severally took up the work of law-finding at the point to which popular agencies had carried it, and developed new law as the popular law-finders had done by interpreting the older law. What is meant by " official " law or " equity " is the law produced by governmental agencies not exclusively nor, indeed, primarily judicial — agencies which set themselves above the previously existing law and not merely supplement but override it. Such agencies are never regarded at the outset as having either law-making or law-finding power; but the body of rules which they persistently enforce come ultimately to be regarded as law. Such agencies were the Roman prætors; the Frankish kings, acting through their counts palatine and their *missi;* and the English kings, acting through their chancellors.

Superficially there was a difference between the way in which the Roman prætors made law and that in which the English chancellors made it. The prætors used the quasi-legislative form of ordinance or "edict "; the chancellors developed new rules as law-finders develop them, by deci-

sions. The Frankish kings used both methods; they made
new rules by ordinance, and they found new rules of equity
in the king's court. When, however, we examine the edicts
of the Roman prætors and consider how their provisions
were applied, the difference almost disappears. The duties
of•the Roman prætor were in the main judicial: it was
his chief business to arrange for the termination of private
controversies. The edict which each prætor set up at the
beginning of his year of office was not a series of commands, but a programme. In it he promised certain
remedies and indicated under what circumstances each
remedy should be given. This programme was carried
out by means of formulas sent to the *iudices*. The formula
was a command: if the *iudex* found certain allegations of
the plaintiff to be true, and did not find certain other allegations of the defendant to be true, he was commanded to
render a certain decision. The English chancellor decided
cases as he saw fit; the Roman prætor caused cases to be decided as he saw fit. A new rule worked out in chancery was
first disclosed in the decision of the special case which suggested it, and any modification of the rule was subsequently
revealed in the same way. Any new rules which the prætor
intended to enforce, and any modifications which he intended
to make in the rules laid down by his predecessors, were announced in advance. Fundamentally, these two methods of
making law are identical; and they both resemble law-finding
rather than legislation. The rules laid down were suggested
by actual controversies, and were amended as new controversies afforded new points of view. In form the Roman
process was more considerate. The complaint of the English common lawyer, that equity was administered according to the length of the chancellor's foot, would have lost
much of its force if the length of the foot had been indicated
in advance.

The similarities in the three movements — the Roman, the
Frankish and the English — are more striking than any such
formal differences. At the outset neither Roman prætor nor

Frankish king nor English chancellor was held to be capable of making or finding " law " or of creating new rights. Each, however, could issue orders and enforce them *in personam* by fine or imprisonment. Each was therefore able to impose new sanctions and to create new remedies; and eventually it was admitted that where there was a sanction there must be a legal rule, and where there was a remedy there must be a right.

Under each of these systems the new law-finding was more purely governmental than the ordinary law-finding which it overrode. The Roman prætor, whenever it was necessary for his purpose, reduced the *iudices* to the position of English civil jurors; *i.e.,* he laid down the rule to be applied, provided the facts were as stated, and the *iudices* had nothing to do but to determine the question of fact. In the administration of equitable justice in the court of the Frankish king, and in the courts of the king's *missi,* the judgments were found in traditional fashion by representatives of the freemen; but these representatives, at the king's court, were usually officers of the royal household, and in the missatic courts they were *scabini* appointed by the counts. The influence exercised by the king and his count palatine and his *missi* upon these judgment-finders must have been very great, because the pleadings, the evidence and the judgment were not governed by folk-law, with which they were familiar, but by king's law. In English proceedings in equity there is, of course, no jury; the judges determine the facts as well as the law.

The rules laid down in the edicts of the prætors and those expressed or implied in English decisions in equity became law by force of custom. The custom that converted them into law was not popular, for the people had no more to do with these movements than the Russian people have to do with the ukases of the czar. The custom was governmental. It was by the iteration of the same rules in successive prætorian edicts (*edicta tralaticia*) that the Roman *ius honorarium* was built up. It was by the observance of precedents and the development of a settled practice that English equity came to be a constituent part of English law. In the same way Frankish ordinances and Frankish equity were becoming law when the process was interrupted by the disruption of the Carolingian empire.[49]

ROMAN IMPERIAL LAW

Ordinary, as distinguished from equitable, law-finding was first governmentalized at Rome in the imperial period. At the close of the republican period, civil judgments were rendered by *iudices*: under instructions from the prætor when the new rules of prætorian law were to be applied; without instructions, when the old civil law was to govern the decision. The *iudices* were popular, not governmental officers; they were selected in each case from a panel of citizens of rank and wealth. Law was actually found, however, neither by the prætors nor by the *iudices*; the instructions or formulas issued by the prætors and, as far as legal questions were involved, the decisions of the *iudices* were actually shaped and controlled by the jurists, and these were in no sense governmental agents. The criminal jurisdiction of the Roman assembly was transferred, towards the close of the republican period, to new criminal courts, the *quæstiones*; but in these courts also, verdicts were rendered by citizen *iudices*.

Under the empire law-finding gradually became altogether governmental. The first step in this direction was taken when the jurists became representatives and agents of the emperors. This change was effected by conferring upon the leading jurists a " right of responding," and by directing the *iudices* to follow the legal opinions given by such jurists. The opinions of these " patented " jurists (to use Muirhead's phrase) now possessed legal authority; and the opinions of other jurists soon lost even the moral authority which they

[49] In the development of king's law as in that of folk-law, says Brunner, " it was repeated and uniform application, *i.e.*, custom (*Gewohnheit*) which . . . showed . . . that a true legal rule (*ein wirklicher Rechtssatz*) had come into existence." *Deutsche Rechtsgeschichte*, vol. i, p. 277.

had previously enjoyed. The next step was to establish new courts, civil and criminal, in which imperial officials heard the pleadings and the evidence and rendered the decisions (*iudicia extraordinaria*). The last step was to transform the surviving courts of the older type (the prætorian courts) into purely governmental courts. This change was initiated by substituting for the independent citizen *iudices* subaltern officers of the court itself — an innovation which seems to have been welcomed by the citizens, since it relieved them from duties which they felt to be onerous and desired to escape — and completed by making it optional with the magistrate, in each case, whether he should try the case himself or delegate its trial to one of these subaltern *iudices* (*iudices pedanei*). When these changes had been made the magistrates became judges in the modern sense.

In proportion as law-finding was governmentalized, it was also centralized. From the decisions of independent citizen *iudices* appeals had never been admitted. From the decisions of imperial officials appeals ran to the emperor, or to such higher officials as he might designate. The emperor had also, as supreme magistrate of the commonwealth, a general original jurisdiction. In fact, his original jurisdiction appeared earlier and developed more rapidly than his appellate jurisdiction. Any case could be brought before him in first instance, and he might either decide it himself, by a decree, or delegate its decision, by rescript, to the ordinary court or to a special court. In case of delegation it was usual, if a doubtful or novel question of law was involved, to state the rule to be applied, assuming the facts to be as represented.

The imperial decisions, whether rendered in first instance or on appeal, were formulated in the imperial council (*auditorium*), which was thus the supreme court of the Empire. At a later period the emperor's appellate jurisdiction was transferred to imperial prefects.

In connection with these changes, all the more important offices of a judicial character came to be filled by the patented jurists. The jurists of the republic had been the extra-legal counsellors of the magistrates and of the *iudices*. Those of the first century of the Christian era were the authorized counsellors of the *iudices*, of the magistrates and of the emperor. In the republic and under the first emperors the jurists might occasionally act as *iudices*, and they frequently became magistrates; but their control over law-finding, although practically complete, was for the most part indirect. The great jurists of the second and third centuries were judges in the modern sense; [50] and it was by their direct activity, *i.e.*, by their decisions, and particularly by the decisions reached in the imperial council, that the law of the empire was chiefly developed. Their decisions were reported and digested in their writings. Their commentaries were, for the most part, digests of case-law; their books of " questions " and "responses " were, as the names imply, collections of cases. To treat all the juristic literature of the empire as " scientific law " or " legal theory," which became law only by popular or professional recognition and use, is to misrepresent its character and its authority.

By the decisions of the imperial jurist-judges, and in the literature in which these decisions were preserved, all the results of the preceding legal development were fused and harmonized; so that, in the fourth and fifth centuries, neither the Twelve Tables nor the subsequent republican legislation nor the prætorian edict nor the decrees of the senate were cited, except as interpreted in the juristic literature, *i.e.*, by the judicial practice of the early empire. This was the *ius* or common law of the late empire. It is not usual

[50] From the close of the first century to the middle of the third, all the principal jurists whose writings were or came to be regarded as authoritative (except Pomponius and Gaius, who were probably teachers of law, and Africanus, of whose career we know nothing) were members of the imperial council, *i.e.*, of the supreme court of the empire. Some of them held other positions of which the duties were wholly or partly judicial, such as praetor, praefectus urbi, and proconsul. Papinian, Paul and Ulpian, extracts from whose writings constitute about five-ninths of the *Digest* of Justinian, were successively praefecti praetorio, *i.e.*, chief justices of the empire.

to call it customary law, nor did the Romans call it unwritten law; [51] but it was judge-made law, and, like the " interpretation " of the republican jurists, it represented the persistent custom of the law-finders.

During the early empire there was relatively little direct legislation. What there was took the form, for the most part, of *senatus consulta*. The emperor had the power of issuing ordinances (*edicta, mandata*) but he was not at first regarded as having legislative power; and the imperial decrees and rescripts, to which legislative authority was ultimately ascribed, were, as we have seen, neither laws nor ordinances, but decisions. After the middle of the third century, when the production of juristic literature ceased, it is often assumed that all legal change was made by direct legislation. As late as the beginning of the fourth century, however, the law was still developing largely by decisions. The imperial rescripts dating from the later part of the third and the early part of the fourth centuries, which constitute so large a part of Justinian's *Codex,* are case-law and, for the most part, very good case-law. It was not until the fourth century that the emperors began to declare that the rescripts issued in single cases were not to be regarded as establishing general rules. [52] Then, indeed, legislation became almost the sole factor of legal development. The change was not the result of a normal evolution but a symptom of degeneration. Decisions ceased to be regarded because jurisprudence had sunk to so low an ebb that they were not worth regarding. [53]

The older case law, however, stood in undiminished honor and authority. Much of it was saved in Justinian's *Digest,* some of it in his *Codex*. Only in this part of the compila-

---

[51] Gaius, *Institutes,* vol. i, p. 2, catalogues the prudentium responsa under the head of the ius scriptum.

[52] Constantine: " Contra ius rescripta non valeant: " *Cod*. Theod., 1, 2, c. 2. Arcadius: *Cod*. Theod., 1, 2, c. 11. Theodosius: *Cod*. Iust., 1, 14, c. 2. Anastasius: *Cod*. Iust., 1, 22, c. 6. Finally Justinian, with his famous " non exemplus sed legibus iudicandum ": *Cod*. 7, 45, c. 13.

[53] So Krüger, *Römische Rechtsquellen,* p. 267. He lays stress also on the extent to which, as is evidenced by contemporary constitutions, decisions were procured by favor or by corruption.

tion of Justinian were there seeds of life; and from the close of the eleventh century to the close of the nineteenth these seeds have yielded renewed and rich harvests.

MEDIÆVAL LAW, SECULAR AND ECCLESIASTICAL

Through the middle ages there was, in the states of continental Europe, no law-finding of the governmentalized and centralized type which had existed in the Roman empire. There were beginnings of such a development in the Frankish empire, not only in the king's courts but also in the county courts; but after the dissolution of that empire law-finding became popular again and particularistic. The arrested development of Germanic law and the degradation of such Roman law as survived to the plane of crude local custom, were due in the main probably to the independence of the local courts and the absence of any controlling central instance in the feeble feudal kingdoms; but these results were also due in part to the character of the law-finders. The old Germanic law-speakers, like the jurists of the Roman republic, were produced by a process of natural selection. They held their unofficial position by virtue of their recognized knowledge of the law and skill in adapting it to new exigencies. When Charles the Great instituted the *scabini,* it is not unlikely that his counts selected as a rule men who had been law-speakers or " advisers." In a sense the change was analogous to that which Augustus introduced when he "patented" the recognized jurists. But when, after the dissolution of the Frankish empire, the office of *scabinus,* like every other secular office, became associated with the holding of land and passed with the land by inheritance, law-finding passed into the hands of men who were not necessarily fit and who often were conspicuously unfit. The contempt which the civil doctors of the twelfth and following centuries expressed for customary law was not unfounded. Much of it was what they called it, " asinine " law, because it had been developed by " men lacking reason."

This was one of the reasons why national law, in its mediæval form of local usage, offered, upon the continent, so little resistance to the invasion of the renascent Roman law at the close of the middle ages. It was largely because national law on the continent had not developed as, in England, its own learned judiciary, that the civil doctors captured the new courts which were established by the absolute monarchy at the close of the middle ages, and carried Roman law into parts of Europe which had never been subject to Roman authority and in which there was practically no Romanic population.

When we turn from the rude secular states of the middle ages to their great ecclesiastical state, the Roman Church, and examine the legislative and judicial manner by which the canon law was developed, we feel ourselves in another age. From the point of view of legal development the difference between the secular and the ecclesiastical courts of the middle ages was as great as the difference between the courts of Saxon Alfred's time and those of English Elizabeth's time. In fact, the ecclesiastical courts perpetuated the judicial organization of the late Roman Empire and furnished a model for the European continental courts of modern times. Law-finding in the church was wholly sacerdotal.[54] The decision rested in the first place with the bishop as *iudex ordinarius* [55] and in the last instance with the pope. Any case, however, could be carried to Rome, not only on appeal but in first instance, for the pope was universal ordinary and had a jurisdiction concurrent with that of every bishop. When a case came before the pope he might either decide it himself or refer it, and he might refer it either to the ordinary judge of the diocese in which it properly belonged, or to a special delegate. In case of reference or delegation, he was likely, if a legal point of any difficulty was involved, to

[54] Popular coöperation in finding the judgment was illegal. Any local custom of the sort was invalid. *Decretal. Greg. IX*, i, iv, c. iii.

[55] The bishop decided, regularly after hearing the advice of his Chapter; but a local custom which permitted him to decide without hearing the advice of the Chapter was valid. Sexti, *Decretal.*, i, iv, c. iii.

send instructions as to the law to be applied, supposing the
facts to be as represented. [56] All this was in accordance with
Roman imperial law and usage.

Like the Roman emperors, the popes had legislative power,
and their decretals might be acts of pure legislation; but the
greater number of the decretals were like the imperial prescriptions, — decisions on questions of law based on actual
cases submitted.   In examining the *corpus iuris canonici*,
one is struck with the predominance of the casuistic element.
Like the *Digest* of Justinian, and that part of Justinian's
Codex which consists of prescriptions, the body of the canon
law is largely a compilation of case law.   It is unusual to call
the codified canon law, or any part of it, customary law;
but the part that rested on judgments was developed in primarily the same manner in which customary law always develops, *viz.*, by the persistent usage of the law-finders.

When the modern states of continental Europe began to
emerge from the political confusion of the middle ages,
the princes took into their hands the administration of justice
and gradually built up courts of the modern European type.
The change was generally accomplished by pouring new
wine into the old bottles, — by associating with the unlearned law-finders, whether these were nobles, citizens or
peasants, new law-finders learned in Roman laws, civil and
canon.   The introduction of these learned judges was the
result of a general conviction that the law of Justinian was
living law; and it was also the chief cause of the effective
reception of that law.   At the same time, the traditional
right of the king to do justice was made effective by drawing
appeals from the local and provincial courts to the king's
court, which ceased to be simply a feudal court of the chief
vassals and became, in part or wholly, a learned court

---

[56] When we speak of the bishop or pope as finding the law, it is in the
same sense in which we speak of the Roman emperor or the Roman president
of a province as a law-finder.   In fact, the bishop's judicial authority was
regularly exercised by a trained canonist, — his surrogate (subrogatus), and
papal decisions were regularly rendered by a council or court of trained
canonists.   The church had developed its own juristic class.

of appeal or of cassation. Gradually, of course, the learned element in all these courts displaced the popular element, and no new representation of the people was introduced until in the eighteenth and nineteenth centuries, jury trial in criminal cases was borrowed from England.

It is not generally recognized on the continent, even to-day, that these new courts made new law. Even in Spain and France, where law-finding was first centralized, the centralization came too late to enable the early courts to develop uniform national law. In Germany and Italy no such centralization was attained until the nineteenth century; all that was accomplished earlier was the establishment of courts of the new type in single German and Italian territories. In theory, the new royal and princely courts applied, in the first instance, existing local and territorial laws and customs, and in the second instance, the Roman civil law with the changes introduced by the canon law. In fact, however, the effective reception of the Roman civil law, wherever it took place, was accomplished by the persistent custom of the new learned courts; much established custom was destroyed by their persistent refusal to recognize and enforce it; and many new developments were attained, on the one hand by reinterpretation of territorial and local customs, and on the other hand by reinterpretation of the case law of Justinian's *Digest*. Broadly speaking, the practice of the new learned courts was, from the close of the middle ages until the end of the seventeenth century when legislation began to flow more freely, the chief agency by which continental law was recast.

VII

PROBLEMS OF ROMAN LEGAL HISTORY[1]

To attempt to recapitulate within the limits of a single paper the unsolved problems of Roman legal history would be an absurdity. Such an undertaking would make it necessary for us to follow the development of the Roman law from the Twelve Tables to Justinian's law books in order to indicate what portions of this millenial movement are still obscure. Even then the survey would be incomplete, since the history of the Roman law neither begins with the Twelve Tables nor ends with Justinian. It begins at that unknown date when Rome began and it has not ended yet.

To select a narrower period and to single out what seem the more important problems would be more feasible; but the mere enumeration of difficulties would be neither interesting nor profitable.

The best excuse for a paper on the problems of any science is the writer's conviction or hope that he may be able to make some contribution towards their solution, if it be only by suggesting unworked lines of investigation which appear to him to promise useful results. It is my belief that for the most important period of Roman legal history — the period in which the ancient Roman law, public and private, reached its highest development, and which extends, roughly speaking, from the middle of the third century before Christ to the middle of the third century after Christ — there is a promising method of investigation or line of approach which as yet has been scantily utilized. The method which I advocate is that of comparison; and the comparison which I suggest is with Anglo-American legal

[1] Read before the Congress of Arts and Sciences, St. Louis, September 21, 1904. Reprinted from *Columbia Law Review*, vol. 4, no. 8, December, 1904, pp. 523–540.

development from the twelfth century to the present day.

The older lines of investigation appear to be worked out. It does not seem likely that new material of importance will be discovered; we can hardly hope for a second find like the fourth book of the *Institutes* of Gaius; and all direct methods of interpreting the existing sources have been so diligently and ably exploited by European jurists, from Cujacius to Mommsen and Lenel, that every student of the Roman law now has the instinctive feeling that a new interpretation is probably a very doubtful interpretation.

The usefulness and the limitations of the comparative method of studying legal history perhaps need more accurate definition than they have yet received. The assumption with which comparative jurisprudence starts, is the essential identity of human nature everywhere. The inference is that social developments among the most different peoples would be identical if all had reached the same stage of development and were living under identical conditions. In this last qualification we have the first and most important limitation upon the comparative method. Conditions are never identical; they are at most broadly similar. The working hypothesis, accordingly, on which comparative jurisprudence proceeds, is that peoples in corresponding stages of social development are likely to approach legal problems from similar points of view and to attempt their solution on similar lines. The inference is that a fully known development in one nation may help us to interpret a partly known development in another nation. Proceeding with proper caution, we may even fill gaps in the historic record of one system by searching for the intermediate links in a similar chain of development in another system. Such reconstructions, it is needless to say, will seldom be indisputable, but they will be more nearly correct than the products of the historical imagination.

Another limitation upon the comparative method, as an agency in historic reconstruction, is found in the fact that different legal systems do not develop in absolute isolation. The history of human law, as of all civilization, is largely a history of borrowings. I think, however, that this limitation is fully appreciated by students, and that there is at the present time little danger that it will be disregarded. The tendency of historical jurisprudence now, as in the past, is rather to exaggerate than to overlook the borrowed elements in each legal development. Because the Romans had certain institutions which were not primitive and which resembled Greek institutions, and because similar institutions existed at a still earlier date in Egypt and in Babylon, there has been over-readiness among students to assume, without sufficient evidence, a series of imitations and an unbroken chain of derivations. A similar process of reasoning has attributed to Roman sources not a few English institutions which on closer investigation appear to be independent products, as truly English as they were truly Roman or, to put it more accurately, neither English nor Roman but human. Their similarity is due to the similar working of the legal mind under analogous conditions.

It may, however, be granted that the comparative method must be used with caution, that the movements compared must be intrinsically comparable, and that allowance must be made for possible borrowings.

Given these limitations, it is not surprising that comparative study of legal institutions for purely scientific purposes has thus far been confined practically to the field of early law. There has been greater safety here, because the conditions of social existence are more uniform among barbarous peoples than among civilized nations, and because there is less chance of imitation of foreign customs.

In this part of the field, the application of the comparative method to the problems of Roman legal history has already yielded valuable results. The comparative study of early law in general has thrown light into many corners which were hopelessly dark to the later Romans themselves. " Not for all things established by our ancestors," wrote

Julian, " can a reason be assigned "; but for quite a number of these things we are now able to assign reasons that are not merely plausible but convincing.

To the later and more important stages of Roman legal development — to the public law of the later Republic, and to the civil and prætorian law of the later Republic and of the early Empire — the comparative method has not been applied, or it has been applied sporadically only and with little result. The reason is very simple. The jurists of continental Europe have rightly felt that the other and more modern legal systems with which they are acquainted are not available for comparison. As regards public law, they have been living under absolute monarchies or under constitutional monarchies in which the monarch is still a real force. They have had no personal and vital acquaintance with republican government conducted on a large scale and maintained for a long period — no such experience as Englishmen have had, in substance, for two centuries and Americans, in form and in substance both, for more than a century. As far as popular participation in national government has been introduced in the larger European states, it has been borrowed from England and adapted to continental conditions. As regards private law, the continental European jurists have had personal and vital acquaintance with only two systems — the remnants of the old Germanic law, a law arrested in its development in the tenth century, and the law of the later Roman Empire, which at the close of the middle ages they borrowed *en bloc* and which they have since been modifying and assimilating. The only Germanic system which has had an unimpeded and continuous development, the only modern system which has an independent history comparable in its duration with that of the Roman law, is to them almost a closed book. On the other hand, the English, who have the data for comparison, have done little serious work in the field of Roman legal history, and the best of that work has been done in the field of Roman public law. In the field of private law they have relied on

French and German writers, not only for the historic facts but for the interpretation of the facts.

But, it will be asked, are the modern Anglo-American and the ancient Roman legal systems fairly comparable quantities? Are there such broad analogies in their general development as to warrant the hope that a minute study of the one will be serviceable in interpreting the other? I grant the differences; they are sufficiently obvious; but I insist on fundamental although less obvious analogies.

I

The constitution of the Roman Republic was substantially an unwritten law, as is the English constitution. It consisted of precedents, *i.e.*, adjustments reached in the political field at the close of political conflicts. Of those adjustments a part, but only a part, was incorporated in declaratory statutes. In establishing their Republic, the Romans retained their ancient elective kingship for ceremonial purposes, housing the King of the Sacra in the old royal palace and treating him as head, or rather as figurehead, of their state church. The real powers of the kingship they entrusted to officials elected by political parties. The English have retained a less shadowy kingship, but they have similarly transferred the most important powers of the crown to a small body of officials who represent the dominant party in an elective assembly.

The American constitution, on the other hand, is indeed a written one, but there has grown up beside it a body of authoritative precedents. The American executive has many points of resemblance, in time of peace, to a Roman consul; in time of war, to a Roman dictator. To the Romans, the chief change which occurred when the Republic was established was that the royal power was entrusted to magistrates elected for short terms. Sir Henry Maine asserts that in their presidency the Americans have perpetuated the monarchy of George the Third. A witty Frenchman, M.

Raoul Frary, tells us that England is now a republic with an hereditary president, while the United States is a monarchy with an elective king. The common element — and the fundamental element — in all three constitutions is the exercise of governmental power by men elected by party organizations.

Great Britain, like Rome, has built up a world empire; and like Rome it has combined domestic liberty with external power by limiting governmental authority at home and permitting it to act freely abroad. The reserve powers of the British crown furnish the constitutional historian with an exact analogy to the war power (*imperium militiæ*) of the Roman consul. The viceroy or governor is the English equivalent of the Roman proconsul or proprætor; and colonial affairs are controlled by the British Privy Council as provincial affairs were controlled by the Roman Senate. The influence of the Roman Senate made for continuity of policy, as does the influence of the Privy Council, and for the same reason. The Romans kept their ex-magistrates in the Senate as the British keep their ex-ministers in the Privy Council. So that the Senate, like the Privy Council, represented the expert political experience of both political parties. As a matter of policy, Great Britain has conceded, as did Rome in the Republican and early Imperial periods, a large measure of local self-government to its subjects beyond the seas. In both empires we find the war power and the control of diplomatic relations in the hands of the home government, the ordinary administration decentralized and left in the hands of local authorities.

The United States, after rounding out its continental domain, has recently acquired possessions beyond the seas. In dealing with them it is somewhat embarrassed by the absence from its written constitution of indefinite and general governmental power — power corresponding to the Roman military imperium or to the residuary authority of the British crown. This difficulty was felt a century ago when the process of continental expansion was beginning;

and each successive exigency has been met, and is being met, by the development in our unwritten constitution of the war powers of the American president. In the administration of its earlier continental acquisitions, the United States, following the example of Rome and of Great Britain, encouraged the development of local self-government; and it is following the same policy in its new insular dependencies.

In the expansion of Great Britain and of the United States, as in the expansion of Rome, the fact of central interest is the upbuilding of empire by a free people; and in the British and American empires — if the insular dependencies of the United States are to be dignified with so high-sounding a title as empire — the fundamental problem is the same which confronted the statesmen of republican Rome, *viz.*, the reconciliation of empire with liberty.

One of the devices of Roman public law for limiting governmental power at home was an elaborate system of checks and balances. The power of almost every official was limited in its practical exercise by the independent and possibly opposing powers of other officials. In the hierarchy of superior and inferior officials which constitutes the administrative system of the modern continental European state, no such checks as these exist; but they are familiar to the English public lawyer, and they have been greatly multiplied in American constitutional law.

The Anglo-American law protects private rights against governmental encroachments not in modern European but in Roman fashion. In the place of administrative control of the inferior by the superior, which is so highly developed in modern European law, the English and American law, like the Roman, has developed control through the ordinary courts. When, for example, a Roman ædile destroyed merchandise which obstructed the public highway, the legitimacy of his action was tested, at Rome, not by appeal to the consul, but by an action to recover damages for illegal destruction of property, just as a similar exercise of police power would be tested in Great Britain or in the United States.

It may finally be noted that contemporary political conditions in the United States help us rightly to understand the dramatic final century of the Roman Republic. When we cease to view that period through the eyes of European scholars, we shall recognize that its salient characteristic was the appearance on a magnificent scale of those political personages whom we call " bosses "; and we shall discover that the Latin word for boss was *princeps*. *Princeps*, Mommsen tells us, was a word commonly used in the later Republic to designate the most prominent citizens. The definition might be made more exact. The citizens who were designated as *principes* — men like Marius and Sulla and Pompey and Crassus and Julius Cæsar — were prominent before all things in political management. They were the men who controlled the machinery of the senatorial and popular parties. The members of the first triumvirate, a body which an American politician would instinctively designate as " The Big Three," were described by Cicero as *principes*. In our federal system of government we have not developed any boss whose authority reaches beyond the limits of a single state; we have no national bosses; and if we had them, our constitutional and administrative arrangements are such that even a national boss could not readily put himself at the head of a large mercenary army in New Mexico or in Alaska and upset the government by marching on Washington. These variations, however, do not affect the substantial identity in political science of our boss and the Roman *princeps;* and this identification enables us to understand that the official theory of Augustus and of his immediate successors — the theory that the free commonwealth was still in existence — did not seem to the Roman public to be a fiction. Through his control of the army the boss had become a military dictator; but the forms of popular government were, for a time, sufficiently preserved to enable intelligent citizens to blink the change, and to leave the majority of the citizens unconscious that any serious change had occurred. To them, Augustus was simply the boss raised to his highest terms. Consuls and prætors and all the other officers of republican government were elected on his nomination and the Senate was filled with his henchmen, but these were familiar accompaniments of boss rule. From this point of view, we can fully understand Pliny's remark, that the very men who were most averse to recognizing anything like lordship (*dominatio*) had no objection to the authority of a *princeps*.

Modern examples of the transformation of the party boss into the military monarch, with more or less careful maintenance of the forms of popular government, are not far to seek, but we must seek them still in the Latin world. English history offers no nearer parallel than the career of Cromwell; but Cromwell, although a party leader, was not a boss, and in the English Commonwealth the evolution of military monarchy remained incomplete.

II

In the field of private law the movement in the early Empire was substantially as well as formally a continuation of that in the late Republic; and during both periods the processes by which the Roman law, civil and prætorian, was developed, were fundamentally the same as those by which Anglo-American law and equity have been developed. This fundamental similarity is not generally appreciated, because the mode in which the Roman law was developed is not commonly understood. We read in every legal history that the Roman civil law was cast into the form of a code, the famous Twelve Tables, about four and a half centuries B.C., and that the further development of this law was accomplished chiefly by interpretation of the Twelve Tables. We read also that the interpretation which was accepted as authoritative, and by which the law was developed, did not proceed from judges, but until the third

century B.C. from a college of priests, and after that time
from a small number of private citizens who were known as
iurisprudentes. The English common law, on the other
hand, as we all know, has been built up by judicial opinions;
it is simply the permanent practice of the courts. At first
glance it does not seem as if these two processes were analogous. On closer inspection, however, the differences are
seen to be superficial. The law of the Twelve Tables was
not a code in the modern sense of the word; it was simply
a collection of the principal rules of early Roman customary
law. From the point of view of comparative jurisprudence,
it belongs to the same class (although to a more advanced
period of legal development) as the early German Leges and
the Anglo-Saxon dooms. It has recently been asserted by a
prominent Italian historian that the Twelve Tables were
probably a private compilation, and that the story of their
construction by the decemvirs and of their submission to
and acceptance by the Roman popular assembly deserves
no more credit than the legend of the slaying of Virginia
which forms a part of the narrative of the decemviral epoch.
Still more recently this thesis has been defended with great
ingenuity by a distinguished French legal historian. I myself have not been convinced by their arguments. I still cling
to the belief that the essential part of the Roman story is
probably correct; that the Twelve Tables were probably accepted by a Roman assembly as the German Leges were accepted a thousand years later by German tribal assemblies.
For my present purpose, however, the answer to this historical question is not material. In the later Republic the compilation known as the Twelve Tables was officially regarded
as a Lex; it was revered as a charter of popular rights and as
" the cradle of the civil law "; but it was interpreted with
as much freedom as if it had been merely a private statement
of the rules governing the administration of justice in a far-
away and semi-barbarous age. It exercised little more real
influence on the administration of justice during the last
century of the Roman Republic than the laws of Alfred

exercised upon the English administration of justice in the time of the Tudors. The compilation had been surrounded for generations by a growing mass of interpretation, which had so modified and supplemented its primitive and scanty provisions that for all practical purposes the interpretation and not the *lex* was the law.

The first alleged distinction between the development of Roman civil and English common law thus disappears. Each represents a development from rude and simple custom to refined and complex jurisprudence by means of interpretation. There remains, however, the apparent difference between the interpreters. What is there in common between the jurists of republican Rome and the king's judges in England? To answer this question we must consider the position and activity of the Roman jurists. They obviously were not judges in the ordinary sense, for they did not hear pleadings or try cases. They rather resembled our lawyers, for they gave advice to all who chose to consult them. They helped their clients to avoid trouble by drafting contracts, wills and other instruments; and when trouble had arisen, they gave opinions (*responsa*) on the legal points at issue. So far at least their activities were those of practising lawyers. But they differed from all other practising lawyers of whom we know anything in two important respects. In the first place, they did not take charge of cases in litigation, either as attorneys or as barristers. They were willing neither to prepare cases for trial nor to argue cases before the *iudices*. Such matters were attended to by professional orators like Cicero. Cicero was a lawyer in our sense, but at Rome he was never regarded as a jurist. In the second place, while the Roman jurists were always ready to furnish opinions, they neither expected nor received pecuniary rewards. The rewards at which they aimed were the gratitude of those whom they had served, the confidence of the public, and eventual election to political office. As practising lawyers they were, accordingly, servants of the public in general rather than servants of their special clients.

To appreciate how far the Roman jurists discharged the same function as the English judges, we must note how controversies were actually decided at Rome and how they are actually decided under the English system. Controversies were actually decided at Rome, not by the magistrate who heard the pleadings, but by *iudices,* who were private citizens. Similarly, controversies have been decided for the last seven centuries in the Anglo-American administration of justice by juries, also composed of private citizens. Neither were the Roman *iudices* nor are the English jurymen supposed to know the law. As English jurymen are instructed by the judges, so the Roman *iudices* were instructed by the jurists. The instruction might be directly addressed to a *iudex* if he choose to ask for it, but it usually came in the form of an opinion obtained by one of the parties. It was of course possible that both parties might have obtained opinions from different jurists, and it was conceivable that the opinions might be conflicting. This, however, was not the rule but the exception; because the Republican jurists, in giving their opinions, were not in the position of paid advocates trying to make out a case for their clients; they were unpaid servants of the public and ministers of the law itself. Differences of opinion, under these circumstances, were no more numerous than those which have always existed in the English and American courts. The republican *iudices* were not bound to follow the opinion of any jurist; they had the powers of English criminal jurors; they were judges of law and of fact alike. In both systems, however, it is noteworthy that the decisions actually rendered by *iudices* or by jurymen have never been cited as authority. What was cited at Rome was the response of a jurist, and what is cited in Anglo-American law is the opinion of the court. Hobbes perceived the fundamental analogy between the Roman jurists and the English judges when he declared, in his *Leviathan,* that the king's judges were not properly judges but jurisconsults.

The Roman law was thus developed, as the English law

has been developed, not by the decision of controversies, as is sometimes said, but by the opinions expressed in connection with such decisions by specially trained and expert ministers of the law. The English judge combines some of the powers of a Roman prætor with the authority of a Roman jurist — he is half prætor and half *iurisprudens;* but his influence upon the development of the law has not been prætorian but jurisprudential.

It should be noted further that single *responsa* did not make law at Rome any more than instructions from judges to juries have ever made law in England or in America. What were regarded at Rome as authoritative precedents were the so-called " received opinions," that is, the opinions which were approved and followed by the juristic class. In England and America, similarly, it is not the preliminary rulings or the final instructions of the trial judges but the opinions of the bench to which cases are carried on appeal that constitute precedents; and it is doubtful whether a decision of even the highest court in a case of first impression really makes law. It seems the better opinion that it is the acceptance of such a decision by professional opinion and its reaffirmation by the court in later cases which makes it really authoritative.

The real difference between the Roman jurists and the English judges was that the Roman jurists, like the law-speakers of our German ancestors, who laid down the law for the folk-moots, were designated by natural selection. It is interesting to note that, before the conversion of the Germans to Christianity, their law-speakers were priests, as were the earliest Roman jurists. After the Germans were Christianized, the law-speakers were those persons who were generally recognized as " wise men "; their position and their authority, like that of the Roman jurists of the later Republic, rested on general opinion, which was itself based on professional opinion. In the Frankish period the law-speakers began to be artificially selected. The Frankish count appointed the " advisers " (*rachineburgi*); and these advisers developed into the *Schöffen* of the middle ages. In other words, the German law-speaker is the ancestor of the European judge. At Rome also, in the Imperial period, artificial selection was substituted for natural selection. Certain jurists received from the Emperor "the right of responding"; and the *iudices* were thenceforth bound to follow opinions given by these certified or "patented" jurists unless divergent opinions were presented. This change brought the Roman jurists a step nearer to the Anglo-American judges. The evolution was completed, as I shall presently indicate, in the second century after Christ; but before describing the processes by which law was made in the Empire, we must consider and compare Roman prætorian law and English equity, in order to see how far the processes by which these systems were developed present real analogies.

III

Roman prætorian law and English equity are in so far analogous as they both represent what the Romans called *ius honorarium* — "official law." In both cases the new law was produced by governmental agencies which were not exclusively nor indeed primarily judicial — agencies which set themselves above the previously existing law and not merely supplemented it but overrode it.

There was a superficial difference between the way in which the Roman prætors made law and the way in which the English chancellors made it. The prætors used the quasi-legislative form of ordinance or "edict"; the English chancellors developed new rules in judicial fashion by decisions rendered in single cases. When, however, we examine the edicts of the Roman prætors, and consider how their provisions were applied, the difference almost disappears. The prætor, like the chancellor, was originally an administrative rather than a judicial officer; but his duties were in the main judicial; it was his chief business to arrange for the termination of private controversies. The edict which each prætor set up at the beginning of his year of office was not a series of commands but a programme. In it he set forth remedies and indicated under what circumstances each remedy would be given. This programme was carried out, as single cases were presented, by means of formulas sent to the *iudices*. The formula was a command; if the *iudex* found certain allegations of the plaintiff to be true, and if he did not find certain other allegations of the defendant to be true, he was commanded to render a certain decision. The English chancellor decided cases as he saw fit. The Roman prætor caused cases to be decided as he saw fit. A new rule working itself out in chancery was first disclosed in the decision of the special case which suggested it, and any modification of the new rule was subsequently revealed in the same way. Any new rules which the Roman prætor intended to enforce, any modifications which he intended to make in the rules laid down by his predecessors, were announced in advance, at the beginning of his year of office. Fundamentally these two methods of creating law are identical, and they both resemble law-finding rather than law-making. The rules laid down were suggested in both systems by actual controversies, and they were amended in both systems as new controversies afforded new points of view. In form the Roman process was more considerate of private interests. The complaint of the English common lawyer, that equity was administered according to the length of the chancellor's foot, would have lost much of its force if the length of the foot had been indicated in advance.

The similarities of the two movements are more striking than the formal differences between them. At the outset of his activity neither the Roman prætor nor the English chancellor was held to be capable of making or finding law or of creating new rights. Each, however, could issue orders, and each could enforce these orders *in personam* by fine and imprisonment. Each was therefore able to impose new sanctions and to create new remedies; and eventually, in both systems, it was recognized that where there was a sanction there must be a rule and where there was a remedy there must be a right. Strictly speaking, the rules laid down in the edicts of the prætors and those expressed or implied in English decisions in equity became law by force of custom. It was by the iteration of the same rule in successive prætorian edicts (*edicta tralaticia*) that the Roman official law was built up. It was by the observance of precedents and the development of a settled practice that English equity came to be a constituent part of the English law.

There was, however, one important historical difference between the two movements. The development of the Roman prætorian law not only made Roman law more equitable, but it also introduced into that law the commercial customs of the Mediterranean — customs which apparently date back in part to the Babylonian empire. A similar reception of European commercial law took place in England, but here it came later, after the development of equity and chiefly through the action of the common law courts. In both cases, however, as Goldschmidt has pointed out, commercial law was not brought in as a distinct and separate system, as in the modern continental European states; the English law was commercialized by decisions of the common law courts, largely rendered in the eighteenth century, just as the Roman law had been commercialized by the prætorian edict in the second and first centuries B.C.

IV

In the Roman Imperial period the processes of law making became more obviously similar to the processes by which law has been developed in modern times. Under the Empire, law-finding gradually became altogether governmental. The first step in this direction was taken, as we have seen, when the jurists became representatives and agents of the Emperors. The next step was to establish new courts, civil and criminal, in which Imperial officials heard the pleadings and the evidence and rendered the decisions (*iudicia ex-traordinaria*). The last step was to transform the surviving courts of the older republican type — the prætorian courts — into purely governmental courts. This change was accomplished by substituting for independent citizen *iudices* subaltern officers of the court itself, mere referees. This last change brought the Roman courts to substantially the same form as the European continental courts of the present day. To describe the change in English phraseology, not only did the magistrates become judges, but jury-trial was abolished.

In proportion as law-finding was governmentalized, it was also centralized. From the judgments of the independent *iudices* appeals had never been permitted. From the decision of the Imperial judges appeals ran to the Emperor, or to such higher judges as he might designate. In the Imperial Council, or rather in that branch of the council which came to be known as the Auditory, the Roman Empire obtained a supreme court of appellate jurisdiction.

In connection with these changes, all the more important offices of a judicial character came to be filled by the patented jurists. During the republican period and under the first emperors, the jurists might occasionally act as *iudices* and they frequently became magistrates, but their control over law-finding, although practically complete, was for the most part indirect. The great Roman jurists of the second and third centuries of the Christian era were judges in a modern sense; and it was by their direct activity, *i.e.*, by their decisions on points of law, and particularly by the decisions rendered in the Imperial Auditory that the law of the Empire was chiefly developed. Their decisions were reported and digested in their own writings. To treat the juristic literature of the early Empire as " scientific law " or " legal theory," which became law only by popular or professional recognition, is to misrepresent its character and its authority. If the eminent European scholars who have written the standard histories of the Roman law were familiar with development of Anglo-American law, they would readily recognize the true character of the law developed in the Roman Empire.

In the early Empire, as in the Republic, direct legislation played only a subordinate part in the development of the law. After the middle of the third century, however, when the production of juristic literature ceased, it is commonly assumed that all legal change was made by direct imperial legislation. As late as the beginning of the fourth century, however, the law was still developing largely by decisions. The imperial rescripts which date from the latter part of the third and the early part of the fourth centuries, and which constitute so important a part of Justinian's *Codex,* are case law, *i.e.,* they are decisions reached by the imperial supreme court, published as imperial rescripts; and for the most part these rescripts are fully up to the level of the previous century. It was not until the fourth century that the Emperors began to declare that rescripts issued in single cases were not to be regarded as establishing general rules. Then, indeed, legislation became almost the sole factor of legal development. This change, however, was not the result of a progressive evolution, it was a symptom of degeneration. Judicial decisions ceased to be regarded because jurisprudence had sunk to so low an ebb that the decisions were not worth regarding. The older case law, however, stood in undiminished honor and authority. Much of it was saved in Justinian's *Digest,* some of it in his *Codex.* Only in these casuistic portions of Justinian's compilations were there seeds of life; and from the close of the eleventh to the close of the nineteenth century those seeds have yielded rich and renewed harvests.

v

The subject assigned me — with which I have been taking certain liberties — is not European legal history nor legal history in general nor comparative jurisprudence; it is Roman legal history; and for this reason I have thus far confined myself, in the main, to indicating how largely the study of English legal history may be expected to help us to a deeper and truer comprehension of Roman legal history. I trust, in closing, that I may be permitted to take a further liberty with my theme, and to indicate that a careful study of Roman legal history will be of great service to the English or American student who desires to comprehend his own legal history. I lay little stress on the point that we may thus recognize what has been borrowed; I desire chiefly to insist upon the point that we may thus better appreciate the true character of English legal history as an independent development. Furnished with a knowledge of the Roman law and of its development, the English investigator will more accurately gauge by comparison the excellencies and the defects of the English law. He may not find that the Roman law is more scientific — a statement which I take to mean that its broader generalizations are thought to be more correct — but he will certainly find that the Roman law is more artistic. The sense of relation, of proportion, of harmony, which the Greeks possessed and which they utilized in shaping matter into forms of beauty, the Romans possessed also, but the material in which they wrought was the whole social life of man. There was profound self-knowledge in the saying of the Roman jurist that jurisprudence was " the art of life."

The comparative student will find also that while the English law has developed in certain directions further than the Roman, the Roman law in certain other respects had attained sixteen hundred or even two thousand years ago a development which seems to go beyond ours. This is true, for instance, in the whole field of commercial dealings. The great regard paid in all commercial transactions to good faith and the instincts of an honest tradesman, and in particular the abandonment by the Romans, two thousand years ago, of the primitive and dishonest doctrine of *caveat emptor* — a doctrine which the English law still unaccountably retains — point out lines along which, I believe, our own law is bound to develop.

Best of all, the comparative student will learn to distinguish between that which is peculiar and therefore accidental in both systems and that which is common to both and therefore presumably universal. It has long been the hope of some of the greatest modern jurists, both in English-speaking countries and in Europe, that by strictly inductive study it may be possible to discover a real instead of an imaginary natural law. The corresponding hope of the legal historians, that it will in time be possible to formulate the great laws that govern legal development, is not, I believe, an idle dream; and I am sure that the minute comparative study of Roman and Anglo-American legal developments will carry us further towards such a goal than any other possible comparison.

VIII

JURISPRUDENCE [1]

Our lives are controlled, to an extent which we do not measure without effort, by rules of conduct which are imposed upon us by our environment and which we may not contravene without endangering our existence, our welfare or our happiness. We do not ordinarily realize the multiplicity of these rules or their coercive operation, because our acceptance of them is largely unconscious and our obedience to them, the leading of a normal or regular life, is largely automatic. When, however, we force ourselves to consider all these rules, and when we attempt to classify them, we see that some of them, such as the rules of healthful living, represent primarily the adaptation of our conduct to our physical environment; others, such as the rules of thrift, adaptation to what may conveniently be termed our physical-social environment, that is, to those conditions which result from the interaction and reciprocal modification of human society and its environment; while a third group of rules, which may be termed social, seems to be imposed upon us by the sentiments or the will of our fellowmen. When rules which we assign to the physical or to the physical-social group appear also, as they often do, in the distinctively social group — when, for example, we find that violations of the rules of health or of thrift are denounced as immoral and are in some instances penalized by law — it still remains true that these rules are not primarily social. They do not originate in social opinion, and disregard of them is attended by risks which society has not created. They receive the additional sanctions of morals and of

[1] A lecture delivered at Columbia University in the series on Science, Philosophy and Art, February 19, 1908. Published by The Columbia University Press, New York, 1908.

law because human interests are so solidary that the individual cannot live or die or prosper or suffer for himself alone.

It may of course be queried whether we have any right to consider human society as a thing distinct from its physical environment, acting independently upon that environment and imposing upon us, as individuals, rules of conduct which are purely social. In the constitution of human society, indeed, there is much that seems arbitrary, and in its action there is much that is incalculable; but it is possible that our inability to forecast social action is due solely to the complexity of the phenomena, and that our impression that society determines in any degree its own constitution and conduct is an illusion. These questions, however, lie outside of the field of jurisprudence. The law with which our science has to do assumes the existence of individual wills and bases its authority upon a social will. Whether the individual will is in any sense free; whether the social will is the resultant of free individual wills or a direct and independent product of the social life; in what degree the social life is itself controlled by forces which men do not create and cannot control — these are questions which the jurist gladly leaves to the psychologist, the sociologist and the philosopher.

Legal rules, even when they are assignable, by virtue of their origin, to the physical or to the physical-social group, belong, as regards their legal quality, in the group of social rules. In the same group we find a second body of rules which we call moral; and in addition to legal rules and moral rules we are aware of a third body of more or less heterogeneous rules which you will permit me, for convenience, to call manners.

What now is the characteristic which differentiates law from manners and morals? Obviously not the field in which it operates, not the matters with which it deals. Law has indeed a field, or a number of fields, in which it operates alone. Law has created institutions of its own; and the rules which shape these institutions and govern their operation had no previous existence in manners or in morals. To a large extent, however, manners, morals and law cover the same field. To knock a man down, for example, or to wrest from him portable valuables is, in most instances, at once unmannerly, immoral and illegal. Especially large is the field which is common to law and to morals — so large, indeed, that many time-honored definitions of law assume a complete correspondence of law with morals, and it has been possible to say, although erroneously, that law is simply applied morals.

It is equally impossible to find the distinguishing characteristic of law in its purpose or end. The primary purpose of law is the maintenance of the social order; but this purpose is also subserved, in large measure, by morals and by manners. The graver disturbances of the established social order are usually stigmatized as immoral. The existence, in the various fields of human effort, of accepted and regular modes of activity does much to lessen the friction of social life; and the established forms of social intercourse, manners in the narrowest sense of the word, take out of the struggle for existence much of its bitterness and perhaps do more than either morals or law to prevent breaches of the peace.

The ultimate purpose of the law, indeed, is not the maintenance of the social order but the assurance of the conditions of social progress. That man shall obtain increasing control over his physical environment; that the relations of men shall become more and more kindly; that human life shall be more and more worth living — these are the final objects of the law. To attain these ends individual effort must not only remain worth while, it must be increasingly encouraged; in other words, competition must continue; and yet anti-social activities must be increasingly restrained and there must be increasing coöperation. The fundamental and eternal problem of human civilization is the reconciliation of individual with social interests. Such progress as has thus far been made towards the solution of this problem has been achieved by raising the plane of competition and by increasing the range of coöperation. In the methods of competition craft has replaced brute force, and fair play is replacing craft. The objects of competition have become and are becoming less and less material: honor is sought rather than wealth, and higher honor is accorded for social service than for personal success. The coöperation of the horde has been replaced by that of the class and, in many fields, by that of the nation; international coöperation exists and is increasing. All these ends, however, are moral as well as legal ends, and higher ethical ideals indicate lines of legal progress.

We gain our first glimpse of the distinguishing characteristic of law, and perhaps of that of morals also, when we note the different results that attach to the disregard or violation of different rules of social conduct. If the rule infringed be one of manners simply, there is usually a social reaction of surprise, attended commonly by ridicule of the offender. If the rule infringed be one of morals, the social reaction is more energetic: it is more than a surprise, it is a shock, and it is attended by more or less heated disapproval, which may range from contempt through scorn to loathing. In the mind of the offender himself there is a reflex of the social disapproval; there is the prick of conscience, the sense of shame; and if he be a religious man and his offense be one that his religion brands as a sin, there will be a sense of divine displeasure. Arnold defined religion as morality touched with emotion; but there is a marked element of emotion in morality itself, independent of religion. All these reactions, it will be noted, are purely psychical, and the penalties which follow breaches of manners and morals operate upon the offender's feelings. Law, on the other hand, encourages certain courses of conduct by the assurance of advantages and discourages other courses of conduct by imposing disadvantages or penalties which affect the property or the person; and these purely legal consequences may be enforced, in case of need, by the entire physical power of the community.

We note further, and this brings us to a second *differentia* of law, that the advantages which follow the observance of legal rules and the disadvantages or penalties which attend the disregard or violation of such rules do not attach solely by virtue of the social sentiment or opinion, but by virtue of the social will. In civilized communities this social will is formulated through special processes and usually by special organs. The processes are mainly political and the organs are for the most part governmental. In constitutions adopted by the people, in acts passed by representative bodies, in orders of administrative officers and in decisions of courts we find, authoritatively stated, the rules of law, the advantages which attach to their observance, the disadvantages or penalties which follow their disregard or violation. The rules of manners and of morals, on the other hand, are not stated in any such authoritative form. In early society, indeed, authority over the entire field of conduct is usually accorded to priests, and in later stages of social development this authority frequently persists in the field of morals; but in an advanced civilization it tends to disappear. It may still be asserted, and it may long command extensive recognition; but the recognition becomes less and less general, and morals, like manners, tend to rest directly upon social sentiment and opinion. They are matters of usage.

To affirm that law is formulated through special processes, and chiefly by special organs of the community, is not to deny that its rules are largely determined by social sentiment. Manners and morals are, to a large extent, antecedent to law, and social usage has always furnished much of the material of which law has been made. In the earliest stages of legal development usage apparently furnishes all the material; it is converted into law simply by adding the support of social force; and in every state of social progress new law is made by the recognition and enforcement of established customs. Manners, morals and law, all appear to rest ultimately upon social utility. The conversion of usage into law, the decision whether any particular rule of conduct shall be supported by the physical power of the community, is clearly a question of social expediency. Social utility or expediency is determined, in the whole field of conduct, by the social judgment, and social force can be exercised only by virtue of the social will. The social judgment, however, is usually inarticulate; it reveals itself as sentiment. In the matters with which the law deals, we call this sentiment the sense of justice. The social will, likewise, is, in most instances, not aimless indeed, but only vaguely aware of its true aim; it manifests itself as impulse to do something, to sweep aside or crush something that is felt to be alien and hostile. As it is the primary function of practical ethics to interpret moral emotion and to give articulate form to the moral sentiment, so it is the primary function of practical jurisprudence to interpret the sense of justice and to formulate in legal rules those ends toward which the social will is blindly groping. Ulpian's " *nomen iuris a iustitia,*" although indefensible from the philological point of view, is good philosophy. In the interpretation of the social sentiment and the social will judges and legislatures have indeed an authority which no men or bodies of men possess in the fields of manners and morals: even when they misinterpret the general sense of justice and thwart the general will, the rules which they lay down are law. Such law, however, has no root, and, if it be not formally abrogated or superseded, it becomes a dead letter. In the long run, general sentiment and opinion control not only the finding and making of law, but also its enforcement.

Persistent disregard of general sentiment on the part of law-finders or law-makers is exceptional; in the democratic state it is almost impossible. Conflicts between general sentiment and positive law arise, as a rule, only when social changes have made the established legal rules unsatisfactory. Such conflicts take the form of agitation for the reform of the law, and they cease when the law is suitably amended. Conflicts between sectional or local or class sentiment and the general law arise, on the contrary, in every type of state, and such conflicts are practically incessant. Powerless, as a rule, to control law-finding or law-making, adverse minority sentiment makes itself felt in resistance to the enforcement of the law; and under favoring circumstances the resistance may result in the nullification of the law. From such results it is sometimes inferred that the physical sanctions of the law are less coercive than the psychical sanction of opinion, even when the opinion is that of a portion of the community only, of a locality or of a social group. It should be noted, however, that when the law is worsted in these conflicts it does not put forth its full power. It is defeated because it binds its own hands. Laws are nullified, for example, because local administrative authorities are legally independent of the central administration, or because juries are permitted by the law to interpret the law as they see fit. It may not be advisable to destroy or seriously to limit local self-government because Sunday-closing laws are locally nullified, or to empower judges to set aside verdicts in criminal cases because business or labor interests make it difficult to punish illegal combinations; but these or similar changes in the law can be made if such be the general will.

The strength of the law lies in the fact that its physical sanctions operate, or can be made to operate, with equal force throughout the entire area of a state and among all classes. The weakness of general opinion lies in the fact that it operates less strongly on men's minds than does the opinion of their locality and that of their class. Especially strong is the influence of group opinion, and it is strongest in the smallest and most homogeneous groups. The pressure of social opinion seems to vary inversely as the square of the social distance. Hence the tendency of all usage to variation and to particularism; hence the lusty growth, at all times, of group morals — morals of the class, of the profession, of the business, of the gang. Left to itself, enforcing itself only by the pressure of social opinion, our existing morality would tend to revert to its primitive form, the usage of the horde. The higher social utilities which the rules of general morals represent could never have prevailed over the interests of the horde or of the tribe or of the class through any appeal to reason or to individual interest; for feeling is stronger than reason and group feeling is stronger than self-interest. The agencies which in the past have slowly subordinated group morals to general morals, and by which general morals were perhaps first formulated, are religion and law. Every religion that has developed beyond the stage of a clan cult has, on the whole, lent its psychical sanction to the more general morals; and the religious sanction, like the legal, can be made to operate with equal force over indefinite areas and upon all social classes. The law, in so far as it has had to deal with moral questions, has likewise put its special sanction, that of physical force, behind general morals. In the early stages of civilization, religion apparently played the more important part in formulating the rules of general morals and in securing their triumph; in later periods and at the present time law has possibly become the more efficient agency. Religion influences the believer only; law coerces even the anarchist. Confessions are divided into sects, and churches are organized, in some instances, along the lines of class cleavage; states grow larger by conquest or by federation, and modern states are becoming increasingly democratic.

Our analysis of social rules and of their operation upon the individual is not complete without a word regarding constraints that are neither purely psychical nor purely physical but economic. A religious association, possessing at the outset no means of securing obedience except those which are purely psychical, may come to exercise so general an influence over the minds of men that individuals cast out from its communion are completely boycotted and can obtain none of the necessities of life. A relatively small num-

ber of persons, united by ties of class interest, may so monopolize land or other means of production that no one can live
by his labor except upon the terms which the group pre-
scribes. A larger number of persons, similarly united by the
ties of class interest, may so monopolize the labor market
that no one outside of their association can obtain regular
employment and that the production of goods becomes impossible except upon the terms which they dictate. There
have been periods in which such associations or groups have
become states, or at least governments. This was the case
in the middle ages with the Christian church, the feudal
nobility and some of the city guilds; and the rules established
by these associations became law in the strictest sense of the
word, since they were generally accepted and were supported
by physical force. In the democratic state, however, with
monarchic or representative government, such associations
are not permitted to exercise permanently an economic constraint which parallels and possibly neutralizes the constraints imposed by the general will and applied through
governmental organs. If the ends which such associations
pursue are approved by the social judgment, the constraints
are legalized, but the associations are brought under legal
control. Otherwise, their efforts to exercise an irresistible
extra-legal constraint are repressed as illegal conspiracies.
The democratic state is rightly jealous of its monopoly of
coercion, for its government alone can be trusted to exercise
coercion in the interests of liberty.

By way of summing up the results thus far reached, I
suggest, with all deference to the superior authority of the
specialists in ethics, that morals is that part of the social
order which is supported by social opinion, touched with
more or less emotion; and, with more confidence, I describe
law as that part of the social order which by virtue of the
social will may be supported by physical force.

Law is in part found, in part made; that is, it is established partly by decisions and partly by legislation. Of

these processes the decision is not only the older but the more important and the more persistent. A decision is not alone the termination of a pending controversy, it is also a precedent for future decisions. To us, to-day, the word suggests primarily a judicial decision; but there were decisions before there were courts, and decisions that make law are still rendered to-day outside of the courts. The primitive human community resembles those lowest forms of animal life which exercise with the whole body a number of functions which the higher animals exercise only through special organs. The primitive decision is a community-decision, and its earliest form is the lynching or running-out of the individual who has violated one of the rules of conduct which the community feels to be fundamental. In somewhat more advanced communities there is another very important form of community-decision. When a man has slain another in self-defence or in rightful vengeance, the community may intervene to protect him from blood-feud, just as to-day the community, acting through special organs, absolves from responsibility the individual who has shot a burglar at night in his bedroom. In both cases the slaying of the wrongdoer precedes the decision that he has been rightfully slain; but in both cases the decision in favor of the man who has taken the law into his own hands recognizes that what he has taken into his own hands is law.

After the establishment of courts, community-decisions tend to disappear in that part of the law with which the courts are competent to deal. In those parts of the law, however, in which the courts are not competent, in political law, for example, community-decisions have continued to establish law in modern times. All unwritten constitutions rest on precedents, and constitutional precedents are set whenever acts of power are supported or accepted by the whole community. And in the international community the only rules that are strictly legal are those which have been enforced in the past, and will therefore presumably be enforced in the future, by the international community, the concert of powers. The rest of what we call international law is as yet only international morals and manners.

The processes by which early society develops judicial and legislative organization have only recently begun to be understood. As regards European communities, we can now say with confidence that neither law-finding nor law-making has any historical connection with the authority of a patriarch to settle disputes of his descendants and to lay down rules for their future conduct. In general, it may be said that the more light we get on the conditions prevailing in really primitive human society, the less we see of anything resembling a patriarch. Ages seem to have been necessary for the establishment of marital and paternal authority, and ages more for the development of the patriarch; nor is any patriarchate so complete as that of the Romans known to have existed among any other European people. The earliest European court was not patriarchal but popular. In it the community still acted collectively, but it acted not as a mob but as an orderly assembly. The assembly court had from the outset special law-finding organs; it gradually developed special organs of decision; and the modification, rearrangement or combination of those organs have produced every type of modern court.

Legislation, as we know it, has two historical roots: formal agreement of the community (which originally, it seems, had to be unanimous) and the order issued by the war-lord to the people under arms. From the power of the military leader to issue orders to his men was derived, when temporary leadership grew into permanent kingship, the power to issue orders in time of peace. Among European peoples, however, such orders were not originally regarded as laws in any proper sense, but merely as administrative measures; and neither among the Germans nor among the Romans could such orders be enforced, originally, by any means other than a fine, legally limited in amount. Only in proportion as a king gained power by conquest did his ordinance power expand into anything like legislative power; and it amounted to general legislative power only when the king became an absolute monarch. In the modern state the executive order has shrunk into something like its original dimensions, while the general power of the people to legislate by agreement is still exercised directly or through representatives.

Even in the earliest stages of legal development, when the social will manifests itself directly in social action — in lynchings, for example — there are experts to tell the community why it acts as it does. These experts are not lawyers only; they belong to the single undifferentiated profession from which have emerged all the professions of civilized life; they are experts in all matters natural, human and divine; they formulate the rules of health, of thrift, of manners and of morals. All this knowledge is one body of wisdom, and all these rules are part of the religion of which these men are the priests. In their undifferentiated activity we are nevertheless able to recognize special fields of legal action. They define not only the cases in which individuals may rightly be slain or be thrust out into the deserts or forests, but also the cases in which clan feud may be rightly raised or private vengeance rightly taken. They also devise the earliest methods of deciding doubtful cases and of terminating controversy. Among the early Romans the legal activity of the priests had become so highly specialized that not only was there a class of priests whose business was chiefly legal, but there were three boards of these priests: one for interstate relations, another for the public law of Rome, and a third for the private law.

After courts of justice were established, the priestly lawfinder was succeeded and displaced, in European legal development, by the secular law-finder, whom the Romans described as the jurisprudent or jurisconsult, the Germans as the wiseman or law-speaker. These law-finders were unofficial persons: they were neither elected by the assembly nor appointed by king or magistrate. They emerged from the body of the people by a natural selection; they were entitled to declare the law because they knew the law. Conclusive, of course, as to the authority of a new law-speaker was the general opinion of the older and recognized law-speakers. These experts were not judges in our sense, nor did they directly decide controversies. In the early European court a governmental chairman heard the pleadings of the parties, but he was not necessarily a lawyer. The decision was rendered originally by the whole body of the freemen, as among the Germans; in a more advanced stage of development it was rendered, as in Greece and republican Rome, by a larger or smaller body of citizens, or by a single citizen; but even when, as at Rome, the decision on the law and the facts was rendered by a single citizen, he was not necessarily learned in the law. The naturally selected unofficial experts informed the chairman of the court whether the pleadings were regular; and it was from such experts that the people or their representatives learned the rules of law which should govern their decisions. Outside of court these experts gave legal advice to individuals. They accordingly combined the functions of the modern law-finding judge and of the modern counselor.

The modern type of court with which we are all familiar was constructed at Rome in the early Empire, and was constructed again a thousand years later in Norman England, by the simple expedient of selecting a jurist or wiseman for chairman of the court. This change substituted for the naturally selected unofficial law-finder an artificially selected official law-finder. In the English type of court popular coöperation in the administration of justice reappears in the jury; but, as the decision of the people in the earliest European court was guided by the instruction of the expert, so the decision of the modern jury is guided by the learned judge.

After the judges were taken out of the general body of experts, the remainder of the legal profession (including certain elements which were not historically derived from the law-speaking or jurist class) was organized either, as in England, in the two groups of barristers and solicitors or, as in imperial Rome and in the United States, in a single undifferentiated body of practising lawyers.

When we say that law is established by decisions, we do not mean that the condemnation or acquittal of a person accused of crime or the rendering of a judgment for the plaintiff or for the defendant in a civil case establishes the law. It is in the determination of the legal question at issue, by the recognition and formulation of the legal rule which governs the case, that the law is established. This, as we have seen, has always been the work of experts. That part of the law which the Romans described as the customary or unwritten law, which we describe as common law or case-law, is, in reality, simply expert opinion. The unwritten law of Rome consisted, in the republican period, of the " responses " of the unofficial jurists, in the imperial period of the responses of the jurists who were authorized to respond and who, for the most part, were imperial judges. Old German tribal law was found in the " wisdoms " or " dooms " of the wisemen or law-speakers; English and American common law consists of the opinions rendered in court by learned judges.

These experts, it should be noted, have always been men engaged in the practical application of the law; and their opinions have always been given in connection with cases actually in litigation and in view of the facts of each special case. It should be noted, further, that the unsupported opinions of single experts have rarely been regarded as authoritative. The response of the single jurist at Rome, the wisdom of the single law-speaker among the Germans, was regarded as establishing the law only in so far as it was accepted by the whole body of legal experts. Similarly, in the latest stage of legal development, the opinions which are cited as authoritative are those rendered on appeal by courts of final instance. It should be added that the modern bench always depends largely on the bar to cast light on all sides of a difficult legal question, and that, in the English and American practice, the authority of a decided case may always be impugned on the ground that it was not fully argued. To make our description of unwritten or case-law completely accurate, we should therefore say that it is deliberate and accordant expert opinion.

While the expert law-finders have always claimed that they were following precedents and abiding by the rules laid down in decided cases, they have always exercised great freedom in the interpretation of earlier decisions. In the development of the customary or unwritten law it has always been assumed that the law which is found in decided cases existed somewhere before the cases were decided. One of the oldest German words for law is *êwa*, that which has always been. Of this eternal law the wisdom or dooms pronounced by the wisemen were simply the accepted statements. This is still the orthodox doctrine of all courts of justice. From it is derived the very important inference that the form in which a rule has been stated in earlier cases is not binding; it is always admissible to re-examine the cases and to restate the rule. The possibilities of change and development inherent in such a theory are obviously very great; they have been sufficient to enable the courts to meet, by constant re-interpretation, most of the needs of a progressive society. It was in fact mainly by interpretation that the Roman law and the English law were developed from rude customs into the stately fabrics beneath whose shelter all civilized peoples except the Chinese and the Mohammedans are now living.

In connection with the development of the rules of the unwritten law there also gradually appears a set of more general rules described as principles. These present themselves as propositions of which the ordinary rules are merely corollaries; and from these principles are frequently derived, in case of need, entirely new rules. The eternal existence of these principles is asserted with even greater energy and persistence than is the eternal existence of the special rules;

but here also it is recognized that no particular statement of a principle is definitive.

When we make abstraction from the time-honored fictions of the law-finders, and consider what European legal experts, priests, law-speakers and judges have actually been doing in the twenty-three hundred years over which our observation extends, it is impossible, I think, to deny that their methods have been scientific — far more scientific than their own description of their methods. The fundamental assumptions upon which all their work has been based are obviously these: that law exists for the protection of social interests, and that social interests are more truly reflected in social feeling, in the general sense of justice, than in any reasoned theories. In their effort to give to the social sense of justice articulate expression in rules and in principles, the method of the law-finding experts has always been experimental. The rules and principles of case-law have never been treated as final truths but as working hypotheses, continually retested in those great laboratories of the law, the courts of justice. Every new case is an experiment; and if the accepted rule which seems applicable yields a result which is felt to be unjust, the rule is reconsidered. It may not be modified at once, for the attempt to do absolute justice in every single case would make the development and maintenance of general rules impossible; but if a rule continues to work injustice, it will eventually be reformulated. The principles themselves are continually retested; for if the rules derived from a principle do not work well, the principle itself must ultimately be re-examined.

The further this process is carried, the more does the conscious recognition of social utility become the real, although unavowed, basis of decisions — " the secret root," as Holmes says in his *Common Law*, " from which the law draws all the juices of life." In novel cases, however, especially when their novelty is due to changed social conditions — in cases, that is, in which the sense of social utility has not yet attained its reasoned justification — the finding of

new law is always controlled by feeling rather than by
reason.

That legal experts have not generally described their
methods as experimental and inductive is probably due to
the fact that the scientific character of such methods has
not been generally recognized until modern times. Through
the ages in which deduction from unquestioned premises
was regarded as the only scientific mode of thought, the
lawyers not unnaturally endeavored to represent their premises as absolute and unchanging and their method as purely
deductive.

Great as are the possibilities of the development, by interpretation, of law which has no objective existence except
in its interpretation, these possibilities are not unlimited.
In all law, and most of all in law established by decisions,
there is a tendency to persistence, a resistance to change.
This is true of all law, because society demands not only
that the rules of law be just, but also that they be certain.
It is especially true of case-law, because the development
of this law is wholly in the hands of lawyers, who are generally more conservative than laymen. Their conservatism
is rational, because they understand, better than laymen,
the meaning and the value of the accepted principles and
rules of the unwritten law; and it is valuable to society,
because these principles and rules represent the abiding
sense of justice, as against momentary gusts of popular
feeling, and the accumulated experience of centuries, as
against impressions derived from situations which are exceptional and which may be transitory. Legal conservatism,
however, is a constant impediment to necessary changes;
if it cannot prevent, it delays them; and the delay which
it causes is most constant in case-law. A current of decisions may be diverted, but it cannot well be made to flow
backward; and if its direction is to be seriously modified, it
will not turn abruptly but will sweep round slowly in a very
long curve. Accordingly, in periods of rapid social change,

law is made by other processes than those which we have been considering.

One of these processes is that by which the prætorian law was developed at Rome and equity in England. In both instances new law was made and enforced by executive or administrative authority, and in both instances this new law was developed experimentally in the administration of justice between litigants. It was thus substantially the same process by which the older law had been developed; but the old precedents were disregarded and a fresh start was made. Both at Rome and in England the new law was framed by experts: at Rome by the jurists who sat in the councils of the prætors, in England by a special court with its own bar. In both instances admirable results were achieved; but in both instances the production of new law through these administrative agencies ceased when the social needs which had set them in motion were satisfied. The prætors and chancellors began to adhere with increasing strictness to the precedents established by their predecessors; the new law became relatively stable; and the ensuing legal development proceeded along the old lines of interpretation until legislation became active.

In modern times, however, the making of law by the decisions of administrative authorities is reappearing. On the continent of Europe there are regular administrative courts, and their decisions not only control the working of the administrative machinery, but affect the interests of individuals. In our country administrative tribunals are multiplying in the form of federal and state commissions, which are clothed with quasi-judicial as well as with quasi-legislative powers and which are meeting new social exigencies by decisions as well as by administrative orders. When, as is the case both in Europe and in the United States, certain matters fall exclusively within the jurisdiction of these administrative authorities, their decisions create new law. In Europe it is recognized that administrative judges should be experts alike in administration and in law. In the United

States, where administrative tribunals are comparatively new and their importance is imperfectly realized, this double qualification is not as yet demanded.

Legislation is confined, in early stages of legal development, to matters of policy and is chiefly employed for the adoption of temporary measures in the face of special exigencies. The abiding social order, the ancient law, is too sacred a thing to be changed consciously and openly. When early legislation touches the field of general law it is usually declaratory, that is, it simply affirms the law already recognized and enforced in the decision of controversies. Such declaratory legislation first appears, in many communities, in connection with early attempts to set forth the law as a whole, that its provisions may be better known. The use of legislation, whether popular, royal or representative, as a means of changing the general law comes late in European political life. The idea that the law stands in need of constant change and that the necessary changes are normally to be accomplished by legislation is an idea that appears only in a very advanced civilization. In the Roman Empire it appeared only in the period of decline and decay. In the West Gothic and Frankish Empires legislation was fairly frequent because of the persistence of late Roman traditions. In mediæval Europe, after the ninth century, there was little legislation except in church councils and in the free cities; and in the cities legislation was active only when they had attained a high degree of economic and political development. In the modern European states there was little reformatory legislation before the eighteenth century, nor did statutory law gain anything like its modern volume before the nineteenth century.

The increasing part played by legislation in late periods of legal development is due in some measure to the increased rapidity of social change, in some measure to an exaggerated faith in the power of law to modify social conditions and to remedy social evils, but in the main, apparently, to the fact that there are certain portions of the law which courts are wholly unable to develop and certain other portions in which judge-made law is less satisfactory than enacted law. Political law, constitutional and administrative, is usually beyond the competence of courts. This part of the law, developed during long stretches of time by community-decisions, is at last embodied in statutes and in written constitutions. Again, that part of the law which expresses interests which are primarily social tends always, and particularly in a democratic society, to be formulated by the direct assertion of the general will. Finally, there is a considerable part of the law which is distinctly arbitrary. Here also there must be rules; but from the point of view of justice it seems immaterial what the rules shall be. Here certainty, not justice, is the imperative social demand, and here the movement toward legislation begins at a very early period.

After ceding all these fields to legislation, a large domain may yet be reserved for the tentative development of law by the courts. To the courts may be left that part of the law which primarily subserves the interests of individuals, which accordingly grants to individuals a large measure of liberty, and which, for this reason, has to deal with extremely varied and highly complex relations. In this part of the law the demand for justice is more imperative than the demand for certainty. This part of the law, roughly speaking, is the law of personal property, of contracts and of torts. To the very end of the Roman Empire this part of the law remained embodied in decided cases, and the same is true to-day among all English-speaking peoples. The belief, so generally held to-day, that in a really advanced civilization legislation must cover the whole field of the law, that the finding of law by courts is a remnant of archaic conditions destined gradually to disappear — this belief has no basis except in the conditions existing to-day in continental Europe and in those countries which have derived their institutions from continental Europe. But in continental Europe, from the dissolution of the Frankish Empire until the establishment of national states, the political and legal development was abnormal. In the Roman Empire, and in England after the Norman conquest, there were at all times organs capable of finding general law as well as organs capable of making such law, and there was always a central authority able to subordinate local law to general law. Both in the Roman and in the English legal development, accordingly, it was possible to create general or common law by decisions as well as by legislation. In continental Europe the national state developed much later than in England: in Germany and in Italy it was not organized until the nineteenth century. Until it was organized there were no efficient organs for finding or making national law. When it was organized, the existing law was in the main provincial or local; and the provincial and local laws were so firmly established that national law could be produced only by legislation, and a complete body of national law could be created only by codification.

The work of the legislator is akin to the work of the judge, in that it is his business to express the social will in the form of rules. In the work of the legislator a higher degree of skill is required than in the work of the courts, because rules laid down in statutes are less easily amended than rules laid down in decisions. A representative legislature, in particular, is a cumbrous piece of political machinery, not easily set in motion; and if a law be ill-considered or badly drawn, it will do much harm before it arouses enough resentment to secure its amendment or repeal. In modern European countries, including Great Britain, these considerations have led to the development of a class of legislative experts, men who are primarily trained lawyers but who are also trained legal draftsmen, and who hold permanent appointments in the governmental service. These experts not only draw all bills which are introduced by the government, but they examine bills introduced by private members of the legislative body; and it is usually impossible for a private member to secure the adoption of a bill unless it be put in such form as the governmental experts deem satisfactory. Under the influence of this body of legislative experts, a scientific theory of legislation has obtained general acceptance. It is recognized that no finite intelligence can anticipate the various situations to which a proposed law may become applicable or the varying conditions under which it may be applied. A modern European statute accordingly lays down the principles that are to be applied or indicates the ends that are to be attained, and leaves the detailed rules which shall give effect to the legislative purpose to be formulated in administrative orders or to be worked out in decisions. In the United States the legislative expert is only beginning to appear and is still in the unofficial stage of development. Under these conditions it is not surprising that our theory of legislation is that of a past age. Our legislators try to do too much, and by attempting to provide for all contingencies they not only embarrass the administration and the courts, but in many cases they defeat their own purposes.

The making of a code, especially of a civil code, which sets forth the rules of the private law, that is, the law of property, of contracts, of family and of inheritance, is the most difficult work in the field of legal science. The successful solution of this problem presupposes a large and well reasoned body of case-law and numerous well digested systematic treatises. No single expert has ever constructed a satisfactory civil code: the work must be done, as it has been done in modern European states, by a commission of experts. The most scientific process which has ever been employed in the work of codification is that which was employed in the German Empire in the construction of the existing civil code. A committee on plan and method was appointed in the spring of 1874. In the autumn of the same year, in accordance with the recommendation of this first committee, a commission of eleven eminent jurists was constituted, with the chief justice of the highest imperial court as its president. In the year 1887 a complete first draft was presented to the government. In 1888 this was published, with five volumes of " motives." An enormous amount of expert criticism appeared in this and the ensuing years. All this criticism was carefully digested by governmental experts. Their digest was arranged in the order of the sections of the draft code and was published in 1894. With the aid of this digest a second commission revised the draft of 1887, and a greatly improved second draft was published in 1895. After further slight revision by a committee of the Imperial Diet, the code was adopted in 1896, and it went into force in 1900.

The occupation of any portion of the legal field by written law, constitutional or statutory, in no wise terminates the activity of the courts in that field; it does not even terminate their law-finding power. Scientific legislation recognizes fully that the detailed rules which are needed to give effect to a legislative policy must be worked out partly or wholly by the courts. Unscientific legislation requires from the courts something more than this subsidiary law-finding; it requires corrective interpretation. The same is true of the most thoroughly considered and most carefully drawn laws, when the social conditions to which they must be applied have undergone serious changes. According to the theory of the separation of powers, the courts should not use their power of interpretation for the purpose of correcting or amending legislation; they should apply the written law as it is written, leaving to the legislatures the task of improving it. Practically, however, this course would result in so much inconvenience and injustice as to arouse public resentment, not against the legislatures but against the courts. The general purpose of the law, it would be said, is evident; why do the courts not endeavor to realize that purpose? This accordingly is what the courts try to do. For more than two thousand years it has been an accepted legal principle that, in interpreting the written law, effect should be given, as far as possible, to the spirit and intent of the law. Here again the possibilities of law-finding under cover of interpretation are very great. A distinguished German jurist, Windscheid, has remarked that in interpreting legislation modern courts may and habitually do " think over again the thought which the legislator was trying to express," but that the Roman jurist went further and " thought out the thought which the legislator was trying to think." Of this freer mode of interpretation Windscheid might have found modern examples. The president of the highest French court, M. Ballot-Beaupré, explained, a few years ago, that the provisions of the Napoleonic legislation had been adapted to modern conditions by a judicial interpretation in "*le sens évolutif.*" " We do not inquire," he said, " what the legislator willed a century ago, but what he would have willed if he had known what our present conditions would be." In English-speaking countries this freer mode of interpretation has always been applied to the unwritten or common law, and it is usually applied to the written law with a degree of boldness which is very closely proportioned to the difficulty of securing formal amendment. Thus the rigidity of our federal constitution has constrained the Supreme Court of the United States to push the interpreting power to its furthest limits. This tribunal not only thinks out the thoughts which the Fathers were trying to think one hundred and twenty years ago, but it undertakes to determine what they would have thought if they could have foreseen the changed conditions and the novel problems of the present day. It has construed and reconstrued the constitution in " the evolutive sense," until in some respects that instrument has been reconstructed.

Every science classifies the phenomena with which it deals. In the law classification is especially necessary because, without classification of persons, of acts and of relations, it would obviously be impossible to lay down any general rules. In the early stages of legal development classification is crude: persons are either fully capable and responsible or completely incapable and irresponsible; acts by which property may be transferred or debt created are limited in number, and such acts are valid or invalid according as certain forms are or are not rigidly observed. In early law certainty is far more important than equity. In the later stages of legal development classification becomes increasingly refined, and, correspondingly, the law becomes more and more equitable; for equity, in last analysis, means discrimination. To this process, however, there are necessary limits. In its most advanced development the law necessarily deals with typical persons, typical acts and typical relations; for if it should attempt to deal specially with variations from the normal type it would lose all certainty. In becoming absolute equity it would cease to be law. Modern society, however, provides special organs of discrimination, in such institutions, for example, as the pardoning power and the jury. The great social advantage of the jury is that it can bend the law in hard cases without creating authoritative precedents.

Every science, again, analyzes the phenomena with which it has to deal. In the law every act is resolved into its inward and its outward elements: crime becomes a combination of wrongful intent and illegal conduct; contract becomes a meeting of two corresponding wills in corresponding declarations. Every legal relation is resolved into its constituent powers or rights; and in spite of the very great variety of legal relations, the variety of legal rights is seen to be limited.

The conception of the legal right is to-day so familiar, and it seems so simple, that we can hardly realize with what difficulty it was attained. But as early law was wholly remedial and the substantive legal order which the remedies supported was only slowly recognized, so the legal right long lay concealed behind the correlative and essentially ethical notion of the duty. Brunner tells us that in the Germanic languages the word *Recht*, whether used in the sense of right or of law, is clearly younger than the other words for law; and Hozumi assures us that the Japanese language had no expression for the legal right until 1868, when a word was coined by a Japanese writer who had studied European law at Leyden. And only in our own time has it been clearly perceived that the legal right, previously regarded as the atom of all legal relations, is itself a combination of a definite interest and a limited power, and that these two elements are separable. This was one of Jhering's great contributions to jurisprudence. Coupling this analysis with Burgess's sharp distinction between state and government, we see that it is in no sense inexact, as has been frequently asserted, to speak of public legal rights. Of course limited powers can not be attributed to the state, because the state is legally omnipotent; but limited powers may properly be attributed to any organ of government, and our public rights are in fact a combination of definite public interests with limited governmental powers. The possible developments of this line of thought in private and in public law are as yet imperfectly realized.

The final task of legal science is the orderly and convenient arrangement of all the institutions and rules of the law, public and private, substantive and remedial, in a logical system. The difficulties of this problem are very great, because of the innumerable points at which each part of the law touches every other part. Interrelations so complicated that the mind must work in a fourth dimension to apprehend them cannot be satisfactorily exhibited along the single line of a topical arrangement.

I have already indicated that the formulation of legal rules and principles has been, in the main, the work of practical jurists, men actively engaged in the administration of justice. The same statement may be made as regards legal classification and analysis, both in Roman and in English law. Not only has most of this work been done in the judicial laboratory, in connection with the discussion and decision of concrete cases, but the results obtained are largely embodied in judicial opinions. Moreover, the literature in which these results are presented has for the most part been produced by practical jurists. Nearly all the juristic writers of the Roman Empire were imperial judges (a few only were law professors), and their writings were substantially digests of the practice of the imperial supreme court. In English-speaking countries the legal literature has been less important; in these countries legal classification and analysis, like the rules of the law, are for the most part to be sought in the law reports; but in these countries, as at Rome, the most valuable contributions in these fields of legal science have been made by practical lawyers, by judges or by members of the bar. In this respect, again, the continental European development, during the middle ages and in modern times, has been different. In consequence of the arrested development of national law, recourse was had to the compilations of Justinian; because of the antiquity of these compilations their study centered in the universities; and from the eleventh century down to the present time nearly all the legal literature was written by professors. These writers were, indeed, by no means out of touch with the administration of justice. Not only were some of them judges, but until comparatively recent times university law faculties were frequently called upon to decide difficult cases. The relation between legal literature and applied law was, however, fundamentally different from that which existed in the most productive period of Roman jurisprudence and exists in English-speaking countries. It was a relation not of dependence but of control. The constructive work of the academic writers was based chiefly on that part of the Roman legal literature which is preserved in the *Digest* of Justinian. In this literature they had at their disposal a rich and admirably reasoned body of case-law. The decentralized administration of justice in the secular courts was producing no case-law comparable with the Roman in range or in quality. For all these reasons, legal literature obtained, and it still in a measure retains, a direct influence upon the decisions of the continental European courts which it did not exercise in the ancient Roman world until the period of legal decadence in the fourth and following centuries, and which it has seldom exercised in the countries of the English law.

On the other hand, attempts to present the law or large parts of the law in systematic treatises have always been made under academic influences. Gaius, who wrote his *Institutes* of Roman law in the second century, and whose arrangement was generally followed, even in English-speaking countries, until the nineteenth century, seems to have been a law professor. The most important systematic works produced in France prior to the nineteenth century were those of Donellus and Pothier, both professors, although Pothier was also a judge. The modern German arrangement (*Pandektensystem*), which is replacing that of Gaius, was developed in university lectures; and a series of academic writers, from Savigny and Puchta to Windscheid and Dernburg, have given the Germans the most admirable body of systematic legal literature that has ever been produced. In England, the attempt to present the whole law systematically was made but once before the time of Blackstone, namely, by Bracton. Bracton was a judge, but he borrowed the whole framework of his treatise from Azo, an Italian law professor. Blackstone was a university professor, and his commentaries were prepared as lectures. In this country the systematic treatises of Story and of Kent grew out of academic instruction.

Philosophical theories of law demand our attention only in so far as they have strongly influenced or are strongly influencing the movement of law or of politics.

The life of man, the Stoics said, is but a part of the universal order. For the individual and for the state there are eternal and immutable natural laws with which human conduct and human laws should be in harmony. As regards human law, it will be noticed that this theory bears a singular resemblance to the orthodox judicial doctrine, according to which every rule of law laid down in a judicial decision existed before it was discovered and enunciated. The natural-law theory gives to this eternal law, if not an objective basis or a demonstrable source, at least a name. The jurist-judges of the Roman Empire accepted the Stoic theory and used the name; and when a new rule was needed for the decision of a novel case, they drew from natural law the rule that seemed to them desirable. The mediæval church accepted the natural-law theory, adding the explanation that the natural order was simply a part of the divine order, so that when divine revelation was lacking the divine will was discernible as natural law. In the Roman Church as in the Roman Empire the discovery and the interpretation of the natural law were wholly in the hands of authorized experts.

Sporadically discernible in the ancient world is a theory that natural law is something more than a reservoir from which supplementary rules may be drawn when needed, that it is a superior law, and that human law that is not in harmony with natural law is of no authority. No Roman lawyer entertained this essentially anarchic theory. It received no countenance from the mediæval church as regarded ecclesiastical law; but it was accepted by the church as regarded secular law. Such law was void not only when it was contrary to the revealed will of God as interpreted by the church, but also when it was contrary to natural law as interpreted by the same authority. When in the sixteenth and following centuries it came to be generally held that neither church nor state had exclusive authority to interpret the divine will or the natural law, the theory that natural law was superior to positive law developed all its latent dynamic qualities. Natural-law theories were employed to legitimize revolution. "*Is* and ought to be " was the revolutionary formula for the assertion of every previously unrecognized right.

The reaction in favor of constituted authority produced both the positivist and the historical theories of law, or at least led to their more precise formulation. The positivist theory, as formulated by Hobbes, was a direct result of the English revolt against the crown. Hobbes did not deny the existence of natural law, but he asserted that it was not " law proper." The law of nature, he neatly remarked, " is become of all laws the most obscure, and has consequently the greatest need of able interpretation." Only the sovereign or the judges to whom he delegates authority are competent interpreters. This of course is the theory which was implicit in the Roman jurisprudence, but Hobbes was the first to make it explicit.

The historical theory was formulated in the reaction against the French revolution. The historical school found its antidote to the natural-law theory, not in the will of the sovereign, but in the authority of the past. According to this theory, presented in the field of public law by Burke, formulated as applicable to all law by Savigny, law is not made, it grows. The judge who declares it, the legislator who seems to make it, are simply interpreters of the national sense of right; and this in its turn is a product of the nation's entire historical existence.

To a certain extent the historical school also represents, at least in English-speaking countries, a reaction against the positivist school; less indeed against the theories set forth by Hobbes than against those formulated by the so-called " analytical " jurists. Confusing, as did Hobbes himself, the state with the government and finding sovereignty not in the crown, as did Hobbes, but in Parliament, the analytical jurists have always been inclined to regard legislation as the normal source of " law proper." Maine and other English adherents of the historical school have not only rehabilitated judge-made law, but they have restored custom to its ancient (and perhaps unduly exalted) dignity and importance.

Whether it is admissible to speak of a comparative school of jurisprudence, in the sense in which we speak of the natural-law school or of the historical school, may perhaps be disputed. It may be urged that comparative jurisprudence has produced no distinct theory of law. In the writings of Jhering, however, we find an interesting and, I think, typical reaction against the historical theory as formulated by Savigny. Without for an instant denying that law is a historical phenomenon, Jhering insists that it is not wholly nor even mainly a national product. Even national law is in the main a world product. The history of law, like the history of civilization, is a history of borrowings and of assimilations. Further, Jhering vehemently denies that law grows and asserts that it is and always has been made. It is a product of conscious and increasingly determinate human will. In this last assertion Jhering approaches the position of the positivists, but he lays less stress than they on the authority by which the rule is established, emphasizing as essential to the concept of law the possibility of enforcement. Noting the assertion of a contemporary writer that a certain custom was really law, only it was not enforced, Jhering replies: " We might as well say: This is fire, only it does not burn."

Each of these theories represents a partial truth. Many of the contradictions disappear when we realize that the natural-law theorists and historical jurists are primarily interested in the substance of legal rules, the analytical jurists and the other positivists in the legal quality of the rules.

The historical study of law did not originate in the historical school of jurisprudence, nor were the laws of different peoples first compared when the comparative school formulated its theories. The extent to which law has always rested on precedents has always made it necessary for the lawyer to look back; and he has always been ready, if he could not find a satisfactory precedent in the near past, to look back as far as any existing record or tradition has made retrospect possible. The use of the historical method in legal literature is also very old; and even that type of history which was recently described, in the non-technical lecture on history, as "morphogenetic" is distinctly visible in the *Institutes* of Gaius, written for the use of first-year law-students more than seventeen hundred years ago. Resuscitated by Cujacius in the sixteenth century, imbued with a due sense of its own importance by Savigny in the nineteenth century, morphogenetic history has been as assiduously cultivated by lawyers as by any other body of scientific men. The comparative method is, if anything, older than the historical. The story that, in the fifth century before Christ, when the Romans were thinking of putting their own laws into written form, they sent to Greece for a transcript of the laws of Solon, may not be true; but the fact that the story was believed in Rome in the early Empire is significant. In fact the Roman lawyers were actively engaged in the last two centuries of the Republic, in studying and comparing the laws and customs of all the Mediterranean peoples, in order to establish a uniform commercial law — a problem which they solved with such success that the commerce of the world has ever since been governed, in the main, by the rules which they then formulated. Historical and comparative study of the law is prosecuted to-day on a more extensive scale and by more scientific methods than in any previous period, but these studies are new things only in the spirit in which they are being carried on and in the way in which they are now combined.

Legal history is being studied not only for the elucidation of existing law but for its own sake. It has become a part of general history, and one of the most essential parts. In political history its importance has long been recognized; in social history its significance is still imperfectly appreciated. For many obscure periods of history, the legal material is the fullest that we possess and by far the most trustworthy. The interpretation of the legal material requires special training, but the results to be gained are well worth the labor. In the course of time the synthetic historian will become aware that the legal material is that which he can least afford to neglect; that without the law of property and of contract, of family and of inheritance, of crimes and of torts, social history is as invertebrate and flabby as is political history without constitutional law.

Comparative legal study also is carried on to-day, not only for the practical suggestions which the legislator may derive from the accumulated and digested experience of other nations, but for its own sake. It has become a branch of the new science of society, and one of the sturdiest and most fruitful branches.

New also — an invention of our time — is the combination of the historical with the comparative method; and the results in every field of social science have been surprisingly rich. The comparative study of early institutions has been actively prosecuted during the last two generations, philologists and jurists, anthropologists and ethnologists, working side by side; and it is not too much to say that our conceptions of the beginnings of civilization have been revolutionized. Comparative work in the later stages of legal development promises a rich harvest.

These lines of study have carried the jurist far away from the practical tasks of interpreting and developing the law of his own time and his own people; and yet we are beginning to see that some of the results attained are of practical value. A vantage ground is being gained from which the existing law of each nation may be objectively examined and criticised. It is becoming more and more possible to see how much of any existing legal system is dead or moribund, how much is vital. It is also becoming possible to see in what respects the law of each nation is in advance of other systems, and in what respects it is suffering from retarded development.

These studies, moreover, are preparing us to meet the great problem of the future — that of establishing world order and assuring the conditions of world progress. Even in the most progressive nations there are many unsolved social problems; but the world problem is forcing itself more and more insistently upon our attention; it will not be evaded or postponed.

The problems of world order and world progress can not be solved by international morals alone. In the international community, the law of the diminishing pressure of widening opinion is conspicuously verified; the influence of world opinion upon the rulers and peoples of the single states is very much weaker than the influence of national opinion upon wants or group action; and the triumph of world morals over national morals can be secured only through international law. Rudimentary as this law is, it has already secured important gains. It has suppressed the slave-trade; it has forced the opening of all doors to world commerce; it has established the freedom of the open and the narrow seas; it has secured to all men the free use of the great navigable rivers of the world. Civilization is being carried into the backward portions of the world through the agency of the single national states, but international law is beginning to define the powers and duties of the states which undertake this mission.

In spite of the highly refined character of many of its rules, international law has as yet hardly reached the stage of development which European tribal law had reached in a prehistoric period; but the development is in rapid progress. In international arbitration the world has taken the first steps towards international adjudication, but arbitrators have as yet no greater authority than is given them by the voluntary submission of the parties. World legislation is still in the contractual stage of development; it comes into existence only by unanimous agreement; an international congress is a Polish diet with the *liberum veto*. International conventions between great groups of states are, however, becoming increasingly numerous and important, and these conventions are reaching more and more into the field of commercial relations; besides the public law of nations a conventional private law of the world is in process of construction. The social force which is necessary to transform international law from a body of usages and agreements, supported only by moral sentiment, into " law proper " exists in the concert of the powers. This force has been exercised, thus far, only against backward or feeble states; but every case in which it is exercised establishes a precedent. All the essential agencies of legal development exist; they are becoming increasingly active; and it can hardly be doubted that the development will be more rapid in the next three generations than in the last three centuries.

At a similar stage in the development of tribal law the task of interpreting and guiding the social will was everywhere in the hands of priests; it was at a later period that the task was transferred to secular law-finders. The world of to-day has many religions; it will listen to the secular jurist alone. It has been listening to him, largely accepting his rulings and his instructions, since the time of Grotius, the first of the world-lawspeakers. In the court of The Hague it is now replacing the naturally selected unofficial expert by the artificially selected official expert, the learned judge. In this new laboratory of world-law the bench will require the constant assistance of a learned international bar, and bench and bar will need all the help they can secure from international legal literature. For centuries to come, perhaps during the whole future existence of the human race, there will be ample fields for juristic activity within the single nations; but the great task of the jurisprudence of the future will be to interpret the social will of federated humanity and to express in increasingly accurate and logical form the universal sentiment of justice.

THE JAPANESE CODE AND THE FAMILY.[1]

JAPANESE law is only beginning to attract the attention it deserves. To the student of comparative legal science it is of interest by reason of its long history and because of the extent to which its development, like that of all important legal systems, has been modified by the reception and assimilation of foreign institutions. To the student of early European law it is of especial value because it shows us in present operation that system of ancestor-worship which did so much to shape the social and political organization of the ancient Mediterranean peoples.

Japanese law was first made accessible to the occidental world by the writings of European and American students resident in Japan. These writings were largely translations of the older chronicles and laws and were published for the most part in the Mittheilungen and Transactions of the German and English Asiatic Societies. Among the pioneers were Kempermann (1873), Chamberlain (1883), Rudorff (1888), Florenz (1892), and Wigmore (1894). During the last fifteen years Japanese lawyers, educated in Germany, in France, in England, or in the United States, have begun to give us the inside view both of Japanese legal history and of the new imperial legislation. The earliest of these publications were the product of German or of Dutch training in research, and in the still scanty literature of Japanese law presented by Japanese writers in European languages the German treatises continue to outnumber the rest.

An examination of some of the more recent of these publications,[2] dealing chiefly with the ancient, mediæval and

---

[1] Reprinted from *Law Quarterly Review*, vol. 23, no. 1, January 1907, pp. 42–67.

[2] The recent Japanese works on which this article is based are: Hozumi, *Ancestor Worship and Japanese Law* (Tokio, 1901), and *The New Japanese Civil Code as Material for the Study of Comparative Jurisprudence* (Tokio,

modern law of the family, awakens in the mind of the student who knows anything of occidental legal development both interest and perplexity. He finds himself interested in the primitive traits which the Japanese family has preserved to the present day, in the persistence of the wider ancient family and in the compromises by which the modern Japanese legislator has attempted to reconcile the traditional solidarity of the house with the principles of modern individualism. The occidental student finds himself perplexed, at the same time, by certain apparent contradictions in the Japanese accounts of their earliest family organization.

I

The great periods recognized by Japanese legal historians are (1) the period of indigenous civilization, which terminated with the reception of Chinese ideas and institutions in the seventh century of our era; (2) the period in which Chinese culture remained dominant, which closed with the year 1868; and (3) the present period of occidental influence. A subdivision of the second period is made at the close of the twelfth century, when the feudal system was fairly established. Until the third period law was not clearly differentiated from social ethics; until 1868, indeed, there was no word in the Japanese language that expressed the idea of a legal right, a fact which indicates that social relations were viewed exclusively from the side of duty.[3] Moreover,

---

1904); Asakawa, *Early Institutional Life of Japan* (Tokio, 1903); Ikeda, *Die Hauserbfolge in Japan* (Berlin, 1903); Tsugaru, *Die Lehre von der japanischen Adoption* (Berlin, 1903); Sakamoto, *Das Ehescheidungsrecht Japans* (Berlin, 1903); Iwasaki, *Das japanische Eherecht* (Leipzig, 1904). Among earlier Japanese publications the writer has examined: Kishi, *Das Erbrecht Japans* (Göttingen, 1891); Araki, *Japanisches Eheschliessungsrecht* (Göttingen, 1893). Among publications by occidental scholars: Chamberlain, Preface to translation of Kojiki, in *Transactions of the Asiatic Society of Japan* (Tokio, 1883); Weipert, Familien- und Erbrecht, in *Mittheilungen der deutschen Gesellschaft für Natur- und Völkerkunde Ost-Asiens* (Tokio, 1890); Gubbins, *The Japanese Family System*, Introduction to translation of the *Civil Code of Japan*, pt. ii (Tokio, 1899). As regards the existing law, the translations of the *Civil Code* by Gubbins and by Lönholm (Tokio, 1898) have been consulted.

[3] Kishi, *op. cit.*, pp. 10, 11; Hozumi, *Civil Code*, pp. 26, 27. The admirable word now used, "ken-ri" or "power-interest," was coined by Dr.

the so-called laws of the emperors and of the feudal princes were not addressed to the people; they were kept secret from the people.[4]   They were instructions addressed to subordinate officials.   Those which touched upon what we should regard as legal relations contained, of course, what we should call legal rules: *i.e.*, they set forth the principles according to which justice was to be administered in controverted cases.   In the second part of the second period, from the close of the twelfth century until the latter part of the nineteenth century, the feudal principalities were independent in legislation and in adjudication, and the development of law and custom was, as in the European middle ages, particularistic.   In 1867 Japan had as many divergent laws and customs as existed in France or in Germany a century earlier. The written laws of some three hundred principalities were modified by local customs of even more restricted validity, and across the territorial laws and customs there ran, as in continental Europe down to the French Revolution, well-defined class distinctions.

Since the re-establishment of the imperial supremacy in 1868 a common national law has been established.   This result has been attained not by the gradual development of a settled practice in central courts of last resort, as in imperial Rome and in Norman England, but by the more rapid process of legislation, as in modern continental Europe.   The Japanese imperial legislation of the closing decades of the nineteenth century, culminating in the civil code of 1898, has effected at the same time a sweeping reception of West European law.   Hozumi characterizes it as a reception of Roman law: Japanese civil law, he says, has " passed from the Chinese family to the Roman family of law." [5]

Tsuda and was introduced in 1868 in his treatise on Western public law. Tsuda's analysis of a right into the elements of power and interest was thus almost contemporaneous with, but apparently independent of, Jhering's well-known definition of a right as a *rechtlich geschütztes Interesse*.

[4] Hozumi, *Civil Code*, pp. 19, 21.

[5] Hozumi, *Civil Code,* p. 19.   According to Hozumi's classification of " families " of law, this statement is correct; but in his classification he confuses historical and present conditions, distinguishing, among others, a

In the Japanese reception of West European law it is interesting to observe that, as in the reception of the law-books of Justinian in mediæval Europe, the completed formal reception was preceded by a theoretical or scientific reception. The whole process was startlingly rapid; Japan passed in single years through stages which in mediæval northern Europe extended over generations; but the stages were the same. In the first stage the schools took the leading part. Japanese students absorbed foreign law at Paris and at the English Inns of Court, at Leyden, Leipzig, and Berlin, just as the North Europeans, seven centuries earlier, had absorbed Roman law at Bologna and other Italian Universities. Almost simultaneously occidental law began to be taught in Japan. In a separate law school attached to the department of justice and in two or three private law schools French law was taught, and also " natural law." This latter " law," it is pretty clear, was simply general west European law viewed from a French angle. English law was taught in the Imperial University of Tokio from 1874. In 1887 legal instruction in the University of Tokio was reorganized in four sections: English law, French law, German law, and "political science." [6] Simultaneously, as in the theoretical reception of Roman law in mediæval Europe, there was an attempt to popularize the foreign law by translations and treatises in the native tongue. In 1870 was established a governmental bureau for the " investigation of institutions," and one of the first products was a translation of the French codes.[7] On the heels of this scientific reception came the practical reception. In 1875 a law was issued providing that judges should decide civil cases according to the express provisions of written law and, in cases where there was no

---

Roman, a Germanic and an English family (p. 16), but recognizing no French or Romance family. As a matter of fact, English, French, and German law, as they exist to-day, are blends of Germanic and Roman law in varying proportions; and in borrowing from existing occidental systems, Japan has joined, not the Roman, but the Roman-German or West European family of law. So Ikeda, *op. cit.*, pp. vii, viii.

[6] *Ibid.*, p. 8.   [7] Hozumi, *Civil Code*, p. 6.

such written law, according to custom. In the absence of both written and customary laws, they were to decide according to the principles of reason and justice. This law flung wide open the door for the ingress of foreign law. . . . The rapidly changing circumstances of Japanese society brought many cases before the courts for which there were no express rules, written or customary, and the judges naturally sought to find out " the principles of reason and justice " in western jurisprudence. The older members of the bench, who had not been systematically taught in western jurisprudence, consulted the translations of the French and other European codes, while the younger judges, who had received systematic legal education in the universities, either at home or abroad, and whose number increased from year to year, consulted western codes, statute books, law reports and judicial treatises, and freely applied the principles of occidental jurisprudence which in their opinion were conformable to reason and justice. Blackstone, Kent, Pollock, Anson, Langdell, Windscheid, Dernburg, Mourlon, Baudry-Lacantinerie and other textbooks and the numerous commentaries on European codes, statute books and law reports were looked upon as repositories of just and reasonable principles and supplied necessary data for their judgments. In this manner occidental jurisprudence entered our country, not only indirectly through the university and other law colleges, but also directly through the bench and the bar.[8]

From 1868 onward imperial legislation also was active, and special laws effected or accelerated the reception of special institutions or rules borrowed from Western Europe. More general legislation, *i.e.*, codification, was hastened by the desire of the Japanese government to abolish the privileges of foreigners and to subject them to the territorial law, and by the counter demand of the foreign governments that the territorial law should be such as their citizens could comprehend and respect.[9] In 1870 a penal code was published; in 1880 appeared a new penal code and a code of criminal

---

[8] *Ibid.*, pp. 18, 19.
[9] *Ibid.*, pp. 5, 6; Ikeda, *op. cit.*, p. 149.

procedure; in 1890 a new code of criminal procedure, a code of civil procedure, and a commercial code; in 1890–1891 a civil code, which never went into operation; in 1896 and 1898 the present civil code; and in 1899 a revised commercial code.

In its first stages the Japanese reception of European law seemed likely to go too far, as did the German reception of Roman law at the close of the middle ages. There was a tendency to accept the foreign law too eagerly and too thoroughly, with an accompanying sacrifice of vital elements of indigenous custom. On this point Sakamoto writes:

> On the one hand, the existence of open places in the [written] private law and the lack of any comprehensive presentation of the prevailing customary law and, on the other hand, the study of the foreign law, especially the French and later the English and German, induced advocates and judges to apply to legal controversies foreign law, preferring it to native custom, and in particular to apply that foreign law in which they had been trained and which they accordingly regarded as the only law that was real value.[10]

The same tendency was displayed in the first drafts of a civil code. These were so largely based on the French civil code as to arouse opposition, not only on the part of Japanese who had studied English or German law, but also on the part of some who had been trained in French law. The critical period of the struggle was reached in 1891, when a code framed in large part by Professor Boissonade, a French jurist, was adopted by the Council of State, to go into force in 1893. In the ensuing agitation for postponement and revision, Hozumi, who had studied in the English Inns of Court and later in German universities, took a leading part. In a treatise on codification he declared that it was a disgraceful thing that the work of preparing a national code should have been entrusted to a foreigner. In the newly-

[10] Sakamoto, *op. cit.,* p. 49.

established Japanese parliament such an appeal to national sentiment found ready sympathy. In 1892 the enforcement of the code of 1891 was postponed, and a committee of revision was appointed of which all the members were Japanese. A subcommittee consisting of three law professors, Hozumi, Ume, and Tomii, was charged with the work of revision. The code submitted by them was accepted with some modifications by the full committee and by the Japanese parliament, 1896–1898, and is now in force. It was not a mere revision of the code of 1891, but a new and independent work. All the principal codes of the modern world were examined, but Japanese conditions and customs were kept steadily in view. In its general arrangement the Japanese code follows German models (*Pandektên-System*): in its substance it is a product of comparison and selection.[11] Hozumi characterizes the struggle between the supporters of the code of 1891 and the revisionists as a conflict between the school of natural law and the historical school, and compares it with the famous German controversy between Thibaut and Savigny. It more closely resembles, however, the later German controversy between the Romanistic and Germanistic schools; for in Japan both parties were in favor of codification, in order to get rid of particularistic laws and customs, and the opposition to the code of 1891 was preëminently patriotic.

II

Of all the social relations with which the new code deals, the family remains least affected by occidental influences. For this reason, the history and present organization of the Japanese family are of special interest to the student of comparative jurisprudence.

Regarding the earliest organization of the family, the writers under review make or accept statements which, to the occidental student, seem not merely inconsistent but irrecon-

---

[11] Hozumi, *Civil Code*, pp. 6–12; Sakamoto, *op. cit.*, pp. 53, 54; Ikeda, *op. cit.*, pp. 148–151.

cilable. Under these circumstances it seems advantageous
first to present those statements which seem to be most
strongly supported by evidence, and which are consistent
with one another, and then to notice the contradictory statements and to endeavor to explain their origin. For such
an analysis, fortunately, the works under review furnish
sufficient data.

In the earliest period, before the reception of Chinese ideas
and institutions, the clan and not the family was the legal
unit.[12] Endogamy and exogamy apparently existed side by
side.[13] In either case the wife remained with her own kinsfolk, although a separate house was commonly built for her
and her children.[14] The word for wife, *shingo* or *shinso*, is
said to mean " new building." [15] The husband was apparently a surreptitious although licensed visitor; the old Japanese term for marriage, *yo-bai*, is said to mean " prowling by
night." [16] That in unions of this description married women
were fairly independent of their husbands, or, if one chooses
so to put it, " occupied a higher place than in later times," [17]
is quite in accordance with all that we know of other peoples
with similar matrimonial arrangements. The legendary first
emperor, Jimmu, is said to have " commanded a vast army of
male and female warriors," [18] and at a later period there are
stories of young girls and grown women armed and fighting.[19]
Women were capable of holding land in their own right.[20]

That under such circumstances there was no polyandry —
and there seems to be no trace of it in myth or legend —

---

[12] Hozumi, *Ancestor Worship*, p. 44 *et passim*. Kishi (*op. cit.*, pp. 19,
20) states that the original land-tenure in Japan was the common cultivation of land by entire villages, which represented " families in the wider
sense."   [13] Weipert, *op. cit.*, p. 100; Asakawa, *op. cit.*, p. 55.

[14] Iwasaki, *op. cit.*, pp. 11, 12; Sakamoto, *op. cit.*. pp. 10–12; Tsuguru,
op. cit., p. 33, note; Asakawa, *op. cit.*, p. 57; Weipert, *op. cit.*, p. 94.

[15] Sakamoto, *loc. cit.*; Araki, *op. cit.*, p. 12.

[16] Iwasaki, *loc. cit.* Weipert (*op. cit.*, p. 94) says, on the authority of
Professor Naito, that the word means " loud calling "; Araki, *op. cit.*, p. 11,
translates it " herbeirufen," and explains that matches were made at rustic
dances, the man calling to the maid to join him. A legend in *Kojiki* (Chamberlain's translation, pp. 20, 21) seems to indicate that in the earliest times
the woman spoke first.

[17] Hozumi, *Civil Code*, p. 28.   [19] *Ibid.*, p. 105.

[18] Asakawa, *op. cit.*, p. 98.   [20] *Ibid.*, p. 73.

confirms the opinion of those students of primitive institutions who regard polyandry as an exceptional form of marriage. Polygyny, however, was common: the position of the nocturnal prowler may be compared with that of the occidental sailor with wives in many ports.[21]

In such a form of marriage we do not expect to find marital or paternal authority; and Ikeda tells us that there was no paternal power in the old Japanese law. The word used in the middle ages for house-power, *katoku*, is borrowed from the Chinese. The purely Japanese word *soryo*, which came ultimately to be used as equivalent to *katoku*, meant originally the authority which the chief house exercised over branch houses [22] — that is, it did not signify house-power at all, but clan headship.

Under such conditions we should expect to find relationship traced only through the mother, and kinship through the father ignored. As a matter of fact, the Japanese legends indicate that agnatic brothers and sisters who were born of different mothers were permitted to marry one another.[23] In *Nihongi* the marriage of an emperor to his half-sister (A.D. 434) is denounced as criminal, but stress is laid on the fact that they were children of the same mother.[24]

The later form of marriage, which gradually became the prevalent form — the entry of the bride into the husband's house and kinship group — was borrowed from the continent. Buddhism made its way from Korea into Japan in the middle of the sixth century of our era; and by the year 624 there were in Japan 46 Buddhist temples with 1385 priests and priestesses.[25] In the reign of the empress Suiko, 593–628, there was an increasing adoption of Chinese political doctrines.[26] The Reform of 645, which all Japanese writers

[21] So in *Kojiki* (Chamberlain's translation, pp. 80, 81) the goddess says to the god: " Thou, indeed, being a man, probably hast on every headland a wife, but I, being a woman, have no man except thee."

[22] Ikida, *op. cit.*, pp. 5–7.

[23] So Weipert, *op. cit.*, p. 95. Several of the Japanese writers under review allude to these legends, and accept their evidence with obvious reluctance. *Cf.* Sakamoto, *op. cit.*, pp. 10–12; Asakawa, *op. cit.*, p. 58; Araki, *op. cit.*, p. 11.

[24] Cited by Asakawa, *op. cit.*, p. 53.

[25] *Ibid.*, pp. 129, 143.

[26] *Ibid.*, p. 253.

treat as the beginning of a new era, was " a confessed adaptation . . . of Chinese political doctrines and institutions."[27] Chinese ethics also made their way into the islands; and the Confucian doctrines of the wife's duty to the husband and the child's duty to the father seem to have exercised the greatest influence in transforming the Japanese family — in developing the patriarchal household and in securing the recognition of agnatic kinship. We gain a clear view of the conditions which obtained before the Reform of 645 in an imperial decree of 646, which undertook to establish a new system of local government, based on local kinship groups (*ko*). In this decree, as is usual in revolutionary pronunciamentos, the old usage is treated as mere abuse: the heads of the local clans, it is declared, have so divided the people that husband and wife and father and child bear different clan names, and that (agnatic) brothers are assigned to different families.[28] As a bit of evidence, this confession of the imperial legislator outweighs all the myths and legends above cited,[29] and is equalled in value only by certain survivals of the older order which are noted below.

The preceding sketch of the earliest Japanese family is not to be found in all its details in any of the writings under review: it is pieced together from scattered statements. And nearly all of the Japanese writers and some of the foreign writers add other and inconsistent statements. It is asserted, for example, that the right of divorce was exclusively marital.[30] That marriages of the sort above described were easily dissolved we may readily believe; but that the wife was not as free to close the door of her house against her husband as was the husband to discontinue his visits to the wife seems highly improbable.[31] It is further stated or assumed by most of the writers under re-

[27] Asakawa, *op. cit.*, p. 4.   [28] *Ibid.*, p. 259.
[29] The distinguished sinologist, Professor Hirth of Columbia University, informs the writer that the earliest Chinese traditions point to mother-right conditions, and he suggests that the Japanese may possibly have borrowed even their legends from China. *Cf.* Chamberlain, *Kojiki,* preface, pp. lxviii–lxx.   [30] Sakamoto, *loc. cit.;* Iwasaki, *loc. cit.*
[31] Hozumi, *Civil Code,* treats the one-sided marital power of divorce as a characteristic feature of the second or Chinese period.

view that the primitive Japanese household was under paternal sway, and that the headship of the family and its property regularly passed, as in the mediæval period, from father to son. It is stated by one writer that a distinction was drawn, even in the earliest period, between the first or principal wife and other wives, and that the son of the first or principal wife regularly succeeded to the father's position.[32] Adoption is said to have been practised, as in the mediæval period, when there was no male heir.[33]

When we examine the evidence adduced in support of this latter group of statements, we find that it is drawn from the history of the imperial dynasty, as set forth in certain chronicles which date from the early years of the eighth century — *Kojiki* and *Nihongi*. Outside of the imperial family, there is no evidence regarding the order of succession to the headship of clan or of household.[34] In *Kojiki* and *Nihongi* we have a complete list of Japanese emperors from 660 B.C. to 592 A.D., and the succession seems to have passed regularly from father to son or, in default of a son, to an agnatic brother or nephew.[35]

These " chronicles " are a mixture of myths and legends with statements which seem on their face to be historical. *Kojiki* was compiled 711–12 A.D., and purports to rest on information orally given by the Emperor Temmu to one Hiyo-no-Are, " a person of strong memory," and subsequently communicated by Hiyo-no-Are to the editors. The Emperor is represented as stating that the existing chronicles [36] are largely false and that, if these falsehoods be not

---

[32] Sakamoto, *loc. cit.* On the other hand, Weipert, *op. cit.*, p. 94; Araki, *op. cit.*, p. 6, and Asakawa, *op. cit.*, p. 54, ascribe this distinction to Chinese influence.

[33] Tsugaru, *op. cit.*, pp. 26–33. Chamberlain, *Kojiki*, preface, p. xli, believes that adoption was borrowed from China.

[34] Ikeda, *op. cit.*, pp. 36–38. Ikeda adds that there are traces in *Kojiki* of an elective headship, but does not indicate the passages on which he relies. He thinks that there may possibly have been female headship. In the following (early mediæval) period he finds evidence of a certain authority attributed to the oldest member of the kinship group, although such member may not be the head.   [35] *Ibid.*, pp. 22–33; Asakawa, *op. cit.*, pp. 56, 57.

[36] Of these alleged earlier chronicles nothing is known. The art of historical writing is said to have been introduced into Japan ca. 600 A.D. Asakawa, *op. cit.*, p. 109.

corrected, the foundation of the monarchy will be destroyed. He therefore commands that the existing histories be revised, " falsehoods being erased and the truth determined." *Kojiki* is especially full and precise as regards events from the seventh century B.C. to the fifth century of our era: after 488 A.D. it begins to lose its narrative detail and it stops at the year 628. Its language appears to be the vernacular of the time of its composition, and the Chinese characters in which it is written are in many instances used phonetically. In some instances the meaning of the characters is disputed. *Nihongi* was compiled a few years later, 720 A.D. It is written, Asakawa says, " in a Chinese style as pure and dignified as its author could make it." The record purports to be based in part on seventh-century sources, and the narrative grows fuller as it approaches the year 697, at which date it closes.[37]

It is universally recognized that *Nihongi* is written with a pro-Chinese bias, but Japanese scholars think that *Kojiki* is to a considerable extent what it purports to be — a record of the genuine traditions of the national life. Chamberlain, however, has no doubt that the older history has been falsified for political purposes.[38] When we consider that both *Kojiki* and *Nihongi* were compiled a couple of generations after the Reform of 645, and when we remember that every successful revolution in the occidental world, ancient or modern, has promptly striven to legitimate itself by falsifying antecedent history, it can scarcely be doubted that Chamberlain's view is correct. Even the mythology seems to show a reaction against Japanese customs and a bias in favor of Chinese views.[39] It seems probable that both these chronicles are revisions of the indigenous tradition in accordance

[37] Cf. Chamberlain, *Kojiki,* preface; Florenz, " Nihongi," preface, in *Mittheilungen der deutschen Gesellschaft für Natur-und Völkerkunde Ostasiens,* vol. v; Asakawa, *op. cit.,* pp. 7–12.

[38] Chamberlain, *loc. cit.,* p. xlv.

[39] For example: the story already cited, in which a goddess takes the initiative in wooing a god, represents the results as disastrous: the progeny was wholly unsatisfactory. Not until the courtship began *de novo* and the god spoke first were proper children born. *Kojiki,* Chamberlain's translation, pp. 20, 21.

with Chinese ideas, and that *Kojiki,* with its alleged imperial inspiration, its interesting figure of the old man of strong memory and its use of the vernacular, is the more adroit of the two reconstructions.

The list of emperors given in these chronicles and the dates of their reigns are things which only Japanese writers can take seriously.[40] From 660 B.C. to 592 A.D. but thirty-two rulers are listed, which makes the average length of the single reign nearly forty years.[41] In those twelve and a half centuries we find but one female ruler — the Empress Jingo, 201–269 A.D. — while in the following 166 years (592–758 A.D., that is, in the period subsequent to the introduction of the art of historical recording) there were no less than six empresses, who ruled collectively for 75 years. The fact that seems really to require explanation is that the corrected chronicles of the prehistoric period failed to eliminate the Empress Jingo; and the explanation seems to be that it was in her reign that Korea was conquered by Japan, and that her name was too firmly embedded in the memory of the nation to permit her to be ignored. All that could be done was to regularize her position, from a Chinese point of view, by making her a mere regent. Accordingly she occupies the throne as the representative of an infant emperor and rules in this capacity for 68 years. The six female reigns between 592 A.D. and 758 A.D. are similarly treated as regencies or are declared to be usurpations. Two of the usurpations present particularly interesting features.[42] The Empress Kokyoku, 642–644 and 655–661, occupied the throne at first as widow of a deceased emperor (so the official history puts it, but we may doubt whether the deceased emperor did not really reign as her consort), and when she went into voluntary retirement she was succeeded by her own son to the exclusion of his elder half-brother, the son of the preceding emperor by another wife. In 748 the father-in-law of

[40] *Cf.* Chamberlain, *loc. cit.,* pp. xlix, liii, liv.
[41] During the period of the hereditary shogunate, the average term of power was less than sixteen years.
[42] Ikeda, *op. cit.,* pp. 19, 20, 25, 26, 28, 29.

the reigning emperor forced his son-in-law to abdicate in favor of his daughter's daughter. If things that smack so strongly of mother-right could be done when Chinese ideas were becoming dominant, what may not have been done in those earlier centuries of which the tradition has been corrected in *Kojiki?*

It seems clear that the Japanese writers are hampered in their reconstruction of the primitive Japanese family by their disinclination to question the work of the Emperor Temmu and thus possibly to imperil " the foundations of the monarchy." It is clear, too, that they are unwilling to admit that the worship of male ancestors was not always a part of the original national religion, Shinto. This religion, which seems to rest primarily on the sentiment of awe in face of all that is marvelous, which has always maintained itself against or in combination with Buddhism, and which has enjoyed especial favor and protection at the hands of the government since 1868, is now largely a system of ancestor-worship, and almost all the writers under review assume that such was its original character. Peculiarly naïve in expression, but essentially typical in substance, is Tsugaru's argument to prove that the adoption of male heirs must have been customary in the earliest times. He assumes that the worship of male ancestors existed from the beginning, that this worship was conducted by men, that the succession to the sacral office passed down the male line and that, if the male line failed, adoption was necessary. For these assumptions he gives no reason except that " women are destined by nature to leave their own religious community in case of marriage." [43] But if, as he concedes, the wife did not enter the husband's house but remained with her own kin,[44] his theory of ancestor-worship implies the existence of sacral family groups distinct from the recognized kinship groups and perpetuating themselves according to a different system — which seems wholly incredible. It is one of the disadvantages of the life-long inside view of religious institutions

[43] Tsugaru, *op. cit.,* p. 26.   [44] *Ibid.,* p. 33, note.

that the devotee finds them so " natural " that he is apt to project them into the remote past. For the rest, Tsugaru seems to think that evidence of any sort of adoption in the earliest period is evidence for every sort of adoption. We may accept his assumption that strangers could be taken into the clan;[45] we may think it probable, as he does, that in some cases the visiting husband may have been transformed into a clan member in good and regular standing;[46] but that adoption was practised, as in a later period, to perpetuate the worship of house ancestors in the male line seems wholly inconsistent with the mother-right structure of early Japanese society.[47]

Of the forms of ancestor-worship which have grown up in Japan, *viz.*, worship of the first imperial ancestor, worship of clan ancestors, and worship of house ancestors, it would seem to an outsider, relying on the evidence which the Japanese give us and the analogies of other national systems, that only the first two forms could have existed in the earliest period. If they existed, the worship of the legendary clan ancestor as a clan god was doubtless the older of the two. Hozumi thinks that it was the chief bond which held the clan together. The clan god, he tells us, was transformed at an early period into the " local tutelary god," [48] who shares with the first imperial ancestor the honors and oblations of the *kamidana* or god-shelf in every Japanese house. The worship of the first imperial ancestor must have been developed later than that of the clan ancestors; for in Japan, as elsewhere, the monarchy was primarily military and national unity was achieved by conquests.[49] This national worship was probably developed by analogy from the worship of the

---

[45] Tsugaru, *op. cit.*, p. 25.   [46] *Ibid.*, pp. 31, 33.

[47] Gubbins (*loc. cit.*, p. iv and note) evidently doubts the primitive character of Japanese ancestor-worship, but subordinates his judgment to the authority of Prof. Hozumi. Prof. Knox of the Union Theological Seminary in New York, one of the first occidental authorities upon Japanese religion, informs me that he has reached, along different and non-legal lines of investigation, the conclusion that ancestor-worship formed originally no part of Shinto, but was borrowed from China.

[48] *Ancestor Worship*, p. 25.

[49] Sakamoto, *op. cit.*, pp. 17, 18; Asakawa, *op. cit.*, pp. 30, 44 *et passim*.

clan ancestors; and through association of ideas the worship of the first imperial ancestor produced the theory that all the inhabitants of the empire were of one blood.[50] In the territorialized clan, community of blood had already become in large measure a fiction, and it was easy to develop a similar fiction for the whole empire. Whether the clan gods were male or female Hozumi does not tell us; but the first imperial ancestor, worshipped as such to this day, was the sun-goddess Amaterasu.

III

The complete reception of Chinese views by the imperial court in the middle of the seventh century is indicated by the character of the imperial legislation during the following sixty years. As regards the family organization it is ordained that a man shall have but one wife. It is assumed that the wife enters the husband's kinship group and that the headship of the group normally passes from father to son. If there be no son a male heir is adopted. At the same time these laws reveal compromises with the older customs, some of which persist to this day. Polygyny is not really abolished; concubinage is recognized, and in the Taiho code (701 A.D.) the concubine is practically a wife of inferior rank. Her children are legitimate and have rights of succession.[51] The husband may enter the wife's household, and when there is no son in that household it is expected that he shall do so. This older form of marriage is brought into harmony with the new agnatic system by means of adoption, which converts the son-in-law into a sacral and legal son. This adoption-marriage (*muko-yoshi*) is still common in Japan.

The new kinship groups (*ko*) rested, like the Chinese family, on the principle that relationship through males takes precedence over relationship through females. The degrees or "ranks" of relationship recognized in the imperial laws were based upon the Chinese law of mourning.

---

50 Hozumi, *Ancestor Worship*, pp. 61, 63; Tsugaru, *op. cit.*, pp. 93, 97.
51 Weipert, *op. cit.*, pp. 107, 108; Araki, *op. cit.*, p. 6; Ikeda, *op. cit.*, pp. 195–197.

It is recognized more or less fully by nearly all the writers, Japanese and foreign alike, that this legislation represented, to a large extent, aspiration rather than achievement. It is fairly certain that it had little operation outside of the imperial family and the families of the nobles; and even in the imperial family, as we have seen, agnatic succession was by no means firmly established before the middle of the eighth century.

The chief agency in the development of the Japanese "house" was feudalism, which grew up in Japan in substantially the same manner as in Europe and assumed similar forms. In Japan, as in the Frankish empire, the military retainers were, originally, dependent members of the lord's household. Entry into such a household took them out of their former families, and gradually the older mother-right clans were superseded by new military groups.[52] When offices and fiefs became hereditary, they were heritable only by sons, born in the house or brought into it by adoption. The legislation of the Shogunate and of the territorial princes in the later middle ages gave to the new patriarchal and primarily agnatic house its complete development. But this legislation, again, affected only the military class.

In the period of transition from the old marriage to the new, from the eighth to the thirteenth centuries, we are told that marriage was arranged with the utmost secrecy, through the mediation of a kinsman of the bridegroom or of the bride, and was consummated with equal secrecy in the house of the bride. Three days later the marriage was publicly celebrated in the bride's house. At this celebration the husband was formally introduced to his wife's parents, "to whom, up to that time, he may not have been personally known."[53] From the fourteenth century on, however, the public celebration of the marriage preceded its consummation, and the celebration took place in the house of the bridegroom. The only reminiscence of the older order, according to Araki, is found in the fact that, in the chief ceremonial act, the

---

[52] Weipert, *op. cit.*, pp. 88, 89.   [53] Araki, *op. cit.*, p. 15.

alternate drinking by bride and groom from the same cup, the bride takes the first draught.[54]

The statement that the new form of marriage was fully established by the fourteenth century [55] seems to be true only of the noble and warrior classes. Among the peasants and the burgesses the new house seems to have developed more gradually, mainly through imitation and under the influence of Confucian ethics. In these classics " bridegroom-entry," *i.e.*, the form of marriage which leaves the bride in her own family, seems to have persisted; and even where the ultimate effect of the marriage was to transfer the wife to her husband's house, the marriage was initiated in the older indigenous fashion. In many localities the secret consummation of the marriage in the bride's house seems to have been usual even in the nineteenth century, the public celebration, with the removal of the wife to the husband's house, occurring only after days or months of cohabitation. In some localities this ceremony took place only when the wife was pregnant or after a child had been born.[56] Such " bride-children " were regarded as legitimate.[57] Among peasants and burgesses, again, *muko-yoshi,* or the adoption of the daughter's husband, seems to have been far more common than in the military class. The husband of an elder daughter was not infrequently adopted as heir to the headship of the house, although there were younger sons in the house already. In the absence of sons the succession to the headship might not only vest in a daughter but might be held by her after marriage, the husband becoming and remaining a subordinate member of the family.[58] Of course, however, the new marriage tended to prevail over the old in all classes. The position of the *muko-yoshi* or adopted son-in-law became more and more difficult; and the position of the husband who was not to be house-head, but was to pass from the household authority of his father-in-law under that of his own wife, was in too violent contrast with the Chinese ideas of feminine

---

[54] Araki, *op. cit.*, p. 18.
[55] *Ibid.*, pp. 15, 16; Iwasaki, *op. cit.*, pp. 13, 18.   [57] *Ibid.*, p. 108.
[56] Weipert, *op. cit.*, p. 99.   [58] Ikeda, *op. cit.*, pp. 126, 129.

subordination and marital supremacy to be in any way satis-factory.[59]

Inasmuch as the new marriage was not worked out in Japan but was borrowed in a fully developed form from China, we should not expect to find the intermediate stages of wife-stealing and wife-purchase which have elsewhere attended the evolution of marital right. The new Japanese marriage, like the old, was apparently consensual from the outset, *i.e.*, it rested simply on the agreement of the households and of the parties concerned. The evidence in favor of capture-marriage, collected by Prof. Naito, and set forth by Weipert, is destructively criticised by Araki; [60] and of the other writers under review Sakamoto alone supports the Naito-Weipert theory. The evidence produced by Sakamoto is valueless: he cites a legend, which shows traces of Chinese origin, and modern laws (1665 and 1863) against abduction.[61] Of purchase-marriage there is no evidence whatever; ceremonial exchange of gifts, which occurs in connection with every type of marriage, of course proves nothing.

In the new marriage, with its fully developed marital authority, the right of divorce belonged practically to the husband alone. In the feudal period, before 1868, the wife's right to a divorce without the husband's consent was recognized in a very limited class of cases,[62] and the chief ground, abandonment, hardly belongs in this class. Concubinage, although it had fallen into disrepute, was legally permissible until 1880, and the son of a concubine took precedence over a legitimate daughter in the succession to the headship of the house.[63]

In its final development, the Japanese house (*iye*) was ruled, like the Roman family, by a single head, who held and managed all the property, and exercised over the other members of the house all the personal authority which in

---

[59] *Cf.* Araki, *op. cit.*, p. 8; Tsugaru, *op. cit.*, pp. 6, 7.
[60] *Cf.* Weifert, *op. cit.*, pp. 94, 95; Araki, *op. cit.*, pp. 9, 10.
[61] Sakamoto, *op. cit.*, pp. 2–4. [62] *Ibid.*, pp. 26, 27, 40, 41.
[63] Araki, *op. cit.*, pp. 5–7; Ikeda, *op. cit.*, pp. 108, 195–197.

more advanced systems is exercised by parents over minor children. Unlike the Roman family, the Japanese house was not divided upon the death of its head. When the head-ship was vacated, either by death or by the retirement of the head from the active direction of the affairs of the house, the authority over the undivided house passed to a single successor. The succession was not exclusively agnatic: it was based on primogeniture with a preference of males. In default of a male successor the headship might vest in a female. If such an heiress were already married her hus-band was already an adopted member of the household; if she married after her accession to the headship her husband entered her household. In either case, at least in the noble and warrior classes, the headship passed to the husband; but since he held it by right of his wife, he lost it in case of divorce.[64]   Like the Roman family, the Japanese house in-cluded the wife and children of the head, his widowed mother, and his unmarried sisters; unlike the Roman family, it might also include his brothers and uncles, with their wives and children. If the succession to the headship had passed as a result of abdication (*inkyo*), the Japanese house might include the father and even the grandfather of the head. Unlike the Roman family, again, the Japanese house was, until 1868, the ultimate unit of public as well as private law. Only house heads could hold office.[65]

The chief bond of unity in this household, we are informed, was (and still is) the worship of the family ancestors. The headship of the house is primarily a sacral office, and the perpetuation of the household is chiefly important for the maintenance of the family *sacra*. As among other ancestor-worshipping peoples, adoption was originally and is still usually resorted to only in the absence of a natural successor to the sacral headship. In the selection of an artificial suc-cessor persons of kindred blood were always preferred, be-cause " the spirit does not receive the offerings of strangers."

[64] Araki, *op. cit.*, p. 8.
[65] Hozumi, *Civil Code*, pp. 43, 64; Ikeda, *op. cit.*, p. 134.

In the Taiho code the adopted son must be a kinsman within the fourth degree. In 1615 it was made possible to adopt any person of the same family name. Before the end of the seventeenth century it was decided that a son might be adopted from another clan. This was justified on the ground that all Japanese were of kindred blood.[66]

IV

The new Japanese legislation represents a compromise between the strict house system and the occidental family system. It represents also a long step towards individualism; for public rights and duties have been made independent of the house organization, and property rights and liabilities are attributed not only to all the adult male members of the house but also to married women and to minor children.

Formally, the house is still the legal unit. Every Japanese is registered as head or subordinate member of a house; and, as in Roman law, every person who was independent of household authority was designated as head of a family, so in the existing Japanese law every isolated individual — the illegitimate child, who is not admitted either into the father's house or into that of the mother, and the person who is released or expelled from one house without gaining admission to another — is registered as " establishing a new house." [67] A person cannot at the same time be member of two houses.[68]

The house is primarily a religious association, and the head is its priest. The ownership of the genealogical records of the house, of the articles used in household worship, and of the ancestral tombs, passes in every case with the headship of the house.[69] The heir to the headship is *heres necessarius* in the old Roman sense: he has not the right of renunciation that is accorded to the heir of mere property.[70] Escape from the burden of house

[66] Hozumi, *Ancestor Worship*, pp. 61, 63; Tsugaru, *Adoption*, pp. 93, 97.
[67] *Civil Code*, §§ 733, 735, 740, 742, 764.
[68] This rule is recognized by implication throughout the code. A corollary of the rule is expressly recognized in § 754.
[69] *Civil Code*, § 987.
[70] § 1020.

headship is made more difficult than it was in Roman law: the presumptive heir may not leave the house even with the consent of its head;[71] nor may the person who has succeeded to the headship resign it until a qualified successor is ready to accept it, nor even then, as a rule, before he has reached the age of sixty.[72]   An exception to these rules is, however, recognized when it becomes necessary for the presumptive heir or actual head of a branch house to assume the succession to the headship of the chief house;[73] and none of the foregoing restrictions apply to the person who has established a new house: he may at any time abolish it and become a member of another and older house.[74]   The relation of these rules and exceptions to the dominant religious principle is obvious.   In a new house there are no house ancestors to worship, and no sacred duty binds its founder to its maintenance; but he who has become head of a house by succession, or is legal heir to the headship of a house, has or will have house ancestors.   If, however, the house is a newer branch house, the duty to the older and principal house may become paramount.

Thoroughly in accordance with ancestor-worship is also the rule that the headship of the house is vacated if the head loses his Japanese nationality.[75]   We have already noticed the theories that all the people of Japan are members of one great family, bound together in the worship of the first imperial ancestor, and that " the spirit does not receive the offerings of a stranger."   If a Japanese ceases to be a member of the collective national family, he necessarily becomes a stranger in his own house and to its ancestors.   It seems probable that the identical Roman rule, by which *capitas diminutio media* entailed *capitis diminutio minima* originated in similar religious ideas.

In addition to its sacral significance, the Japanese house has protective and disciplinary functions.   The head of the house is bound to support its needy members and to edu-

---

[71] § 744.
[72] §§ 752, 762.
[73] §§ 744, 753, 762.
[74] § 762.
[75] § 964, cl. 1.

cate their children; although at present, when all the property of the household group is no longer held by the head, his duty is secondary to the reciprocal duties of husband and wife and of ascendant and descendant.[76] In the absence of a natural or testamentary guardian, the head of the house is the legal guardian of minors and of persons interdicted from the management of their own affairs.[77] Without the consent of the head, no person can come into the house, except the legitimate children of its members, nor can any member sever his connection with the house. From this principle it follows, in particular, that the consent of the heads of the houses affected is necessary in all cases of marriage and adoption, without regard to the ages of the parties.[78] The head of the house, moreover, determines the residence of all its members.[79] It should be noted, however, that the marriage or adoption which takes place without the consent of the head or heads concerned is not invalid,[80] and that the subordinate house-member who changes his residence without such consent is not brought back to the residence assigned to him. The extreme penalty which attaches to such disregard of the authority of the house head is expulsion from the house.[81]

Succession to the headship of the house vests primarily in a lineal descendant of the last head. Preference is given: (1) to the nearest in degree; (2) to males; (3) to legitimate children; (4) to recognized illegitimate children; (5) as between persons who in other respects fall in the same class, to the senior in age. Legitimized children and adopted children are in the same class with legitimate children born in the house, but as regards seniority they are treated as if born at the moment of legitimation or adoption.[82] If there be no lineal descendant or adopted child capable of succeed-

---

[76] §§ 747, 955.   [77] *Vide, infra.*   [78] §§ 741, 750.
[79] § 749.   [80] §§ 776, 849.   [81] §§ 741, 749, 750.
[82] §§ 970 *et seq.* The preference of the nearest in degree, taken alone, would vest the succession in a younger child to the exclusion of the child of an elder predeceased child; but the principle of representation is expressly recognized in § 974.

ing, the head of the house may appoint a successor by act
inter vivos or by testament.[83]   Failing such appointment,
the law makes very elaborate and complicated provisions for
the choice of a successor.[84]   The organ of choice, in the
majority of cases, is the family council (see below), and
the choice is made, primarily, from among the members of the
house, the wife of the last head being preferred to his collateral relatives.   If it be necessary to go outside of the house, a
member of an allied house (main or cadet branch of the
house in question) is to be preferred.   From the order of
preference indicated by the law the council may, however,
depart with the permission of the proper court.[85]

Within the house, the law recognizes the modern occidental
family, *i.e.*, the group consisting of husband, wife, and children; and it accords to the husband as such, and to parents
as such, an authority which is independent of that exercised
by the head of the house.

Marriage and divorce are consensual: they are based upon
the agreement of the parties,[86] supplemented, in case of persons under certain defined ages, by the consent of the parents.[87]   The only formal requirement for the validity of
these acts is the entry of the marriage or divorce upon the
civil register.[88]   If one of the parties to a marriage desires
a divorce and the other party refuses his or her consent, judicial divorce may be obtained on certain legally specified
grounds.[89]   Here the wife is still apparently at a disadvantage, for the grounds on which she may demand divorce are
fewer than those upon which the husband may sue.   Uxorial
infidelity, for example, is a ground for divorce; marital infidelity is not.   One of the grounds, however, on which
either party may sue, *viz.*, such ill-treatment or insult that

---

[83] §§ 979–981.   [84] §§ 982–985.

[85] The provisions above summarized are complicated by special rules
which take effect in case there is in the house a parent of the last head. Such
a parent, and not the family council, chooses the successor from among the
members of the house, and upon such a parent the succession itself devolves
if there be neither wife nor collateral relation to assume it. §§ 982, 984.

[86] §§ 778, 808.   [88] §§ 775, 810.

[87] *Vide, infra.*   [89] §§ 813–819.

the maintenance of the matrimonial relation appears intolerable,[90] is so broad that it may well establish a practical equality.

In addition to the form of marriage which brings the wife into the husband's house, the *Civil Code* recognizes the older form of marriage which has the opposite result. Marriage may be preceded or accompanied by the adoption of the prospective son-in-law by the bride's parents (in which case he is termed *muko-yoshi*), or marriage may be immediately followed by the entry of the husband into the wife's house (in which case he is described as *niu-fiu*).[91] If the wife be presumptive heir to the house headship, the *muko-yoshi*, by virtue of his sex, takes precedence over her and becomes presumptive heir in her stead.[92] If the wife be already head of her house at the time of her marriage, the *niu-fiu* becomes head by virtue of the marriage, unless the contrary is stipulated.[93] If the adoption-marriage be annulled, the adoption of the husband may be annulled; if the marriage be dissolved by divorce, the adoption may be dissolved;[94] and the *muko-yoshi* who has become presumptive heir or house head by virtue of adoption, loses this status as a result of the annulment or dissolution of the adoption. The *niu-fiu* who has become house head by virtue of his marriage simply, loses this status when the marriage is dissolved by divorce.[95]

We have seen that concubinage was not illegal in Japan until 1880, and that the child of a concubine occupied a position midway between that of a legitimate and that of an illegitimate child. The word used to designate the concubine's child was *shoshi*.[96] In the existing Japanese legislation, the *shoshi* is described as an illegitimate child recog-

---

[90] § 813, cl. 5.   [91] § 788.

[92] The *muko-yoshi* does not take precedence over any presumptive heir except his wife; *cf.* § 973.

[93] § 736.   [94] §§ 858, 866, cl. 9.

[95] § 964. Ikeda's statement (*op. cit.*, p. 252), that the *muko-yoshi* who has become house head and is subsequently divorced does not cease to be house head, means that the divorce as such does not effect such a *capitis diminutio* as in the case of the *niu-fiu*.

[96] The distinction between the *shoshi* and other illegitimate children was apparently the same which the Romans drew between *filii naturales* and *spurii*.

nized by the father;[97] and under this definition the status of the *shoshi* seems to be nearly the same as in mediæval Japanese law. If the parents of the *shoshi* marry, the *shoshi* obtains the status of a legitimate child.[98] If the father's wife is not the *shoshi's* mother, the relation between this quasi-stepmother (*chakubo*) and the *shoshi* is treated as legally equivalent to the relation between parent and child.[99] The *shoshi* inherits property *ab intestato;* has, like legitimate children, a legal portion of which he or she may not be deprived by testament: and even where there are legitimate descendants, the *shoshi* takes half the share of a legitimate child.[100] The *shoshi* is capable of succeeding to the headship of the house, taking precedence over illegitimate descendants; and it is a disputed question whether the male *shoshi* does not take precedence over a legitimate female descendant.[101]

Within the narrower family (as distinguished from the house) the authority of the husband over the wife, as defined in the *Civil Code,* is not very great. The wife is bound to live with the husband,[102] but any hardship resulting from this rule is apparently tempered by the facility with which she may obtain a judicial divorce. For all legal acts which seriously affect the wife's property rights, or which impose upon her serious personal obligations, she must obtain her husband's permission;[103] but this permission is not necessary when the husband has disappeared, or is incapable of managing his own affairs, or when the interests of the husband and wife conflict.[104]

Parental authority — exercised primarily by the father, but in his absence or incapacity by the mother[105] — is very generously measured: in some respects it is greater than

---

[97] § 827.   [98] § 836.   [99] § 728.

[100] §§ 1004, 1131. Under these sections, however, the *shoshi* enjoys no greater rights than those attributed to other illegitimate children.

[101] This was the mediæval rule. After the prohibition of concubinage in 1880, but before the present *Civil Code* was in force, the Japanese Imperial Court decided, April 13, 1897, that the legitimate female descendant preceded the male *shoshi*. The *Civil Code* apparently re-establishes the mediæval rule; for in the order of preferences laid down in § 970, the preference of males precedes the preference of legitimate descendants. Ikeda adopts this interpretation, but cites a contrary opinion. See Ikeda, *op. cit.,* p. 196.

[102] § 789.   [103] § 14.   [104] § 17.   [105] § 877.

the authority attributed to the head of the house. Without parental consent, males under thirty and females under twenty-five may not validly marry; nor may a husband or wife under twenty-five agree to a divorce; nor may any person validly adopt or be adopted.[106] The historical predominance of the house over the natural family is nevertheless recognized in the rule that no parental authority exists in these or in other matters unless the parent and the child are members of the same house.[107]

In the mediæval Japanese house there was as little room for guardianship as for parental authority, because the head of the house not only held all the property of the house, but also exercised over its subordinate members all the personal control now attributed to parents or to guardians. Only when the headship devolved upon a minor, or when the adult head became incapable of managing the affairs of the house, could the authority of a parent, as such, become of legal importance,[108] or, in default of a parent, would a supplementary guardianship be necessary. In other words, guardianship existed only as house regency. At the present time, however, since the law has developed separate property and parental authority within the house, guardianship has become necessary for all minors not under parental authority and for all persons incapable of managing their own affairs. By way of compromise with the older system, however, the law vests the guardianship of minors not under parental authority in the head of the house, unless a guardian be named by parental testament.[109] In the case of persons of full age interdicted from the management of their own affairs, guardianship devolves primarily upon the father or mother; or, if the person interdicted be married, primarily upon the husband or wife and secondarily upon the father or mother; failing any such guardian, this guardianship also devolves upon the head of the house.[110]

[106] §§ 772, 809, 843, 844, 857.
[107] §§ cited, and also § 877. An exception to the rule in § 845.
[108] Moral authority seems always to have been attributed to the parent.
[109] §§ 901, 903.   [110] §§ 902, 903.

Distinct from and independent of the house, an even wider family was recognized by older custom and laws, and is recognized by the existing legislation. This widest family, which one is tempted to describe as the " sib," includes all persons related to a given individual by blood or by marriage within certain defined degrees.[111] It includes also all members of the same house,[112] some of whom may be connected with the given individual by adoption only. Through the agency of a representative council,[113] consisting always of three persons, this widest family discharges important legal duties, particularly as regards minors. If there be no one to exercise parental authority over the minor, and no legal or appointed guardian, the family council selects a guardian.[114] Under analogous circumstances, it appoints a guardian for an interdicted person. The council supervises the administration of all guardians,[115] including the administration of the head of the house when he acts as legal guardian. Certain parental powers, *viz.*, consent to marriages, to divorces by agreement, and to adoptions, are exercised by guardians only with the approval of the council,[116] and may apparently be exercised by the council directly.[117] Even when parental authority exists, if this authority be exercised by a stepfather or stepmother or *chakubo,* the family council must assent to the giving of a child under fifteen in adoption;[118] and it may authorize marriage, divorce, or adoption in the case of a stepchild or *shoshi,* when the consent of the step-parent or *chakubo* is withheld.[119] When parental authority is exercised by a mother, the assent of the family council is required for acts affecting the property interest of the child;[120] and in all cases where the interests of parents and children are in conflict, the council appoints a representative to safeguard the interests of the child immediately con-

[111] Within the sixth degree of consanguinity or the third of affinity, § 725.   [112] § 945.
[113] §§ 944–953. A good description of the family council and its functions is given by Gubbins, *loc. cit.*, pp. vii–ix, xxxvi–xxxviii.
[114] §§ 904, 905.   [115] §§ 909–938.   [116] §§ 772, 809, 846.
[117] § 772, cl. 3, is differently translated by Gubbins and by Lönholm.
[118] § 843.   [119] §§ 773, 809, 846.   [120] § 886.

cerned.[121]   It will be perceived that the powers and duties of the Japanese family council are more extensive and important than those of the European family council — that it exercises much of that " over-guardianship," as the Germans term it, which in occidental countries is entrusted to the courts.   " It is true," Mr. Gubbins writes, "that in all cases there is an ultimate appeal from the decision of a family council to a court of law, but, apart from the natural reluctance of most people to take this step, the chances of success are too remote to favor its frequent adoption." [122]

In certain contingencies, the powers of the family council extend over the house itself.   When the head of a house is incapacitated, and there is no parent or guardian to act in his stead, the family council exercises the rights of house-headship;[123] and when the headship is vacant, and there is no legal or appointed successor, the family council, as has been noted above, chooses a successor.[124]

The members of the family council are regularly appointed by the proper court; but a council for a minor may be appointed by parental testament.[125]

In the foregoing survey of the three family groups in which the Japanese live — the narrow family, consisting of husband, wife, and children; the house, which may include several such families; and the still wider body of kinsfolk — we have noted only the legal incidents of membership in these organizations.   All these groups, however, like the occidental family, are primarily social, not legal; and in addition to the obligations which the law recognizes, the traditions of each group impose ethical restraints, while an elaborate etiquette develops and maintains the habit of deference to authority.   Japanese life has assuredly little of that sort of liberty which Caesar found among the Suabians, " cum a pueris nullo officio aut disciplina assuefacti nihil omnino contra voluntatem faciant." [126]

---

[121] § 888.   [122] Gubbins, *loc. cit.*, p. xxxvi.   [123] § 751.
[124] §§ 982, 983, 985.   [125] §§ 944, 945.
[126] *Bell. Gall.*, vol. iv., p. i.   That Caesar found in the Suabian " libertas vitae " one of the causes of their " immanis corporum magnitudo," suggests,

As regards property, however, Japanese legislation has broken through all these concentric social rings: it has vested all property rights in the individual. The subordinate house-members have become *sui iuris*. The property of the married woman is not merged in that of the husband's house; it is not even merged in that of the husband. In the absence of ante-nuptial contract the husband manages the wife's property and may expend the income, but only " in accordance with the uses to which it may rightly be applied." His position is that of a trustee, unless his wife is head of the house, in which case he is merely her agent.[127] By ante-nuptial contract the matrimonial property relations may be adjusted in such other manner as the parties may desire.[128] Property acquired by minor children is managed by the father (or by the mother under the control of the family council), but such property is not in parental usufruct: the powers and duties of the parent are those of a natural guardian.[129]

It is an interesting fact that the capacity of a subordinate house-member to hold property was first recognized, in Japan as at Rome, in the case of *peculium castrense* and *quasi-castrense, i.e.,* as regards salaries and annuities of military and civil officers.

Succession to property is in large measure independent of the house organization, but concessions are made to the older system. If there is no testament, the inheritance devolves primarily upon the descendants of the deceased, *per stirpes,* and without any preference based on sex or age. In the absence of descendants, the inheritance goes to the surviving husband or wife; in the absence of a surviving consort, it goes to the ascendants.[130] The power of a testator to modify this order of succession is limited by the right of the intestate heirs above mentioned to a legal portion, which in the case of a descendant amounts to one-half of

---

in view of the small stature of the Japanese, speculations which are probably more curious than impórtant. The valuation of his theory may be left to the anthropologists.   [127] §§ 798–807.   [128] §§ 793 *et seq.*
        [129] §§ 884 *et seq.*   [130] §§ 994 *et seq.*

the share which he or she would have received *ab intestato,*
and in the case of a surviving consort or an ascendant to one-
third of such share.[131]   All this is thoroughly European; but
there are two additional rules which give the house head a
privileged position.   (1) If the inheritance in question is
that of a subordinate house-member; if there is neither descendant, surviving consort, nor ascendant; and if no contrary provision has been made by testament, the head of the
house takes the entire estate.[132]   Brothers, sisters, and other
collaterals have thus no rights of succession *ab intestato.* (2)
If the inheritance is that of a house head, his successor in the
headship, if a descendant, is entitled to one-half of the estate, no matter how many other descendants there may be;
and if the successor be not a descendant, he is entitled to
one-third of the estate.   These shares, moreover, are legal
portions, of which the new head cannot be deprived by testament.[133]

Subject to the limitations imposed by the rules regarding
legal portions, the power to dispose of property by testament
is fully recognized, and the law of testaments is elaborately
formulated.   As yet, however, testament has taken no firm
root in Japanese custom.   " What is done in Europe and
America by will is done in Japan by adoption.   Instead of
giving away property to another person by will which becomes effective after death, a Japanese takes another person
into his house by adoption during his lifetime, and makes
the latter the expectant successor to his property." [134]

In comparing the Japanese house with the Roman patriarchal family, Japanese writers insist on the differences between the two organizations as well as on the resemblances;
but they have not formulated what seems to be the fundamental difference.   The Japanese house apparently repre-

---

[131] § 1131. This section, at least in the translations, is not accurately
worded; but in view of §§ 994, cl. 2, and 995, it must apparently be interpreted as above.   [132] § 996.

[133] § 1130. But where there is no descendant, the house head may appoint the successor to the headship by testament.   § 979.

[134] Hozumi, *Civil Code,* p. 58.

sents an earlier stage of social development: it may be regarded as an intermediate link between the clan and the purely patriarchal family. The further back its history is traced, the more like a little clan does it appear. If we attempt to summarize the Japanese development, we may say that, within the territorialized clans which had taken form in the mother-right period, there grew up, apparently as a result of Chinese influences, patronymic groups which were practically inchoate father-right clans. If Japan had not at that time already passed beyond the clan state of civilization; if the individual, instead of looking for protection to his kinsfolk exclusively, had not begun to look to a feudal lord; these new groups would apparently have developed into clans. As it was, the new houses soon began to throw off branch houses; but unlike the Roman patriarchal family, the Japanese house did not, and does not now, split into new houses as often as the head disappears: it throws off branch houses, apparently, only when it becomes, or threatens to become, unwieldy.

Recent Japanese legislation leaves the historic house formally intact; but its economic basis has been seriously weakened, and the personal authority of the head of the house has been diminished. Within the house, the modern occidental family has obtained at least a partial organization. It was perhaps the expectation of the Japanese legislators that this narrower family, developing within the house, would ultimately replace it. In considering, however, the probable development of this family and the importance which it is likely to attain as a social agency, it must not be forgotten that the modern European family was characterized, in its formative period, by the concentration of all the economic resources of its members in the hands of the husband and father, and by greater authority of the husband over the wife and of the father over the children than is accorded to the Japanese husband and father; nor must it be forgotten that this family rested on the permanent union of husband and wife. In the existing occidental family, the disintegrating influences of separate property rights and of facile divorce are already discernible; and the importance of the family as a social unit rests largely on traditions established in earlier times. It now resists further disintegration chiefly by a sort of *vis inertiae*. It may therefore well be questioned whether the new Japanese family, modelled as it is on this latest and feeblest phase of the occidental family, and rendered yet feebler by a greater facility of divorce than any occidental state at present concedes, will really take the place and discharge the social functions of the historic house. If the Japanese house is destined to disappear, it seems probable that the decisive agency in its disruption will not be the new family, but the individualistic tendencies which the legislation of the last generation has called into activity; and the future development of Japanese society will bring the individual in increasing measure face to face with the national state, without important intermediate authority or protection.

X

THE DOGMA OF JOURNALISTIC INERRANCY.[1]

A YEAR or two ago a letter was printed on the first page of the New York " Sun " with the startling editorial head-line: " Right You Are; Wrong Were We." Those who read the letter discovered with a shade of disappointment that the mistake which the editor admitted was a trifling one: he had described a football as an "oblate spheroid." Still, his response made a grateful impression and lingered pleasantly in the memory; for admissions of editorial fallibility are most unusual, and the promptness, completeness and cheerfulness of this admission made it unique.

That newspapers rarely admit mistake is notorious. They are far from willing to correct statements of fact, and they are very unwilling to withdraw or modify expressions of editorial opinion. Many persons find this attitude unreasonable; some pronounce it absurd. Fundamentally, however, the policy of the newspapers is sound. It may even be shown to be necessary. It was not originally adopted because of any conviction that news was accurate and editorial opinion conclusive; on the contrary, it was forced upon the daily press by the inevitable inaccuracy of its news and the necessary inconclusiveness of its judgments.

News, of course, presents itself as matter of fact, but it is in reality only matter of impression. News of an occurrence reflects, at best, a one-sided superficial first view of a part of the facts which make up the occurrence. The difference between facts and news becomes most evident when we compare the methods by which facts are ascertained and those by which news is gathered. The most efficient agencies which the wit of man has devised for ascertaining facts are scientific investigation and judicial inquiry. Both agencies

[1] Reprinted from *The North American Review*, vol. 187, no. 627, February, 1908, pp. 240–254.

have found it necessary to develop special and highly technical processes and to take plenty of time — processes which journalism could not employ if it would, and time which the journalist has not at his disposal.

A comparison between judicial inquiry and news-gathering is the more legitimate because the work of courts is in some respects akin to that of newspapers. Many matters which figure first as news become in time objects of judicial investigation. Courts disentangle their facts, as journals get their news, from testimony. Like news-gathering (and unlike scientific investigation) judicial inquiry is conducted under some limitation as regards time: except in police courts the work is not hurried, but controversies must be terminated and the calendar must be cleared. The methods of the news-gatherer, however, are very different from those employed by courts. The reporter, as a rule, hears but one side, and very little of the evidence on that side. He hears testimony which a court would exclude as irrelevant or misleading. He often relies wholly on hearsay. He does little if anything in the way of cross-questioning witnesses or determining their freedom from bias, and he seldom investigates their reputation for veracity. The crudity of his processes is attributable mainly to haste. Where courts (police courts again excepted) have days or weeks, he has minutes or, at best, hours. The pace at which he must work is quickened by competition; for news is spoiled if a rival journal publishes it in an earlier edition. The correspondent labors under much the same difficulties as the local reporter, and has little opportunity to test the statements which he transmits.

The difference between facts and news is increased, in many instances, by political or economic bias. A reporter hesitates to bring in matter which makes against the policy of his newspaper, and he is inclined so to color the matter which he does turn in as to render it acceptable.

The most important factor of variation, however, is the news-gatherer's duty to make a "story." This duty is not imposed upon him by arbitrary editorial policy; it is imposed upon the newspaper by the news-readers; and all that the editor decides is how far he shall go in meeting the public demand. Nor is the public desire for " true stories " a new desire created by the newspapers; it is as old as human society. Rumors about great people and great events, gossip and scandal about people of all sorts — these have always been demanded. And from the outset the gatherers and distributors of such news — village gossips, town barbers, travelling peddlers and strolling bards — have been constrained to put their news into artistic form; they have gained a hearing not because their stories were true, but because their news was always a story.

The news-story must, of course, maintain a close connection with the world of fact. News, no matter how fictitious, deals with real persons in real places, and is usually based on actual occurrences. Pure fiction is the younger rival of news; it tries to tell a better story by freeing itself wholly from the trammels of fact. In so doing it gains in artistic quality, but it loses something of verisimilitude. Even in pure fiction an illusion of reality is essential to enjoyment; and news, because it preserves an apparent connection with fact, retains the advantage of readier and stronger illusion.

It seems a far cry from village gossips and wandering story-tellers to the modern daily press, with its costly plants, its myriads of workers, its national and international organization; but, at bottom, modern journalism satisfies the same social demand with the same supply — rumor, scandal and gossip. Some of the more respectable newspapers limit their output of scandal; some of them refrain, except in the case of prominent people, from publishing gossip; a few endeavor to exclude unauthenticated rumors of the " interesting if true " type; but others cover the whole field and achieve thereby the largest sales. The modern daily press has unquestionably whetted the appetite for fiction that masquerades as fact, because it has made the supply as regular as that of our daily bread; and the demand that news

shall be interesting has grown more urgent as the interest
of news has been enhanced by increasing skill in its presentation. More strictly than ever before the news-gatherer is
held to-day to the duty of making a story. If the occurrence
which he has to describe is not interesting, he must supply
interest. If the details do not group themselves dramati-
cally, they must be regrouped. Omission or addition of incidents is governed, not by a desire to make the picture correct, but by the obligation to make it striking. To the
journalism that gives freest play to the artistic impulse of
imaginative reconstruction, we apply the term " sensa-
tional "; but it is not commonly realized that sensational-
ism is only an exaggeration of what we are accustomed to
regard as legitimate journalistic practice, and that even in
the most respectable newspapers there is a great and inevitable difference between facts and news.

Editorial comments are based on current news. If, as
is commonly the case, the news is inaccurate, the comments
are necessarily inconclusive. And the editor, like the reporter, works under the lash of timeliness. It is expected
of him that he shall emit opinions promptly. The function
of the leading article is to relieve readers who are mentally
indolent and readers who are busy and therefore preoccu-
pied — and nearly all readers fall into one or the other of
these classes — from the task of forming their own opinions
or finding fit expression for their own emotions. This function must obviously be discharged before the readers have
either made up their minds or forgotten the news. Once in
a while, a very conscientious editor, confronted with a very
difficult or a very important question, announces that the
newspaper prefers to reserve its judgment until fuller reports
are obtained; but even such an editor is rarely able to wait
until all the relevant facts are approximately established.
To reserve judgments is, on the whole, injudicious. It not
only disappoints the reader of the editorial page, but it tends
to discredit the snap judgments presented in adjacent columns. Bismarck's aphorism seems as true of journalism as

of politics: that it is often less dangerous to do the wrong thing than to do nothing.

Under such conditions, editorial utterances, if not dictated by partisanship or other prepossessions, are more often reflections suggested by the current news than anything approaching judgments, and more often expressions of emotion than exhibitions of thought. The editor's safest course is to voice what seems likely to be the general feeling of his readers. The most dangerous course that he can follow is to try to formulate a judgment.

The legal view of news and of newspaper comment — a view that is entitled to consideration — is clearly reflected in the care with which, in criminal cases, all such matter is withheld from the jurors.

If the preceding analysis of the functions of daily journalism is substantially correct, the general policy of newspapers is evident. With facts as such, they have nothing to do. Statements of fact concern them only when the matter is timely and the form interesting. The great metropolitan newspaper should steadily roll off from its cylindrical presses its endless picture of daily life, having less regard for truth of line and of color than for general effect; never looking backward except to point out that on such a date it published " exclusively " some interesting piece of news. On its editorial page it should record the thoughts suggested and the feelings excited by the news of the day; never reverting to its past utterances except to remind its readers that on such a date it expressed an opinion which fuller information has confirmed.

The course of conduct here outlined is that which the ablest newspapers regularly follow; and they would doubtless follow it without exception, were it not for a factor of disturbance which is practically constant — the letter to the editor.

By tradition, and in consonance with certain established (although disputable) theories regarding the relation of newspapers to the public, every individual who alleges misrepresentation or misjudgment of his acts or utterances has a right to a modest amount of space in which to present his grievance and to ask for redress. This right is akin to the commoner's right of petition in a monarchic or aristocratic state, and it is correspondingly sacred. Such letters, if they be not too long, must be printed; they must be printed with scrupulous exactness; and, as a rule, they must be answered.

These petitions the newspaper is bound to resent and to resist. They intrude belated facts. They call upon the journalist to turn aside from his business of publishing the news and making comments on the news and to go into the opposite business of publishing facts and rendering judgments based upon facts. To cater to such demands would be bad journalism. To make the situation perfectly clear, let us imagine that the newspapers received every such petition in a friendly spirit; that they investigated every alleged grievance in a judicial temper and with an open mind; that if, on full consideration, it did not appear that any misrepresentation had been made or any misjudgment recorded, they announced this finding in such a manner as to inflict upon the unsuccessful petitioner the least possible pain; that if, on the contrary, the grievance were found to be real, they granted prompt and full redress, corrected the erroneous statement, modified or withdrew the misjudgment, and made the correction, modification or withdrawal as prominent as the original item or comment. What would be the result? Everynewspaper would be deluged with petitions. To deal with them, the working force would have to be increased and the paper itself enlarged. To discharge its new duties fully and conscientiously, every important newspaper would probably be forced to organize a second staff, composed of men not primarily interested in news but in facts — men of judicial temper and scientific training; and it would probably be found desirable to issue with the daily newspaper a supplementary fact-paper. In the fact columns of this supplement the reader would find corrections, first, of yesterday's news; second, of day-before-yesterday's news; and so on back for

weeks, for months, and possibly for years, for in some instances no satisfactory approximation to the truth could be
attained until years had elapsed. On the editorial page of
this fact-paper would appear the sober second thoughts of
the fact editors, touching the opinions expressed weeks,
months or years before by their colleagues in the news department.

This fantastic picture of a journalistic house divided
against itself is of value as a further illustration of the difference between news and facts. It shows that a serious and
persistent pursuit of facts would carry the journalist into
the field of the historian. The picture is of chief value, however, as a demonstration that the demands of individuals for
the correction of misstatements or for the withdrawal of mis-
judgments are unreasonable demands, which the newspapers
are compelled to resist. Any considerable concessions to
these demands would be distinctly injurious to the essential
interests of journalism. In theory, such concessions would
be admired by all who praise truth and justice; in practice,
they would gratify only the comparatively small number
of persons whose wrongs were righted, and they would dis-
please almost all other newspaper readers. Frequent corrections of yesterday's news would annoy the news-reader
by compelling him to doubt the news of to-day. The illusion
of reality might in the end be so weakened as to rob news
of the only advantage which it possesses over other forms of
imaginative literature. Nor would the reader of newspaper
comment be pleased by frequent modifications or reversals of
the editorial attitude. The average man does not care to appropriate tentative conclusions; he wishes, for the sake of
mental tranquillity, to be provided with judgments that
seem final. To lose confidence in his newspaper would drive
him to formulate his own prejudices and to find reasons for
defending them; and this would be irksome.

The illusion of reality as regards its news and the illusion
of finality as regards its opinions constitute what is commonly called the " prestige " of a newspaper. The word is

apt, for its original meaning is " illusion." In eighteenth-century English it was used in no other sense; Johnson defined " prestiges " as " illusions, impostures, juggling tricks." To-day the word has come to suggest something like reputation, but it does not mean reputation: it implies nothing more than successful appeal to the imagination. Reputation for accuracy of statements no newspaper possesses; for every one knows that news is not accurate, and that the only difference between reckless and cautious journalism is in the degree of inaccuracy. Reputation for soundness of judgment no newspaper possesses; for every moderately intelligent person knows that snap judgments cannot be uniformly wise. Popular illusion on this point is more persistent only because the readers of each newspaper share its views; they read it because it voices their prejudices; but for this very reason no general illusion obtains as to the wisdom of any particular paper. " Prestige " in these matters newspapers do possess in varying degrees; and the statement that " a newspaper must preserve its prestige " is axiomatic. The maintenance of illusions which are dear to the public and useful to the newspapers is a necessary aim of journalism; and the newspaper is bound to save what an Oriental would call its " face."

If it be admitted — and it is hard to see how it can be denied — that the petition for justice is a disturbing factor in the life of a newspaper, it must be conceded that sound journalistic policy demands that such disturbances be reduced to a minimum. It follows that the petition must be so answered that the petitioner shall not be likely to repeat his offence. No satisfaction is to be given him, for that would encourage him to write again as soon as any of his acts or utterances should again become an item of news or a subject of comment. Moreover, any satisfaction given him would encourage other aggrieved persons to write to the editor. It is clear, therefore, that, even if the petitioner happens to be in the right, he must be so answered as to be put in the wrong. This is not difficult to any practised disputant, and to an editor it is particularly easy. Both for the special purpose of putting the petitioner in the wrong and for the general and really essential purpose of withholding satisfaction, the editor has means at his disposal which the ordinary disputant does not command. Not only has he the defensive position and the last word, but the attack is necessarily made on ground which he selects and with weapons which he furnishes. He decides in what part of his paper and in what type the letter shall be printed. If it contain arguments which seem convincing, or if it be so written as to appeal strongly to the sympathy of the public, he can print it in a part of the paper where few readers will notice it. He always puts it into the smallest type. He selects the heading for the letter, and is thus enabled to give a false impression of its contents to those who do not read it and to bias the minds of those who do. The heading and the answer — if any other answer than the heading be deemed necessary — are printed in larger type, the heading usually in heavy-face type. This difference in type fitly symbolizes the fundamental advantage of the editorial position. The attack upon the paper is made by the weak individual " I "; the defence is conducted by the strong institutional " We." Were not vital interests of journalism at stake, the inequality of the contest might well move editors themselves to compassion.

To most American editors the denial of petitions for justice seems insufficient. They are clearly of the opinion that petitioners not only must receive no satisfaction but should be punished for the attempt to interfere with the regular business of the newspaper. This attitude is intelligible, but it is not prudent. If the newspapers are adequately protected by making petitions fruitless — and this seems to be the case — it is unnecessary, and therefore impolitic, to give petitioners an additional grievance. Passive hopelessness should not be converted into active hatred. In any case, there is a choice among punishments; and it may be asserted with confidence that no form of punishment should be selected which tends to arouse sympathy for the petitioner.

If it be deemed necessary to punish him at all, the safer course is to make him ridiculous.

The refusal of satisfaction is of course necessary; and this involves refusal to admit mistakes. This, in its turn, involves an assumption that mistakes are not made; and this assumption is the Doctrine of Journalistic Inerrancy. It is obviously a fiction; but, like many fictions of the law, it furnishes a convenient statement of a working rule. It formulates a policy based on expediency, and it admits such exceptions as expediency may require.

It is well known that doctrines expressing policies tend to harden into dogmas presented as truths. With this tendency every student of government or of law or of religion is familiar. To this peril journalism also has succumbed. The Dogma of Journalistic Inerrancy converts a maxim of policy into a tenet of faith. It asserts that the newspaper is always right; and from this premise it deduces invariable rules of journalistic conduct. To show how this result has been reached, it is necessary to consider the manner in which the peculiar nature of journalistic activity, especially its preoccupation with first impressions to the exclusion of facts and with sentiment to the exclusion of judgment, reacts upon the minds of the journalists themselves.

Journalists of the highest mental type develop a philosophy which is by no means unknown outside of their profession. They hold that truth is not ascertainable, and that, if it could be ascertained, it would probably be valueless. Applied to journalistic problems this theory produces very convenient inferences. Since the facts which constitute an occurrence can never be fully ascertained, one view of the occurrence is presumably as good as another. The first impression may indeed be modified by a second, but the second in turn may be modified by a third; and in many cases, after long investigation, the first impression is re-established. As for editorial opinions, they are probably sounder and assuredly not less sound than other opinions. The only value of opinions, in any case, is the influence which they exercise upon conduct; and if an editorial opinion makes for desirable conduct, it is better than a more deliberate judgment which may have undesirable results. It follows that there is really no reason why any plausible statement should be corrected or any laudable opinion modified.

Among journalists of another and inferior mental type, a conviction develops that the news which they publish is fairly accurate, and that the views which they take are the only correct ones. The fact that their statements are seldom denied and their opinions seldom disputed, the ease with which the few who attempt to correct them are discomfited, the apologies and flatteries with which the experienced letter-writer approaches them — these things tend to create and to strengthen self-esteem. They forget that their comparative immunity from criticism is due to hopelessness, and that the deference shown them is evoked by fear. The conviction of their own truthfulness and wisdom is of course most rapidly and most strongly developed among the most respectable journalists. The newspaper that is able to give thanks in public that it is not as other journals are — forgers of rumors, scandalmongers, " yellow "— develops a spiritual pride which darkens its judgment; and its relative accuracy and wisdom seem to it almost or altogether absolute.

Among all newspaper men the transformation of the doctrine of inerrancy into a dogma is furthered by constant association with one another and by the resulting formation of a general journalistic opinion which is incomparably stronger and more uncompromising than is the opinion of any individual journalist. The same influences produce like results in all compact, like-minded social groups — in cliques and in parties, in faculties and in churches. Loyalty to the group makes the interests of the group paramount and converts the rules of conduct which subserve these interests into articles of faith. If one may invert Schiller's famous distich, the good cow which provides its attendants with butter becomes to them a goddess, gracious and holy.

Between acceptance of the doctrine of inerrancy as a

statement of policy, with clear consciousness that it is a fiction, and assent to the dogma, with conviction that it embodies a truth, many mental attitudes are conceivable; and it is probable that most newspaper men occupy intermediate positions; but the general conduct of the American daily press shows that the average editor stands much nearer to the dogmatic than to the rational point of view.

The dogmatic attitude reveals itself primarily in unbroken adherence to the rule that mistake is not to be conceded. It is only by journalists of the rational type that admission of error is ever made. Even from them such admissions come seldom, and the mistakes which they acknowledge are hardly ever of any importance.

The degree to which the dogmatic attitude has been substituted for the rational is reflected in the treatment of letter-writers who ask for an editorial correction or retraction. To journalists of the agnostic and indifferentist type, the aggrieved individual who forces his way into their columns is a fussy little man whose grievance is of no real consequence. Of course, no satisfaction is to be given him, but it is unnecessary to take him seriously or to treat him very badly. Such journalists defend themselves with the weapons of wit and of humor, in the use of which they naturally excel. To the thoroughgoing dogmatist, on the other hand, the outsider who denies journalistic inerrancy is a miscreant, who is to be punished, not merely for the general purpose of repressing infidelity, but also because of his personal sin against the light. The journalist of the self-righteous type is peculiarly vindictive in his treatment of such offenders. What does it profit him that he is scrupulous beyond others, if he is to be reproved as are the publicans of the press? These journalists are not happy in the use of humor or of wit; for the humor of an earnest man is heavy and the wit of an angry man is blunt. Outsiders who question the opinions of an editor of this type in matters of any consequence are often treated with unwise brutality. They are trampled and gored by the Sacred Cow.

Dogmas are dangerous, not only to those who deny them, but also to those who accept them. Policy admits variations; dogma excludes them. Sound journalistic policy demands that the disturbance of newspaper business by petitions be reduced to a minimum; but the interests of journalism also require that petitions be occasionally submitted. Newspapers, like governments, are bound to do things that arouse resentment; resentment must have an outlet; and for newspapers, as for monarchic and oligarchic governments, the safest outlet is by petition. If petitions should cease, the public would clearly perceive that its right of petition had been nullified. It is for this reason that it seems unwise to inflict punishment on petitioners. The aim of punishment goes beyond the discouragement of offenders; it goes to the total repression of offences. It may, indeed, be said that the repressive aim of punishment is never fully realized; it may be urged that, for the sake of bringing to public attention the facts as they view them, some aggrieved persons will always brave certain ridicule and probable insult; but it must be recognized that the tendency of punishment is to reduce petitions below the minimum of safety to journalism itself.

The dogmatic attitude and the course of conduct which it dictates are directly dangerous to journalism by reason of the resentment which they arouse. In primitive social conditions those who insult and defame others incur bodily danger; and in some parts of our country the journalist is still exposed to private vengeance. As civilization advances, the person who injures another by spoken, written or printed words is protected against violent reprisals; but this is not done for his sake, nor does the law which protects him represent any social solicitude for his life or limbs. The law is concerned solely with the maintenance of the peace. The persistent social attitude was clearly expressed by Franklin — himself a journalist — when he intimated that complete liberty of the press should logically be accompanied by complete liberty of the cudgel. The law has deprived the public of its cudgels, but in exchange it has given actions for defamation and prosecutions for libel. The check upon journalistic activity persists; it has simply assumed a new form. Journalists gain something by the change. The legal remedy is more costly in money and in time than the private vengeance which it replaces, and it is less certain in its operation. Moreover, the law is conservative; and new forms of insult, which in an earlier step of social progress would have found redress by the cudgel, are only slowly met by an extension of the established legal remedies. But the advantages which journalism enjoys in the present stage of legal development are not necessarily permanent. More effective enforcement of the remedies which the law provides may be secured by associated effort. Societies might well be formed which for a moderate annual premium would in-sure their members against defamation. Able counsel would be retained; every grievance alleged by a member would be promptly investigated; and, whenever sufficient ground for action should be discovered, legal proceedings would be in-stituted and carried through at the cost of the society. Once formed, such organizations would probably extend their field of operations; they would become associations for the re-form of the law. Doubtless cases would be brought before the courts in the hope of securing a judicial construction of the law more favorable to the protection of the individual reputation. Efforts would be made to obtain statutory changes of similar tendency. The laws of other countries would be examined, and it would be ascertained that in many respects these give more efficient protection against misrepresentation than is afforded by the laws now in force in our States. It would be found in particular that most foreign legislations do not require allegation and proof of pecuniary damage, but only of such misrepresentation as affects the reputation. In some legislations it is provided that, when-ever a newspaper has been guilty of misrepresentation, it must publish the full text of the judgment in the same part of the paper and in the same size of type in which the original misrepresentation appeared. Statutes of this character would be demanded, and in the present state of public feeling such statutes might be passed. Encouraged by success, the protective associations might press for legislative recognition of the right of privacy; and they might secure the adoption of laws penalizing the publication of statements regarding private and family life, except in cases in which written authorization could be shown or a legitimate public interest demonstrated. In our States it is notoriously easy for an organised minority to secure almost any sort of legislation; and it is evident that the libel-insurance societies would take care that the new laws should not sleep in the statute-books.

It need hardly be pointed out that such laws, effectively enforced, would seriously interfere with the existing liberty of the press. Journals would still appear, but they would bear little resemblance to the American newspapers of the present day. They would rather resemble those staid journals of Continental Europe, which the American newspaper man has always derided for lack of enterprise and dearth of interesting news. Journalists there would be, but of a new and humdrum type. They would lack the glad freedom in the exercise of irresponsible power which now makes the career of the American newspaper man attractive.

To most American journalists the dangers here indicated will probably seem unreal. Accustomed to arousing resentment and skilled in making its outbursts appear ridiculous, they naturally underrate the forces which they are arraying against themselves. They forget that the misrepresented, weak as individuals, may become strong through organization. They do not appreciate that the irritation of the misrepresented is rapidly increasing, partly because grievances are never redressed, but chiefly because petitions for redress are so often dismissed with frivolity or with brutality. Least of all do they appreciate that the perilous course which they are following is due to a gradual change in their own mental attitude — to the elevation of the doctrine of journalistic inerrancy to the position of a dogma.

Gossips and scandalmongers have always been feared; bards were formerly feasted in the halls of heroes whose deeds they were expected to celebrate and welcomed in the courts of princes whose acts they might condemn; but the power of the modern daily press is, in its magnitude, a new thing. Like all new power, it is over-confident: it does not realize its limitations, foresee its perils, nor discern the policy which it should pursue to minimize or neutralize hostility. It might well learn something from the history of political power; and it might consider with especial profit some of the many wise things which Machiavelli says about the absolute prince.

The prince, Machiavelli argues, cannot safely be virtuous, for of the recognized virtues many would make his career difficult and some would make it impossible. But, inasmuch as men praise virtue and censure vice, the prince should always seem virtuous. To this end, he should always claim for himself the moral qualities which as a rule he cannot display in his conduct. This, however, is not enough; he must occasionally do conspicuously virtuous acts. The occasions should be carefully selected, so that his good deeds shall involve the least possible sacrifice of political interest and make the greatest possible impression upon the public imagination.

Up to a certain point, newspapers instinctively follow the course which Machiavelli mapped out for the prince. They cannot be accurate, but they claim accuracy; they cannot render unbiased, deliberate and conclusive judgments, but they assert that their comments possess these qualities; they cannot deal justly with petitions for the redress of grievances, but they say that they are just. Obviously they should go further. In rejecting petitions, they should assume an appearance of fairness; and once in a while they should grant redress of a grievance, and grant it in such a manner as to make the act of justice especially striking. Once in a while a letter protesting against misrepresentation should be followed by the curt editorial statement: " The reporter who misled us has been discharged." More rarely, but still once in a while, a newspaper should relieve an individual from an aspersion cast upon him in its editorial comment; and, since he who gives quickly gives twice and he who gives cheerfully gives twentyfold, the aspersion should be retracted at the earliest possible moment and with the ungrudging alacrity of the "Sun's" confession: "Right You Are; Wrong Were We."

The dismissal of a reporter for misrepresentation is not wholly without precedent; but the cases in which such action has been publicly announced are very rare. In such dismissals, undue consideration has possibly been given by some editors to the question of the reporter's culpability. Private dismissals, except for offences against the newspaper itself, and consideration of the reporter's culpability as regards outsiders are equally inconsistent with sound newspaper policy. A reporter who has turned in a good story should never be dismissed because his story is not true, but only because the interests of the newspaper require a vicarious sacrifice on the altar of justice; and, since such sacrifices are designed to allay resentment and to create a general illusion of journalistic truthfulness and justice, they should be made with the utmost publicity.

The prompt, undisguised and cheerful withdrawal of an editorial aspersion is probably without precedent. The editor who should first take such a step would doubtless be censured by almost all other journalists, but their opinions would not appear in print. In the public mind, the truthfulness and justice of his paper would be so securely established that subsequent rigorous adherence to normal journalistic policy would not seriously impair this new prestige for many years. Upon the advertising value of action so unusual it is unnecessary to insist.

A second editorial retraction could not produce the same sensation as the first, and repeated dismissals of reporters would also yield diminishing returns of illusion; but since such departures from established custom could never become common, they would never fail to produce the desired effect. An annual dismissal or a triennial retraction, if properly staged, would cause the murmurs of discontented thousands to pass unheeded.

These suggestions will doubtless be regarded as revolutionary, but they are in reality conservative. Occasional departures from the traditional policy not only will be of advantage to journalism, but are necessary for its safety. The Doctrine of Journalistic Inerrancy must of course be maintained, but the Dogma should be abandoned.

XI

THE NATURE AND THE FUTURE OF
INTERNATIONAL LAW [1]

RETURNING, in the early days of the war, from a belligerent
Germany, through a mobilized Switzerland and a partly
mobilized Italy, to an America that was still unperturbed
and unprepared, I revisited the famous Museum of Naples.
In one of the central corridors, I noticed an ancient mural
inscription, which I had doubtless seen before without ap-
preciating its significance — an inscription of the time of
Augustus: " To perpetual peace." Thus even in warlike
Rome, and more than nineteen centuries ago, after a series
of wars that had shaken the then civilized world from the
Alps to the African deserts and from the Pillars of Hercules
to the Nile, as after every great war that has since devastated
Europe, men's minds were turning with inextinguishable
hope to the vision of a warless future.

I

To keep the peace is the prime and perpetual problem of
law. From prehistoric ages, when loosely aggregated tribes
first sought to limit feuds between kinship groups and to
substitute compensation for vengeance, to our own day, when
we are still striving to check the unregenerate human reversion to violence in economic struggles, and to persuade or
compel the adjustment of labor troubles through negotiation
or arbitration, the fundamental command of the state has
been the prætorian *vim fieri veto*. This is also the goal, yet
unattained, of that body of law, ancient in its beginnings but
still imperfectly developed, which we call the law of nations.

[1] Presidential address, at the annual meeting of the American Political
Science Association, Philadelphia, December 28, 1917. Reprinted from *The
American Political Science Review*, vol. xii, no. 1, February, 1918, pp. 1–16.

To describe a law that is construed and applied in the courts of every civilized state and in international courts of arbitration; a law whose rules are to be found not only in recorded precedents but also in resolutions of international congresses; a law that has been elucidated for three centuries by the labor of hundreds of trained jurists, until its sources and literature form a library far larger than that of many an existing system of national law — at least twenty times larger than the library used in compiling the law books of Justinian — to describe such a law as imperfectly developed seems paradoxical. Many writers, however, go much further, denying that the law of nations deserves the name of law. They call it international morality. Others deny that it merits even this name. Recognizing no world ethics, they assert that international law is nothing more than a body of usages, morally binding upon the single state only in so far as the state accepts them, supplemented by agreements which each state concludes of its own free will and cancels at its own sovereign pleasure.

All these writers, of course, admit that in so far as any state binds itself by international agreements, and so long as it adheres to these agreements, and in so far as the rules of international morals or international usage are recognized by the legislatures or courts of the single state and enforced through its own administrative or judicial processes, what we call international law is indeed law, but only because it is national law. When a controversy arises between states, treaty provisions that are repudiated by either of the parties and rules that are not binding upon both parties by their own domestic law are not law at all, because there exists no superior organized force to constrain obedience.

The assumption that underlies these assertions is that no rules of social conduct can be regarded as legal rules unless they are supported by superior force, exercised by some generally recognized and relatively permanent superior authority. It is further maintained, by many writers, that law, properly so-called, not only must be enforced, but also must be established by such an authority. To this last contention, however, legal history lends no support. Little national law was originally established by organized political authority, unless recognition is to be regarded as establishment. Usages older than courts or legislatures were interpreted by the earliest courts and embodied in the earliest legislation. Even in the later stages of legal development changes of usage have been similarly recognized.

Among the writers who maintain that international law is really law, some insist, and with truth, that physical coercion is not the only means that a society employs to insure obedience to its laws, nor is it always the most effective means of coercion. Ridicule of unusual conduct and disapproval of anti-social conduct exercise a psychical pressure that is often more effective than fine or imprisonment. If social disapproval is sufficiently strong to entail ostracism, and if this begets a boycott, a society exercises the same economic pressure that a state employs when it supports its laws with pecuniary fines or with confiscation of property. Even in the modern state, the law that is made or recognized by political authority would be far less generally observed if the penalties that are imposed on anti-social conduct by the physical power of the state were not supplemented by the pressure of. public opinion. These writers point out that international law has an effective sanction in the sentiments and opinions of civilized mankind, and that no state, however powerful, can without serious risk antagonize the civilized world.

Between those who assert that rules enforced by psychical pressure may be regarded as legal rules, and those who insist on the criterion of forcible coercion by a political superior, an intermediate position may be taken. It may be admitted that social imperatives can properly be regarded as legal only when they are supported in last instance by force, without admitting that this force must needs be exercised by an organized political authority. If a society that has no political organization, or none that is efficient, exercises physical coercion, either through spontaneous general action or through extemporized organs, to punish acts that are regarded as anti-social, or if it recognizes the right of its individual members to exercise physical coercion against offenders and protects them against retaliation, it may well be maintained that social usages thus sanctioned are legal.

From this point of view it is possible to distinguish tribal law in its earliest stages of development from tribal manners and morals, and to find in early tribal usage a core at least of true law. From this point of view it may also be said that some at least of the rules that govern the relations between independent modern states are to be regarded as legal rules.

Not a few writers have compared international law in its present stage of development with national law in its infancy or adolescence. In the law of nations, as in all early law, the greater part of the recognized rules rest on precedent; they are customs. In either system, law may be supplemented or even changed by agreement, and agreement must in principle be general. Decision by a majority of voices was no more recognized in the Teutonic folkmoots or in the Polish Diet than in the international congresses of today. Agreements bound only those that agreed. In both the historic instances cited, however, the principle of general consent was modified by the greater influence of the more important members of the community. In the Teutonic folkmoot, a handful of common free men would hardly attempt to groan down a proposal supported by all the chiefs. In the Polish Diet an ordinary nobleman would hesitate to interpose his *liberum veto* against a resolution supported by all the magnates. Today the general agreement of the more important states sometimes suffices to establish a new international rule.

The most striking analogy between the soicety of nations and early tribal society is to be found in the fact that the early tribe was not primarily a society of individual human beings, but a society composed of more or less independent groups. The Teutonic tribe, for example, was a society of kinship groups. The legal molecule was the *Sippe*, for which you will permit me to use the good old Saxon word " sib." The atoms in this social molecule were disregarded. As in the society of nations a wrong to an individual is a wrong to his state, so in the Teutonic tribe an injury inflicted on an individual was an injury inflicted on his sib. The absence or imperfect development of superior political authority inevitably leaves the redress of wrongs to self-help; and in the Teutonic tribe this was the affair of the sib, as in the society of nations it is the affair of the state. In the one case the ultimate means of redress was sib feud; in the other, it is war. To the Teutons, feud between sibs and war between tribes were essentially the same thing; the only difference was in the scale of operations.

As early as the fifth century, however, and probably earlier, the Teutonic tribe had taken a step forward which the society of nations is today endeavoring to take. It had suppressed feud in the case of minor injuries, compelling the injured sib to come into the popular court and demand penalty. It permitted feud only in cases of " blood and honor." And even here, if the injured sib was willing to waive vengeance and sue for penalty, the offending sib was forced to answer in court.

Again, in dealing with acts that clearly injured not only a sib but also the whole tribe, the Teutons had established in a prehistoric period the rule that such an act put the offender out of the peace of the tribe, and that any freeman might slay him with impunity. In such a case the slain man's sib was restrained from raising feud. The list of offenses recognized as crimes against the tribe was indeed a short one, but the list of offenses recognized today as crimes against the world is still shorter. Piracy is perhaps the only clear case. The attempt to assimilate the slave trade to piracy has not been fully successful.

A very important difference between modern international and early national law is found in the fact that early society was working out slowly and with infinite travail those notions of substantive right that are today familiar to every civilized human being. Courts were instituted to terminate controversy; justice has been a by-product. From this point of view, we may compare the society of nations to a community of at least moderately civilized human beings that has no political organization or none that is able to maintain order. Such was the situation — if I may cite an ancient instance taken from records readily accessible but less frequently consulted than they should be by modern students of politics — of Israel, in the days when it had escaped from its long Egyptian bondage and had not yet developed any political organization superior to that of the tribe. In Egypt the Israelites had become acquainted with a higher civilization, but after conquering and settling Palestine they had, as we are told, " no king, and every one did that which was right in his own eyes." An outrageous breach of hospitality, that is, a breach of the customary law which alone made intertribal intercourse possible, a breach coupled with rape and murder, so stirred the anger of all Israel against the tribe of Benjamin, in whose territory the outrage occurred and which refused to surrender the criminals, that all the other tribes united to exact reparation. Although the allied tribes raised by conscription forces superior to those of Benjamin, they encountered bitter and obstinate resistance. Benjamin seems to have been exceptionally prepared for war. It had what may be called superior artillery; it had " seven hundred men, left-handed, who could sling at an hair-breadth and not miss." The allies suffered two serious defeats, but they prosecuted the war until Benjamin was conquered. Then the chastened tribe was restored to its place in the society of the tribes of Israel.[2]

In continental Europe, in the later middle ages, there were many countries in which law was not efficiently enforced by determinate political superiors. In this period we have repeated instances of the formation, in emergencies, of

[2] *Judges*, ch. xix–xxi.

leagues to enforce peace. Some of these, such as the Hansa, developed into powerful federations. Others like the Vehm, which may be described as a great central European vigilance committee, served their temporary purposes and disappeared. The Vehm developed no determinate superior that could be called sovereign, but the rules it enforced, until it succumbed to internal corruption and decay, were well recognized legal rules and their enforcement was as efficient as in the average modern state.

We have had similar experiences in our own country. In the settlement and development of the West, men imbued with notions of civilized justice were thrown together, in frontier settlements and in mining camps, beyond the pale of organized political authority. They enforced such rules as were necessary for efficient coöperation by reverting to primitive processes, to self-help and to lynching. In some instances, notably in California, they organized vigilance committees. Whether the rules they enforced, and enforced very effectively, should be called law, is of course a question of definition. An apparently prosperous New York business man once told me that he did not believe in government or in law; he thought they did more harm than good. In his youth he had lived in western mining camps and had found that "they got on much better before the law came in." I asked him what they did with claim jumpers and with horse thieves. He replied that claim jumpers were usually shot and horse thieves usually hanged. He was unacquainted with the formal philosophy of law or of politics; but he was one of Touchstone's "natural philosophers," and his theory of law was that of the analytical jurist of the most formalistic type.

In the society of nations, the redress of an international wrong by the concerted action of a number of states is a significant step. Such action has been taken more than once against small states, and against nations imperfectly organized or temporarily disorganized by internal conflicts. The most recent illustration is the concerted action of the Powers to protect their legations in China against the Boxers. That such concerted action is possible against more powerful offenders has been demonstrated in this war, in the gradual extension of the alliance against the Central European Powers. Germany and Austria expected to fight two European Powers and two or three small European states. Today they see arrayed against them six Powers and thirteen states containing the majority of the inhabitants of the civilized world. This vast league of nations has been called into being and into action by Germany's disregard of treaties and of international law. The moral reaction began with the rape of Belgium; but more decisive than this or any other offense Germany has committed in arousing the active hostility of the world — clearly decisive in bringing the United States into the war — is the ruthless and indiscriminate destruction of enemy and neutral merchant vessels. German submarine warfare against ocean commerce not only affronts the general sense of justice and outrages the universal instincts of humanity, it also disturbs the economic intercourse of the world. It not only inflicts material damage, direct and indirect, in every quarter of the globe, it also imperils to an unprecedented degree the agencies of intercourse which gave birth to civilization and by which civilization is still chiefly maintained. This is the principal, although not the only reason, why Germany finds itself confronted by something very like a World Vigilance Committee.

In every such concerted action of the still unorganized society of nations, we find, if I may revert once more to the analogy between international and early national law, a forward step resembling that taken by the tribe when it began to react in its entirety against offenses for which there had been previously no redress except by feud. In the development of tribal law, such reactions indicated that offenses previously regarded as torts were beginning to be viewed as crimes. Concerted action by the society of nations against an offending state seems to imply a recognition that a state may be held accountable, not only to other single states which it has directly injured, but also to the world for a crime against civilization.

II

There is today a widespread feeling that the fabric of international law has fallen into ruin and that it must be rebuilt from the foundations. This feeling is not new; it has appeared in every general European war; it was widely expressed during the Napoleonic wars. When men's minds are engrossed by war, they forget that the rules they see overridden are only a part, and not the most important part, of the law of nations. It is only the law of war that is menaced; the law of peace is unassailed and will resume its sway when peace returns. And it is a hasty judgment that affirms that even the law of war has broken down when, as is the case today, many of the combatants have been drawn into the struggle by Germany's disregard of the restrictions imposed upon warfare between civilized nations and are fighting, in part at least, for the maintenance of the law of war. Only if Germany wins and its offenses remain unpunished, will it be possible to assert that in this world war the law of war has been overthrown.

After this war, it will doubtless be necessary to fill some gaps in the law of war. The use of submarines and of aircraft must be regulated. The right of retaliation must be defined and limited. It must be made clear that the violation of neutral rights by one belligerent gives the other no right to violate the same or other rights of the same or other neutrals; and even as between belligerents some check must be imposed upon reprisals that cannot properly be called retaliations, upon reprisals that are clearly disproportionate in their illegality or in their inhumanity to the alleged offenses by which they are evoked. In the Brussels conference of 1874, it was proposed that " the choice of means of reprisal and their extent should bear some relation to the degree of violation of law committed by the adversary," that they " should not exceed the violations committed." Without some check, reprisals and counter reprisals, each exceeding the other in illegality and inhumanity, tend to carry warfare back to its earliest and most barbarous form. There must also be an examination and a limitation of the conception of military necessity. An unlimited right of reprisal and a right to violate the rules of war whenever, according to a purely military judgment, there exists a necessity for their violation — these alleged rights reduce all rules of war to scraps of paper.

Acceptance of such restrictions will be facilitated by the experience of this war. There seems to be a growing recognition that excessive cruelty and inhumanity do not pay. The Austrian jurist, Lammasch,[3] has recently written:

After the conclusion of this war, all parties will have sufficient occasion to consider whether the direct advantages they have derived from acts justifiable or excusable only from the point of view of reprisal or of necessity outweigh the indirect disadvantages that they have incurred.

He cites the German jurist Zitelmann as saying: "In the great political game of the future every concession to humanity, the avoidance of rivalry in cruelties, will bring rich gain."

There is indeed one branch of international law that needs to be built up from the foundations, not because it has been overthrown in this war, but because its construction had hardly begun. This is the branch of the law that deals with the maintenance of peace. Its development will require limitation of the war-making power of the single states, not solely by self-imposed restrictions, but also by the law of nations. Proposals that are in process of formulation in many countries contemplate the prohibition of war in what are termed justiciable cases and the postponement of war in other cases. If a controversy between states turns upon a disputed interpretation of international law or of a treaty, or upon disputed facts, the matter is to be referred to a court

---

[3] *Das Völkerrecht nach dem Kriege* (Christiania, 1917), pp. 17 *et seq.*

of arbitration. If the controversy springs from a collision of interests, there is to be no resort to war until an attempt has been made by mediators to discover a settlement that may prove acceptable to both parties.

In the outbreak of most wars another factor is notoriously operative — a factor which may be associated either with disputed questions of law or of fact or with collisions of interests — the point of honor. In the opinion of some writers, the point of honor should be disregarded. This, in the present state of general feeling, seems impossible. According to other writers, this point also should be submitted to arbitration, in order that it may be determined by an impartial authority whether the honor of the aggrieved state has been impaired and how it shall be rehabilitated. It is well known that in some countries, where duels are still fought, at least in certain social classes, similar arbitrations are found possible; but it must also be noted that, in many if not in most cases, the so-called courts of honor find that the only possible redress is by conflict. The majority of writers appear to hold that the point of honor can be dealt with only through mediation.

This program closely follows that by which feud was checked in early tribal society. Adjustment of quarrels without armed conflict was originally obtained only by direct negotiations or by mediation. Submission of such controversies to a court was originally a matter of agreement; it first became compulsory in minor cases; ages passed before feud was suppressed in cases of " blood and honor." It was not deemed cowardly that the offender should buy his peace, but that the wronged party should sell his vengeance seemed base. National feeling today is quite similar. When, for example, Italian citizens were lynched in New Orleans, our government was prompt to offer pecuniary compensation; but Italy was loath to accept any satisfaction save the punishment of the murderers.

All these proposed rules may be established by treaties. The United States, for example, has already negotiated many such treaties. They may be established by international congresses; but the resolutions of these congresses will be no more than treaties between each ratifying power and all the others. What security will there be against breaches of such treaties?

In minor matters such treaties will doubtless be generally observed. Nations rarely go to war for trifles; if trifling causes have been alleged, these have been pretexts. What guaranty will there be, however, that in disputes not justiciable, in collisions of interests in which national passions are fired by the assertion that the national honor is at stake, a powerful state will stay the march of its armies until mediators have considered alleged grievances, investigated disputed statements of facts and submitted to each nation concerned their findings and their plan of settlement? What convincing arguments can be opposed by statesmen to the military authorities, if these allege, as they always allege when they think themselves better prepared than their adversaries, that every day's delay strengthens the prospective enemy and lessens their own chance of victory?

It is proposed today in many quarters that the society of nations shall act collectively through permanent organs to enforce submission to the proposed rules. More or less elaborate schemes have been formulated for the establishment of the requisite organs. The idea is not new, nor is there much that is novel in these plans. Similar proposals have been made from time to time during the past six centuries. What is new is the wide support given to these plans and the endorsement they have received from responsible statesmen.

The crucial question is that of sanctions. We shall gain relatively little, it is urged, by establishing new international organs unless it is possible to give something more than moral authority to their decisions and mandates. The decision that a controversy is justiciable must be followed by some joint action of the civilized world against the state that refuses to submit its case to arbitration. The prohibition of hostile action in other cases, until reasonable time has been given for mediation, must be followed by some joint action against the state that refuses to obey the injunction. The first question is: What shall be the nature of the joint action? When this question is answered, a second arises: Can the joint action required be secured? Who shall coerce unwilling neutrals to join in coercing their quarrelsome neighbors?

This last question needs only to be stated to be answered. In the society of nations, as it exists today, any such general coercion is unthinkable. All that can be deemed feasible is to affirm the legal right and the moral duty of nations not primarily interested to join in penalizing breaches of the proposed rules. How far they will recognize such a duty and exercise such a right will depend in part upon the nature of the action they are expected to take.

On this point, there are many proposals. It is suggested that joint action should be confined to measures short of formal war. In case one party accepts and the other rejects arbitration; in case either party, after arbitration, refuses to accept the judgment of the arbiters; in case a state disregards the injunction to refrain from hostile action pending mediation, the states not primarily interested are to have the right and it shall be their duty, upon the outbreak of the war, to say to the offender: We shall allow no goods to be exported from our territories to yours and we shall permit you to float no loans within our jurisdiction. To the other party involved in war, they may and should say: You may draw from our territories whatever supplies you need, including munitions of war, and you may borrow from our citizens whatever funds they are willing to lend you. This differential treatment, it is suggested, may be carried further: the citizens of states not primarily interested may be forbidden to enlist in the army or navy of the offending state and may be encouraged to offer their services to its enemy.

Other supporters of coercion go much further. According to their plans, it shall be the right and the duty of the society of nations to take military action against the offending state. The economic sanctions are to be supported by the sanction of physical force. It is even suggested that a world army and a world fleet, composed of contingents furnished by the several states, shall be organized and held in readiness for immediate use against states that disregard the proposed international rules regarding arbitration and mediation. This proposal is not infrequently coupled with schemes for the reduction of national armaments.

It is to be noted that some at least of these proposals involve the establishment of a world government. It is not proposed to organize a world state with federal government, but there is to be something approaching a world confederacy. If this confederacy is to hold periodical legislative congresses; if it is to have a supreme court, a council of mediation, and a board clothed with a certain degree of executive authority — a board which in one of the plans is called (most unwisely, it seems to me) a " ministry " — and if it is to have a federal army and navy, it will have much of the outward semblance of a world state; and its powers — on paper, at least — will not be sensibly inferior to those exercised by some of the looser national confederacies that have existed in the past and that have finally developed into federal states. They will not be sensibly inferior to those exercised by our own Union under the Articles of Confederation.

That some such world organization will ultimately be established is not improbable. The development of law has always been accompanied and conditioned by the subjection of smaller to larger groups — of kinship groups to tribes, of tribes to small states, of small states to national states — and the development of international law may well bring similar subordination of the single states now sovereign to the authority of a world league. That any such world organization will be developed in the near future, few students of history and of politics will deem probable. The subordination of smaller to larger groups has always encountered intense and obstinate resistance — a resistance based on that human instinct which is most essential to efficient coöperation, the instinct of loyalty. When we remember what stretches of time have been needed to transfer allegiance from each smaller to each larger group, when we recall that, in most cases, this transfer of allegiance has been accomplished only through war, we may well conclude that it will be no easy task to imbue the people of the great modern national states with the conviction that they owe any real allegiance to humanity, and that it will be even harder to convince them that this allegiance is in any respect higher than that which they owe to their own national states.

It will be easier to carry resolutions through international congresses and to secure their general ratification than to establish new methods for their enforcement. It will be easier to obtain general recognition of the right of disinterested states to insist on arbitration or on mediation, when war seems imminent, and to participate in joint action against an aggressive state, than to secure formal pledges of eventual participation in such action. It will be less difficult to secure pledges to join in a boycott against future offenders than pledges to take part in military action. It will be far less difficult to establish permanent boards for arbitration, for investigation and for mediation, than to clothe them with real powers. Plans for facilitating voluntary coöperation will encounter far less opposition than proposals that suggest the establishment of anything resembling a world government.

In pointing out some of the obstacles that will be encountered in any effort to organize the society of nations and to give more efficient sanction to its laws, it is far from my purpose to discourage such efforts. If they are wisely directed, I believe that substantial progress may be achieved. The temper of the world is far more favorable to such efforts than at any former period. Never before were the nations so closely knit together by material and spiritual bonds of every kind as in the years immediately preceding the outbreak of this war; never before has it been so convincingly demonstrated as during the past three years that the common interests impaired by war outweigh any separate and selfish interests that war can possibly promote; never before have neutrals so clearly seen that they have a vital concern in the maintenance of the world's peace. Until now, the attitude of neutral governments towards a war has resembled that taken in 1439 by the authorities of Namur towards a local feud. " If the kin of the slain man will and can avenge him, good luck to them, for with this matter the Schöffen have nothing to do, nor do they wish to be reported as having said anything about it." [4] In the present war our government found such a neutrality of thought and of word increasingly difficult, and neutrality in conduct was ultimately found to be impossible.

For the successful working of any international organization to maintain peace it is essential that every civilized state should not only claim the right but should also recognize the duty of aiding in its maintenance. This involves the acceptance of the international point of view, the development of the international mind. In this matter all who teach and write in the fields of history, sociology, economics, politics and law have grave duties. Never before, except possibly in the period of the French Revolution, have the dynamic potencies of what seemed abstract theories been so strikingly revealed. Many of the theories we have held are being tested, as never before, in the furnace of this greatest and most terrible of wars. Some of them have developed unforeseen and deplorable corollaries. It is our duty today to reëxamine our theories from the point of view of the interests of humanity. Let us ask ourselves whether they work for the welfare and the progress of the world; whether they tend to further the immemorial effort of humanity to rise from the mire of brute struggle for survival to the clean heights of a noble rivalry in common labor for the general good.

[4] Brunner, *Deutsche Rechtsgeschichte*, vol. 1, § 21, note 11 (p. 150).

XII

THE GROWTH OF THE AMERICAN UNIVERSITY [1]

Fellow-students — for we are all in this class, the president and my colleagues as well as the undergraduates.

Most, but possibly not all of you, know that in the waterways about New York City the only point that is called a gate bears the unattractive, not to say ill-omened, name of Hell Gate. In coming from Hell Gate to Golden Gate one is conscious of a marked change in the moral as well as in the physical environment — a change that is, in a way, symbolized by the names of the two sea gates. I do not mean to suggest that New York is in any sense an inferno. Hell Gate got its name, not because it was a way into New York, but because of a dangerous reef in mid-channel, which caused it to be regarded by early mariners as a way leading too frequently into another and worse world than ours. I think, however, that there is something symbolic in the retention of the name in spite of the fact that the reef was long ago blown up and a safe channel dredged. I do not think that such a name would be tolerated in San Francisco or in any Californian port. In its retention there is a certain humor, but the humor is cynical and has its root, like all cynicism, in pessimism. Along our eastern coast, perhaps because of its closer touch with Europe, there is in fact something — and too much — of the weary Old World's pessimism. America, which is nothing if not optimistic, begins, as Emerson said long ago, west of the Alleghanies.

In further progress along the westward course of empire, in crossing the Rockies, a dweller on the eastern coast feels another change. He is again on the edge of an ocean. Civili-

[1] An address delivered September 15, 1922 at the University of California. Reprinted from the *University of California Chronicle*, vol. xxv, no. 1, February, 1923, pp. 43–98.

zation, as every student of history knows, is not a national
but an international product. It started everywhere by the
sea and, until the development of railroads, it was carried
first along the routes of sea trade, and only slowly found
its way into inland regions. The earliest trade meant an
interchange of spiritual as well as of material goods; as a
great legal historian, Rudolf von Jhering, has strikingly put
it: "The ship that carried goods brought back gods." But
however cosmopolitan your moral atmosphere, it is still
as American as that of the great central hinterland between
the Alleghanies and the Rockies. Thoroughly American, for
example, is an inscription I saw the other day on an arch
through which the traveler passes from the railroad station
into a town in the San Joaquin Valley: "Modesto. Water,
Wealth, Health and Contentment." In these days of world-
wide unrest it is cheering to find that in one spot at least
there is contentment. If a stranger may trust his first impressions, this genial optimism prevails throughout your
state. Your moral atmosphere seems as golden as your air.

For the students in this University, as for students in
all the leading American universities, there is one ground
for contentment which is perhaps not fully appreciated by
those of you who belong to the younger generation, who
are undergraduates. To you the opportunities offered by a
modern American university may well seem a matter of
course. Unless you have studied the history of American
education you cannot fully realize how new are these opportunities nor how great they are as compared with those
offered to American students fifty or even forty years ago.
At Columbia, for example, and the state of things at Columbia was fairly typical, we had, in 1880, a little college
of the old type, with a rigid plan of study. We had also
a school of engineering. Loosely attached to these were
schools of law and of medicine. In the three professional
schools the instruction was narrowly practical. The engineering courses, organized by men who had studied in
Europe, extended over four years. For medical education

three years were deemed sufficient. Preparation for the practice of the law was compressed into two years. The collegiate and the professional curricula were parallel, in that the requirements for admission were substantially the same — for some of the professional schools a little lower than for the college. These fragments of the future university, separately organized and independently developed, were uncorrelated, with a resultant waste of effort in instruction. For example: In the schools of medicine and of engineering the first year of study was largely devoted to general courses in some of the natural sciences, for the reason that no high-school graduates and few college graduates had received adequate preparation in these subjects. In several of these subjects substantially identical instruction was given separately in the professional schools and in the college.

Similar conditions existed throughout our country. Except for the traditional professional schools of divinity, of law, and of medicine, and the newer schools of engineering and of agriculture, sometimes attached to the old colleges, often standing alone, there was, half a century ago, only sporadic provision for professional training. In the University of Pennsylvania there was a school of dentistry which drew students from foreign countries. In 1880 there were but three schools of architecture in the United States, and ambitious would-be architects were still streaming to Paris. Hence the saying, current some twenty years ago, that American architecture was either *Beaux-Arts* or bizarre.

Students who desired a broader training in medicine, in law, or in theology than was offered in this country went likewise to various European centers.

For those who desired a more advanced training in non-professional subjects than could be obtained in our colleges there was practically no provision. Nor was there provision for training in research, either in the natural or in the social sciences. For those who desired such training it was not simply advantageous, it was necessary, to go to Europe. Even before the middle of the last century there was a growing body of American students in the German universities, partly because of the opportunities there offered, partly because many of the requirements imposed upon the German youth were relaxed or waived as regarded foreign students. The first attempts to fill some of these gaps in our educational system were made in our colleges. To find room for necessary and neglected studies, the rigid scheme of college study was relaxed and, in some colleges, abandoned. The elective system was introduced, at first in the senior year, in some institutions finally even in the freshman year.

The elective system has its advantages for the earnest student who has a definite goal in view and is willing to accept expert guidance in reaching it. In most of our colleges, and particularly in our eastern colleges, the proportion of such students is small. Many desire to enjoy to the full the social advantages of the college and to devote as large a portion of their time as possible to extra-curricular student activities. Then there is everywhere a certain proportion of distinctly indolent students. For getting through college along the lines of least resistance the elective system offers special facilities. Observation of the results led President Stanley Hall of Worcester University to remark, some years ago, that the college seemed to have become an institution for the artificial prolongation of the period of adolescence. And a former colleague of mine at Columbia, Professor Woodward, afterwards president of the Carnegie Institution at Washington, was moved to describe the elective college program as "four years of aimless discontinuity." President Eliot of Harvard, the leading champion of the elective system, was fond of saying that the intrinsic merits of that system could not be better stated than in the words of Shakespeare:

No profit grows where is no pleasure ta'en.
In brief, sir, study what you most affect.

When any utterance of a dramatist is cited, it is worth while to consider in what sort of a mouth the words are put. The advice cited, which you will find in *The Taming of the Shrew,* is indeed addressed to a young Italian gentleman who has come to Padua to study philosophy, but it is given him by a comic scamp of a servant, who is afraid that, if his master takes his university work too seriously, neither of them will have a good time.

These disadvantages of the elective system have to a degree been remedied in various ways; for example: by assigning to each student a faculty adviser; by insisting on prerequisites for more advanced courses; by increasing the number of prescribed courses; and by the so-called group system, which perhaps comes nearest to securing coherence and continuity of work.

One result, however, which I for one greatly regret, is the progressive disappearance from our college education of the study of the classics. I regret this chiefly because our civilization is so largely a continuation of the ancient Mediterranean civilization. As Sir Henry Maine put it, modern civilized nations are those that have taken their religion from Judea, their arts and philosophy from Greece, and their law from Rome. I am not of those who believe that all that is worth while in the ancient culture has been so thoroughly assimilated that the records of that culture can be thrown into the educational scrap-heap. No architect or artist would assert that the Parthenon could be dynamited or that the Venus of Milos and the Hermes of Olympia could be removed from the public galleries in which they stand and sold to private collectors of antiquities without loss to the world; and I feel that we still need in equal measure the inspiration to be derived from the classical literatures.

The attempt to make provision for studies previously neglected by introducing them into the college curriculum proved unsatisfactory, not only for the reasons above noted, but also because many of these studies require a background of knowledge and a maturity of mind which college undergraduates rarely acquire before the senior year.

A different and more satisfactory solution of the problem has been worked out during the past fifty years. For advanced study of the natural and social sciences provision has been made in non-professional graduate schools. In these, training in research had been developed. New professional schools have been established. In these, and also in the older schools, professional training has been increasingly liberalized, partly by requiring preliminary college study, partly by enabling and encouraging professional students to devote some part of their time to related subjects in the non-professional graduate schools. At the same time there has been a general lengthening of the periods of professional study. All these parts of the university have more and more been correlated with one another. These changes have been facilitated by the very general adoption of the so-called "combined courses" of college and professional study, in which, as is sometimes said, the college and the professional schools are "telescoped." This innovation has been of advantage not only to the professional schools but also to the colleges. It has brought into the colleges something of the more earnest spirit of professional study.

In this development no single university has assumed a sole leadership. Johns Hopkins University was established, nearly half a century ago, exclusively for graduate study. An undergraduate college was a later addition. Harvard was the first university to require for admission to its law school a preliminary college training. In both of these movements Columbia University was an early second. Columbia was the first to permit its college students to elect in their senior year a full professional course of study, and it has since placed all its professional schools on a basis of two or three years of college study. The University of California has taken an interesting and important further step in establishing, in concurrence with its three-year program of professional legal study, a four-year program in its school of jurisprudence.

James Bryce pointed out that one great advantage of our federal form of government was the possibility of independent political developments in the single states. Our state governments, he said, were so many political experiment stations, in which we could try all things and hold fast to that which proved good. The even higher degree of autonomy in our educational system which comes from the existence of privately endowed as well as of state universities provides a very much larger number of educational experiment stations. Of these California has become one of the most important, one whose experiments are watched with closest interest from the Pacific to the Atlantic.

XIII

THE PRINCIPLE OF NATIONALITY [1]

My interest in Chinese civilization, and particularly in Chinese government, was aroused at an early period, forty-five years ago, when I was studying law in Berlin. It was awakened by acquaintance with a scholar and diplomatist who was at the time a secretary of the Chinese Legation at Berlin, Mr. Lo Feng-luh. He had previously been connected for several years with the Chinese Legation in London, and later, I understand, returned to England as Chinese Minister. Lo Feng-luh was intellectually one of the most remarkable men I have known. His mind worked rapidly and at the same time accurately. He had what James Russell Lowell, writing of Abraham Lincoln, described as a " sure-footed mind." We became good friends. " A difference of taste in jokes," George Eliot says, " is a serious bar to friendship." One of the things that drew Lo Feng-luh and me together was an identical sense of humor. During my three years of study in Germany I knew no German with whom I stood in equally intimate relations nor any German, except one of my law teachers, whose personality impressed me so strongly and has remained so vivid in my memory.

In our talks he asked me many questions about occidental society, literature and religion — rather, I think, to corroborate his own impressions than to enlarge his knowledge, for he understood Europe. I, in turn, asked him many questions about Chinese society and government, and I always got from him frank and illuminating replies.

I recall one statement of his which I shall make the text of my remarks this evening. " To me," he said, " Eng-

[1] Paper read before the Chinese Social and Political Science Association, October 5, 1923. Reprinted from *The Chinese Social and Political Science Review*, vol. vii, no. 4, October, 1923, pp. 226–233.

lishmen and Frenchmen, Italians and Spaniards, Germans and Russians seem rather varying types of a single race than distinct peoples." He found no greater difference between these European peoples, in speech, in customs, and in ideas, than exists between the peoples of the different provinces in China.

In the nineteenth century it became an axiom of occidental political philosophy that the only proper and secure basis of political organization is a substantial identity, within the territory of each state, of ideas, customs and speech. The principle of nationality, in this narrow sense, obtained and still enjoys almost undisputed recognition. If this be the last word of political philosophy, the Chinese Empire was, and the Chinese Republic is, a political anomaly. And yet the Chinese Empire existed for centuries before the Roman Empire had been established, and in comparison with it the oldest existing national states of Europe are modern things and many of them are mushroom growths. China has repeatedly seemed on the verge of dissolution, the disappearance or overthrow of a dynasty has repeatedly produced periods of anarchy, but always its unity has been reestablished, as I hope and trust that the unity of the Chinese Republic will be reestablished.

What are the bonds that have held China together? Speaking with diffidence, on the basis of the information derived from my first Chinese teacher, Lo Feng-luh, and, since that, from my Chinese students — many of whom have been at the same time my teachers — I gather that the positive bond of unity is a common written language, through which common views of ethics, of economics and of politics have been diffused among the educated classes, who in China, as always and everywhere, have been the leaders of thought and through whom these common views filtered down through the people of all the provinces. A negative bond of union — if I am rightly informed — was found in a wise tolerance of provincial divergences in matters not essential to political unity. There was no attempt to impose a common speech upon all the provinces. There has been tolerance in the matter of religion. There has been little, if any, interference with local customs. While the government of the several provinces was entrusted to officials appointed by the emperors, it appears to have been necessary for these governors, if they wished to retain their positions, not only to discharge satisfactorily their duties to the Empire, but also to live on good terms with the provincials. And strictly local government, if I am correctly informed, was left largely in the hands of representative local groups, such as merchants' and farmers' guilds.

Why has the course of European history been so different? To answer this question fully in a brief address would be impossible. History is constantly being rewritten from the point of view of the latest developments; and for at least a century it has been the effort of historians to show that no union of the peoples of continental Europe under any form of government could endure, because such a union would violate the principle of nationality. To try to show that this assumption is untenable, or unquestionable, it would be necessary again to rewrite European history. I shall endeavor only to outline what seem to me the chief causes of European disunity. Two thousand years ago a unity was achieved which endured for five centuries. Not Europe alone, so far as Europe was civilized, but also the entire area of western civilization was included in the Roman Empire. When the northern barbarians, eager for their place in the sun, swept across the Rhine, the Danube and the North Sea and gained control of Italy, Gaul, Spain and Britain, they had no notion that they were overthrowing the Roman Empire. They regarded it as still existing; their kings were governors of Roman imperial provinces and their armies were imperial armies. Many of their kings sought imperial recognition of their authority — from the emperor at Rome, so long as there was such an emperor; later, in several instances, from the emperor at Constantinople. As has repeatedly happened in the history of China, the northern conquerors accepted, and to some extent assimilated, the superior civilization of the conquered southern world. They were already, or soon became, Christians. Those Germans whose territories had never been ruled by Rome retained their speech, but, under the guidance of the only educated class, the Christian ecclesiastics, their kings organized their governments more or less on Roman lines. The Germans who settled in Gaul, Spain and Italy not only accepted Roman institutions but also, ultimately, the speech of the Roman provincials.

Meanwhile, Christendom had been split by religious dissensions into two great churches — the Roman Catholic and the Greek Orthodox. The East Roman or Byzantine Empire, which lasted a thousand years longer than the Western, was thus severed from Western Europe, the Eastern Slavs were Christianized by Greek missionaries, and these two regions developed for centuries along different lines. In Western Europe, in spite of political disunion, the tradition of unity remained strong; and when in the Frank Empire all the Christian peoples of Western Europe, except the English, were brought under the rule of a single monarch, it seemed natural and fitting that Charlemagne should be crowned emperor at Rome. In the early part of the ninth century there seemed to be a fair chance that Western Europe, recognizing one supreme secular ruler and one spiritual head, the Roman Pontiff, would remain united.

Before the close of the ninth century this empire went to pieces, not, as modern German historians explain, because of the development of distinct nationalities, but because of the increasing power of local magnates and because of disputes regarding the succession to the throne. When this empire was dissolved, Western Europe was not divided into national states, in any proper sense of the term. As a result of the development of feudalism, it was divided into kingdoms, in which the kings at first had little power, and it was sub-divided, as regarded real political authority, into an extraordinary variety of larger and smaller units.

A feudal seigneur, even if his holding was hardly larger than that of an American farmer, was practically, in most cases, king of his own little domain. Through the later Middle Ages the sense of nationality was weak. The noble, the knight, the priest, the scholar, the trader, the artisan even, felt himself first of all a member of his class. He had more in common with men of other classes who spoke his own language. For all educated men there was still a common European language, the Latin. In Germany there was no attempt to write even local laws and customs in the German language until the thirteenth century.

At the close of the Middle Ages Western Europe was divided, as it had previously been separated from Eastern Europe, by religious dissension — by the Protestant revolt against Romanism. This was not exclusively a German movement; Protestantism was strongly developed in French-speaking countries also.

It was not the sense of nationality that created the modern national states: it was rather the growing power of kings and the formation of strong national states like the English, the French and the Spanish that developed the sense of nationality. The establishment of strong central governments in these states made for internal peace and order, but gave rise to greater and more destructive European wars. For the safety of each state it was felt to be essential that none should gain such territorial expansion and power as to dominate Europe. The prime object of statesmanship, and the most frequent cause of war, was the maintenance of the balance of power. The result of these balance-of-power wars was summed up by Dean Swift, after the war of the Spanish succession, in a couplet that might have been written at any time in the last four years:

> Now Europe's balanced; neither side prevails,
> For nothing's left in either of the scales."

It was in the nineteenth century, which witnessed the establishment of Greek independence, the separation of Belgium from the Netherlands and of Norway from Sweden, and the belated unification of Italy and of Germany, that the principle of nationality, the doctrine that unity of speech was the true basis of political union, became axiomatic. The problem of maintaining the balance of power — which in plain English means jealous fear and periodical warfare — has had indeed some good results. It has protected many of the smaller states, like Switzerland. It failed, however, to protect Belgium against invasion, and it kept, and still keeps, the Turk in Europe.

In the nineteenth century the principle of nationality ran mad. It came to mean the claim of every territory, however small, which had its own language, or even its own dialect, to complete independence. With the establishment of four independent states in the Balkan peninsula came the notion that no one of these must be strong enough to menace the others; and forty years ago there was a balance-of-power war between Serbia and Bulgaria. Today the principle of nationality has broken up a natural economic area — that of the former Austro-Hungarian Empire — into four independent states. The first result of this extreme assertion of the principle of nationality was that each of these four states, prompt to demonstrate its independence, established a protective tariff against the others. These new customs barriers became, however, so injurious to each of these new states that, two years ago, their governments were forced to negotiate commercial treaties.

A permanent cause of hostility and of warfare between the national states of Europe was the difficulty, amounting in many cases to an impossibility, of drawing national boundaries along the lines of language. Around most of these states there were districts of mixed speech. That identity of speech is not the only conceivable basis of political unity was, however, clearly demonstrated in the case of Alsace. This was always, and is still, a German-speaking land; but for a century its people have been loyal to France. In other parts of Europe the problem of drawing language lines is insoluble. In Bohemia, for example, German-speaking and Czech-speaking areas alternate like the black and white squares of a chess board. The Czechs resented the rule of the German-Austrians; the German population to-day resents the rule of the Czechs.

The notion that government must rest primarily on identity of speech has had hateful results. It has led repeatedly to the attempt to change the speech of alien elements within a national state. This doctrinaire effort was as unwise as it was tyrannical. The effort of Prussia to Germanize its Poles and its Danes, and the effort of the German Empire to Germanize Alsace-Lorraine, only intensified the hostility of their unwilling subjects.

If political principles were treated like scientific theories as working hypotheses, to be tested, modified, and even abandoned in the light of results — the principle of nationality would long ago have been discredited. That it has been so obstinately held in Europe is the more remarkable in view of the fact that Switzerland has given for centuries, as it still gives to-day, conclusive proof that a state may exist and be firmly based on the loyalty of its citizens, although they are united neither by a common speech nor by a single religion. If Switzerland were to be dealt with according to the principle of nationality, the larger part of its territory would go to Germany, a very considerable part to France, a smaller part to Italy, and the inhabitants of the Valley of the Inn, who speak a distinct language and have a literature written in that language, would be organized as an independent and sovereign state.

If the Austro-Hungarian government had not been based on the rule of the Slavic and Italian elements by German-Austrians and Magyars, if all its peoples, like those of Switzerland, had been given home rule under a federal system of government, and if each area had its proportional representation in the Central Government, it seems probable that this empire would have held together. If the Slavs in this empire had had any voice in the direction of foreign policy, there could hardly have been an Austro-Serbian war. It would perhaps be pushing an hypothesis too far to say that the recent world war would then have been averted; but the immediate issue which precipitated that war could hardly have arisen.

If it had been generally recognized in Europe that a federal system of government enables people of varying speech, customs and religion to live together in harmony, it seems probable that most of the political troubles which have afflicted Europe for centuries, and have recently imperilled its civilization, might have been averted. And it seems clear that the establishment of federal unions would solve many of Europe's immediate problems.

For China, in the light of its own history and in that of European history, a federal system of government seems essential. I say this with the less hesitation because so many Chinese of thought and of experience are expressing the same conviction. I have read with great interest the detailed plan of federal government which Dr. Bau recently presented to your Association. With my limited knowledge or rather almost unlimited ignorance of Chinese conditions, it would be audacious for me to criticise the details of his plan, but I believe that in its main features it is sound.